The politics
of the British
constitution

MANCHESTER
UNIVERSITY PRESS

Political Analyses

Series editors: Bill Jones and Michael Moran

The politics
of the British
constitution

Michael Foley

Manchester University Press

Manchester and New York

distributed exclusively in the USA by St. Martin's Press

Copyright © Michael Foley 1999

The right of Michael Foley to be identified as the author of this work has been asserted by him in accordance with the Copyright, Designs and Patents Act 1988.

Published by Manchester University Press
Oxford Road, Manchester M13 9NR, UK
and Room 400, 175 Fifth Avenue, New York, NY 10010, USA
http://www.man.ac.uk/mup

Distributed exclusively in the USA
by St. Martin's Press, Inc., 175 Fifth Avenue, New York, NY 10010, USA

Distributed exclusively in Canada
by UBC Press, Univeristy of British Columbia, 6344 Memorial Road, Vancouver, BC, Canada V6T 1Z2

British Library Cataloguing-in-Publication Data
A catalogue record for this book is available from the British Library

Library of Congress Cataloging-in-Publication Data applied for

ISBN 0 7190 4551 7 *hardback*
      0 7190 4552 5 *paperback*

First published 1999

05 04 03 02 01 00 99   10 9 8 7 6 5 4 3 2 1

Typeset in Photina by
Northern Phototypesetting Co, Ltd, Bolton
Printed in Great Britain
by Bell & Bain Ltd, Glasgow

Contents

Figures and tables

Series editors' foreword

The *Politics Today* series has been running successfully since the late 1970s, aimed mainly at an undergraduate audience. After over a decade in which a dozen or more titles have been produced, some of which have run to multiple copies, MUP thought it time to launch a new politics series, aimed at a different audience and a different need.

The *Political Analyses* series is prompted by the relative dearth of research-based political science series which persists despite the fecund source of publication ideas provided by current political developments. In the UK we observe, for example: the rapid evolution of Labour politics as the party seeks to find a reliable electoral base; the continuing development of the post-Thatcher Conservative Party; the growth of pressure group activity and lobbying in modern British politics; and the irresistible moves towards constitutional reform of an arguably outdated state.

Abroad, there are even more themes upon which to draw, for example: the ending of the Thatcher–Reagan axis; the parallel collapse of communism in Europe and Russia; and the gradual retreat of socialism from the former heartlands in Western Europe.

This series seeks to explore some of these new ideas to a depth beyond the scope of the *Politics Today* series – while maintaining a similar direct and accessible style – and to serve an audience of academics, practitioners and the well-informed reader as well as under-graduates.

To Jenny and Edmond
for their example in rising above adversity

1

The constitution in question

The 'politics of the British constitution' is a conspicuously unorthodox phrase in the British political system. Political activity in the United Kingdom is normally conceived as being unerringly accommodated within the structures and processes of a settled constitutional order. Just as British political life is widely seen as a phenomenon occurring in, or through, a distinctive pattern of constitutional forms, so the constitution itself is interpreted primarily as a medium of political exchange, even to the extent of equating political capability with constitutional legitimacy. Constitutionalism in the British system, therefore, is often reduced to the notion of a constitution of British politics – i.e. a summation of political experience expressed through forms, processes, traditions and developments, and substantiated by longevity, continuity, assimilation and adaptation. It is because of this instinctive conviction in the spontaneous existence of a determinable constitution, and in the trustworthiness of a political class in maintaining the constitution's operational integrity, that politics has traditionally not been translated into constitutional dispute. Just as the term 'unconstitutionality' has little meaning in British politics, so the idea of a genuine politics of the British constitution has remained a thoroughly unconventional precept in a system of governance characterised by convention.

Far from a politics of the constitution, the British system has traditionally been characterised as one in which the constitution is simply assumed to exist as a self-evident entity. In fact, it is the very absence of a developed form of constitutional dispute and speculation that is seen as symptomatic of a living constitution. The British constitution, therefore, is a presumptive construction. Its notoriety as an unwritten, unassembled and imprecise collage of discrete parts is turned into a virtue of collective experience and consensual expression. Only a mature and effectively functioning political community could operate and maintain such an ethereal set of rules. The constitution evokes a basic political settlement rather than embodies one in any documented frame of reference. In this way, a circular type of constitutional culture is fostered in Britain. Just as the constitution is assumed to exist from the presupposition of a basic political settlement and the presence of a political community, so the latter are taken as read from a constitution that could only remain operational with the benign support and mutual trust of just such a settled community. A particular historical process had produced and legitimised a particular political process which in its turn validated and reaffirmed the historical continuity of constitutional practice. Given this background, the acceptance of constitutionality in the British system can be said not only to precede the notion of an actual constitution, but to determine the very nature of the British constitution to the extent that it has remained less a textual anchorage and more a projection of social temperament and tradition. Politics is certainly facilitated by such a constitution, but because the 'rules of the game' themselves are mostly immune to direct and sustained political argument, the British constitution is normally thought to transcend politics and to provide by implication that extrapolitical dimension which is the essential characteristic of constitutionalism.

The ambiguity surrounding the origins and meaning of the British constitution has always generated doubts over the nature and status of such a constitution. Apart from the anomalies and disjunctions which might be said to compromise its integrity as a system of government, the constitution is vulnerable to the charge of being driven by the exigencies and practicalities of contemporary politics. The latter is not so much the instrument by which the constitution is discovered, as the independent variable controlling the shape and operation of the constitution. Just as the interplay and consequences of British politics is assumed to be constitutional, so the constitution can be seen as being reducible to the needs of prevailing political forces. Because the constitution gives emphasis to a government being permitted to govern, and because of the doctrine of parliamentary sovereignty that makes no qualitative distinctions between statute and constitutional law, it is alleged that the principles of the government and constitutional constraint are either weak or absent in the British constitution. What restraint exists comes more from the mutual convenience, collective interest or political prudence of the political participants – rather than from the effect of any autonomous and authoritative dimension of constitutional principle. According to such a perspective, the British constitution is too responsive and assimilative to be an authentic constitution. It is said to fall foul of Thomas Paine's celebrated criteria of a constitution – namely, that it should be an antecedent of government; that it should define the authority of government; and that where the distinction between the constitution and the government is not observed there is in effect no constitution.[1]

The British constitution is also criticised for its dependence upon precedents and history. It is not only an acclaimed derivative of experience, but represents an active construction of fragmented past practices into a singular entity. To its detractors, this process remains chronically incomplete and unsuccessful. Just as a summation of experience cannot be said to be synonymous with constitutionalism, so the extrapolation of discrete rules and customs into a general aggregate can be claimed to fall far short of an authentic constitution. It may provide a collective *ex post facto* characterisation, but it does not amount to a corporate whole founded axiomatically upon first principles and with a separate existence to the political realm. Such a constitution, based as it is upon conditioned impulses, historical improvisation and fluid practices, can and has been said to be no constitution at all – echoing Alexis de Tocqueville's celebrated dictum that the 'English constitution has no existence'.[2] According to this perspective, the reason why Britain has had such a dearth of political argument and activity surrounding its constitution is simple. It lacks an identifiable constitution and with it a distinct constitutional dimension.

In Britain, such ontological distinctions are traditionally seen as the irrelevant trappings of an empty debate. The controlling premise is one of a working constitution whose existence is verified, rather than thrown into doubt, by its characteristic flexibility and adaptability. The British Constitution has no pretence to pure forms, immutability and precision. Its defining condition and chief virtue is one of evolutionary change. So much so in fact, that the main device for conveying and explaining the British constitution has traditionally been one of describing change and tracing recent developments.[3] The equanimity with which the constitution is reduced to reportage and 'pure description',[4] without the safety net of an entrenched framework, is seen as evidence of a settled political process which confers legitimacy upon its outcomes – even when they have a substantial effect upon the process itself. The customary British view of their own constitution, therefore, is essentially minimalist in character. It is a set of institutions, procedures, rules and conventions. This has encouraged an open-ended and pragmatic view of constitutional change, which has occasionally prompted even British commentators to concede the difficulty of reconciling the constitution with the normal logic of constitutionalism. It is often alleged, for example, that because of 'the absence of legal criteria that distinguish constitutional law from other laws, the definition becomes so broad that it defines nothing at all'.[5] But such problems rarely disturb the body politic. Indeed, it has become almost part of the British constitutional tradition that having acknowledged the constitution's unorthodox independence from fundamental frameworks of organisation and rights, it is customary to dismiss the deficiency as being in any way significant.

The priority of description over prescription within the British constitution is itself reflected in British constitutional analysis, where the emphasis is normally laid upon the functional value of current constitutional arrangements and the desirability of evolutionary developments over any premeditated excursions into large-scale reform. It is customary to refer to the absence of any tradition of continuous political dispute over the structure and operation of the constitutional system. It is equally common to acknowledge the difficulties of politicising the British constitution in any direct and concerted way. A particular problem in this respect has been the influence of the common law tradition with its emphasis upon a non-statutory and judge-made dimension of law. This tradition has fostered the principle that liberties pre-exist law and are judicially maintained without recourse to any formal declarations of freedoms up to and until they are limited by legislation.[6] The core value of parliamentary sovereignty may provide a point of access to constitutional inquiry, but at the same time its axiomatic authority and finality amount to a method of foreclosure that pre-empts the need for, and the relevance of, constitutional debate.[7] Both the common law tradition and the 'absolute supremacy'[8] of parliament generate a basic 'unfamiliarity with discussing the constitution in broad conceptual terms'[9] and a related discomfort with both the language of constitutional dispute and the intellectual analysis of government.

But perhaps the most significant difficulty of all is simply the severity of the logistical problems involved not merely in using constitutional change as a way of acquiring political leverage, but in operationalising the constitution as a political issue in its own right. And underlying all such difficulties is the cultivated sense of needlessness that surrounds attempts to transform the constitution into an accessible issue. Effective politics is not thought to require constitutional argument. On the contrary, constitutional debate is traditionally seen as an unnecessary distraction and a waste of political resources. Because the constitution is assumed to be basically neutral in operation, to be conditioned by the rule of law and to be run in accordance with indigenous precepts of reasonableness, the British have grown to be 'profoundly uncurious about the rules of the political game as it has been since the franchise was completed between 1918 and 1928'.[10] The conventional outlook is the one described by Sidney Low in 1904: 'We live under a system of tacit understandings. But the understandings themselves are not always understood.'[11] If this often quoted aphorism on the British constitution is accurate, then what is more significant than the lack of understanding is the lack of concern and disquiet over such an ostensibly dangerous ambiguity. Even the lack of understanding appears to be 'understood' (i.e. in the sense of tolerance and acquiescence) as a necessary and, therefore, tolerable concomitant of what is taken to be the inherent imprecision of a functioning constitution. Given such a context of implicit reciprocity and collective restraint, a politics of the constitution has remained conspicuously underdeveloped in the British system. This is not so much because of the absence of any tangible constitution, but because such a politics has traditionally been seen as being superfluous and unworkable in a constitution that already appears to fuse process with purpose, change with continuity, and movement with stability.

The central tradition of the British constitution has been one of a settled political order formed and rationalised in the nineteenth century and bequeathed with minor adjustments to the twentieth century. This is not to say that the constitution has been devoid of subsequent reforms, crises and major adjustments but these have been conspicuous by their comparative rarity and their episodic nature. They have punctuated, rather than under-mined, the constitutional tranquillity of the British government. As a con-sequence, a basic immunity to sustained analysis and challenge has been the hallmark of the British constitution for much of the twentieth century. Despite the many anomalies and ambiguities that were implicit in what was largely a pre-modern constitution set in a rapidly developing industrial state, the fundamental precept of the constitution remained one of instinc-tive functionality. It worked in spite of itself because of the social consensus that supported it and foreclosed speculation about its content and integrity. The key component of Albert Venn Dicey's classic and highly influential eulogy to the 'Edwardian constitution' was the convention of acceptance that the constitution had arrived at a state of systematic settlement.[12] The constitution could be viewed as an integrated expression of unified mean-ing and a conclusive source of political legitimacy.

Even as late as the middle of the twentieth century, '[c]ommentators assumed that there could scarcely be any improvements ... The conventions and practices of the late Victorian period were not considered as merely true for that time, they were regarded as proper or normal.'[13] Britain still 'adhered to the democratic doctrines enunciated by the late nineteenth-century liberals' and maintained its faith that all 'unanswered questions would resolve themselves'.[14] In spite of the growing disjunctions between constitutional theory and practice, 'the political class were quite happy to carry on as before, putting constitutional or structural questions into the too dull, too difficult or irrelevant categories'.[15] Satisfaction with the politi-cal opportunities afforded by the constitution overcame any anxieties over its internal disjunctions. The British constitution was simply 'regarded as clear, predictable, settled and rather boring to discuss'.[16] Anthony Lester describes the constitutional insouciance of the era:

In the 1950s there was broad satisfaction in Britain with our constitutional arrangements. ... [They] were still generally regarded as a glorious example, to be envied by less fortunate nations, of a flexible and adaptable method of gov-erning a modern democracy with the consent of the governed and with free-dom under the law. In the world of 1950, even a perceptive and critical student of government and law could be forgiven for giving our constitution, with all its charming historical anachronisms and anomalies, a clean bill of health. This is what many students would have been likely to read and believe'.[17]

Britain may well have been a declining world power but at a time when the number of new nations was rising sharply, the country could still pride itself as being the fountain-head of the Westminster model – a constitutional template self-consciously attributed to a 'process of adaptation covering a period of over a thousand years'.[18] Even in the 1960s and early 1970s, when various gestures towards the need for marginal reform were being made, the basic outlook remained that of assuming 'without really thinking about it, that our political system would remain essentially unchanged';[19] and that since 'everything had operated without fuss within an unwritten and flexible constitution',[20] political life would continue in much the same way.

The post-war tranquillity of Britain's constitutional arrangements, however, did not survive the mid-1970s when the multiple assaults of stagflation, industrial strife, social unrest and economic decline began to erode not merely the political consensus on policy but also the traditions surrounding the structure and operation of the constitution. The British constitution appeared to have suddenly stopped working and to be in a state of terminal decline. Whereas in the 1960s, 'there was almost a concern to avoid the problem of the British state', by the 1970s 'there was agreement that British politics had slipped beyond the explanatory grasp, and the control of the established constitutional theory'.[21] The stark realism of the 1970s stripped away the comfortable securities of the 1950s and laid bare the problematic status of the many changes which the British system had accepted but hardly assimilated over the many years of its development. In the process, 'constitutional fundamentals had been opened up with a vengeance'.[22] Doubts over the real substance of ministerial responsibility, cabinet government, civil service neutrality and parliamentary accountability suddenly erupted into concern and even anxiety that the protocols of constitutional management no longer could, or should, disguise the analysis of the political system. The highly charged atmosphere of public unrest and political volatility generated a level of profound scepticism over the British constitution which brought to the surface a range of fundamental issues that had previously been kept in a state of dormancy through a process of strategic neglect on the part of the constitution's participants and operatives. As the level of consciousness rose over the inherent connection between the constitutional process and political action, or inaction, the British constitution experienced the novelty of becoming an object of widespread analysis, discussion and complaint. The period was 'remarkable for the number of issues of constitutional significance that [were] the subject of political debate; remarkable given the previous absence of such debate'.[23] Judges and statesmen joined academics and commentators in licentious speculations over the integrity, and even the remaining viability, of the constitution. Alistair Buchan predicted 'a generation's work of reform ahead of us, analogous to that between 1832 and 1870'.[24] It was a prediction that typified the disquiet at the time over what was seen in many influential quarters to be the chronic unsustainability of the constitution.

It is true that much of the rancour that was generated by severe social and economic unrest, and which became attached to the constitutional debate in the mid-and late 1970s, subsided during the 1980s. Nevertheless, the issue of the British constitution did not fade away. It was maintained throughout the succeeding period and has continued to the present day. While the political circumstances and motivating forces may have changed in nature, the impulse to systematic dissent and structural prescription has remained in operation. Far from degenerating into a rump of pre-Thatcherite gadflies, constitutional critics and reformers have grown both in number and organisation, and in experience and sophistication. The objects of constitutional concern have also become more diverse. They range from assertions that the electoral system no longer legitimises its product of parliamentary sovereignty to the increasing public interest in establishing entrenched rights of citizenship to afford a point of reference for individuals seeking legal redress against the government; from concerns over governmental insensitivity over basic freedoms to anxiety over the impoverished standards of personal conduct by those in positions of political influence and responsibility; from the demands for greater participation and self-government in the constituent regions and nations of the United Kingdom to claims that 'central control has tightened'[25] and has as a result 'diminished local and regional counterweights and alternative centres of influence',[26] permitting insensitive, and even arbitrary, executive behaviour; from doubts over the plausibility of parliamentary and ministerial responsibility and over the extent to which it can be, or has been, replaced by a system of market accountability generated by independent government agencies to complaints over how, or even if, the public interest is served by privatised utilities and the creation of 'quangocracy'; from the imposed restrictions on the powers of local government and the operation of local democracy to the ramifications of European Union membership, which along with other regional and global developments, place Britain's political autonomy and national identity in doubt. The effect of so many anxieties on so many fronts means that while the 'British Constitution used to be the envy of the world, ... [t]oday it is difficult to find any writer who is not critical of our institutions. There is hardly any element of the constitution which has not come under attack.'[27] Even the crown is no longer immune to assault as the financial costs, personal morality and cultural authority of the royal family have become regular objects of public scrutiny.

Interest in constitutional issues can no longer be dismissed as either intermittent pulses of popular agitation prompted by temporary political frustration, or the effect of an intellectual *avant garde* attempting to substitute genteel constitutionalism for 'real politics'. On the contrary, the meaning, organisation and performance of the constitution has become synonymous with the real politics of the 1990s. Constitutional reappraisal and reform has become a permanent and integral part of the British political agenda. It is an issue which now enters into the political and electoral calculations of interests, parties, bureaucracies and governments. Just as the British public has become accustomed to the vocabulary of constitutional analysis and prescription, so it has become acclimatised to the future possibility of significant constitutional change. For example, after being seriously proposed for twenty years, the idea of a bill of rights for Britain has largely lost its capacity to shock. It has now begun to look more like a common-sense remedy and one that is already acquiring something of a *de facto* presence by way of decisions from British courts and more especially from the European Court of Human Rights. Constitutional speculation, therefore, has entered the mainstream of political activity. It is seen as being both relevant and legitimate. Its practitioners have no doubts as to its centrality. To Ferdinand Mount, for example, 'most people with any degree of intellectual honesty or seriousness will admit to some unease about the prospects for our [c]onstitution as it now is'.[28] In Peter Hennessy's view, '[t]here is a whiff of constitutional reform in the air and it is more rational, determined and prescriptive than at any time in living political memory'.[29] As such, 'the question is' in David Marquand's opinion, 'no longer whether the familiar but increasingly dilapidated Westminster model should be overhauled. It is how change should come and what sort of change it should be'.[30] Such statements would have been dismissed as mere rhetoric until very recently. Today they appear to be realistic and credible assessments.

Calls for constitutional reform have become utterly conventional. For example, in the period preceding the 1997 general election, the leader of the opposition reaffirmed his attachment to the cause of constitutional reform. Despite the likelihood of a change of government after a protracted period of unbroken Conservative rule and despite Tony Blair's position as the chief prospective beneficiary of the established constitutional order, the Labour leader continued to insist that the agenda for constitutional reform was politically prudent and that the argument for systemic change to the constitution had already been won: 'Changing the way we govern, and not just changing our government is no longer an optional extra for Britain. So low is popular esteem for politicians and the system we operate that there is little authority for us to use unless and until we first succeed in regaining it ... Times have changed. Constitutional issues are now at the heart of political debate. We gauge that constitutional conservatism is dying and that popular support for change is tangible and steadfast.'[31] By September

1997, even Charles Powell, one of Margaret Thatcher's closest lieutenants, was ready to concede that the constitutional status quo was unsustainable: 'The idea which has dominated the post-war years, that our parliamentary democracy is so infinitely superior to that of any other country as to be incapable of improvement, will no longer do ... many of the proposed changes are plainly overdue.'[32]

Although the cause of constitutional reform has until recently remained largely one of potential rather than fulfilment, the issue has had a marked influence on the conduct and agenda of British politics. Its impact has been plural in nature and wide-ranging in scale. Constitutional reappraisal has now become a consistent feature of, and a concerted force within, the interplay of British politics. The onset of a Labour government committed to a raft of constitutional reform proposals and to the objective of national and democratic renewal through constitutional modernisation exemplifies the current salience of the issue and its effect upon political mobilisation, party calculation, policy positioning and the organisation of political argument. And yet because of the British constitution's characteristic capacity for unheralded and unattributed change, the ramifications of such a rapidly developing issue have barely been recognised, let alone analysed. It is no exaggeration to state that a flourishing politics of the constitution is now present within contemporary Britain. And yet, the nature of its existence and the significance of its wider implications are quite obscure.

The purpose of this study is to elicit the meanings and properties of such a politics. The intention is to draw together the separate components of what is often a highly fragmented set of critical and reformist impulses, in order to produce a systematic analysis of the properties and dynamics of the constitutional issue. At present, most of the commentaries on this issue imitate the nature of the constitutional debate itself – i.e. critical appraisal, reformist prescription and defensive reaction. These elements are highly significant but they are often presented as discrete and one-dimensional components with little critical awareness of the complex and contingent aspects within each element, or of the intricate inter-relationships between them. The objective of this analysis is to provide an understanding of the dynamics which structure and animate what has become of the political issue of the British constitution. The study will consider the methods employed to exert, or to resist, pressure in the area of constitutional reform; the ways in which political agendas are formed and reformed in response to constitutional issues; the respective positions, arguments, language and strategies of the main participants in the constitutional debate; and the relationships that exist between types of political motivations and objectives on the one hand and the kind of constitutional positions which are adopted on the other.

Chapter 3 focuses upon the political themes and controversies which have aroused public interest in the operational integrity of the constitution.

It seeks to clarify the complex causes of critical constitutional introspection by offering an analytical typology of what are termed 'constitutional fuels' – i.e. discernible stimulants to constitutional inquiry that have distinctive properties in both cause and effect. The chapter makes a rigorous examination of each one of these fuels and their contribution to the political substance and motive forces of the constitutional debate. Chapter 4 considers the various ways in which these fuels have prompted a politics of constitutional dissent and reform. It examines the thematic variables and organising methods in channelling disapproval and objection not only into a programme for reform but into a campaign establishing constitutional change on the national political agenda. The deployment of argument and resources against the prospectus of purposive reform is the subject of Chapter 5 which reviews the differing nuances and techniques of resistance, together with their relationship to the varying strategies of both left and right of centre.

Chapter 6 reviews the impact of the constitutional reform programme upon the interplay of party politics and, in particular, upon the political calculations and electoral strategies of the main parties preceding and during the 1997 general election. Because the circumstances of this election provided the optimum conditions for achieving constitutional reform, it warrants the closest attention in order to acquire an accurate assessment of the penetrative properties of the constitutional reform issue and the level of dependence it has upon the governing precepts and political resources of New Labour. The final chapter looks at the transition from constitutional reform as a feature of opposition politics to its role both as a set of manifesto commitments mandated by electoral success and as an organising principle of a government's policy programme. The chapter examines the continuing pressures and arguments for and against reform set within new and unaccustomed conditions. It identifies what is in effect a new matrix of conditions which will set the parameters of constitutional development and determine the usages, applications and implications of the growing constitutional perspective in contemporary British politics. But before proceeding to plot the course of what has been and remains an accelerating politics of the British constitution, it is necessary to provide an outline of Britain's traditional constitutional context which has not only conditioned our constitutional development, but until recently effectively defined our very understanding of what constitutionalism entails. Our long-established limitations in the concepts, language and potential of a constitutional dimension in Britain are discussed in Chapter 2.

Notes

1 Thomas Paine, *The Rights of Man* (London: Everyman's Library, 1966), p. 66.
2 Quoted in C. H. McIlwain, *Constitutionalism: Ancient and Modern*, rev. edn (Ithaca: Cornell University press, 1947), pp. 8–9.
3 See the regular 'The British Constitution in ...' articles by Donald Shell in *Parliamentary Affairs*. See also Rodney Brazier, *Constitutional Practice*, 2nd edn (Oxford: Clarendon, 1994).
4 Nevil Johnson, *In Search of the Constitution: Reflections on State and Society in Britain* (London: Pergamon, 1977), p. 41.
5 F. F. Ridley, 'There is No British Constitution: A Dangerous Case of the Emperor's Clothes', *Parliamentary Affairs*, vol. 41, no. 3 (1988), p. 341.
6 See Alan Ryan, 'The British, the Americans, and Rights' in Michael J. Lacey and Knud Haakonssen (eds), *A Culture of Rights: The Bill of Rights in Philosophy, Politics, and Law – 1791 and 1991* (Cambridge: Cambridge University, 1991), pp. 366–439; Robert Alexander, *The Voice of the People: A Constitution for Tomorrow* (London: Weidenfeld and Nicolson, 1997), ch. 2.
7 Cheryl Saunders, 'Evolution and Adaptation of the British Constitutional System' in Joachim J. Hesse and Nevil Johnson (eds), *Constitutional Policy and Change in Europe* (Oxford: Oxford University Press, 1995), pp. 67–94.
8 *Ibid.*, p. 69.
9 Philip Norton, *The Constitution in Flux* (Oxford: Martin Robertson, 1982), p. 1.
10 Peter Hennessy, 'Searching for the "Great Ghost": The Palace, the Cabinet and the Constitution in the Post-War Period', inaugural lecture as Professor of Contemporary History, University of London, 1 February 1994.
11 Sidney Low, *The Governance of England* (London: Fisher Unwin, 1904), p. 12.
12 Albert Venn Dicey, *Introduction to the Study of the Law of the Constitution*, 10th edn (London: Macmillan).
13 John P. Mackintosh, *The Government and Politics of Britain* (London: Hutchinson, 1971), pp. 12, 14.
14 *Ibid.*, pp. 29, 30.
15 Peter Hennessy, *Never Again: Britain 1945–1951* (London: Vintage, 1993), p. 196.
16 Bernard Crick, 'Pandora's Box, Sovereignty and the Referendum', *Political Quarterly*, vol. 46, no. 2 (1975), p. 123.
17 Anthony Lester, 'The Constitution: Decline and Renewal' in Jeffrey Jowell and Dawn Oliver (eds), *The Changing Constitution* (Oxford: Clarendon, 1985), pp. 273–4.
18 J. Harvey and L. Bather, *The British Constitution* (London: Macmillan, 1964), p. 12.
19 Anthony King, foreword in Anthony King (ed.), *Why is Britain Becoming Harder to Govern?* (London: British Broadcasting Corporation, 1976), p. 6.
20 David Butler, 'Politics: The Vanishing Uncertainties', *Sunday Times*, 17 April 1977.
21 John Dearlove and Peter Saunders, *Introduction to British Politics: Analysing a Capitalist Democracy* (Cambridge: Polity, 1984), p. 81.
22 *Ibid.*

23   Norton, *The Constitution in Flux*, p. v.
24   Alistair Buchan, 'The Cure Cannot Begin Until the Sickness is Identified', *The Times*, 2 January 1976.
25   Anthony Sampson, *The Essential Anatomy of Britain: Democracy in Crisis* (London: Hodder and Stoughton, 1992), p. 154.
26   *Ibid.* p. 8.
27   Gabriele Ganz, *Understanding Public Law* (London: Fontana 1987), p. 9.
28   Ferdinand Mount, *The British Constitution Now: Recovery or Decline?* (London: Mandarin, 1993), p. 28.
29   Peter Hennessy, 'We Need a Constitutional Crisis', *The Independent*, 3 July 1991.
30   David Marquand, 'A Dilapidated System in Crisis', *The Independent*, 26 September 1991.
31   Tony Blair, 'Blair on the Constitution', *The Economist*, 14 September 1996.
32   Charles Powell, 'Thatcher's Unfinished Revolution', *The Times*, 4 September 1997.

2

The British constitutional tradition

It is a characteristic of the British political tradition that the constitution is simply assumed to be present. In this light, a constitution is a presupposition – there to be discovered rather than devised. Certainty of existence, however, is acquired at the price of uncertainty over content and application. The British constitution is renowned for being unwritten, or at best unassembled into a coherent form. It is conspicuous for the absence of exact arrangements and precise properties. And yet in spite of its evident lack of a tangible and documented form, the British constitution is traditionally characterised as the object of a profound cultural attachment – an intrinsic belief in the very idea of a pervasive and controlling constitution. Such an allegiance amounts to more than the Aristotelian conception of constitutionalism which lays emphasis upon the general nature of a regime. The British sense of its constitution has always incorporated the conviction that it represents a distinctive and substantive code of political life which not only organises and rationalises government, but restricts the exercise of power to agreed limits. In doing so, it is thought to have successfully reconciled *libertas and imperium*.

A constitution like this is both descriptive and prescriptive at one and the same time. Empirical observations of working practices, supportive attitudes and governing arrangements are translated into depictions of the rightful and proper conduct of government. Likewise, attempts to define the governing principles of the British constitution have traditionally proceeded not from *a priori* concepts or formulated objectives, but from a pragmatic compression of political and administrative experience. With this type of aggregative constitutionalism, the British constitution has always had a reputation for developmental fluidity which has thrived not in spite its unwritten nature but precisely because of its freedom from any core documentation. This notion of a viable and even superior constitutionalism set within a system without a unified textual basis makes the British constitution in essence an exercise in interpretation. The constitution as a single entity has no existence other than by interpretation. Just as it is seen as being eminently interpretable so it is always regarded as being in need of interpretation. The depth of conviction in its quality as a constitution has, therefore, been closely associated with the belief that a unifying nature can be elicited by observation and interpretive construction.

This tradition of intuiting an underlying constitutional ethos from a mass of political and institutional exchanges became established in the eighteenth century. Mining the British system for its constitution became one of the main extractive industries of the era. The repercussions of the Glorious Revolution (1688), the Bill of Rights (1689), the Act of Settlement (1701) and the Act of Union (1707) were widely regarded as having fostered a 'matchless constitution', described by John Adams as the 'most perfect combination of human powers in society which finite wisdom [had] yet contrived and reduced to practice for the preservation of liberty'.[1] The main virtue and chief operating principle of this constitution was believed to be one of harmonious balance. 'The seventeenth century saw the constitution as ancient and balanced'.[2] The ethos of balance was originally drawn from the classical theory of mixed government which assumed that the three classes of society (i.e. monarchy, aristocracy and democracy) could be melded into government, where an array of reciprocal checks would ensure that the interests of each of the tripartite elements were addressed and protected. In the British context, the notion of a mixed and balanced government was evoked by the existence of the monarchy, the House of Lords and the House of Commons in their separate forms as distinctive institutions and in their blended form as the supreme authority of the 'King/Queen-in-Parliament'.

Since the Civil War (1642–49), this venerable source of balanced government had been variously coupled with the more rigorous and radical doctrine of the separation of powers. While the separation of powers was normally employed as a supportive device for mixed and balanced government, its emphasis upon the functional categories of government at the expense of the class foundations of traditional mixed government gave it a potentially iconoclastic logic that implied separate but necessarily incomparable and, therefore, unequal powers. The general theme of separate powers could help to engender a sense of balance but the logic of the doctrine could also be carried to the point of assigning priority to the legislative function and giving proportionate weight to that point of government in which the democratic element was present. In doing so, it would also relegate the position and prerogative of the crown to that of a merely executive role. M. J. C. Vile sums up the underlying tension between the two concepts :

> The separation of powers was essential to the balanced constitution, for the notion of a *balance* necessarily assumed a basis of *separation*, but this necessity

imposed upon the theory of the balanced constitution the burden of maintaining the source of its own destruction; for the separation of powers was eminently suited to the needs of the rising middle class, which was attacking monarchic and aristocratic power, but wished to maintain limits to the exercise of government power even when the government was dominated by an elected legislature. Thus movements towards a greater degree of democracy had the effect of stripping away the monarchical and aristocratic elements of the theory of the balanced constitution, leaving the separation of powers as the only basis of a theory of constitutional government.[3]

The varied problems generated by the confluence of these two constitutional precepts were bequeathed unresolved to the eighteenth century.

If the hallmark of constitutional propriety and authority in the eighteenth century was one of balance, it was equally the case that there was no certainty as to what amounted to balanced government, or how it was to be acquired and maintained. While the two doctrines of mixed government and separated powers were associated to a greater or lesser degree with the notion of balance, their proximity to one another generated ambiguity and confusion rather than clarity and order. It was only in very general terms that the composition of the balance was understood. In contrast to the customary pictures of the eighteenth century as a tranquil era in which Britain enjoyed the benefits of settled government bequeathed by the Glorious Revolution, the century was characterised by a continual debate over just this issue of balanced government. Not only did the principle lend itself to heated constitutional argument, but political disputes were invariably translated into efforts to legitimise one interpretation rather than another concerning the real nature of the balance in the British constitution. Appropriately, it was also a period when the constitution was subjected to intense scrutiny by commentators and observers, each seeking to explain its mysteries and to account for the relationship of its constituent parts to one another. In essence, it was a time when the arrangement for governance following the Glorious Revolution began to be treated as an entity capable of being comprehended and rationalised as a systemic and functioning constitution through a process of empirical and inductive generalisations.

It was Montesquieu who provided what became the best known of the eighteenth century's attempts to elucidate the operation of the constitution. In *The Spirit of the Laws* (1748), Montesquieu commended the British constitution for its capacity to produce moderate, stable and lawful government through its indigenous devices for checks and balances.[4] To Montesquieu, these constitutional mechanisms were founded more upon the differentiation of government functions (i.e. legislative, executive and judicial) than upon the categories of social class associated with such functions. It was Montesquieu who clarified the terminology over government functions and used the British constitution as an illustrative example of the way in which the separation and interdependence of functionally distinct institutions precluded the decline of liberty and the onset of governmental corruption. Within this schematic conception of British government, the executive was clearly differentiated as a separate branch of government and the judicial function was isolated as analytically distinct from, and comparable in significance to, the other two functions.[5]

The affirmed co-existence of three functionally distinguishable and interactive elements in British government was regarded not only as an empirical vindication of Montesquieu's conception of three generic functions within all governments, but as an actual expression of the normative principle of balanced government. Montesquieu's thesis has always been surrounded by controversy. For example, arguments persist over whether Montesquieu idealised the British constitution for the purposes of constructing a conceptual model; over the extent to which he ignored the growth of cabinet government to protect the integrity of the three separate powers; and over whether he employed functional categories to redefine and reaffirm a balance of social classes and in particular to preserve the intermediary position of a threatened nobility.[6] Despite such controversies, Montesquieu's widely celebrated eulogy of Britain's constitution injected an altogether more mechanistic view of balance than that associated with the traditional conflation of mixed government. In doing so, he gave the British constitution a universal significance as the exemplar of balanced government, based not upon exceptional social circumstances and idiosyncratic arrangements but upon its revealed condition as an epitome of general analytical categories of government.

Montesquieu may have been the most celebrated expositor of constitutional balance but he was by no means the only commentator who felt the need to account for the existence of an equilibrium within the British constitution. William Blackstone, for example, perceived to a much greater extent than Montesquieu did the role of the judiciary as an actual power and institutional force distinct from the other two branches. Montesqiueu had limited the judicial element to a function of government. Blackstone on the other hand believed it possessed a 'distinct and separate existence'[7] as both a function *and* an institution. In the *Commentaries on the Laws of England* (1765–69), Blackstone presented the concept of a three-way balance in which both the monarchy and the judiciary had indigenous sources of power separate from the corporate entity of the Parliament. Although parliamentary sovereignty over law-making remained an unassailable principle to Blackstone, its supremacy was conditioned by an institutional differentiation that explicitly compounded some of the substance of a separated powers framework with the more familiar forms of mixed government. Blackstone's reference to 'true excellence of the English government, [being] that all the parts of it form a mutual check upon each other',[8] was strongly suggestive of the presence of institutional, rather than simply social, checks within British government.

William Paley was another who expounded the virtues and practicality of balanced government. In *The Principles of Moral and Political Philosophy* (1785), he asserted that the British constitution remained a genuinely mixed one. It sustained its balance through the influence exerted upon the House of Commons by both the crown and the House of Lords. Such an influence was legitimate, as it allowed the monarchy and the aristocracy to defend both themselves and the equilibrium of the constitution by preserving their institutional autonomy against the growing constitutional weight of the House of Commons. Another well-known eighteenth-century commentary on the British constitution was produced primarily for a continental audience by Jean L. de Lolme. In the *Constitution of England* (1771), de Lolme placed so much emphasis upon the quality of balance in the British system that he tended to allow his observations to be determined by this central supposition. He stressed the separation of powers as the key doctrine embodied in the constitution and saw the balance produced as a stalemate between the three rigorously distinct and independent institutions. De Lolme's excessively schematic depiction of constitutional reality not only revealed a marked predisposition towards balance as a principle of government in its own right, but demonstrated the different ways by which just such a balance could be interpreted. Whereas de Lolme regarded constitutional deadlock as the touchstone of balanced government, William Paley, for example, saw as a condition of balanced government the need to erode the divisions within its structure and to achieve a more positive equilibrium through linkages and interaction – even to the point of condoning royal patronage as a source of parliamentary influence. If the effect of de Lolme's balance was immobilism, the cause of Paley's more dynamic government was 'an interlocked constitution, calculated on the model of a cantilever bridge, [which] was necessarily static'.[9]

But perhaps the best illustration of the extent to which the concept of balance had not only become bound up with constitutional propriety, but also implicated in contemporary political dispute, was that provided by Henry St John Bolingbroke.[10] Bolingbroke was a constitutional theorist who characterised the British constitution in the following mixed government terms:

> It is by this mixture of monarchical, aristocratical and democratical power, blended together in one system, and by these three estates balancing one another, that our free constitution has been preserved so long inviolate ... It secures society against the miseries which are inseparable from simple forms of government, and is liable as little as possible to the inconveniences that arise in mixed forms'.[11]

Bolingbroke, however, was also a polemicist and not averse to adapting constitutional doctrines for political purposes – even if this was at the expense of his own intellectual consistency. In Bolingbroke's vituperative campaign against Robert Walpole's ministerial system, he refused to regard this form of monarchical influence as an integral feature of mixed government, and castigated Walpole's system as a corruption of the balanced constitution. To drive the point home, it has been argued that Bolingbroke shifted his position significantly in the dispute and, as a result, sowed the seeds of the separated powers principle in Montesquieu's mind by advocating a clear demarcation of the three constituent branches of government in respect to the functions with which they were primarily associated.[12] Bolingbroke claimed that 'in every kind of government some powers must be lodged in particular men, or in particular bodies of men, for the good order and preservation of the whole community'.[13] According to this view, Bolingbroke, under the pressure of political controversy, was quite prepared to employ the principle of separated powers in order to retain constitutional balance which, in his opinion, was being increasingly threatened by the contemporary developments in the British system's traditional format of mixed government. If this was a measure of Bolingbroke's adherence to balanced government, it was also a reflection of the degree to which balanced government had become the recognised rationale of the British constitution. While his opponents declared the need for monarchical-ministerial influence upon Parliament, in order to preserve a balance of interdependence,[14] Bolingbroke sought to alleviate this 'corruption' of the constitution by pressing the intrusive branch back towards its appropriate role, in order to restore the equilibrium that was thought to have existed before the encroachment of the monarchy. Such was the authority and compulsive quality of the term 'balance' in the language of eighteenth-century British politics that it was employed by both sides in contemporary political disputes – by traditionalists and reformers, Whigs and Tories, and by court and country factions alike.[15]

'If the theory [of balanced government] was evident and unanimously agreed upon, the mechanics of the operation were not'.[16] The different permutations of balance between and amongst a variety of components available in the British system became so central to the constitution's meaning that the principle of equilibrium ultimately provided the only common frame of reference for traditionalists and radicals alike. How best to maintain an ancient equilibrium, or to restore the constitution's lost heritage of balance, exercised the most gifted political and legal minds of the day, as each sought to acquire legitimacy for its position by what had become the constitution's primary prescriptive feature. Balance permeated the political vocabulary of eighteenth-century Britain. It dominated the rules of engagement between political adversaries to such an extent that a structure of balanced powers and mutual control came to be recognised as the indispensable guarantor of Englishmen's rights and liberties.[17]

The social and economic transformations that characterised the nine-teenth century placed an increasing burden upon the plausibility of balance as the defining quality of the constitution. With the progressive extension of the franchise in the 1832, 1867 and 1884 Reform Acts and with the commensurate shift of emphasis towards the House of Commons in general and majority party government in particular, the notion of equilibrium became more problematic as a central reference point. The feasibility of bal-ance on grounds of both mixed government and separated powers was increasingly compromised not only by the evident institutionalisation of cabinet government and the marginalisation of even a constitutional monarchy, but by the sheer logic of democracy with its expansive nature and potentially illimitable legitimacy. Nevertheless, the ideal of balance remained in place and constituted a nostalgic and usable counterweight to the burgeoning modernity of representative government.

At the beginning of the nineteenth century, the British constitution was increasingly coming under strain. On the one hand, the excesses of the French Revolution and the calls by domestic radicals such as Thomas Paine to extend natural rights into radical democracy prompted a reaction against the type of open and popular dissent that had been tolerated in the eigh-teenth century. On the other hand, it was becoming evident that the 'matchless constitution' was politically dependent upon patronage, sinecures, rotten boroughs and a system of brute social deterrence against property crimes.[18] Far from being an idyll of Augustan civility, the eigh-teenth century had in reality been a society coarsened by violence and the rise of arbitrary executive power in suppressing riots. Subsumed under the rule of law was a draconian penal code in which minor crimes were pun-ished by whippings, transportation and public execution. '[T]he unleashing by Europe's most moderate ruling elite of Europe's most barbarous criminal code upon some of the best-natured and most patient poor in Europe'[19] accounted for 7000 executions between 1770 and 1830. The notion of a self-governing balance of socially based institutions evoking an equilibrium between classes in society began to look less credible and more tenuous.

The Whig philosophy of evolutionary and progressive history culminating in the Glorious Revolution of 1688 also looked less relevant in the nineteenth century when the central constitutional issue was no longer one of liberty against royal despotism. During the first half of the century, the Whigs were pressured not merely by Tory reaction but by a radical impulse provided on an intellectual level by the liberal rationalism of the utilitarians and on a pop-ular basis by the Chartists who wished to revive the link between English republicanism and the liberties and rights of an ascribed 'ancient constitu-tion'. It is true that the Whigs were able to exploit the links between royalty and Toryism to press a reform agenda that led to Catholic emancipation, the repeal of the Test and Corporation Acts and, most significantly, of all the

Great Reform Act of 1832, which doubled the electorate, swept away rotten boroughs and established middle-class political participation on a more regular basis than before.[20] It is also true that Whig apologists such as Lord Macaulay were highly adept at presenting such reforms in eighteenth-century and even seventeenth-century terms – namely, as a vindication of the traditional balanced constitution. To Macaulay, history demonstrated that the constitution could peaceably assimilate and adapt to change while preserving its forms and traditions.[21] The continuity of change might alter the relationships between the component elements of the whole constitution, but the integrity of the structure would not be compromised. Because the constitution was allegedly so amenable to change – i.e. equable change within an equilibrium – reform was possible without revolution or recourse to revolutionary ideas like democracy, republicanism and egalitarianism.

While such accounts of the constitution's capacious potential for imperturbable change were popular amongst the mid-Victorians, they were also complacent over the way they refused to acknowledge and address the political implications not only of the Reform Act but of the movement towards widening the franchise in general. While Tories had condemned the Reform Act as effectively marking the end of mixed government in Britain, they together with many Whigs hoped and supposed that this one electoral adjustment would eliminate the pressure for further change and foreclose any additional reforms. 'The old system was fundamentally indefensible, and, if the landed class was to preserve any part of its old ascendancy, concessions had to be made to popular demand.'[22] But in pressing for such a putative restoration of balance, the reform's sponsors had in fact opened a Pandora's Box, the complex ramifications of which were to pervade political argument and constitutional development for the rest of the century – and arguably throughout the following century.

In one respect, the 1832 Act can be seen as setting in motion a cumulative set of reforms leading inevitably to universal suffrage. The House of Commons had always been different from the monarchy and the House of Lords in that it represented, rather than embodied, its power base. Once that representational basis had been called into question and altered to reflect social interests in a different way, then it opened up the prospect of speculation over further changes to remedy successive problems of political authority. After the opaque, irregular and anomalous form of eighteenth-century and early-nineteenth-century representation had been impugned – whether on grounds of precedent, justice, utility, prudence or equity – the nature of representation in the House of Commons became progressively open-ended in scope, in process and in purpose and meaning.[23] For example, as the assumptions of 'virtual representation' gave way to claims of actual representation, the interpretive and corporate nature of the representative process was opened up to the direct translation of interests, and ultimately, of sheer numbers. Trusteeship of the general welfare evolved into a condition in which benevolent responsibility became more closely interwoven with political pressures, actively imposed by the previously passive recipients of such paternalism. This emphasis upon representative will rather than a presumptive welfare was further encouraged by the utilitarian drive towards maximising liberty and social benefit through the calculus of rational government. Despite the rational implications of such motivating forces, they could nevertheless be construed as being ultimately compatible with the British constitution. Indeed the principles and impulses of a widening representative base became a characteristic feature of Victorian progress and one that could be claimed to reaffirm the constitution's capacity to acknowledge contemporary forces and to absorb forms and interior traditions.

But this view was very much a product of retrospection. At the time, the expansion of the electorate fostered another and altogether more sceptical and even negative interpretation of the constitutional consequences. While acknowledging the practical and moral difficulties of opposing electoral reform, and while recognising the contribution that voting could make to each individual's self-development, even the advocates of change were disquieted over the extent to which a mass electorate could reduce government to a democratic ascendancy of uninformed and prejudiced opinion, that would overwhelm government with issues relating to 'the condition of the people question'. In such circumstances, the old ideal of a balanced constitution seemed to be at risk not only because the traditional co-existence of classes within government would be compromised by the enhanced vigour of the lower house, but because the governing ethos of parliamentary sovereignty would be co-opted by the legislative supremacy of an insurgent House of Commons. The 1832 Reform Act revealed the potential supremacy of the people over the House of Commons, and of the latter over the House of Lords. It could even be claimed that the Act had already introduced an external check upon a government precariously balanced from within. The prospect of further reforms would only serve to transform the lower house from a chamber of communities to a literal House of Commons whose authority would be reduced to numerical values – the result of which would be to undermine the qualitatively different power bases of the monarchy, the lords and the propertied middle classes. What was seen in many quarters as the successive appeasement of the 'lower orders' induced intellectual anxieties over the prospect that representativeness would lead to a process of equivalence in which Members of Parliament would become the unmediated agents of the popular will unrestrained by any selfless notions of traditional trusteeship and responsibility for unrepresented sectors of society. The propulsion towards a democratic rationale of government threatened to overwhelm the old checks of common law, precedent and convention and to expose parliamentary sovereignty as an internally regulated form of power that could not possibly withstand the incursion of an allegedly alien mass culture within government.

> If Parliament was sovereign, and the House of Commons could claim an increased legitimacy and independence within the constitutional structure through representing a wider cross-section of the community, then the representatives of the people could annex the determination of public policy. Furthermore, once the principle of an equal right to vote was conceded, then the majority of those representatives might be elected by the working classes. If they imitated the monarch, and followed a natural propensity to rule in their own interests, they might trample on the liberties of others. That was the fear in the nineteenth century.[24]

In the same way that majority rule was thought to be unassimilable within the contemporary institutional structure, so the ethos of constitutional liberty was considered incompatible with the egalitarian impulses of mass democracy. The majority could no longer be anonymously subsumed under the auspices of trusteeship. It was not even feasible to think that it could be consciously incorporated within the traditional configuration of government. 'Whig and Liberal leaders could appreciate the logical force of the arguments for a further and much more radical extension of the franchise', but even they 'felt that the ignorance of the multitude was an insurmountable barrier to such a reform'.[25] To such sceptics, if measures were not taken to ameliorate this incipient democracy, then it would utterly transform the British constitution. In doing so, it would risk the prospect of those republican excesses of conformity, intolerance, illiberalism and instability described by Alexis de Tocqueville as 'majoritarian tyranny' – i.e. a consequence of the fact that the 'very essence of democratic government consists in the absolute sovereignty of the majority; for there is nothing in democratic states which is capable of resisting it'.[26] John Stuart Mill, for example, was committed to the proposition that Parliament should reflect the full range of social opinions and that the vote was a form of political education in its own right. Nevertheless, he wanted the franchise limited to literate and tax-paying citizens and he prescribed that democratic leadership be lodged securely in the reliable hands of the middle classes. Mill also distinguished between the ultimate power vested in a representative government and the actual translation of such power in the form of governmental functions. He described it as 'a radical distinction between controlling the business of government and actually doing it'.[27] But perhaps the figure that best exemplifies the dilemmas raised by the prospect of mass democracy and representative government and who typifies the internal strains between traditional constitutional structures and contemporary political developments in mid-Victorian society is Walter Bagehot.

Bagehot's perspective was both modern and traditional; realistic and for-malistic. At one level, he was an iconoclast seeking to lay bare the actuali-ties of cabinet government, the distinction between 'efficient' and 'dignified' parts of government, and the extent to which 'a republic [had] insinuated itself beneath the folds of monarchy'.[28] At another level, he was a tradi-tionalist keen to protect the functional utility of custom, protocol and even political theatricality. Bagehot frankly acknowledged the actual and poten-tial advance of democracy. At the same time, he remained utterly sceptical of the mass's inherent capacity for government. 'The masses of Englishmen', he wrote, 'are not fit for an elective government; if they knew how near they were to it, they would be surprised, and almost tremble.'[29] Bagehot pos-sessed a thoroughly hierarchical conception of society that compared com-munities to 'great mountains' containing 'primary, secondary, and tertiary strata of human progress'.[30] In a developing democracy, a disjunction existed between the modern access of the masses to electoral power and their rudimentary and even primitive understanding of politics. Bagehot turned this deficiency into a virtue of constitutional stability by drawing attention to the importance of the system's 'dignified elements' in providing a form of mass political engagement that did not threaten the social order. Bagehot's defence of the monarchy, for example, was not based upon any Tory attachment to divine right or on any genuine appreciation of its mys-tique. It was an irreverent rational assessment of the institution's digressive capacity not only in distracting the multitude from the real business of gov-ernment, but in providing government with a 'comprehensible element for the vacant many'.[31] Its actual use, therefore, came from its apparent use-lessness. Its cosmetic qualities and its gift of introducing irrelevance into public life disguised a more serious capacity of embodying a political ideal, and elevating the citizenry by an 'interest, higher, wider and deeper than ordinary life'.[32]

Bagehot had a distinctly sociological conception of the constitution. While the separation of powers may have been compromised by the efficient secret of the links between the executive and legislative branches, elements of the old mixed government scheme were evident in his emphasis upon social equilibrium. Different classes possessed different levels of political experience, perception and consciousness. As such, they could effectively be blended together in the cause of good government. His elitist attachment to hierar-chy together with his wish to postpone democracy, or at least to defer its effects, led him to support the proposition that the British constitution could absorb change. To Bagehot, the assimilative properties of the constitution were not the same as Macaulay's eulogy to the basic imperturbability of structures. Bagehot distinguished between substance and forms; essence and effects. The British constitution was in the throes of change but this was effectively disguised by a 'dignified' super-structure of tradition and custom that performed a constraining and stabilising function. Just as the ignorance and credulity of the masses effectively counterbalanced the incipient force of numbers, so the multitude's association with the dignified elements of government allowed the middle classes to retain their hegemony for the benefit of the constitution. Whether such a position was construed as one of balance or managerial manipulation, the end result to Bagehot was a constitution dependent upon social temperament, artful ambiguity and mass narcosis.

The fears and anxieties engendered by the spectre of mass democracy in the nineteenth century ultimately proved to be unfounded. The Reform Acts were not preludes to social instability and political dissolution. On the contrary, the extension of the franchise had come about as a consequence of a graduated process of incorporation consisting of a successive relaxation of property qualifications, rather than any sudden and complete collapse in restrictions. Such a cumulative transformation could not only be couched as evolutionary in character, it was in many ways directly experienced as a progressive exercise in assimilation that exerted change but which did not overtly defy established practices and constitutional authority. Despite the rapidity of social and economic change and the radical implications of an enlarged franchise, the conduct of politics continued in its traditionally practical and unself-conscious manner. To G. H. L. Le May, 'English politicians have been readier to work their system of government than to analyse it in its full complexity.'[33] In this respect, the Reform Acts made no difference. 'Political debate in the nineteenth century was mainly concerned with what ought to be done and who ought to do it; the political machinery was accepted as more or less adequate for its task by most of the serious parties to the argument.'[34] The sense of underlying flux was not translated into any revised conception, or understanding of the constitution. Myriad changes generated a comfortable myopia over the totality of their effect. For those who were concerned over the direction and meaning of constitutional change, and over the contemporary state of constitutional principles, Albert Venn Dicey provided the reassurance of definite answers. While Bagehot may have 'burst through the veils and masks of the useful fictions which [had] concealed the dramatic alterations in the disposition of powers',[35] it was left to Dicey to rework the disorder of such exposure into a realistic redefinition of constitutional theory, operational precision and systematic value.

In *Introduction to the Study of the Law of the Constitution* (1885), Dicey asserted that the British system of government rested upon three main principles. The *first* was the doctrine of parliamentary sovereignty which incorporated a fundamental acceptance of the legal supremacy of the 'Queen in Parliament'. It meant that Parliament had 'under the English constitution the right to make or unmake any law whatever' and that nothing or no-one was 'recognised by the law of England as having a right to override or set aside the legislation of Parliament'.[36] Just as the jurisdiction of Parliament was absolute, so its legal actions amounted to sovereign law that could not be constitutionally challenged by any other body on the basis of any other source of law. Within this framework, there was no point of access for subjecting Parliament to a claim of *ultra vires*. Constitutional law was no different to statute law and *vice versa*. This was another way of saying that the British constitution was one large derivative emanating from the single uncontested and irrefutable point of parliamentary sovereignty – i.e. 'the one fundamental law of the British constitution'.[37] That law was not in itself a product of Parliament. It possessed the immunity of a separate source, in that it was a common law principle based upon historical precedent and given contemporary meaning by the judiciary's traditional and professional attachment to parliamentary supremacy and statute law. The constitution's 'fundamental law', therefore, was in essence a legal doctrine owing its existence to the courts' continued recognition of it.

To this extent, Dicey followed the Blackstonian mix of valuing common law but also of giving due recognition to the fact 'that absolute despotic power ... must in all governments reside somewhere'.[38] But unlike Blackstone, Dicey had to contend with the nineteenth century's transformation of the franchise and with the related change in both the nature and scope of the House of Commons's authority. In his desire to give recognition to the claims and accomplishments of an advancing democracy and also to integrate them into the framework of established principle, Dicey sought to make a distinction between 'legal sovereignty' and 'political sovereignty'. The former approximated to the traditional model of an institutionalised parliamentary sovereignty. The latter rested upon a recognition that the concept of parliamentary sovereignty could not easily be limited to an 'in-house' arrangement, but had to be reconciled with the evident existence of a mass electorate that the House of Commons was now progressively embodying rather than merely reflecting. To Dicey, 'legal sovereignty' remained intact but it was now set within the electoral parameters of political sovereignty which conditioned and limited its exercise. While judges remained unaware of such terms as 'popular will' or 'electoral mandate', the electorate nevertheless now possessed the ultimate sanction and with it the capacity to enforce its will – albeit indirectly through the medium of Parliament. In Dicey's view, parliamentary democracy not only should, but actually did, provide a fusion of sovereignties. 'The essential property of representative government is to produce coincidence between the wishes of the sovereign and the wishes of the subjects ... This, which is true in its nature of all real representative government, applies with special truth to the English House of Commons'.[39] Democracy may have been a *fait accompli* but to Dicey it was as assimilable as other constitutional developments because 'political sovereignty' was ultimately reducible to the terms of 'legal sovereignty'.

Dicey's sanguine views of democracy and its unavoidable links to the legal absolutism of parliamentary sovereignty were based upon the *second* main theme of his influential interpretation. To Dicey, the 'rule of law' was both a normative principle and an empirical condition of the British constitution. The prevention of arbitrary government and the presumption of individual rights and liberties were secured by the system's attachment to a set of legal procedures and working assumptions that cumulatively produced the condition of a rule of law. The specified conditions of such a rule were as follows. A person could only be arrested and subsequently punished for a clear breach of what was clearly a law. Guilt had to be determined by a court of law working through authorised procedures. The law had to be ascertainable, in order to allow individuals to incorporate their conduct and plans within the bounds of legality. Another principle was that all persons were to be considered equal before the law. Irrespective of rank, position or class, everyone should be universally subject to the same law administered by the same system of courts. As such, there could be no distinction between ordinary citizens and officers of the state. Their legal status was level within a single jurisdiction. As a consequence, an individual's freedom could only be infringed when the powers invoked by the authorities were backed by law and exercised according to authorised procedures designed to limit the discretion of officials and preclude the possibility of arbitrary government. Finally, the entire administration of law should be informed by a respect for the law and a concern to protect justice against those who abuse the power of the state.

Dicey had no hesitation in confirming that the British constitution satisfied all of these conditions. Indeed, Dicey's whole purpose in reducing the concept of a rule of law to a set of distinguishable properties was designed to demonstrate Britain as the epitome of such rule. Dicey's acceptance of parliamentary sovereignty and representative government, therefore, was amalgamated with a pronounced emphasis upon law and the spirit of legality as the defining feature of the constitution. It was evident that the modernity and expansiveness of party government in the House of Commons were at the very least qualified by the tight traditionalism of common law and the independence of the judiciary. This was a point that was made clear in Dicey's conclusion:

> [T]he general principles of the constitution (as for example the right to personal liberty, or the right of public meeting) are ... the result of judicial decisions determining the rights of private persons in particular cases brought before the courts ... [W]ith us the law of the constitution, the rules which in foreign countries naturally form part of a constitutional code, are not the source but the consequence, of the rights of individuals as defined and enforced by the Courts ... thus the constitution is the result of the ordinary law of the land.[40]

In contrast to 'continental' forms of government like that of France, officials in the British system had no immunity from the normal legal framework. There was no specialised body of law peculiar to public administration. Civil servants, like policemen, remained citizens in uniform. Dicey also took pride in what he took to be the clear superiority of judicially recognised and enforced rights over the allegedly precarious nature of mere paper rights drawn from abstract declarations. The immediacy of Britain's rule of law was 'for practical purposes worth a hundred constitutional articles guaranteeing individual liberty'.[41]

The system's dependence upon conventions provided the *third* element of the British constitution. Conventions referred to those informal rules and customs that not only complemented the formal structures and procedures, but ensured that they were operated effectively in line with the accepted standards of fairness and legitimacy. In Dicey's view, conventions were clearly distinguishable from law in that no legal means existed to enforce them. Nonetheless, they were distinguishable both for the degree of binding moral obligation they instilled and for the widespread perception that they were indispensable to the constitution's integrity as a system of government.[42] Among these conventions were that money bills should not originate in the House of Lords; that the sovereign must assent to any bill passed by both houses of parliament; that a ministry resigns if it no longer commands the confidence of the House of Commons; that in any difference of opinion between the House of Lords and the House of Commons, the latter should prevail; and that the cabinet is responsible to Parliament for the general conduct of government. Despite being central to the machinery of the rule of law, such conventions were unknown to it. As tacit understandings, they were effectively non-justicable. And yet with the assistance of the common law tradition, such conventions were effective in shaping the conduct of government. They were testaments to what was and remained a dynamic process of institutional development.

Dicey was realistic enough to see that his theme of a constitutional rule of law would not be credible without addressing the self-evident imprecision in the structural, procedural and legal relationships at the heart of government. Conventions, built up by usage and legitimised by precedent, provided that element of consistency and predictability. Half-castes they may have been in that they were neither wholly law nor wholly impulse; nevertheless, they filled the interstices of the formal system and animated it into an integrated scheme of government. Dicey's conventions made a virtue out of a vice by allowing a code of practice to compensate for an absence of constitutional law. Fundamental ambiguities over the content and distribution of institutional powers, over the levels of permissible encroachment by institutions upon one another and over the scale of their discretionary authority were allegedly resolved in all but law by the social orthodoxy of conventions. Law, however, always remained in the background with the understanding that if an established convention were breached it would 'almost immediately bring the offender into conflict with the courts and the law of the land'.[43] Major or more widespread breaches were likely to lead to corrective legislation. By the same token, Dicey's principle of parliamentary sovereignty was also implicit in the maintenance of constitutional conventions. Because conventions were regarded by Dicey as mediating agents linking formal structures with changing political conditions, they were instrumental in the structure's adaptation to a mass franchise. Conventions facilitated the hegemony of the House of Commons within government and, in so doing, they underwrote the primacy of the electorate's political sovereignty. Their 'one ultimate object' in fact was 'to secure that Parliament, or the Cabinet which is indirectly appointed by Parliament, shall in the long run give effect to the will of that power which in modern England is the true political sovereign of the state – the majority of the electors or (to use popular though not quite accurate language) the nation'.[44]

Dicey's interpretation of the British constitution quickly acquired an authority that has remained largely intact to the present day. This is not to say that the premises and properties of the Diceyan perspective have been immune to criticism. On the contrary, Dicey's now traditional schema of government has brought in its wake a host of well-established criticisms. For example, it is often alleged that Dicey's conceptions of parliamentary sovereignty and the rule of law are logically and operationally incompatible with one another. Dicey himself had tried to pre-empt just such a criticism by claiming that they were quite consistent with one another – 'the sovereignty of parliament as contrasted with other forms of sovereign power, favours the supremacy of the law'.[45] Parliamentary sovereignty may once have been necessary to establish the rule of law over and against the arbitrary exercise of power by the crown, but once that threat had been eliminated the power of Parliament itself – or rather the party controlling the House of Commons – was quite able to exert power arbitrarily through the law. Far from being an absolute principle, the rule of law was dependent not only upon subjective interpretation but upon contemporary usage and political pressure. As such, the rule of law was not quite the constitutional anchorage portrayed in Dicey's analysis. Dicey refused to recognise the 'difficulty of reconciling the power of Parliament – which at a whim could destroy it – with the rule of law',[46] because in his view, Parliament would not exploit such an opportunity to infringe the rights and liberties of others, or to alter the basic framework and procedures of government. Echoing Blackstone, Dicey implied that Parliament could not do what it ought not to do: 'The theoretical possibility of tyranny was trumped by its practical and political impossibility. Whatever may have been the case in the past, a modern Parliament would never embark upon despotic measures ... Legal sovereignty was bounded and conditioned by the realities of political sovereignty. What *could* be done, *would* not be done.[47]

Equally subjective in nature and problematic in application were Dicey's constitutional conventions. They have spawned an entire critical literature on what constitutes a convention, how conventions can be discerned, what bases of obligation they are linked to, and how conventions coming into effect can be distinguished from those passing out of use. The same circular pattern that linked the existence of rules with the very obligation to comply with them, and which blended a process dependent upon conditions with the very presence of such conditions, was evident in Dicey's conception of the rule of law and its relationship to parliamentary sovereignty. Even though there was no necessary connection between his conception of a rule of law and the process of government, Dicey proceeded upon the assumption of a basic liberal consensus in Victorian society which effectively ensured that parliamentary sovereignty would faithfully reflect the values of civil liberties and minimal governmental intervention. Because Dicey had apparently missed the signals of a more collectivist role for government, he is regularly accused of having adopted an excessively narrow construction of the constitution – i.e. one that was not only confined *by* law but *to* 'law' and in particular to Dicey's conception of the law. As a consequence, he was considered blind to those developments of the modern state that were transcending and undermining his libertarian categories of constitutional law. For example:

> There can be little doubt that the absence of wide discretionary power which, for Dicey, was essentially the same as opposition to arbitrary conduct, was so closely associated with the rule of law and the British constitution that they became almost indistinguishable concepts. What might be thought extraordinary is not that Dicey and his contemporaries could unite to oppose unaccountable discretion and the possibility of factions holding the nation hostage but that he was unaware of the existence of such possibilities in the England of his time. The likely explanation is that Dicey saw the constitution in terms of individual liberties and nothing else. Regardless of the accuracy of his faith in the fact of British civil liberties, it was laissez-faire that seemed to him to represent the cornerstone of constitutional guarantees'.[48]

> Unfortunately Dicey's account of the Rule of Law, which was not really adequate in his own day, is now quite unacceptable. It is no longer true that government has no wide arbitrary discretionary power; equality before the law may be a necessary part of the Rule of Law, but it does not go very far by itself; and the notion that basic constitutional rights have to be derived from ordinary case law in order that a country be considered subject to the Rule of Law would mean that the United States was not subject to the Rule of Law. There seems something perverse in arguing that constitutionally guaranteed rights are actually inconsistent with the Rule of Law.[49]

Dicey's account of the constitution, therefore, has not been without its critics. It has been assailed for its empirical limitations, its logical disjunctions, its fusion of description and prescription. its political *naïveté* and its myopia towards constitutional development. These criticisms have in their turn prompted various attempts to revise, displace or demolish its position as an authoritative depiction of constitutional reality. The most concerted attempt to challenge the status of Dicey's exposition remains analysis Ivor Jennings's in *The Law and the Constitution* (1933). While the title was almost identical to the popular shortened title of Dicey's work (i.e. *The Law of the Constitution*), it was pointedly different in that it did not equate the constitution with law. In fact, Jennings's objective was to demonstrate that the constitution was rooted in benevolent power and popular consent.

In contrast to Dicey, Jennings did not equate official discretion with arbitrary power. On the contrary, Jennings located the constitution directly within the context of the positive state with its wide discretionary powers, its collectivist organisation and its obligation to social provision. In Jennings's view, the Whiggish conception of Dicey's constitution was ideologically motivated. The rule of law was merely a static legal device for achieving political stasis. As a consequence, Dicey had failed to 'consider the *powers* of authorities. He seemed to think that the British constitution was concerned almost entirely with the *rights of individuals*. He was imagining a constitution dominated by the doctrine of *laissez-faire*.'[50] Jennings sought to reverse this weighting by showing that the rule of law was not a legal principle so much as a purely subjective entity designed to accommodate the personal political philosophy of its originator. To Jennings, the rule of law was rooted in power.

> Its powers are not only wide, but unlimited. In most countries, not only the administrative authorities but also the legislature have powers limited by the constitution. This one would think, is the most effective rule of law. In England, the administration has powers limited by legislation, but the powers of the legislature are not limited at all. There is still, it may be argued, a rule of law, but the law may at any moment be changed. Strictly speaking, therefore, there is no constitutional law at all in Great Britain, there is only the arbitrary power of Parliament.[51]

Because of his attachment to liberal dogma, Dicey's constitution could be dismissed as an anachronism which failed to discern the contemporary corporatism of the bureaucratic state and the impulse for social justice through government intervention.

In line with this emphasis upon political realism, there was no essential difference in Jennings's eyes between constitutional conventions and legal rules because they were both reducible to 'general acquiescence'.[52] It was not simply that 'many conventions were as important as any rules of laws'.[53] It was that they were essentially 'rules whose nature did not differ fundamentally from that of positive law'.[54] By the same token, the control of Parliament and its ability to give contemporary definition to the 'rule of law' ultimately lay with the supreme power of the electorate. This was not Dicey's electorate of core liberal opinion but a heterogeneous electorate of competing and often polarised views leading to governments constantly conditioned by the need for re-election. Jennings was concerned with the political contingencies that lay behind legal formalism. To him, the supremacy of Parliament was a common law 'legal fiction'[55] made into fact by the actual and deterrent effect of political and electoral forces. Such a supremacy leads to 'a strong executive, capable of taking decisions and, within the limits of political expediency, forcing them upon the country'.[56] As a consequence, the 'Government does in truth govern'.[57]

While Dicey essentially assimilated change as an affirmative condition of Britain's rule of law, Jennings's more active endorsement of the central state, and the mobilisation of mass consent as the basis of legitimate government action, opened up the prospect of an altogether more instrumentalist view of the constitutionalism. Dicey's equation of law and constitutionalism was confronted by a conception of the constitution rooted in politics and geared towards political change and programmatic reform. The principles and framework of limited government appeared to give way to an expansive utilitarian state that responded to social and economic needs irrespective of nineteenth-century liberal structures. Jennings sought to demonstrate that the established process of the British constitution would not always produce the same outcomes. The rule of law in itself would not prevent the occurrence of radically variable consequences, especially given the emphasis that was laid on party supremacy and legal positivism. To Dicey, such an infrastructure of rules and procedures could only ever be consistent with a liberal conception of limited government. The laws of the constitution were directed to this overall law of the constitution. It was a matter of substance and internal logic. Just as Dicey had provided a corrective to prior constitutional conceptualisation, so Jennings attempted to correct Dicey in the light of a rapidly developing central state. Whether Jennings is interpreted as transcending or extrapolating Dicey, the net effect was to show that both the law and the constitution were reducible to politics in a less than consensual society. Jennings agreed with Dicey that the constitution was essentially a derivative of processes but disagreed as to the nature and direction of such a derivative.

Jennings's sceptical view of both the existence and the value of a liberal rule of law constitution showed how susceptible the British constitution was to a political construction. It introduced the concept of a 'political constitution' in which the constitution was conceived as a direct expression of political exchange in a society divided by conflict. In such a constitution, there could be no division between constitutional and political questions; they were simply inter-changeable with one another. A political constitution not only underwrote the explicit politicisation of constitutional legitimacy upon the structure and operation of the political framework and whatever it produced in decisions and outcomes. Harold Laski, for example, dismissed all concerns over the rise of the bureaucratic state prior to, during and following World War II. To Laski the delegation of legislative powers to ministers and civil servants was inevitable. The constitution needed to reflect the purposiveness of government. 'The first and most vital function of the electorate is to choose a House of Commons the membership of which makes possible the creation of a Government which can govern.'[58] From this first principle it was wholly justifiable for the executive to use whatever political means were available to force through government programmes of social and economic regulation. To Laski, the growth of administrative jurisdiction was no threat to the rule of law. Turning Dicey on his head, the real danger to the rule of law came from judges and their social prejudices.

> [T]he judges seem to me to have used in their approach to most problems of administrative Law canons of statuary interpretation which have been intended not only to preserve the full amplitude of their jurisdiction over question of *vires* but, also, to strike down in the realm of social policy changes in the direction the law has begun to take which they cannot easily reconcile with the doctrines that men like Holt read into the Common Law as they began to adapt it to the habits of a society increasingly dominated by the power of business men.[59]

In Laski's view, the constitution should facilitate rather than limit electorally sanctioned political action. Constraint would always be present in the form of class conflict, party opposition and electoral deterrence. There was no need and no reason for additional restraint to be artificially perpetuated within the political system through structural checks and balances or antiquarian codes of practice.[60]

This reconstruction of constitutional probity into comprehensive political realism is probably best exemplified in J. A. G. Griffith's seminal article 'The Political Constitution'. Like Ivor Jennings, under whom he studied, Griffith was motivated by the intellectual and political need to strip the constitution of its pretensions as an autonomous and self-sustaining medium of political value and structural management. To Griffith, that fiction had been exposed in the 1920s and 1930s when those who continued to use the

> language of the old liberal democracies ... were seen at worst as elaborate facades deliberately constructed to fool most of the people most of the time or at best as out of date pieces of stage paraphernalia which someone had forgotten to clear away with the other impedimenta of Professor Dicey's England ... We sought therefore to free ourselves from the tentacles of the natural lawyers, the

metaphysicians and the illusionists who gave the impression that the working of constitutions was something all done by mirrors, by sleight of hand, and the use of nineteenth-century language based on eighteenth-century concepts.[61]

But while Griffith and many of his contemporaries may have been duly emancipated, the liberal construction of the constitution remained.

The British constitution continued to be characterised as an equilibrium of powers affording a process of governmental self-limitation that was amenable to the assumptions of liberal pluralism as it was accommodating to the more hierarchical and authoritative strategies of Tory democracy.[62] Griffith remarks that even in the last quarter of the twentieth century '[i]t is still quite common to hear the constitution described – even lovingly described – as a piece of machinery cleverly and subtly constructed to enable the will of the people to be transmitted through its elected representatives'.[63] In his drive to expose the moral neutrality of law and to demonstrate that 'law is not and cannot be a substitute for politics' ... ,[64] Griffith asserts that the 'constitution of the United Kingdom lives on, changing from day to day for the constitution is no more and no less than what happens. Everything that happens is constitutional. And if nothing happened that would be constitutional also.'[65] Attempts to wrap the constitution in a rule of law are therefore regarded as deceptive fallacies concealing a Whig counter-revolution to reverse the effect of a mass electorate.

It may be thought from the now conventional critiques of Dicey and from the consequences of a more widely acknowledged 'political constitution' that Dicey's conception of the British constitution had been superseded by contemporary developments – i.e. that it had evolved into a different entity by the very adaptability to which Dicey himself had given much emphasis. But this is simply not the case. Notwithstanding the various empirical and normative challenges to Dicey, his construction of the constitution has remained conspicuously intact. Dicey is still distinguished for having provided a 'classic constitutional statement'.[66] The allusions to classicism continue to be commonplace. While Dicey is credited with having established the 'classical definition'[67] of the rule of law, so he is also said both to have provided 'the classical statement'[68] of the principle of parliamentary government and to have given the 'classical exposition of the significance of the constitutional conventions in England'.[69] '[R]arely has a single book on the constitution reaped such acclaim and dominated the field so thoroughly.'[70] As a result, Dicey's three cardinal principles amounted to 'the nearest thing to a written constitution that England has ever recognised'.[71] Dicey's significance, however, is not confined to the past. 'Shades of Dicey are still in evidence casting an influence over present day constitutional and administrative law.'[72] Parliamentary government 'receives its best known modern statement'[73] in Dicey's work. Furthermore, 'any modern discussion' of the rule of law 'must begin with the theory of Professor A. V. Dicey ... because discussion of the concept in this country has for the past century centred round his ideas'.[74] Dicey's influence upon the legal study of the British constitution therefore remains undiminished. It is said that the 'great value of Dicey's work in this field has been to provide lawyers and jurists with an ideal'.[75] Others refer to the fact that for 'students of the British constitution ... the rule of law pre-eminently means Dicey's doctrine of the rule of law'.[76] The 'extraordinarily influential'[77] nature of *The Law of the Constitution* means that for the constitution 'Dicey's account ... is still the starting point for discussion today'.[78] Some even maintain that it remains the finishing point as well in so far as it is 'still widely used in the definitive description of the British constitution'.[79]

Dicey's academic influence has in its own turn generated a persistent force within contemporary politics and public life. His 'landmark work of constitutional interpretation became the twentieth century orthodoxy, from which generations of students – and even, through the public language of politics, a citizenry – learned an understanding and appreciation of the distinctive characteristics of the British unwritten constitution'.[80] Consequently, Dicey's constitutional propositions and the 'basic ideas they express have been, and still are, very real in their influence on government'.[81] Even though, his principles and methodology are regularly challenged therefore, 'it is right to take Dicey seriously – and not just because of the profound influence of his account in shaping a twentieth-century doctrine of the constitution',[82] but because many of his 'views have not been superseded and his description of the authority of Parliament still represents the general orthodoxy'.[83] In the words of his biographer, 'no individual since Blackstone has had such an impact as Dicey on the development of constitutional law'.[84] He concludes: 'No other scholar has taken his place. His facility of expression has kept his doctrines alive. Dicey has dominated the discussion ... [and] has framed the boundaries within which all later debate has taken place. Modern revision has not eroded the solid foundations Dicey provided for his doctrine.'[85]

To assess Dicey's contemporary authority as a constitutional commentator, a random selection of eight widely used works on the British constitution was taken and the number of references to Dicey was compared with the number of references to other historically established constitutional commentators. The results are presented in Table 2.1 It is immediately evident from this table that Dicey continues to hold a pre-eminent position as Britain's most authoritative constitutional interpreter. In each of the eight works there are more references to Dicey than to any other individual commentator. The preponderance of references to Dicey is even clearer when the numerical differential and proportional ratio between the first and the second rankings in each book are taken into account. In five out of the

Table 2.1 *The relative prominence of Albert Venn Dicey as a contemporary commentator on the British constitution*

Commentators	(a)	(b)	(c)	(d)	(e)	(f)	(g)	(h)
				*Selected books**				
				Number of page references				
Leo Amery	0	0	0	0	1	0	0	2
Walter Bagehot	7	14	0	9	3	4	0	6
William Blackstone	1	1	13	0	2	0	2	0
Lord Bryce	0	0	1	0	1	0	0	0
Albert Venn Dicey	8	42	18	30	11	8	21	17
J. A. G. Griffith	3	0	0	0	6	0	0	1
Ivor Jennings	0	4	6	3	5	2	0	0
Harold Laski	4	0	0	0	0	1	0	3
F. W. Maitland	0	2	5	0	0	0	2	0
J. D. B. Mitchell	0	0	2	0	0	0	0	0
O. Hood Phillips	0	0	0	0	4	0	0	0
E. C. S. Wade	0	7	0	0	2	0	0	0
Dicey's Ranking	1	1	1	1	1	1	1	1
Ratio of Dicey's references over those in second place	1.14	3.00	1.38	3.33	1.83	2.0	10.50	2.83
Dicey's share of all references	34.8%	60.0%	40.0%	71.4%	31.4%	53.3%	84.0%	58.6%

* (a) John Dearlove and Peter Saunders, *Introduction to British Politics: Analysing a Capitalist Democracy*, 2nd edn (Cambridge: Polity, 1991); (b) Ian Harden and Norman Lewis, *The Noble Lie: The British Constitution and the Rule of Law* (London: Hutchinson, 1986); (c) O. Hood Phillips and Paul Jackson, *O. Hood Phillips' Constitutional and Administrative Law*, 7th edn (London: Sweet and Maxwell, 1987); (d) Peter Madgwick and Diana Woodhouse, *The Law and Politics of the Constitution of the United Kingdom* (Hemel Hempstead: Harvester Wheatsheaf, 1995); (e) Philip Norton, *The Constitution in Flux* (Oxford: Martin Robertson, 1982); (f) Gillian Peele, *Governing the UK*, 3rd edn (Oxford: Blackwell, 1995); (g) Stanley de Smith and Rodney Brazier, *Constitutional and Administrative Law*, 7th edn (London: Penguin, 1994); (h) Tony Wright, *Citizens and Subjects: An Essay on British Politics* (London: Routledge, 1994).

eight books, the references to Dicey are more than double the references to his nearest rival. In one commentary, Dicey outstrips his nearest rival by a ratio of 10.5:1. Dicey's share of all the references to constitutional commentators in each item never drops below 30 per cent and in three books it accounts for 60 per cent or more of the citations. The second most widely cited commentator is Walter Bagehot but he is a poor second with only 43 references compared to Dicey's 155. Moreover, Bagehot's study of the constitition was published 18 years prior to Dicey's analysis. Ivor Jennings, who conciously sought to displace Dicey as the pre-eminent commentator on the constitution, and whose book was published nearly 50 years after *The Law of the Constitution*, registers only 20 references. With 54.6 per cent of all the refences to those commentators cited in the eight-book sample, Dicey remains the single most authorative source of interpretation on the fundamental nature of the constitution. If Dicey was originally distinguished for demonstrating that the British constitution of the late nineteenth century was susceptible to being reduced to a classic statement of principles, the prevalence of Dicey in modern constitutional interpretation reveals that, even in the face of radical change and wholesale criticism, no effective substitute for Dicey has emerged. Over time, *The Law of the Constitution* has become less of a classic exposition and more of a constitutional construct in its own right.

The continued orthodoxy of the Diceyan perspective is attributable to two main reasons. First, Dicey's critics are very often arguing at cross-purposes with what they believe to be the Diceyan misconception of the constitution. In many respects, they set up a false dichotomy, in which the distance between themselves and Dicey is needlessly inflated and dramatised. This is most evident in the distinction that is habitually made between Dicey's apparently exclusive pre-occupation with law and the critics' professed realism in recognising and assimilating the inter-connectedness of law and politics. But this is a misconception as one of the main thrusts of Dicey's work was precisely the relationship between the legal and political dimensions of sovereignty and, in particular, the constitutional facilitation of electoral democracy. Even though Dicey is reputed to have been wedded to the principled individualism of nineteenth-century liberal doctrine, his open recognition of parliamentary sovereignty and the role of conventions in 'ensuring the supremacy of the House of Commons, and ultimately ... of the nation'[86] bears witness to his acceptance of a political constitution. It is true that Dicey believed that such a political constitution would normally produce a limited state because this embodied the prevailing public philosophy. The dynamic was similar to what is known in American jurisprudence as 'substantive due process' in which constitutional procedures are not regarded as being neutral but are seen as being designed to protect and maximise a particular set of values.

In effect, Dicey's political constitution was a tight loop in which the liberal principles of government both reflected and reinforced the liberal principles of society as a whole. As we have already noted, this integrated correspondence between a liberal consensus and the rule of law broke down in the face of an increasingly divided society and an expansionary central state. In their wake came a more robust and a notionally open-ended view of a political constitution. And yet, on closer inspection, Dicey's loop of substantive due process is still present in the commentaries of Jennings, Laski and Griffith. The loop may be bigger, looser and more irregular in nature than Dicey's tightly closed system but an implicit belief in the existence and value of certain anchorages of restraint still informs, conditions and disciplines the apparently uninhibited interplay of politics within a political constitution. Despite the partisan and ideological divisions that characterise contemporary politics, it is clear that even the most avid proponents of an emancipated political constitution proceed on the understanding that certain core principles of government conduct will be maintained by political rather than legal means. John Griffith, for example, dismisses a bill of rights, and its corollary of a supreme court, as a wholly unnecessary and unworkable device because restraint of such a nature should emanate from political decisions taken by politicians working within the pressures of representative and accountable government.[87] Although the concept of constraint in Griffith's political constitution depends rather more upon the hidden hand of political exchange than upon an explicit liberal solidarity, the reasoning behind it bears a very close resemblance to the substantive due process arguments advanced by Dicey in condemning continental adventurism in natural law and abstract rights.

The second reason behind Dicey's prominence in modern accounts of the British constitution lies in the sheer tranquillity that his perspective has invested in the form and operation of the constitution. It is not merely that Dicey formulated an authoritative commentary on the British constitution, or that he provided an otherwise disordered assemblage of rules and themes with a set of fundamental organising principles through which a functioning constitution could be identified and made accessible as a single entity. It is that Dicey made the constitution, and with it the idea of constitutionalism, a safe and secure subject. The constitutionality of the British constitution could be taken as read as it was simultaneously both an object and an agent of a basic consensus. While the exact nature of that consensus may have changed, the consequences of its existence have remained intact. This is reflected in the studied British disinterest in the theory and practice of their own constitution. The British constitution is presumed simply to exist. It is even afforded respect and affection on the basis of a utilitarian regard for something workable, or at least not evidently unworkable. To deploy constitutional arguments against it as a constitution is considered pointless because the system is devoid of the arenas, or even the criteria, through which such arguments might purposefully be engaged and evaluated.

Dicey was instrumental in propagating this constitutional outlook not merely because of the content of his work but also because of the way his construction of the constitution became orthodox to the point of foreclosing serious debate over the nature of its operation. The very success of Dicey's archetypal constitutional commentary, and the fact that it remained effectively unchallenged for so long, revealed a basic disposition against constitutional speculation. In essence, Dicey was significant not simply for providing a way of looking at the British constitution but for disclosing a British way of looking at constitutions. This often quizzical, usually indifferent and occasionally jaundiced approach to the constitutional dimension continues to be an integral element of British political debate, which remains conspicuously deficient in the vocabulary of constitutional meaning and validity. The sense of bemused perplexity over the theory and practice of constitutionalism is well captured in the comments by Norman Stone, Ferdinand Mount and Tom Nairn:

> To most people, constitutions are a bore – a cause taken up by earnest, waggling beards, preaching about 'devolution' and 'Europe' and other such detumescent subjects ... [These are] goods that are very, very, difficult to sell to the masses: there is no demand for constitutional reform here.[88]

> [W] ho runs the show and how they do it ... [T]his is the only kind of information that men of affairs want or need to know. Anyone who has ever been asked to brief a leading industrialist or politician will know how quickly their eyes glaze over once this essential information has been provided, how little interest they have in questions of theory or structure and how anxious they are to press on to other topics ... Constitutional writing in this country since Bagehot has had a prosy, commonplace lack of ambition about it. And it is not, I think, coincidental that our understanding of our Constitution has become both attenuated and atrophied over the same period.[89]

> The whole trade of commentary upon the Constitution is ... a realm of quasi-legal necromancy in Britain. It is performed on a mist-shrouded academic plateau by a specially-evolved breed of academic lawyer-philosophers, whose totemic lore is remote from everyday politics. An ancient goat-track connects it with Westminster, and ends there; mutual exchanges of gifts do take place (customarily in the shape of finely wrought footnotes rather than tomes), but rarely more than once in each generation. The task of these upland shamans (it should be recalled) is to 'interpret' an historical transubstantiation almost as miraculous as the one patented in Palestine: how the Sovereign authority of the English Monarchy was conveyed to Parliament, and thence bestowed in wisely reluctant doses upon the people. God's descent into History is recorded

in no written constitution. How could it be? This was an unique advent, which since then others have merely sought to copy with their abortive revolutions, bureaucrats and batteries of pathetic 'principles'.[90]

These comments reflect the essence of the British constitutional tradition – i .e. a presumptive belief in the presence and operational integrity of a coherent constitutional structure. Dicey's bequest is the notion of an underlying and unyielding rule of law which not only amounts to a normative subtext to British political life, but effectively directs empirical enquiry into the constitution towards a single preconceived base point. The constitution is taken to be a matter of fact, but it is a fact driven by faith. To argue against the constitution has traditionally been regarded as socially unconventional and even subversive. Criticism can be tantamount to 'un-British activities' in that it jeopardises the constitution's functional utility as a scheme of government by challenging its master convention of preferring principle and consistency over scepticism. As a consequence, the British constitution has become closely associated not only with a political system that tends to restrict access to constitutional questions and to pre-empt constitutional debate, but with a political culture that condones and even encourages such self-imposed analytical limitation.

Contemporary constitutional attitudes in many ways imitate Dicey's own methodology. He was ostensibly an inductivist working to extract a set of simplifying and unifying constitutional principles from a mass of complex legislative and political material. His method in its turn was comparable to what he considered to be the nature of the British constitution itself 'where the principles of the constitution are inductions or generalisations based upon particular decisions pronounced by the courts'.[91] To Dicey, both these inductivist processes culminated in the emergence of a coherent whole. Dicey can be criticised for always seeing a constitutional sculpture concealed within the political rock. He was perhaps too ready to make large inductive leaps into universalist positions, thereupon engaging in deductive applications from the general to the particular. Nevertheless, he set the pattern for what was to come.

The popularity, authority and protracted longevity of his commentary encouraged a widespread, and deductively generated, contentment with the particularistic dimension of constitutional existence. In Britain, while the constitution is taken to be a single entity, it is almost invariably discussed in its component parts. Reports and articles on constitutional development are traditionally presented in the form of lists of discrete and free-standing events with little or no consideration given to their theoretical or systematic implications. The now conventional reflex of Dicey's inductive leap results in the implicit assumption that 'recent developments' conform to a pre-existing template of constitutional integrity. Developments are necessarily constitutional as they are the direct consequence of an arrangement that continues to be seen as exemplifying the principle of substantive due process. This circular relationship of constitutional cause and effect continues to envelop the constitution and to suffuse British polities with the reassurance of inherent and intuitive constitutionality. It is this sense of an underlying constitutional settlement, and the belief in the durable nature of its balances between political and legal sovereignty, public and private interests, and between state power and civil liberties, that fosters the equanimity with which even the fundamentalist advocates of a political constitution press their case. Dicey's old safety net retains its significance and like any safety net, it is not the objective entity of a constitution so much as the social and cultural security drawn from its perceived existence that has defined the orthodox idea of British constitutionality.

Notes

1   Quoted in Bernard Bailyn, *The Ideological Origins of the American Revolution* (Cambridge, Mass.: Belknap, 1967), p. 67.

2   J. G. A. Pocock, 'Macchiavelli, Harrington, and English Political Ideologies in the Eighteenth Century', *William and Mary Quarterly*, vol. 22, no. 4 (1965), p. 572.

3   M. J. C. Vile, *Constitutionalism and the Separation of Powers* (London: Oxford University Press, 1967), p. 99.

4   C. L. de S. Montesquieu, *The Spirit of the Laws*, trans. T. Nugent, intro. Franz Neumann (New York: Hafner, 1949), Book XI.

5   Montesquieu, *The Spirit of the Laws*, pp. li–lix; Vile, *Constitutionalism*, ch. 4.

6   Raymond Aron, *Main Currents in Sociological Thought* (Harmondsworth: Penguin), pp. 30–5.

7   Quoted in Herbert J. Storing, 'William Blackstone' in Leo Strauss and Joseph Cropsey (eds), *History of Political Philosophy*, 2nd edn (Chicago: Rand McNally, 1972), p. 599. See also Ernest Barker, 'Blackstone on the British Constitution' in Ernest Barker (ed.), *Essays on Government*, 2nd edn (Oxford: Clarendon, 1951), pp. 120–53.

8   Quoted in Storing 'William Blackstone' p. 598.

9   Ernest Barker, *Traditions of Civility: Eight Essays* (Cambridge: Cambridge University Press, 1948), p. 253.

10 Isaac Kramnick, *Bolingbroke and His Circle: The Politics of Nostalgia in the Age of Walpole* (Cambridge, Mass.: Harvard University Press, 1968), ch. 6; J. H. Burns, 'Bolingbroke and the Concept of Constitutional Government', *Political Studies*, vol. 10, no. 4 (October 1962), pp. 264–76.

11 Henry St John Bolingbroke, 'Mixed Government' in Philip W. Buck (ed.), *How Conservatives Think* (Harmondsworth: Penguin, 1975), pp. 39–40.

12 Robert Shackleton, 'Montesquieu, Bolingbroke and the Separation of Powers', *French Studies*, vol. 3, no. 1 (January 1949), pp. 25–38.

13 Ibid., p. 35.

14 W. B. Gwyn, *The Meaning of the Separation of Powers: An Analysis of the Doctrine from Its Origin to the Adoption of the United States Constitution* (New Orleans: Tulane University Press, 1965), pp. 96–9.

15 See Vile, *Constitutionalism*, pp.98–118; *Gwyn*, Separation of Powers, pp. 82–128; Stanley Pargellis, 'The Theory of Balanced Government' in Conyers Read (ed.), *The Constitution Reconsidered* (New York: Columbia University Press, 1938), pp. 37–49; Francis D. Wormuth, *The Origins of Modern Constitutionalism* (New York: Harper, 1949), pp. 169–83.

16 Bailyn, *American Revolution*, p. 71.

17 See Michael Foley, *Laws, Men and Machines: Modern American Government and the Appeal of Newtonian Mechanics* (London: Routledge, 1990), chs 1, 2.

18 See Ian Gilmour, *Riot, Risings and Revolution: Governance and Violence in Eighteenth-Century England* (London: Pimlico, 1993); V. A. G. Gatrell, *The Hanging Tree: Execution and the English People, 1770–1868* (Oxford: Oxford University Press 1994); Peter Linebaugh, *The London Hanged: Crime and Civil Society in the Eighteenth Century* (London: Allen Lane, 1991).

19 Gilmour, *Riots, Risings and Revolution*, p. 163.

20 Michael Bentley, *Politics Without Democracy: Perception and Preoccupation in British Government* (London: Fontana, 1989); Norman Gash, *Aristocracy and People: Britain 1815–1865* (London: Edward Arnold, 1979); David G. Wright, *Democracy and Reform, 1815–1885* (Harlow: Longman, 1970); Stephen J. Lee, *Aspects of British Political History, 1815–1914* (London: Routledge, 1994).

21 Thomas B. Macaulay, *The History of England*, vol. 2 [1855] (London: Dent, 1967), pp. 342–80

22 Robert Blake, *The Conservative Party from Peel to Churchill* (London: Fontana, 1972 p. 16.

23 A. H. Birch, *Representative and Responsible Government: An Essay on the British Constitution* (London: Unwin, 1964), chs 2–5.

24 Jon Roper, *Democracy and its Critics: Anglo-American Democratic Thought in the Nineteenth Century* (London: Unwin Hyman, 1989), p. 122.

25 Birch, *Representative and Responsible Government*, p. 55.

26 Alexis de Tocqueville, *Democracy in America*, trans. Henry Reeve, ed. and intro. Henry S. Commager (London: Oxford University Press, 1946), p. 182.

27 John S. Mill, 'Representative Government' in John S. Mill, *Utilitarianism, Liberty, Representative Government* ed. H. B. Acton (London: J. M. Dent, 1972), pp. 229–30.

28 Walter Bagehot, *The English Constitution*, intro. R. H. S. Crossman, (London: Fontana, 1963), p. 94.

29 *Ibid.*, p. 97.

30 *Ibid.*, p. 63.

31 *Ibid.*, p. 85.

32 *Ibid.*, p. 63

33 G. H. L. Le May, *The Victorian Constitution* (London: Duckworth, 1979), p. 2.

34 *Ibid.*, p. 2.

35 Ferdinand Mount, *The British Constitution Now: Recovery or Decline?* (London: Mandarin, 1993), p. 45.

36   Albert Venn Dicey, *Introduction to the Study of the Law of the Constitution*, intro. E. C. S. Wade, 10th edn (London: Macmillan, 1959), pp. 39–40.

37   O. Hood Phillips, *Constitutional and Administrative Law*, 6th edn (London: Sweet and Maxwell, 1978), p. 46.

38   Quoted in Storing, 'William Blackstone', p. 598.

39   Dicey, *The Law of the Constitution*, p. 84.

40   *Ibid.*, pp. 195, 203.

41   *Ibid.*, p. 199.

42   *Ibid.*, chs 14, 15.

43   *Ibid.*, p. 446.

44   *Ibid.*, p. 429.

45   *Ibid.*, p. 406.

46   John F. McEldowney, 'Dicey in Historical Perspective – A Review Essay' in Patrick McAuslan and John F. McEldowney (eds), *Law, Legitimacy and the Constitution: Essays Marking the Centenary of Dicey's Law of the Constitution* (London: Sweet and Maxwell, 1985), p. 59.

47   Tony Wright, *Citizens and Subjects: An Essay on British Politics* (London: Routledge, 1994), p. 16.

48   Ian Harden and Norman Lewis, *The Noble Lie: The British Constitution and the Rule of Law* (London: Hutchinson, 1986), p. 44.

49   P. S. Atiyah, *Law and Modern Society* (Oxford: Oxford University Press, 1983), p. 66.

50   W. Ivor Jennings, *The Law and the Constitution*, 3rd edn (London: University of London Press, 1943), pp. 54–5.

51   *Ibid.*, pp. 56, 64.

52   *Ibid.*, p. 117.

53   *Ibid.*, p. 84.

54   *Ibid.*, p. 74.

55   *Ibid.*, p. 149.

56   *Ibid.*, p. 169.

57   *Ibid.*

58   Harold J. Laski, *Reflections on the Constitution: The House of Commons, the Cabinet, the Civil Service* (Manchester: Manchester University Press, 1951), p. 58.

59   *Ibid.*, p. 45.

60   Anthony Wright, 'British Socialists and the British Constitution', *Parliamentary Affairs*, vol. 43, no. 3 (July 1990), pp. 330–5.

61   J. A. G. Griffith, 'The Political Constitution', *The Modern Law Review*, vol. 42, no. 1 (January 1979), pp. 5–6.

62   See L. S. Amery, *Thoughts on the Constitution, 1873–1955* (London: Oxford University Press, 1964).

63   Griffith, 'The Political Constitution', p. 5.

64   *Ibid.*, p. 16.

65   *Ibid.*, p. 19.

66   John Greenaway, Steve Smith and John Street, *Deciding Factors in British Politics: A Case-Study Approach* (London: Routledge, 1992), p. 48.

67   J. A. Corry, 'The Prospects for the Rule of Law' in W. J. Stankiewicz (ed.), *Crisis*

in British Government: The Need for Reform (London: Collier-Macmillan, 1967), p. 3.

68 Graeme C. Moodie, *The Government of Great Britain* (London: Methuen, 1964), p. 105.

69 K. C. Wheare, *Modern Constitutions* (London: Oxford University Press, 1966), p. 122.

70 Richard A. Cosgrove, *The Rule of Law: Albert Venn Dicey, Victorian Jurist* (London: Macmillan, 1980), p. 75.

71 Charles Townsend, *Making the Peace: Public Order and Public Scrutiny in Modern Britain* (Oxford: Oxford University Press, 1993), p. 47.

72 McEldowney, 'Dicey in Historical Perspective', p. 42.

73 Moodie, *The Government of Great Britain*, p. 15.

74 D. C. Yardley, *Introduction to British Constitutional Law*, 7th edn (London: Butterworths, 1990), p. 74.

75 *Ibid.*, p. 78.

76 O. Hood Phillips and Paul Jackson, *O. Hood Phillips' Constitutional and Administrative Law*, 7th edn (London: Sweet and Maxwell, 1987), p. 36.

77 H. Calvert, *An Introduction to British Constitutional Law* (London: Blackstone, 1985), p. 28.

78 C. R. Munro, *Studies in Constitutional Law* (London: Butterworths, 1987), p. 82.

79 Greenaway *et al.*, *Deciding Factors in British Politics*, p. 48.

80 Wright, *Citizens and Subjects*, p. 15.

81 J. Harvey and L. Bather, *The British Constitution* (London: Macmillan, 1964), p. 399

82 Wright, *Citizens and Subjects*, p. 18.

83 Geoffrey Marshall, 'Law or Convention?' (review of *The Rule of Law* by Richard Cosgrove), *Times Higher Education Supplement*, 5 June 1981.

84 Cosgrove, *The Rule of Law*, p. 86.

85 *Ibid.*, p. 78.

86 Dicey, *The Constitution*, p. 431.

87 J. A .G. Griffith, 'The Political Constitution', pp. 1–21; J. A. G. Griffith, *The Politics of the Judiciary*, 4th edn (London: Fontana, 1991), ch. 6.

88 Norman Stone, 'Reformal Logic' (review of *The British Constitution Now* by Ferdinand Mount), *Sunday Times*, 10 May 1992.

89 Mount, *The British Constitution Now*, pp. 46, 47.

90 Tom Nairn, *The Enchanted Glass: Britain and Its Monarchy* (London: Vintage, 1994), p. 362.

91 Dicey, *The Law of the Constitution*, p. 197.

3

Constitutional fuels

Over the past 20 years, the constitutional dimension of civil authority has become more conspicuous either as a conclusion to, or as a premise of, political exchange and argument. The protective disciplines of ambiguity and evasion have eroded as the emphasis has shifted away from a largely self-contained regime of political accommodation between the main parties to a more plural and porous context in which a variety of impulses and outlooks interact at different levels to produce an altogether more critical awareness of the structural and procedural factors that condition the conduct of government. It is now recognised that the equanimity with which the British constitution used to be regarded has been shaken by a set of anxieties over the contemporary nature and operation of constitutional processes.

The traditional dependency of what was conceded to be a 'political constitution' upon the distribution of political forces, tempered by social norms of self-restraint, once assured the public of a system that could be relied upon to provide responsiveness, adaptability and efficiency in government, while remaining in a notional equilibrium of collective limitation. It is this benign conception of the system which has increasingly been subjected to public criticism on the grounds that its balances are no longer reliable or even operative in such a rapidly changing social and political environment. Whether this scepticism owes more to a genuine unease over the underlying principles of governmental performance, or to the need for an alternative strategy of political opposition to a government that had remained in office for 18 years, the net effect is the same – namely, a growing realisation that the constitution amounts to a substantive issue in its own right. The cultural and political inhibitions against resorting to constitutional arguments and critiques have conspicuously relaxed. The previously subliminal properties of the constitutional underworld have deteriorated into the critical light of public attention. The British constitution which used to be taken as read is now viewed with suspicion because it evokes a growing sense of systemic maladjustment with the effects of a society in accelerated development.

It is commonplace for the constitution to be criticised for being both too adaptable and insufficiently responsive. It not only attracts complaints that it fails to provide a set of principled points of reference, but draws criticism that it suffers from excessive entrenchment. Like the British constitution itself, the critiques of it are as manifold and segmented in design as they are mercurial in motivation and intention. The constitution evokes dissent in its own image and, as such, the turmoil surrounding the contemporary constitution is characterised by discrete and disparate forms of selective complaint. It has already been noted that the singular entity of the British constitution disguises a melange of laws, customs, norms, conventions, precedents and understandings. Similarly the anxieties and indictments generated by the constitution have no organising principle and have to be conceived and analysed as distinct responses to distinct stimuli – with only an incidental relationship to one another. The constitutional debate in Britain is essentially fuelled by several discernible themes which are closely related to substantive political issues and which together constitute a multiple assault upon what has traditionally been seen as an aggregate constitution. These fuels have disturbed the old tranquillity surrounding the constitution and they continue to generate an agenda for constitutional change.

The objective of this chapter is to make a searching examination of each one of these fuels, to demonstrate the distinctive nature of their separate properties, to locate each fuel within its political context and to explain the driving force of such fuels in raising constitutional issues and in transforming the old norm of constitutional politics into the now established unorthodoxy of a politics of constitutional dispute.

Fuel No. 1: ELECTORAL INEQUITY

Implicit in the idea of a representative democracy are the notions of a filter and a microcosm. In a mass society, it is regarded as not only a necessary but also a positive benefit that the volatile nature of raw public opinion should be refined through an electoral process that gives representatives the opportunity to deliberate and to exercise their judgement free from factional interests or majority intolerance. By the same token, a representative democracy has to approximate closely to the society it seeks to represent, in order to maintain its legitimacy as a system of government. In Britain, the electoral system is heavily criticised for operating such a strong yet arbitrary set of filters that it not only impugns the representative integrity of the government but throws into doubt the status of its democratic credentials.

The well-rehearsed indictment of Britain's 'first-past-the-post' (FPTP) system normally includes the following charges. British electoral arrangements are said to discriminate against smaller parties in favour of the two major parties. Although there is nothing inherently discriminatory in the FPTP system, the net effect of its operation in Britain disproportionately favours the two main parties. For the most part, third parties are disadvantaged because their supporters amount to dispersed minorities that are rarely able to achieve electoral superiority over the one or other of the two main parties. It is true that the system will reward highly localised third parties whose support is sufficiently concentrated to prevail in a limited number of constituencies (e.g. Plaid Cymru, Scottish National Party). But the FPTP system does make it difficult for any nationally organised third party (e.g. Liberal Democrats) to secure parliamentary seats in proportion to its popular vote. In 1983, for example, the Social Democratic Party–Liberal Alliance secured 25.4 per cent of the national vote, coming second in 313 constituencies but winning only 3.5 per cent of parliamentary seats (i.e. 23). In 1992, the Liberal Democrats acquired 17.9 per cent of the popular vote but were only able to translate their 6 million votes into 3.1 per cent of the seats in the House of Commons (i.e. 20). The net effect of such results in 1992 meant that on a national basis it took an average of 41,930 votes to elect a Conservative MP and 42,657 votes to elect a Labour MP, while it took an average of 209,855 votes to elect a Liberal Democrat to Parliament. The capricious nature of the system was reaffirmed in the 1997 general election when the Liberal Democrats doubled their parliamentary representation from 20 seats in 1992 to 46 in 1997, even though the party's share of the vote actually declined from 17.8 per cent to 16.8 per cent.

The relative strength of a third party leads to other forms of inequity. It is common for over half the seats in a general election to be won by a plurality rather than a majority of votes. At the national level, this translates into governments being elected by a minority of voters prevailing over a majority with preferences against such an outcome. It is true that no government since 1935 has been voted in office with the support of an absolute majority of the popular vote. To this extent, the FPTP system has a long record of producing what could be termed minority governments. It is only with the advent of a serious third force in the shape of a Liberal resurgence and the formation of the Social Democratic Party that the disjunction between majority status and minority support becomes more explicit as the percentage of the popular votes required to achieve governing status has declined by several points. A succession of Conservative governments elected with 43 per cent to 45 per cent support (1979, 1983, 1987, 1992) served to highlight the underlying problem of an electoral system that promotes a two party system together with a correlated expectation of majoritarian government, while at the same time producing anti-climactic results in which victories are conclusively secured by conspicuous minorities. In 1983, for example, the Conservatives won 42.4 per cent of the popular vote which secured 61.1 per cent of the parliamentary seats, providing an emphatic majority of 188 seats over Labour. The tide was reversed in 1997 when with 43.2 per cent of the popular vote Labour won 63.7 per cent of the seats, yielding a majority of 254 over the Conservatives. When such a minority of voters is translated into a proportion of the electorate as a whole, then it is evident that governments in the 1980s and 1990s were regularly voted into office with the support of less than a third of the country.

Other anomalies include the way that the FPTP system in single member constituencies leads to a preponderance of electorally safe white male and middle class candidates and a corresponding underrepresentation of women and ethnic minorities in Parliament. The system also encourages the use of tactical voting in which citizens do not vote for the party of their choice but negatively for the candidate most likely to prevent the least preferred outcome. Another form of inequity inherent in the system is the underrepresentation of Labour voters in safe Conservative seats and Conservative voters in predominantly Labour constituencies. Given that three-quarters of parliamentary seats are safe Conservative or Labour strongholds with a very low probability of change, it means for example that most Labour voters in the South East or Conservative voters in the North can never hope to be represented by an MP of their choice. The same effective disfranchisement is evident in the rural/urban split between the two main parties. The Conservative strength in the shires is not matched in the metropolitan areas where in 1992 the party won only 17 of the 105 seats accounted for by inner London and the 13 largest city areas. Minority votes in such areas are said to be consistently wasted as they fail either to contribute to the process of election, or to feed into the representation of opinion. The preponderance of safe seats also means that the selection of a governing party will be determined by marginal shifts of party preferences within the small minority of marginal constituencies. The disproportionate influence of a minority of swing voters within a minority of disproportionately influential constituencies casts doubt on the representativeness of the electoral system and the legitimacy of the winning party's mandate.

The present electoral system, therefore, generates a variety of complaints based upon inequity and unfairness. Vernon Bogdanor sums up the indictment:

> The first past the post system, then, fails to perform either of the two functions required of an electoral system. It gives power not to the majority but to the strongest minority; and it fails to ensure that all significant minorities are properly represented. It represents minorities not according to their electoral strength, but according to the geographical structure of the vote of minority parties, favouring those whose support is concentrated at the expense of those whose vote is more evenly spread.[1]

Its chief redeeming feature used to be that it produced cohesive and purposeful government, but at the price of an entrenched system of adversarial politics with the attendant risk of pendulum swings in public policy as governments alternated between the two main parties. Apart from the fact that the system has clearly failed to produce a reliable alternation of government, even the functional benefit of decisive majoritarian government now seems in doubt. This is because the two major parties are increasingly drawn to the gravitational centre of electoral opinion, It is also due to the fact that the exaggerative effect of small swings of opinion has diminished with the decline in the number of marginal seats. Moreover, government majorities have tended to become more vulnerable because of the trend towards successive by-election defeats for governing parties.

Vernon Bogdanor points to another indictment of the FPTP system's capacity to produce decisive outcomes. Because of demographic and geographical factors, there has arisen a decreasing correlation between the popular vote and the distribution of parliamentary seats amongst the two main parties. This mainly works to the detriment of the Conservative party in that while it needs an overall lead of approximately 4.8 per cent in the popular vote to secure a majority of seats, Labour requires only around a 2.1 per cent level. Any result between these margins leads to a hung parliament. Notwithstanding the Labour 'landslide' of 1997, therefore, the FPTP system under current conditions would have ensured that half of all post-war parliaments would have been hung parliaments.[2] To the extent that the FPTP system can no longer always assure clear winners and decisive governments, then the case for maintaining the system is proportionately diminished. Even if a change to a more proportionally based system might risk the onset of coalition governments, it would at the same time raise awareness of the already coalitional nature of the main parties and of the possible representational benefits to be accrued by a desegregation of such organisations held together for so long by the electoral pay-offs of size and unity in the present system. The issue is also affected by the fact that the chief sponsor for any reform will invariably be a minority party seeking to challenge the current duopoly on the basis of natural justice but finding it difficult to mobilise public opinion on a fundamental constitutional principle without appearing to be as self-serving as the two main beneficiaries of the present system.

When a majority is not required to prevail in a system whose legitimacy is dependent upon equitable and democratic procedures, then both the system and its democratic identity are vulnerable to damaging criticism. The current electoral system suffers from a host of indictments on precisely these grounds of inequity, injustice and unrepresentativeness.[3] The strength of the electoral system as a constitutional fuel, however, is dependent upon party politics. It is at the same time also weakened by the logic of these same party dynamics, whereby each party seeks to maximise its chances of securing power by fusing self-interest with principle either for sustaining, or for reforming the system. Realistically, the Labour party is the only real source of reform towards a more proportional electoral system but, as Peter Kellner notes, 'throughout its history, Labour's approach to electoral reform [has been] conducted according to the party's imminent needs, rather than according to the compelling call of some higher democratic principle'.[4] The substantive criticism of the present system and the urgency of reform are consequently dependent upon calculations drawn from opinion poll projections, the likelihood of hung parliaments, and the needs of opposition forces for structural assistance. The normative complaints against the electoral framework are also conditioned by the way the issue only arouses concentrated public concern during and immediately following a general election – precisely when the immediate prospect or the *fait accompli* of governmental power precludes any serious political consideration of the ethical objections to the means of acquiring it. Just as the governing party will have no incentive to change the system that brought it to power, so the opposition will condition its outrage against minority government with the hope of capitalising upon the same system in the future, or as a last resort to speculate upon the possibility of electoral reform as a long-term contingency in order to maximise the political potential of an anti-government coalition in the fallow season between elections.

Fuel No. 2: GOVERNMENTAL EXCESS

Another major fuel for constitutional dispute has been the idea of the government exceeding its remit of authority. Governmental excess is an inherently subjective notion but one which has come to have an increasingly material influence upon how governmental motives and behaviour are perceived and how such perceptions can arouse unease, suspicion and even dissent. The idea of governmental excess, in what is a duly constituted democratic government operating under the rule of law, is at best an elusive concept. This is especially so in a system with an unwritten constitution and where political legitimacy is based upon electoral sanction and parliamentary majorities.

In one sense, it is not possible to have governmental excess in a political constitution because any government decision or activity must by definition represent a self-evident political capacity, and with it the necessary political authority, to pursue its chosen course. But notwithstanding this self-validating form of reductionism, a case can be made for government excess on two main grounds. First is the technical claim of *ultra vires* when government exceeds the powers available to it under law. Second, and far less well defined, is the claim that the government has transgressed the bounds of acceptable conduct related to the conventional sphere of governing authority. Without a written constitution, the British system has grown to be dependent upon a range of customs, protocols and traditions that prevent the gaps and ambiguities of the constitution from being exploited by governments. Even when government has the power to overcome the system's checks and balances, it normally remains obligated to the social restraints of 'club government'[5] which provide an interior sense of collective discipline to prevent governments from exceeding the bounds of public tolerance or liberal principle. Because the exact lines of acceptability are always imprecise and because governments are always under pressure to maximise their freedom of manoeuvre, all governments are susceptible to exerting themselves to the point where they risk a backlash against what is alleged to be the arbitrary power of the state.

The practical, functional and utilitarian imperatives of government preoccupied with the socio-economic drives of political support and policy agendas can lead to insufficient care being given to the pluralist and especially libertarian objections to government action. Labour governments in the past have not been immune to charges of excess where individual rights have been involved. The 1974–79 Labour government was at the centre of some notable controversies involving immigration, censorship and press freedom. Nevertheless, it was the Thatcher administrations, whose rationale was paradoxically one of emancipation from the state, which were instrumental in fostering a culture of dissent that translated political opposition into a pronounced consciousness over the condition of constitutional liberties in relation to state power. It was common to hear not only that 'personal liberty lost ground during the years of Margaret Thatcher's government',[6] but that the 'worst examples of the attack on liberty [had] occurred in the last decade [1979–90], and Margaret Thatcher and her government [were] more open in their indifference to liberty than their predecessors'[7] had been. As a result, civil liberties 'played a much more prominent part in constitutional debate than in any other period since the end of the war'.[8]

The scale and radicalism of the Thatcher programme combined with the urgency and conviction of the calls for change by the Thatcher administrations aroused concern over the extent to which Margaret Thatcher's style of government amounted to a *de facto* reorganisation of the state. The anxiety over 'ungovernability' in the 1970s turned to a fear of governmental over-capacity as Margaret Thatcher appeared repeatedly to prevail over the system's checks and balances in the drive for economic freedom and public order. The subtleties of civil society seemed to be secondary to a political project that closely reflected the prime minister's strident self-assurance, her political intransigence and her impatience with opposition. As a consequence, the Thatcher administrations were responsible for a range of measures which had serious implications for the state of civil liberties in Britain. In addition to the diminution of local government, the Thatcher governments secured a succession of reforms to trade union structures and processes that reduced their legal immunities and effectively weakened their position.[9] Police powers of arrest, detention, search and seizure were significantly expanded; extensive restrictions on the freedom of assembly and public protest were introduced; and the powers of the security services in the interception of communications were enlarged. The substance and usage of legislation in the area of immigration, nationality and citizenship were widely regarded as being excessively discriminatory in nature and criminal prosecutions under Section 2 of the Official Secrets Act were brought against individuals (e.g. Sarah Tisdall in 1984, Clive Ponting in 1985) to deter further disclosures of sensitive government information. Press and broadcasting freedoms were curtailed. For example, the government imposed a ban on the broadcasting of personal representatives of proscribed organisations such as the Irish Republican Army, the Irish National Liberation Army, the Ulster Volunteer Force, the Ulster Freedom Fighters, Sinn Fein, and the Ulster Defence Association. The BBC and ITV were subject to government criticism over news content (e.g. Thames Television's *Death on the Rock* in 1988; BBC's coverage of the United States's bombing of Libya in 1986) and even to pressure to drop programmes altogether (e.g. a BBC *Panorama* programme on the SAS in October 1988; and in 1985 an episode in the BBC's *Real Lives* series dealing with Northern Ireland). On one highly publicised occasion in January 1987, the BBC's Glasgow office was raided by police officers in search of materials relating to *The Zircon Affair* – a programme in the series *The Secret Society*.

The fact that such policies could be put into effect by government came increasingly to be regarded as proof positive of a weakness in the constitution – or more precisely of the existence of a government which was prepared to exploit such weaknesses in a more unself-conscious and intransigent manner than previous governments. Critics perceived a crisis in the constitution. Complaints tended to be divided into two categories. First was the belief in malicious intent; namely, that Margaret Thatcher was engaged in an ideological crusade in which civil liberties were actively treated as secondary, peripheral and ultimately expendable. Second was the more measured conclusion that the government's incursions into the sphere of civil liberties were rather the unintended consequences of policy commitment and political convenience, where the reduction of rights constituted collateral damage in a wider engagement over authority, order and social change. Whether the government's actions were purposive or not, the net effect in a constitution with no procedural or substantive distinction between extraordinary change and ordinary legislation was a heightened anxiety over the issue of governmental excess – a fear that an accumulation of small but significant changes could amount to a serious depletion of liberty.[10] Government might claim that 'excess' was a meaningless concept in a historically evolving and politically responsive set of constitutional arrangements, and that the common law continued to provide a vast residuum of presumptive freedoms. But sceptical opponents saw the government's methods as throwing into dramatic and unaccustomed relief the precarious underlying nature of liberty in contemporary Britain.

Thatcherism changed the emphasis in civil relations towards a more mechanistic zero-sum relationship between the state and individual liberty. This shift was accordingly taken up by her critics who increasingly interpreted government action in terms of the tenuous and contingent nature of liberty in the face of an invasive state. If freedom was the obverse of the state in this equation, then the clear imputation was that the *effect* of any palpable loss of liberty must necessarily be synonymous with the *cause* of excessive government. This inference became part of the currency of political debate during the Thatcher era. It led to charges that in Britain 'a shortfall in its respect for human rights ... still exist[ed] in far too many areas'[11] and that 'civil liberties in Britain [were] in a state of crisis'[12] because of the government's 'arrogance in the use of power'[13] and its 'widespread spirit of intolerance'.[14] The Thatcher governments were said to have exposed the long-standing disjunction between 'expectations about openness, democracy [and] public accountability' and the existence of 'traditions and practices concerning the day-to-day doing of the nation's business which live very uneasily with these expectations'.[15] In many quarters, unease turned to dismay in a constitution increasingly exposed as possessing no points of permanent reference. In the British context, it was not technically possible to ascertain whether or not the constitution was being stretched by government excess. Nevertheless, the widespread suspicion at the time was that the government was usurping power and altering the internal balance of the constitution – that something was being lost either by accident or by design and that what was replacing it was open-ended and of doubtful legitimacy.

That suspicion was not lifted when Margaret Thatcher left office. John Major's administrations aroused similar, if less personalised, anxieties over the state of the constitution's checks and balances; over the level of ministerial self-assurance after 17 years of continuous Conservative government; over successive populist campaigns by government for ever more stringent law and order measures; over the conspicuous rise in judicial review cases concerning the executive; and over the general deterioration in the relationship between the government and the judiciary.[16] As the government continued to make inroads into traditional freedoms especially in the field of criminal justice (e.g. the erosion of the right to silence) and as it continued to suffer from a series of defeats by the European Court of Human

Rights, the issue of government excess and the state of liberty in Britain continued to provide a powerful stimulus to constitutional debate.[17] Concern continued to grow over the state of civil liberties, the meaning and value of citizenship, the effectiveness of political accountability, and the extent to which a 'democratic deficit' could be said to exist in the United Kingdom.[18] Notwithstanding the demise of Margaret Thatcher's government, therefore, it is alleged that succeeding British governments 'have repeatedly failed ... to meet minimal standards of conduct when it comes to respecting the rights of individuals'.[19] And even without Thatcher's radical iconoclasm, the widespread belief remains that '[a]s we approach the turn of the century the authorities are turning back the judicial clock and destroying basic rights and freedoms that have taken centuries to put in place'.[20] The anxiety induced by a sense of lost continuity and an unease over the extent to which encroachment has become a habit, has led to an altogether more highly developed public consciousness over the reach of governmental power and over the fragility of civil liberties. It has prompted a broad interest in how liberties are eroded, whether they are recoverable through the same means by which they were originally curtailed, or whether different forms of protection (e.g. a bill of rights) are now required to restore and even raise the level of government restraint.[21]

Fuel No. 3: CENTRALISATION

The perception of power shifting to a central and, therefore, more distant, uniform and coercive location has always been a stimulus to constitutional awareness. Traditionally, Britain has been distinguished by its cohesive political system and the 'fundamental unity of political authority'[22] within the Union. It has had a reputation for social homogeneity, administrative standardisation, central governmental machinery, and a 'common (mass) culture arising from centralisation in London of the channels of mass communication and all cultural agencies'.[23] And yet in spite of this reputation, the British system has always acknowledged the constitutional legitimacy of multiple intermediate centres of power, the existence of a territorial dimension to British politics requiring separate arrangements for Scotland, Wales and Northern Ireland, and the value of civic participation and democratic accountability provided by various tiers of local government. As such, implicit both in Britain's centralised governmental apparatus and in its attachment to the principle of a balanced constitution has been a pluralist conception of power distribution that operates to prevent central government from substituting excess and dysfunction for efficiency and utility.

In the late 1970s there was serious concern that the British government was becoming too large, too costly and too centralised in nature. Central pressures were thought to threaten not only the countervailing powers within the system but also the pluralist ethos which had traditionally co-existed with the principle of unitary government. Government expenditure, which was consuming 45 per cent of GDP in 1979, was widely alleged to be not only inflationary but a pervasive drag on the national economy. The programme of the Thatcher government was to reverse the trend in public spending, to reduce the dependency relationships of groups upon government, and to enlarge social choice and civic responsibility by de-centralising government. This radical crusade did produce outcomes that could be construed as enlarging the scope of personal liberty by reducing the scale and penetration of the state. Whether it was the privatisation of public utilities and the concomitant expansion in share ownership, or the drive to de-regulate the private sector of industry and commerce, or the establishment of a right of tenants to purchase council houses, or the choice given to parents over where to send their children to school, the Thatcher governments claimed to have reversed the trend towards state centralisation. Notwithstanding the counter-argument that the de-centralising features of such reforms were more apparent than real, the main complaint concerning the Thatcher period was that such achievements were in fact more the exception than the rule.

Far from de-centralising the state, the policies of successive Thatcher administrations are widely regarded as having actually increased the degree of centralisation in British government and society.[24] The public sector continued to account for as much GDP as it had done under the last Labour government in 1979. When Margaret Thatcher discovered that her stated objective of liberalisation through a devolution of governmental power would not achieve the required outcomes because of the opposition of other levels of government and sectors in society, her administrations increasingly resorted to liberalisation by central direction. Operating on the principle that it was necessary to acquire power in order to diminish or delegate it, the Thatcher governments set out to reorientate, neutralise, replace or simply to annex these intermediate entities that stood between the citizen and the state. In the words of Samuel Brittan, Margaret Thatcher's policies and methods of decision-making amount to a 'blitz on intermediate sources of power ... [including] not only unions but local authorities, employer associations, universities and even the Church'.[25] Such a 'centralisation of state power' was seen by Brittan to be 'incompatible with the dispersion of authority and influence, which is just as much part of a wider liberalism as free markets themselves'.[26] The problem for Margaret Thatcher was that there was no necessary connection between the structural features of pluralistic democracy and her ideological objective of liberalisation. Other centres of power threatened to impede and to subvert the Thatcherite cause and, as such, were seen as illiberal enclaves of restrictive practices and irresponsible oligarchies which needed to be limited for the greater benefit of the general public. Although centralisation was never a self-conscious principle of Thatcherite governments, the accumulated consequences of policy decisions led to an appreciation of the political and economic benefits to be accrued by enhanced central control. Under the Conservative government, the process of liberalisation became associated with the use of the centre to diminish the checks of pluralism, to reduce the responsiveness and influence of other power centres, to erode the boundaries between the public and private sectors in the interests of efficiency and to inject the disciplines of public choice and market accountability into government-financed institutions. Nowhere was this impulse to defeat or circumvent the pervasive obstructionism of such pluralistic structures more evident than in the Thatcher governments' response to local government.

Because local governments were believed to be undermining the Thatcherite crusade against the state, central government moved on several fronts to alter the financial functions and structure of local authorities. In 1986, it even went so far as to abolish the metropolitan counties and the Greater London Council with the specific aim of eliminating known pockets of municipal socialism and, thereby, removing sources of political opposition to government policy. Local governments in general were made more dependent and consequently more accountable to central government through a range of measures designed to reduce local autonomy by removing functions from local government control and by imposing central disciplinary standards on the activities and expenditures of local authorities. Local finance was in essence centralised. The traditional powers of local authorities over health, education, housing and the police were effectively reduced in favour of central regulation and direction.[27] Areas of policy and administration normally performed by elected local governments were increasingly reserved to non-elected agencies devised and appointed by central government.[28] By the end of Margaret Thatcher's period in office the number of appointees in local administration exceeded the number of elected officers by a factor of two to one. The sheer weight and uniformity of central standards together with the implicit democratic centralism of Whitehall's insistence that its conception of the public interest should prevail prompted Simon Jenkins to conclude that:

> No country in Europe, indeed few in the world, have as little autonomy vested in subordinate local institutions as has Britain ... There is no worse commentary on democracy in Britain than the 30-40 per cent turnouts at local elections, less than anywhere else in Europe. This not the 'fault' of local government, but of a constitution that has casually left it unreformed and denuded of power, and of a custodian of that constitution, the British cabinet, that has revelled in so denuding it.[29]

The centralisation that characterised so much of the Thatcher period continued under John Major's premiership. Central control in areas such as law and order, the National Health Service, schools, higher education and housing reduced even further the scope for variation from government standards. While central budgetary controls were strengthened, performance targets and league tables generated further movement towards uniform national standards and with them centrally imposed rewards and penalties. The discretionary powers of local authorities were further squeezed by the council tax which accounted for less than one-fifth of local government expenditures; by the restrictions on local variations from central budgetary norms on local spending; and by the maintenance of the uniform business rate which was in effect a national property tax levied at the direct expense of the revenue-raising powers of local councils. Schools now taught the national curriculum and administered a regime of national testing. New central service organisations (e.g. the Child Support Agency, the Crown Prosecution Service, the National Lottery the Student Loans Company) were established by government to administer policy at a distance from electoral sanction or political accountability. The centralisation within the government machine itself was also continued under John Major with the Treasury, the Cabinet Office, the Whips Office and Number 10 Downing Street all maintaining their influence over the executive bureaucracy. By 1995 Major was showing signs of further centralisation with attempts to concentrate power in his office and the Policy Unit at the expense of the Treasury and other departments.[30]

It is true that centralisation is not peculiar to the Conservative party or to the Conservative governments of Margaret Thatcher and John Major. It has been an integral component of the British government for at least the last 50 years and Labour party philosophy has traditionally promoted the rational and equitable nature of planning and redistribution from the centre. Others would go further and claim like Will Hutton that Britain's 'quasi-feudal state [has been] handed down intact from the seventeenth century'.[31] As a consequence:

> 'Its lack of checks and balances has produced the most centralised state in the industrial world ... More than that, British public authority is incapable of being anything other than top-down and centralised ... Britain has been unable to construct the dense skein of intermediate public institutions between the centralised state and the market that other successful capitalist economies possess.[32]

Even with Britain's long experience of central government and the unitary state, the centralising properties of such a radical government established in office for so long fostered a widespread concern over the sphere of government and the commensurate state of civil liberty in contemporary Britain. The centrality of one party's reform agenda held in place for so long raised the prospect not just of an irreversible change in public policy, but of a preclusion of any serious alternative to the public philosophy established over the period of Conservative rule. Notwithstanding the rhetoric of empowerment and freedom of choice, the sweep of central, distant and inaccessible controls not only generated specific complaints over the nature and trends of such controls, but exerted at a deeper level a general unease over the operational integrity of the constitution. Anthony Sampson had no doubt that despite the liberalisation of entrepreneurial energies, 'the arena of power ha[d] become narrower and bleaker'.[33] Writing in 1992, he observed that the 'gap between government and governed looms wider than ever [because] Britain is run by one of the most centralised and least accountable systems in the industrial world'.[34] John Gray agreed and drew attention to the current 'tendency to increasing centralisation [which had] become evident in many aspects of policy'.[35] He regarded such a tendency as ominous: 'The danger now is that in the ruins of a project of limited government a corporatist monolith is being built up, which in the inevitable effluxion of time will be inherited by an administration (of any party) that, by conviction or by force of circumstance, will regard the claims of individual liberty with indifference or hostility.'[36]

Centralisation, or at least the perception of progressive centralisation, has always been a powerful generic stimulant to constitutional consciousness and thought. Although it is true that the British constitution has traditionally accommodated a strong central government, the record of recent administrations has generated sufficient suspicion over the level of centralisation to organise complaints and criticisms of government around the theme of a quantum shift towards the centre. That such an alleged shift could have occurred either authentically within the constitution, or external to its customary parameters, raises the constitution as an object of political analysis, argument and reform. The centralisation of the state becomes a key constitutional litmus test. It makes other issues more constitutionally accessible because of its status as the theoretical and practical antithesis of constitutionalism. The very notion of centralisation implies a calculable transformative process within the constitution that is logically and ethically unconstitutional in character. When centralisation becomes a term of political complaint, it draws upon an unease that some qualitative property is being lost through a quantitative agency of change. Centralisation gives form to an abstract, elusive and intuitive sense of loss and transgression. Centralisation can refer more to the attributed causes of change, or to the perceived state of altered conditions. But whichever way centralisation is construed and used, it has the capacity to become a substantive instrument of critical constitutional inquiry. It has also increasingly given rise to demands for corrective action. In the words of Vernon Bogdanor, Britain has been 'less well-placed than any other Western European democracy to fight the depredations of centralism because the institutional underpinnings of local democracy in Britain are so weak'.[37] As a consequence, the perception of centralisation has fuelled an array of reform ideas ranging from Scottish, Welsh and regional devolution and the reorganisation of local government to re-creation of self-governing community cultures through the stimulus of measures designed to enhance democratic participation and active citizenship (e.g. citizen juries, elected mayors, local referendums).

Fuel No. 4: GOVERNMENTAL MISUSE

The misuse of government amounts to a qualitatively different fuel to the abuse of power encompassed within the category of governmental excess. Both fuels are rooted in political autonomy but while governmental excess infers the de-legitimation of governmental authority through decisions and actions that either are, or are alleged to be, *ultra vires* in nature, the misuse of government relates to behaviour which contravenes the government's own rules of conduct. As such, it is not the government's formal authority which is in question, so much as its general character in coming to decisions. The emphasis in governmental misuse is less upon the content of policy and more upon what government actions and choices reveal about the nature of its operating ethos and interior dynamics. This can take the form of a critical disclosure either of a specific government or of the government machine in general. Given the right political conditions, a discrete incident or decision can trigger a concerted public interest in the operation of government. It can inflate the concern for constitutional forms and procedures to abnormally high levels, and lead to a ramifying critique of government which can undermine the political authority of both the individual government concerned and the political system in general. Episodes of alleged misuse of governmental power are usually associated with a pre-existing public outlook of *prima facia* suspicion towards the conduct of a government. Undefined doubts and anxieties can quite suddenly become focused into an indictment of governmental behaviour and political ethics. This may relate to the personal activities of individuals within government, or to the exposure of the *realpolitik* which always conditions the operation of government but which is normally concealed behind the ostensible propriety of democratic values. Such glimpses of personal or structural impropriety may be motivated by party or electoral interests but the net effect is the generation of disquiet over the integrity of government and over the uses to which the legitimate authority of government may be put.

It is the mixture of high public interest and high politics devolved upon an accessible case that can be used to give material expression to a wider predisposition to doubt the government's management of its own power. The fuel of governmental misuse is not normally associated with ideological choices, or administrative failures, or with simple policy mistakes. Governments are traditionally assaulted for such conduct on straight political grounds. The transformation of a particular measure from the normal medium of political exchange into the wider dimension of intensive constitutional inquiry is the relationship between the measure in question, the context of public concern over the working style of a government and the political will to unravel the issue in constitutional terms. Arthur M. Schlesinger's assessment of the Watergate scandal's significance to American government is particularly apposite in this respect: 'The expansion and abuse of presidential power constituted the underlying issue – [i.e.] the issue ... that Watergate raised to the surface, dramatized and made politically accessible. Watergate was the by-product of a larger revolutionary purpose. At the same time, it was a fatal mistake that provoked and legitimized resistance to the revolutionary Presidency.'[38] It is the instrumental value of the defining episode, rather than its intrinsic substance, which is the distinguishing characteristic of this type of resonating issue. Over recent years, there have been a number of episodes in British politics that have incited widespread constitutional anxiety over how government conducts itself within the parameters of its rightful power. The controversies generated by the Pergau Dam scandal and the Westland affair typify the genre.

In the Pergau Dam affair, it was not the facts that were in question so much as the construction placed upon them. In 1988, the British government instigated a foreign aid package to Malaysia which centred upon the construction of a hydro-electric scheme. Britain pledged £234 million of 'soft' concessionary loans to the Malaysian government in support of the dam. The arrangement, financed by the budget of the Overseas Development Agency (ODA), represented the largest sum ever to be attached to a single aid project. The commercial viability of the scheme and the environmental consequences of its construction were questioned not least by the ODA whose initial agreement was made conditional upon a full economic appraisal of the scheme. On the basis of this appraisal, the ODA in February 1990 declared the Pergau Dam to be a 'very bad buy at the price'[39] and that it would lead to an increase rather than to a reduction in the price of electricity for Malaysian consumers. The subsequent Whitehall battle led Douglas Hurd, the Foreign Secretary, to override the ODA's objections because of 'an undertaking at the highest level'[40] to honour the original commitment which had international and trading implications that reached well beyond the project in question. The ODA continued to oppose the measure in 1991 with Sir Thomas Lankaster, the ODA's Permanent Secretary, warning senior ministers that the scheme was 'uneconomic' and 'not ... a sound development project'[41] as it 'would not be consistent with policy statements by ministers to Parliament about the basic objectives of the aid programme'.[42] In effect, the government was being accused of breaking its own rules. Lankester even refused to write the cheques transferring ODA funds to the project until he was formally directed to do so by the Foreign Secretary. The suspicion that the government's support for the project was being governed by the commercial interests of the main British contractors (i.e. Balfour Beatty and Cementation International) and their Malaysian agents was increased by the knowledge that the Pergau funds were being channelled from the Aid and Trade Provision which was that part of the overseas development budget specifically designed to assist British companies in acquiring third world contracts.

But the greatest injection of suspicion was provided by allegations that the aid deal was linked to the sale of Tornado aircraft, two corvettes, two Martello radar systems, a command, control, communications and intelligence system and two army bases to the Malaysian government. There is no doubt that inter-governmental agreements to both the Pergau Dam project and the arms sales coincided with one another in March 1988. Even though the Defence Secretary, George Younger, later sought to clarify the situation by means of a letter to Dr Mahatir Mohamed, the Malaysian premier, formally de-coupling the two elements, the circumstantial evidence in support of a link remained strong. George Younger himself acknowledged in 1994 that each party 'had its own perception of whether there was a linkage and each was happy to keep its own perception. The British refused to make a connection but the Malaysians said there would be no military contract without the aid project.'[43] The higher and controlling level to which Mr Hurd had deferred in his decision to override the ODA's objections in 1991 was widely suspected as being Margaret Thatcher and Dr Mohamed, who in September 1988 signed a 'memorandum of understanding' (MOU) thought to contain details of the arms sales and their explicit link to British aid for the Pergau Dam. The contents of the MOU remained highly classified and attempts by the House of Commons Public Accounts Committee in 1989 and 1994 and the House of Commons Foreign Affairs Select Committee in 1994 to gain full access to the protocols were conspicuously unsuccessful. Despite the evasion and ambiguity surrounding the issue, it is widely accepted that a personal and moral commitment to an 'aid with trade' deal was made by Margaret Thatcher during her visit to Malaysia in 1988 and that any subsequent attempt to challenge such a linkage would have been severely detrimental to British commercial interests in Malaysia.

Such sensitive high-level policy considerations did not, however, deter those who questioned the legality of using overseas development aid on such a project, irrespective of any linkage to military sales. In a case brought to the High Court by the World Development Movement (WDM) in November 1994, the Court declared the government to be in breach of its own rules. Section 1 of the Overseas and Co-operation Act (1980) empowered the Foreign Secretary to authorise aid payments only 'for the purpose of promoting the development or maintaining the economy of a country or territory outside the United Kingdom, or the welfare of its people'.[44] The WDM argued that in this case a 'decision was motivated by improper purposes' and that political considerations prevailed over the stated criteria. The Court agreed, pointing out that if Parliament had 'intended to confer payments for unsound development purposes it could have been expected to say so expressly'.[45] The Court's decision, which prompted Douglas Hurd to consider resigning from the Foreign Office, highlighted the government's actions in infringing its own statutory authority in an area of highly sensitive public policy. But the Pergau Dam affair was more significant than a simple case of *ultra vires*. It raised a series of questions concerning the ethics of overseas aid provision and the relationship of trade to foreign policy objectives. It revealed the interior operation of government and the devices by which legitimate discretionary power could be misused on grounds of *realpolitik*. The Scott Inquiry (1994–96) into the sale of military equipment to Iraq revealed a similar pattern of behaviour when it was disclosed that parts of the government were privately pursuing a policy at variance with the government's collective public pronouncements on the issue.[46] In like manner, the most penetrative constitutional issue raised by the Pergau Dam controversy was the governing ethos of government itself and the way in which functional discretion could be stretched to confound stated principles of conduct and policy.

The crisis over the Westland helicopter company stemmed from a running dispute in 1985 between two cabinet ministers over a minor policy decision but one with major symbolic significance. The Secretary of State for Trade and Industry, Leon Brittan, supported a rescue package for the ailing company that was to be financed by the American helicopter manufacturer Sikorsky. The Secretary of State for Defence, Michael Heseltine, believed that such an option was being rushed through without adequate consideration being given to a rival bid made by a European consortium.[47] Ministerial and departmental conflict was heightened by a personal and ideological dimension that pivoted upon Margaret Thatcher's support for Leon Brittan's non-European option and her opposition to Michael Heseltine who was not only a strong supporter of the European Community, but also a highly ambitious 'wet', whose loyalty had been thrown into doubt after his advocacy of state aid to depressed areas following the outbreak of riots in 1981. As the dispute became more public, it appeared that the prime minister was not in a position to control her cabinet.

Michael Heseltine's preferred European option was always a rearguard action which required time to become viable. As such, his strategy was one of delaying a final decision by public advocacy and private pressure. It was clear that Margaret Thatcher believed the decision had already been taken in principle and that the continued uncertainty surrounding the issue had damaging commercial, international and political implications. Differing perceptions of meetings, conventions, ministerial licence and cabinet government led ultimately to Michael Heseltine's dramatic resignation from the cabinet on 9 January 1986. He believed that both he and his European option had been discriminated against by Margaret Thatcher's management of the cabinet committees and the cabinet itself. In Michael Heseltine's view, he had been deliberately prevented from presenting his case to the cabinet by the prime minister. Even his objections had not been minuted. Accordingly, in the public interviews following his resignation, he made explicit allusions to the constitutional irregularities in Margaret Thatcher's style of cabinet government: 'This was not just a case of a senior minister justifying his withdrawal from government on spurious grounds. He deliberately invoked constitutional impropriety because it had become such a potent term of political dissent.'[48] In one interview alone, he referred to 'a setting aside of the constitution', 'a breakdown of constitutional procedures' and 'an affront to the constitution'.[49]

The dispute was further compounded by the speculation that the prime minister had secretly conspired against Heseltine by colluding in the public release of a law officer's letter to him pointing out a number of 'material inaccuracies' in his position. Ultimately it was Leon Brittan who felt constrained to accept political responsibility for the leak that discredited his adversary. He immediately resigned on 24 January 1986. The subsequent inquiries into the leaked letter, and Margaret Thatcher's own part in engineering Heseltine's resignation through the manipulation of cabinet committees and the Whitehall machine, led in turn to an emergency debate in the House of Commons on 27 January 1986. It was in effect a motion of censure against the prime minister. Margaret Thatcher managed to resist the charges of making misleading statements and engaging in a 'cover-up', but it was 'by far and away the most serious of the difficulties of her second term. It was the nearest she came to nemesis'[50] prior to her resignation in November 1990.

The Westland affair raised a series of controversies concerning ministerial accountability, collective responsibility, civil service anonymity, cabinet organisation, prime ministerial style, constitutional conventions and the methods of assigning culpability in government.[51] At one level, it concerned the rightful disciplining of a recalcitrant cabinet minister. In Margaret Thatcher's own view, 'unless he [Heseltine] were checked, there were no limits to what would do to secure his objectives at Westland. Cabinet collective responsibility was being ignored and my own authority as prime minister was being publicly flouted. This had to stop'.[52] At another level, the affair revealed the private inner world of government at the highest reaches, and especially its dependence upon discreet and subtle protocols of decision-making and administration. As the Westland crisis deepened these protocols were shown to be susceptible to political manipulation and even subversion not so much over what was done but how it was done. The Thatcher government was temporarily de-stabilised because it was seen to be engaged in duplicity, conspiracy, hypocrisy and evasion. If Michael Heseltine was guilty of challenging the interpretation of the convention on collective responsibility as set out in *Questions of Procedure for Ministers*, the prime minister and her closest aides were seen to be responsible for the greater misdemeanour of surreptitiously using power to break its own rules of conduct, in order to discredit an opponent, to prevail in a political dispute, and to bury the precise truth as to 'who did and knew what and when'. Westland may have been an esoteric dispute whose arcane complexities were largely lost outside Westminster and Whitehall, but it 'converted semi-covert insider objections to the Thatcher style into a glowing neon sign'.[53] In doing so, it provided a point of access to Margaret Thatcher's style of government and allowed political dissent, normally geared to the political morality of her government's policy output, to reorganise around the interior morality of her government's conduct.

From these examples, it is clear that the category of governmental misuse has the potential of being as broad, or even broader, an area of constitutional speculation as governmental excess. While it is true that govermental misuse is often ostensibly narrow in focus compared to the implicit dramas of usurpation and exceeded authority, the actual effect of governmental misuse as an analytical agent can be one of unrestrained extrapolation into the deepest and most subtle questions of government. Speculation into governmental abuse will normally stop at the boundaries of legitimate authority – a lawful exercise of power retards constitutional inquiry. Governmental misuse, on the other hand, can transcend such constraints and give expression to less formal and legalistic concerns. The misuse of power will not only stray into the customs and conventions of government but can ramify into the personal ethics of participants and the problematic morality of governmental conduct in such areas as the arms trade and foreign aid. Purely legal authority can be compromised by a heightened consciousness of the ethical ambiguity of the area within which it is being exercised. On occasions, such areas can be extended to the ambiguous morality of government itself – i.e. the Machiavellian concept of a necessarily separate morality of power. The category of government misuse, therefore, can not only raise questions concerning the misapplication of established authority but can engender deeper inquiries into the nature, meaning and legitimacy of such authority. Just as misuse infers a knowledge of rightful use, so the constitutional fuel of government misconduct can generate profound questions of constitutionality that reach beyond the legal construction of enumerated procedures and powers.

Fuel No. 5: SECRECY

Secrecy is habitually referred to as not merely a distinguishable characteristic of British government but its defining condition. As a constitutional
fuel, it is always present either as an implicit generalisation of British governance, or as an explicit instrument of statecraft in which access to specific information is openly denied. Whether references to government
secrecy rest upon cases of actual non-disclosure or on the inference of
secrecy based upon the restricted accessibility of information, the 'British
way of governing has been characterised by an extraordinary secrecy, unri-
valled amongst comparable Western democracies'.[54] It may not be possible
to produce conclusive proof of such a proposition. By the same token, the
numerous allusions to a 'secret state' or a 'secret constitution' are not fal-
sifiable because of the way the British government succeeds in 'preserving
the greatest secret of all, the extent of government secrecy. Non-disclosure
conceals not only the content of information, but also its very existence'.[55]
Secrecy is a notoriously difficult property to define and to assess but the balance of argument and probability lay fairly on the side of an institutional
complicity to conceal information of public interest, of national security and
of the organisational integrity of the government machine itself.[56]

Given that 'Britain has one of the most extensive systems to control the
flow of official information of any Western democracy'[57] and given that
there is no general right of public access to government information in
Britain, it is not difficult to confront instances of governmental secrecy in
the day-to-day operation of British government. Whether it is the prerogative powers of the security services, principles of anonymity and confidentiality in the civil service codes, the thirty-year rule on the release of public
records, the issue of public interest immunity certificates, or the protection
of commercially sensitive information and research in such areas as nuclear
power, environmental pollution, pesticides, pharmaceuticals, food additives
and consumer product safety, the scale of, and the potential for, secrecy
always remains close to the surface of public life. Even when the blanket
restrictions of the Official Secrets Act of 1911 were amended after 78 years
and the new legislation reduced the categories of information whose disclosure could lead to criminal prosecution, any notion of a monopoly reforming itself into at least an oligopoly was quickly dispelled. Of the five
categories in question (i.e. (1) defence, security and intelligence; (2)interna-
tional relations; (3) confidential information received from other countries
and international organisations; (4) information useful to criminals; and (5)
information relating to the interception of telephone calls, mail and other
forms of communication), three do not even require a test of actual harm
incurred for any disclosure to constitute a criminal offence. Harm is taken
either to be integral to the very act of disclosure, or to be a necessary con-

sequence of such disclosure. Furthermore, the revision 'ruled out any general public-interest defence, on the grounds that the protection of the proposed limited categories of official information was already demonstrably in the public interest and any further public-interest defence would be inappropriate'.[58]

That secrecy exists in British government is not at issue. It permeates the system and acts as a controlling technique of policy and administration. What is even more significant is the way that it is legitimised on systemic grounds of (a) constitutional virtue, (b) functional value and (c) social culture.

First, restricting public access to information is formally condoned and accommodated through the constitutional device of ministerial responsibility. This central feature of the constitution is said to provide a chain of public accountability stretching from government departments to Parliament on the basis of ministers being personally accountable for the general conduct of their particular departments. Just as authority flows from the top through ministers as elected officers of the crown and as representatives of the majority party in Parliament, so accountability is deemed to float to the surface with ministers answering questions, defending policies and protecting the records of their departments. The convention of ministerial responsibility is designed to shield the civil service from political influence and public pressure and to provide ministers with the authority to control their departments and to exert discipline upon their officials. Because the convention recognises the nexus between parliaments and the executive and assigns an abstract global accountability to ministers for the actions of their departments, it tacitly condones the withholding of departmental information based upon the ministerial role as public trustee. As long as ministers are ultimately accountable for the policies, acts or omissions of their departments, then the doctrine gives positive encouragement to ministerial discretion in the retention of internal information. In effect, ministerial responsibility offers the threat of sudden blood sacrifices in the form of exposures, resignations, reshuffles and electoral defeats in lieu of a continual stream of open information. The convention of ministerial responsibility not only recognises the historical decline in the power of Parliament to extract information from an executive increasingly organised according to party discipline, but supports the executive's professional claim to the exclusive control of government information in the interest of the nation.[59]

The second rationale that lends principle to the practice of secrecy is the functional utility of confidentiality in an organisation that relies upon private candour and open advocacy. Secrecy is claimed to liberate the process of decision-making within departments, thereby leading to better informed and more balanced decisions than would prevail in conditions of greater public access to information. This is one of the main motivating drives behind the principle of ministerial responsibility. The logic of the relationship is explained by Rodney Brazier in the following terms: 'The extent to which a Minister will carry the can for the errors of his [*sic*] civil servants is bound up with the aim of preserving the anonymity of civil servants, for only by making them reasonably secure from (and their political masters open to) public censure can they give frank advice to successions of Ministers.'[60] To the advocates of confidentiality in government, the restriction of information and the various rules against unauthorised disclosures make an indispensable contribution both to the efficiency of decision-making and to the collective ethos of a functioning government. In the view of Lord Armstrong, the former Cabinet Secretary, 'effective government depends upon a high degree of frankness and openness within the processes of discussion and decision-making'.[61] But as Lord Armstrong makes clear:

> That frankness and openness would be severely inhibited if the whole of those processes were open to public inspection as they occurred or very soon thereafter. Civil servants and other advisers would in some circumstances be reluctant to give the full information and dispassionate advice which it is their duty to give, if it was going to be exposed immediately to the public gaze. Ministers ... [would] be reluctant to commit themselves to positions, or to change or adjust positions once taken, for fear of the possible consequences of their being publicly known to be doing so.[62]

According to this perspective, greater disclosure of public information would inevitably lead from the background or content of decisions to the way in which particular decisions are made. Such a progression would be antithetical to good government and, as such, it is necessary to erect as many forward defences as possible to prevent government from degenerating into incoherence. Secrecy is defended on these grounds as the minimal precondition to a productive exchange of impartial information and a necessary technique of governmental competence.

The third major reason for supporting secrecy in the British system is not constitutional or instrumental so much as cultural in origin. Government secrecy is seen not only as a distinguishing feature but also as a contributory factor to the private and enclosed world of administrative hierarchies. Given the close relationship that has traditionally existed between the senior civil service and the established elites of British society, secrecy in government is also said to reflect a deep trait in British social attitudes towards decision-making and discretion. But whether secrecy comes from a 'longstanding national genius for confidentiality',[63] or is derived from the more prosaic imperative of club government and insider professionalism, secrecy remains a key component in the governmental machine. Some like Peter Hennessy would say that secrecy is the central property which defines government as a functioning social culture:

Secrecy is the bonding material which holds the rambling structure of central government together. Secrecy is built into the calcium of a British policy-maker's bones ... It is the very essence of the Establishment view of good government, of private government carried beyond the reach of faction or political party, the tunnel-vision of pressure group and the impertinent curiosity of the journalist. The rule is that the fewer people who know, the better, including insiders ... Of all the rules, secrecy is the most sacred.[64]

Clive Ponting's insider knowledge of government's interior leads him to the same conclusion:

Most top Civil Servants subscribe to a view ... that a closed decision taking system is better because it is more rational. The Civil Service, as the guardians of the State, are able, it would be argued, to analyse a problem objectively and, free from illegitimate outside pressure, reach the best solution in the interests of the nation ... This secretive atmosphere leads to a very claustrophobic world ... Battles between departments, protecting themselves from outside attack, is all that matters. Policy-making thus becomes a great mystery which cannot and must not be exposed to outsiders who have no right to know how this activity is carried on.[65]

Even though confidentiality can be, and regularly is, defended principally on liberal grounds as protecting the privacy of individuals and organisations, the instinctive drive for security within government is generally thought to be motivated more by cultural drives to prevent the dissemination of information to outsiders and, with it, the risk of compromising the policy-making process. This emphasis upon the 'need for exercising the strictest discretion'[66] by all those with access to confidential information is captured in *Questions of Procedure for Ministers* which states that '[c]are should be taken to see that no discussions of Government policy are held in places where they may be overheard'.[67] More substantively, it applauds secrecy as 'an attitude of mind which puts first the interests of the Government as a whole and subordinates everything to that end.[68]

The power and authority of these systemic forces favouring secrecy are not immune to critical assault. The premises of ministerial responsibility, for example, have been shown to be questionable as it becomes increasingly apparent that civil servants are not anonymous functionaries and that ministers cannot be expected to accept personal culpability for the mass of decisions that emanate from their departments. Given that a practical corollary of the theory of ministerial responsibility is a minister's general control of departmental information, then the whole premise of answerability to Parliament is compromised. The conundrum is succinctly put by James Cornford:

The dependence of the Executive on Parliament is fundamental: parliamentary questions, select committees and the ultimate deterrent of votes of confidence serve to hold government to account and to limit their freedom of action. But given the extent of prerogative powers derived from the Crown, the effective control of the procedures of Parliament, the mastery of the civil service, and the ability to manipulate and bully the media, there need to be some counter-vailing measures to shift the balance towards Parliament and the public.[69]

Even when information is forthcoming, evidence from the Scott Inquiry shows that it may be wholly misleading, in order to conceal the precise nature of policy in particularly sensitive issue areas.[70] Critics of governmental secrecy claim that the Scott Report was symptomatic of an ingrown system of information retention and formalised neutrality. They allege that the absence of open government is part of an overall democratic deficit in which citizenship, participation and scrutiny are constructed by the confidentiality that is implicit in such a top-down structure of policy provision and public administration. 'What is at issue here ... is the extent to which there is a public interest, a citizen interest, distinct from the interest of governments or parties and needing to be built into the process of politics and government. Much of the dissatisfaction with British constitutional arrangements turns on their failure sufficiently to acknowledge and incorporate this distinction'.[71]

It is true that when pressured, governments have moved to relax the criteria for the release of information both in specific circumstances (e.g. John Major's decision to approve the publication of *Questions of Procedure for Ministers*, and to release information on the system of cabinet committees and the structure of the intelligence services) and in relation to general conditions (e.g. the Croham Directive of 1977 and the Code of Practice on Access to Government Information of 1994). Governments have also positively encouraged a greater volume and range of material to appear in the public domain as a result of Select Committee inquiries, Citizen's Charters, performance league tables and the onset of Next Steps executive agencies with their more horizontal structures of public management. Nevertheless, despite these incremental advances, British governments have traditionally stopped well short of anything approximating to a Freedom of Information Act and with it the underlying principle of compulsory disclosure. In fact they have been instrumental in preventing the passage of private members' bills (e.g. Archy Kirkwood's Freedom of Information Bill in 1992) that are designed to establish some form of a 'right to know' in British law.

Freedom of information has all the appearance of being a self-evident good in a democratic society. It is captivating in its radical simplicity, its axiomatic status and in the ease of its popular appeal which regularly draws the support of over 80 per cent of respondents in opinion polls.[72] Public access to information held by a government based upon popular consent seems a logical corollary to the basic precepts of a democratic system. To reform the system by establishing freedom of information provisions may appear to be nothing more than correcting a disjunction between theory and practice, but in reality it would represent a profound change in the sources and usage of power within the governmental system.[73] It would amount to a shift in the balance of the constitution towards Parliament and the public by disrupting the normally closed ranks of ministerial responsibility. More significantly still, an entrenched right of information would demarcate nothing less than a transformation in the British conception of sovereignty away from the intermediary role of an entrusted parliamentary sovereignty and towards the more direct and continuous claims of a popular sovereignty. As Anthony Barnett makes clear:

> [F]reedom of information means that government papers belong to the public. We pay for them to be generated by public servants on our behalf. They are ours. We have the right to see everything, the presumption is always in favour of release, the government must justify secrecy. In terms of political culture, it means that civil servants serve the public – that we, not they, are the masters.[74]

Any such resolution to the problem of government secrecy would represent a profound change in the culture and process of government. Government secrecy is a constitutional fuel that relies upon cultural distaste, public suspicion, individual frustration and opposition party politics. The promise of reform normally exceeds the end product because governments are reluctant to subvert the very principles of sovereignty upon which they acquire and sustain power. Given that confidentiality is such an integral instrument in the management of the British state, the likelihood is that governments will always be reluctant to allow any libertarian 'right to know' to supplant the hierarchical suppositions of the 'need to know'.

Fuel No. 6: PERSONAL MISCONDUCT

The constitutional fuel of personal misconduct derives its force from the behaviour of individuals in politics and, in particular, from the relationship between on the one hand the principles and standards of public life, and on the other hand the extent to which they are upheld by those participating in it. In contrast to the categories of governmental excess and governmental misconduct which give emphasis to the abuse and misuse of political authority, the notion of personal misconduct relates to the behaviour and morality of individuals in positions of public prominence and trust. The issues raised by the theme of personal misconduct are in many ways wider and more unpredictable than governmental excess or misuse. They relate to a broad and diffuse sense of social morality where the personal conduct, sexual behaviour or financial affairs of individual politicians can suddenly give focus to general anxieties about the contemporary state of social and personal ethics. This is not say that cases of governmental misconduct do not devolve upon the behaviour of individuals, or reflect personal codes of morality. Clearly they do, but their significance is rendered secondary by the political or policy substance of the government's corporate context. It is when individual politicians are seen to engage in individual actions and seek to use their individual positions for personal advancement or protection that they are propelled from the dimension of political morality into the more volatile and populist realm of public morality. When a heightened state of public morality is suddenly mobilised and applied to such a chronically ambiguous arena as political life, the result can produce a destructively critical force.

In cases of personal misconduct, a dynamic can develop that links the individual, or the particular, to a notion of what is general. The revelation of individual impropriety therefore can be both driven by, and contribute to, an altogether more generic suspicion of contemporary political conduct. The circularity of such a dynamic means that what might have been regarded as an idiosyncratic case can be taken, in a period of suspicion and disillusionment, as symptomatic of a deeper malaise, thereby prompting further inquiries and uncovering additional cases that reaffirm the original litmus test. A mood of ramifying public condemnation becomes indiscriminate as grosser forms of impropriety are rendered indistinguishable from the more customary types of social ambiguity. In other words, discrete incidents of misconduct can fuel a sweeping form of public suspicion and intolerance that may settle as easily upon the acquisitively corrupt as on the unexceptionally unconventional. When the tide of public morality shifts in relation to the behaviour of politicians, it leads to the sudden exposure of abnormal behaviour as well as to the denunciation of previously tolerable behaviour precisely because of the public prominence of the individuals concerned.

Shifts in the public outlook towards politicians and politics in general were particularly evident during John Major's second administration. Against a background of general anxiety over the social and ethical implications of privatisation, de-regulation, 'fat cat' salaries, quango patronage and the performance-related incentives of an increasingly commercialised public service, the government was periodically afflicted by a series of minor scandals, which through a process of accumulation, built up an impression of a government that was directly or indirectly responsible for an atmosphere of systemic misconduct or sleaze in public life – i.e. 'an insidious blurring of the edges between what is correct and what is not ... the grey area between what is strictly legal and what is not';[75] 'the selfish use of public office for personal advantage ... involv[ing] bending the rules without breaking them'.[76] As a consequence, moral outrage and accusation became part of the armoury of political attack against an often ailing administration. References to sleaze was a particularly effective device in confronting a government that had been in office for over 15 years and which had presided over a radical change in public philosophy. Sleaze implied a large-scale sub-version of ethics for which the government could not evade responsibility. Sleaze was also a suitably ambiguous term that closely corresponded to the ambiguity of its subject with the effect that it could be applied indiscriminately. The association of an arrogant and complacent government with declining standards of social morality led John Major to make periodic attempts to inject a renewed moral consciousness into society from the top (e.g. the 'Back to Basics' campaign launched in the autumn of 1993), but these crusades were always undermined by fresh revelations of personal impropriety at the political centre. Something of the drip-feed nature of the exposures during this period can be gauged from the following selected examples:

- September 1992, David Mellor (Secretary of State for National Heritage) resigns after tabloid stories of an affair with the actress Antonia de Sancha and of revelations that a holiday, paid for by Mona Bauwens, the daughter of a member of the Palestine Liberation Organisation, had not been declared in the register of MPs' interests.
- June 1993, Michael Mates (Northern Ireland minister) resigns following allegations of financial relationship with the fraudulent businessman Asil Nadir.
- January 1994, Lord Caithness (Department of Transport minister) resigns following his wife's suicide and allegations of his negligence and infidelity.
- January 1994, Tim Yeo (Department of Environment minister) resigns after admitting that he had fathered an illegitimate child.
- February 1994, Stephen Milligan (Parliamentary Private Secretary) accidentally strangles himself while engaging in a bizarre sexual act.
- May 1994, Michael Brown (government whip) resigns after allegations that he had a homosexual relationship with a student.
- January 1994, David Ashby (Parliamentary Private Secretary) resigns after admitting sharing a hotel bed with another man while on holiday in France.
- February 1994, Hartley Booth (Parliamentary Private Secretary) resigns after revelations of an affair with a House of Commons researcher.
- July 1994, David Tredinnick and Graham Riddick (both Parliamentary Private Secretaries) suspended following the 'cash-for-questions' disclosures by the *Sunday Times*.
- October 1994, Tim Smith (Northern Ireland minister) admits receiving payments from Mohammed al-Fayed and not declaring the financial association.
- October 1994, Neil Hamilton (Department of Trade and Industry minister) is accused of having an undeclared financial relationship with

Mohammed al-Fayed and of benefiting from his hospitality at the Paris Ritz Hotel.[77]

In the 1992–97 parliament, allegations like these concerning the private or business behaviour of individuals led to the departure of 16 ministers and parliamentary aides. Some clearly had to resign because of the nature of their actions (e.g. David Tredinnick, Graham Riddick, Tim Smith); others were more marginal cases of collateral damage where the sudden exposure of personal failings in an atmosphere of aroused public scrutiny prompted resignation to prevent further political embarrassment to the government (e.g. Tim Yeo, Hartley Booth, Lord Caithness).

Even though it did not involve serious figures or resignations, the most significant and far-reaching single episode of personal misconduct during this era was the 'cash -for-questions' scandal. This centred upon allegations made by the *Sunday Times* in July 1994[78] that two MPs (David Tredinnick, Graham Riddick) had been prepared to accept £1000 each to table questions in the House of Commons related to commercially valuable government information. The ensuing controversy over the laxity of standards and regulations concerning members' financial interests, and further allegations concerning MPs' and ministers' close proximity to outside interests, prompted John Major in October 1994 to set up the Nolan Committee on Standards in Public Life. The Nolan Report drew together many separate strands of public anxiety and produced a critical overview of political ethics. It referred to a 'culture of moral vagueness'[79] and a 'pervasive atmosphere of "sleaze", in which sexual, financial and governmental misconduct were indifferently linked'.[80] The Committee could not ascertain whether there had been any actual decline in public standards but it recognised the public's perception of such a decline and the commensurate increase in the attention given to the conduct of individuals in public life.[81]

> The amount of media interest in the subject of misconduct in public life ... has certainly intensified. In recent years there have been periods when instances of real or imagined malpractice seemed to be reported in the newspapers every few weeks. There is no precedent in this century for so many allegations of wrongdoing, on so many different subjects, in so short a period of time. It is not therefore surprising that opinion polls suggest that people believe that there is more actual misconduct than in the past.[82]

Polls also showed the consequences of such perceptions with 64 per cent of voters in a 1994 Gallup survey believing that 'most MPs make a lot of money by using public office improperly'; only 46 per cent took such a view in 1985.[83] Given that the boundaries of acceptable conduct had been indistinct, and that public confidence in the integrity of representative government was in decline, the Report called for 'urgent remedial action'[84] in the form of a wide-ranging set of regulative proposals covering, MPs, quangos, ministers and the civil service.

The Nolan Committee's very existence – its remit and its subsequent decision to enlarge the original brief – graphically illustrated the constitutional potential of the personal misconduct issue. In a specific sense, many of Nolan's proposals have extensive constitutional implications such as the introduction of an element of outside intervention in the regulation of MPs' interests through the appointment of a Parliamentary Commissioner for Standards; the establishment of transparent vetting procedures for the employment of former ministers; the creation of a partially independent panel to advise ministers on quango appointments; and the regulation of appointment procedures within government departments by a new independent Commissioner for Public Appointments. In a more general sense, the Nolan Committee broke the 'delicate membrane that conceals the ethical conduct of public figures in Britain'.[85] Simon Jenkins's view of the implicit iconoclasm of such a committee publicly inquiring into previously sacrosanct areas is shared by Peter Hennessy who believes that Nolan marked the end of the tacit understandings integral to the '"good chap" theory of government'. Hennessy believed the implications to be profound:

> Not only does this represent the most formidable advance towards institutionalised probity and decency in public and political life since the late 19th century, it does, in a little noticed fashion, also proclaim the beginnings of a written constitution for those particular public activities ... Henceforth standards must be written down, adhered to and monitored.[86]

It was a reflection of the decline in public confidence in the individual integrity of key political participants that culminated in the creation of the Nolan Committee's grand inquest and in the government's acceptance of both its recommendations and its continuing brief to review further areas of public ethics. The Nolan project amounted to a continuing corrective in a constitution based on the principle of continuous adaptation. Personal misconduct had fuelled a pronounced public scepticism over the efficacy of a constitution dependent upon personal good conduct and self-regulation and, as a consequence, the Nolan Committee was able to have 'a real impact on those constitutional practices which for so long had been taken for granted – if, indeed, they had been thought about at all'.[87]

Fuel No. 7: SYSTEMIC DYSFUNCTION

Some governmental decisions and actions produce a more widespread sense of dismay than that engendered by the normal range of governmental choices. Such governmental behaviour will most likely incite conventional forms of criticism and opposition through the traditional dynamics of Britain's adversarial system of party competition. Nevertheless, these types of governmental action possess an additional dimension that is distinct from government either superseding its powers (i.e. *governmental excess*) or abusing them (i.e. *governmental misuse*). The property in question is the capability of such issues to generate a serious decline in public confidence over the political system's capacity for good government. Governments make mistakes which often lead to policies having to be duly amended in response to pressure. But other mistakes are seen as representative of a deeper malaise within the system as a whole. As a consequence, they are regarded as mistakes that should never have been permitted to occur – that they did so is interpreted as a collective failure of the political system itself and in particular of the machinery for consultation, negotiation and constraint which, had it been operating effectively, would have precluded such outcomes. In these circumstances, there is no question that the government possesses the legitimate authority to take such decisions. That is not at issue. The constitutional fuel of systemic dysfunction relates to governmental behaviour which prompts widespread doubts over the operational reliability of the political system to provide rational, balanced, responsible and coherent policies. Although performance criteria like these will always be open to subjective interpretation, some decisions will be seen to be so notoriously inequitable, or so poorly drafted, or so bitterly opposed that they will generate a perception not merely of political maladoitness but of a deeper malfunction within the political system.

At one level, it can be said that any 'failure highlights the defects of our system of government'[88] in a generalised and undefined sense of remote culpability. At a more immediate level, some failures go beyond political miscalculation, or imprudence, or the arbitrary nature of unintended consequences. They raise the issue of the political system in a direct and critical way. In highlighting the concept of an underlying and integrated system of political dynamics, such issues normally generate a critical construction of the system's operational and procedural integrity. In effect, the enhanced public profile of a political system is directly related to a widespread need to condemn it on structural grounds. When political decisions become incomprehensible, they give rise to allegations of systemic malfunction as the only plausible explanation for egregious outcomes. They prompt the response that such decisions *could* have been avoided and that the dynamics of the system *should* have prevented such outcomes. It is not only the public that requires protection from the governing powers. It is the government itself which needs to be protected by a political system that will screen policy decisions and legislative proposals for signs of the impracticable, the unworkable and the unacceptable. These anxieties, and types of responses they give rise to, have become more conspicuous in British politics over recent years. Whether they are due to the effects of one party government over such an extended period, or to the depth of conviction and self-assurance that has characterised the Conservative project in government since 1979, or to the weaknesses of parliamentary scrutiny and opposition review, or simply to the sheer scale and complexity of the administrative state, the central role of government in making policy and formulating legislation has come under growing criticism for producing maverick decisions and anomalous outcomes.[89] Some legislation like the 1986 scheme to encourage individuals to switch from SERPS (i.e. State Earnings Related Pensions Scheme) to private pension schemes is simply so flawed in principle, content, design, execution and effect that it had to be abandoned.

The Child Support Act (1991), for example, was widely supported in principle but when it came into effect it quickly became clear that it was a badly flawed piece of legislation. It aroused intense criticism and provoked a series of public demonstrations against the inequitable effects of the assessment formulas used to determine the level of financial support owed to children by absent fathers. The complicated and formulaic nature of the Child Support Agency's (CSA) decision-making process was compounded by the fact that no right of appeal existed against assessments made by the agency. It quickly became apparent that the Child Support Act was afflicted with drafting problems that could have been foreseen and avoided had the government consulted more closely with those groups which were experienced in the area of family policy (e.g. National Council for One Parent Families, National Association of Citizens Advice Bureaux). But at the time of passage the government was in a hurry to pass what was a controversial piece of high profile legislation and it did not wish to lengthen the time scale of the proposed legislation either in committee or on the floor of the House of Commons. Because parliamentary time is such a valuable resource and because a general election was imminent, the government drove the legislation through Parliament at speed, accepting only one amendment to what was a highly complex bill. MPs were later to be haunted by the legislation in the form of burgeoning constituency case-loads caused by the Child Support Agency's decisions which quickly acquired a reputation for being unfair, impractical and even nonsensical.

Another example of the system's failure to foresee the damaging implications of a piece of legislation came with the Dangerous Dogs Act (1991). The government was once again seeking to respond decisively to an identified problem. A series of highly publicised attacks on adults and especially children by pit-bull terriers and rottweilers led to a tabloid campaign for government action. Even though a range of large breeds (e.g. Staffordshire bull terriers, Dobermans, greyhounds, rottweilers, alsatians) were responsible for the bulk of everyday attacks on children, Kenneth Baker, the Home

Secretary, singled out the pit-bulls for special treatment. The importation of the breed was banned. Remaining pit-bulls had to be neutered, registered, insured, fitted with a micro-chip and muzzled in public at all times. The law opened up a Pandora's box. Crossbreeds could not effectively be distinguished from pure-breeds for the purposes of the Act. 'Close-breeds' could be, and were, seized by the police for the appearance of being dangerously out of control in public. Aggrieved dog owners founded organisations to repeal the legislation and funded extensive appeals to save their pets from being destroyed. Animal welfare groups turned against the law because of the arbitrary nature of its application in which dangerous dogs from breeds classified as non-dangerous were left to roam in public areas while docile family pets could be placed on a dogs' death row because of a technical charge such as being caught without muzzle. The cost of implementing the Act exceeded £30 million and led to hundreds of court cases including six appeals to the European Court of Human Rights. As a consequence, the legislation came to be regarded as an expensive and tragic failure. In a key case, the Act was condemned by Mr Justice Rougier as bearing 'all the hallmarks of a badly thought out piece of legislation'. He continued: 'The Act was no doubt drafted in hasty response to pressure groups. Add to that an observant and zealous policeman and the result is a perfectly inoffensive animal being sent to the gas chamber. It would take the pen of a Voltaire to do justice to this situation.'[90]

Some legislation simply contains unfathomable gaps, like the omission in the rail privatisation bill which had the effect of denying to the Transport Police its traditional jurisdiction over railway property, including the powers of arrest. It is true that mistakes of this order can be rectified by subsequent parliamentary action but this does not prevent the onset of long-term consequences in the form of legal challenges and claims for redress. Other legislation requires a succession of Acts of Parliament to achieve a sustainable and coherent public policy. Between 1987 and 1994, for example, five Criminal Justice Acts entered the statute books, leaving the impression that legislation was only provisional, pending further measures to correct previous mistakes or misjudgements. The Criminal Justice Act of 1993, for example, was passed as a direct response to the unforeseen and chronic problems generated by with the 'unit fines system' which had been introduced in the 1991 Criminal Justice Act.

Without any doubt the prime example of legislative failure remains the fiasco associated with the community charge or 'poll tax' during the 1986–92 period. What was the flagship policy of a government with a fresh mandate from the 1987 general election became a policy disaster that generated deep political divisions, threatened to subvert the entire structure of local government finance, and undermined the central government's authority to such an extent that it had to engage in an ignominious retreat at an estimated cost of £20 billion. After being intransigently committed to the reform, the Conservative government ultimately had to concede defeat in 1991 when the poll tax was repealed and replaced with a property-based tax, similar to the old rating system which the community charge had originally been designed to supersede in 1988. The sheer impracticality and inequity of the poll tax not only incited an insurgency movement against it but prompted numerous inquiries into how such a deficient policy could ever have been passed into law.

> An ingenious but flawed initiative of the first importance was allowed to go ahead unchecked, despite all the safeguards and filters of the policy-making and legislative processes. Despite the legendary resources of the British State and law-abiding nature of its people, it proved virtually impossible to implement, mobilising popular resistance to a degree unprecedented since the General Strike of 1926.[91]

Given that it was such a conspicuous and high profile policy, that it represented the most extensive reform of local government this century and that it was such an incontrovertible and costly failure, there is little doubt that it amounted to a serious indictment of the British system of government. The checks and balances which should have identified the existence of such a defective measure and forced the government to review its stance were clearly ineffective. Parliamentary scrutiny could not withstand the presence of a reform which the government insisted on driving through the legislative process and which had already been worked out in detail before even being presented to Parliament. A bill with such 'profound constitutional significance ... reveal[ed] minimal parliamentary impact'.[92] The definitive study of the issue draws the following conclusion:

> In the case of the poll tax, ministers acted after cursory investigations and virtually no consultation with interested parties. Civil servants at the Department of the Environment developed the policy with barely a word of warning to ministers. Parliament was a rubber stamp. Opposition parties and outside interest groups counted for nothing. Local government, the creature of statute, was powerless to withstand a radical reconstitution of its powers and tax base.[93]

While the original choices may have been based upon the personal convictions and prejudices of the measure's leading advocates, the enactment and application of the policy amounted to a clear evidence of a 'system failure'.[94]

Dysfunctions can occur on the micro level and on the macro level; they can be seen as the consequence of government responsiveness or government unresponsiveness; and they can be construed as the result of procedural inefficiency or procedural efficiency. The common factor is a disjunction between intentions and consequences, leading to a scepticism of the political process and a declining sense of legitimacy for the law. Inadequate public consultation, impoverished legislation, administrative muddle and emergency revision provide a specific category of constitutional fuel in which the emphasis is laid upon the performance measure of basic governmental competence. While it may not always be possible to disengage systemic failure completely from the effects of political imprudence or negligence in the creation of poor legislation, enough weight is attached to the former irrespective of the latter to make it an identifiable cause for constitutional concern. In other words, the idea of a functioning and democratically based political system implies an arrangement of consultation, negotiation and accommodation that should counteract the political and administrative ineptitude of government. Evident failures in the basic function of government, therefore, can be interpreted as systemic faults giving rise to systematic critiques of governance and to an aroused consciousness of the constitutional dimension. Concern may be front-loaded, moving from policy failures to generalised outlooks upon government as a whole, or back-loaded, tracing constitutional critique and reform to key examples of government malfunction. Both forms depend upon, and give pronounced weight to, the concept of government as a machine and with it the analytical corollary of government being prey to mechanical faults, flaws and even breakdowns.

Fuel No. 8: TRANSCENDENT INNOVATION

The chief distinguishing characteristic of the British constitution has traditionally been that of adaptive change. The conventional British perspective is for a constitution to be repeatedly authenticated by a succession of changes that allegedly suggest viability through evolutionary modification. Change in this sense is a corollary of permanence in that it is construed as a device for preserving the central organising principles of the constitution. Change is intuitively confined, and reduced to, new versions of old orthodoxies rooted in the ultimate constant of parliamentary sovereignty. The reassuring nature of such change, however, has recently come under assault from a number of different sources that have generated new conditions which are not so readily amenable to the traditional precepts of the British constitution. Such changes disrupt the normal incrementalism of constitutional development by giving the appearance of transcending the constitution rather than being necessarily assimilated within it.

Judicial review is a particularly conspicuous example of this type, transformative innovation. As the public demand for the courts to rule on the lawfulness of government action has grown, judges have become far less reluctant than they once were to subject government to critical scrutiny. It has led to an increased incidence of judicial review and to a number of high profile cases involving senior ministers.[95] These developments have in their turn led elected politicians to complain that judges are straying into the political arena by allowing personal dispositions to shift the act of judgement from legal to policy grounds. But the behaviour of judges is not simply a matter of personal idiosyncrasy. The role of the judiciary is changing because of developments in the political system. For example, judges are now empowered to strike down an Act of Parliament where it conflicts with European law. Furthermore, when judges are applying European Union (EU) law, they have to use decisions of the European Court of Justice (ECJ) to inform their adjudications. To this extent, British judges are already operating in a framework external to Parliament.

In the view of Robert Stevens, judges have also adapted to a changing environment in more overtly political ways. The onset of a radical right government in 1979 brought in its wake the decline of the civil service, the erosion of the patrician element of the Conservative party and the dramatic shift to the left by a diminished Labour opposition. As a consequence of these dynamics:

> There was a vacuum of power in the centre and, consciously or not, the judiciary began to move into it. The judges began taking liberties, both inside and outside the courtroom. The Conservative government pursued a remarkably powerful agenda, explicit or not, of centralisation. Faced with this ambience, how could the judiciary not expand judicial review, pine for a Bill of Rights, encourage the notion that in implementing EU law it was serving as a constitutional court and even dream of fundamental laws?[96]

It can also be claimed that the judicial role has been altered through social influences, with judges becoming more internationally minded as a result of their experience with constitutional innovations in the Commonwealth and their increasing contact with European techniques of drawing judicial solutions from broad principles. But whether the origins are structural, political or professional, judges are succeeding in widening public access to the courts; they are becoming more professionally oriented to issues of fairness, justice and human rights; they are transforming judicial review from a pragmatic exercise into an altogether more principled and open-textured rule of law within the formal structure of parliamentary sovereignty. Britain is the only signatory of the European Convention on Human Rights (ECHR) neither to have incorporated it into law nor to have its own bill of rights, and yet it does appear, in the light of contemporary trends, that its judges are attempting to compensate for these deficiencies by a *de facto* rights-based conditioning of judgements. The expansive role given to EU law and the reliance upon the ECHR to inform decisions have helped to fuel controversy that Britain is moving stealthily towards a separation of powers with the judiciary assuming constitutional authority at the direct expense of Parliament.[97]

Another innovation that confounds traditional constitutional arrangements is the rise of 'public interest' pressure groups and the effect they have had upon the structure and style of political activity in Britain. The political parties have lost their monopoly in political allegiance and mass organisation. As disillusionment with party politics and with Westminster ritual has increased, as party support has become more volatile and as overall party membership has declined, the shortfall in participation and commitment has been made up by and even exceeded by high profile organisations like the Friends of the Earth with a membership of 200,000 and Greenpeace with a membership of 350,000. Political activism has diversified into a growing profusion of single issue groups determined that political energy should not be dissipated by incorporation into a larger mass. They offer focus, commitment and penetration. They employ modern methods of communications and media management to publicise issues and to pressure large organisations in both the public and private sectors. The established parties find it difficult to co-opt such groups because they operate in issue areas which transcend the normal designation of left and right, and which are able to appeal to a public increasingly sceptical of party-based panaceas and governmental assurances. In a study of what is commonly termed the 'new opposition', the *New Statesman and Society* listed 225 organisations many of which had their own web-sites and e-mail facilities.[98] When these public interest groups are combined with the influence of think-tanks which are now widely regarded as providing the policy ideas and even the political theory once generated exclusively by the parties, the result is a form of populism in which the intermediary structures of politics are becoming increasingly miniaturised and diversified.

The downsizing of political organisation and activity has not been confined to the national level where 'middle class energy, money and time'[99] have led the way with sophisticated campaigns designed to exploit the new channels of expression and representation (e.g. the World Development Movement's successful court action to subject the government's behaviour in the Pergau Dam affairs to judicial review, see pp.60–1). Britain is also experiencing the spontaneous eruption of 'do-it-yourself' citizen organisations at the local level. Community groups, tenant associations, campaign clubs, religious organisations and protest committees are rapidly multiplying. Very few of them are nationally known. They operate in a political underworld below conventional local government and even further below the attention levels of Westminster, Whitehall and the national media. Their relationship with the formal structure of the democratic system is a highly ambiguous one. Andrew Marr sees them as insurgency movements, critical of local authorities and conventional charities and intent upon direct self-help within their own communities. The established parties find it difficult to co-opt such groups because they have little interest in conventional politics.

They are overwhelmingly working class, have very little interest or past involvement in party politics and are strikingly idealistic ... [T]hey have changed the policies of supermarkets and building societies, forced local councils to clear illegal tipping sites, campaigned on homelessness and repossession, persuaded businesses to move and helped to alter policing tactics. [They succeed by] being legal troublemakers, picketing, jamming up offices, haranguing company directors and local politicians. From Bristol to the North of England, they have filled halls and given MPs angry meetings to contend with, of a kind most politicians rarely encounter.[100]

While the impulse behind such groups may be rooted in the anti-politics of alienation and exclusion, the net effect is one of another set of improvised points of political intermediation between individual and government.

The mass media's penetration into the political system represents an additional and highly significant innovation, whose full implications remain unfathomable in the long term. Already evident is the rising status of the media both in the presentation of politics and in the strategy of political calculation. As the House of Commons becomes more marginalised with its debates barely reported even in the broadsheets and with its capacity for constraint having been eroded by such an extensive period of one party rule, traditional opposition has increasingly been superseded not only by the media's own arenas of argument and analysis, but by its aggressive investigative reporting into incompetence, waste, sleaze and hypocrisy in British public life. The *Sunday Times*, for example, has campaigned vociferously for a bill of rights and freedom of information legislation. Its revelations of MPs' behaviour led to the 'cash-for-questions' scandal in 1994 and to the government's urgent response in the form of the Nolan Committee's inquiry into the ethical standards of public life. Like many other newspapers in this climate of abrasive openness, the *Sunday Times* has often ostentatiously proclaimed to be not merely the alternative opposition but the real opposition in British politics. While being something of an overstatement, the sentiment does capture the thrust of the media's competition not just with the traditional lines of political communication but with the established centres of political representation and debate. This populist instinct is particularly conspicuous with the electronic media's pervasive reporting of political news and its invasive coverage of previously closed or restrictive political arenas. There have been deliberate attempts on the part of television organisations to imitate the House of Commons by devising various formats in which the public can express views and debate issues as representatives of a mass audience (e.g. Channel 4/*The Observer*'s 'The People's Parliament'). With the onset of satellite and cable television, the increasingly competitive pressure for political news and debate will ensure that the media will continue to transcend and even supersede constitutional arrangements as polit-

ical institutions and parties persistently have to adapt to the rising imperatives of news management and public presentation.

Associated with this form of disruptive innovation is the growing 'presi-
dentialisation' of British politics. This refers not just to the rising prominence
of party leaders within their party organisations, but to the increased per-
sonalisation of party differences through the imagery and symbolism of individual leaders. Like presidents and presidential candidates, contenders for
the British premiership now have to distance themselves from their parties
in order to cultivate a personal rapport with the public and to mobilise support on a broad basis in an electorate which is increasingly volatile and de-
aligned from the point of view of party loyalty. The requirements of public
prominence and individual identity generate a nexus between the leader
and the public. This can provide opportunities for new and independent
sources of political authority that can be deployed inside a party by a leader
and inside the government by a prime minister. While sitting prime ministers play the presidential card of dealing with the affairs of state through
international summitry and high profile meetings with foreign leaders,
opposition leaders must seek to emulate such symbolism with their own
efforts to fuse the national interest with individual merit. This continuous
political manoeuvring by leaders in what is fast becoming a continuous
election campaign generates a full-scale politics of leadership in which leadership attributes rank as separate and substantive categories of political
evaluation. Such a politics focuses not merely upon the relative merits and
competitive behaviour of leaders, but on the meaning, usefulness, value,
sources and location of leadership in the political system.

There are many other developments whose relationship with the traditional principles of the British constitution remain ambiguous and even
problematic. The process of privatisation, for example, lodged enormous discretion in the hands of each industry's regulator who can control prices,
investment and standards of service. As such, regulators are regularly
accused of making policy rather than simply enforcing it.[101] The scale of
their authority far exceeds the techniques of public accountability assigned
to them. This is essentially the same problem as that generated by the new
public management techniques pioneered by the Next Steps executive agencies. The emphasis upon de-centralised, proactive and quasi-independent
units geared to service delivery, consumer responsiveness and performance
targets has revolutionised the civil service, but has also confounded the lines
of political accountability. For example, a deep ambiguity exists between the
autonomy of the chief executive and the role of the minister in providing a
definable centre of accountability for the services performed by the agency.
Although the formalities of accountability are served by the standard reductionism of the minister's ultimate responsibility to Parliament, the real
nature of the accountability remains open to doubt because of the impreci-

sion that exists between the chief executive's responsibility for operational decisions and managerial control and a minister's formal responsibility for overall policy. Next Steps agencies and their chief executives occupy a twilight area in the British constitution because of the way they appear to confound the logic of its controlling principles.[102] Even though such agencies supervise the bulk of public expenditure, they can be, and have been, criticised for short-circuiting the traditional lines of responsibility between citizen and minister. Gerald Kaufman is one who believes that non-departmental government represents a very serious threat to Britain's constitutional arrangements:

> [I]f a citizen of this country cannot, by consulting his or her constituency Member of Parliament, have a grievance considered by a Minister of the Crown, then the whole basis of representative Parliamentary democracy is being insidiously eroded. What we have is the increasingly burgeoning structure of an unaccountable, undemocratic, corporate state.[103]

Similar problems of governmental functions at one remove from the government exist with the 5500 quangos deployed to administer large slices of national policy at both the national and local level (e.g. health, education, housing, training). Concerns over the sheer numbers and cost of quango appointees (approximately 70,000) and the scale of government patronage related to this 'quangocracy', combined with the complaints over unaccountability, have created severe anxieties over how government is administered in Britain and in particular whether it any longer has a recognisable shape.[104] In David Walker's words: 'Instead of a steady withdrawal, the state has taken new forms. Here new islands have risen from the waves; there the sea has receded leaving unexplored land; elsewhere the waters have covered over some old territory.'[105] In a much wider sense, it is precisely these new forms which create a sense of the British constitution being transcended rather than confronted by change. The new developments co-exist within the traditional precepts and structures of the constitution. They are acknowledged as contemporary features of British government and the genuine products of autonomous processes within the political system. Yet they remain unassimilated and continually open to the charge that they are intrinsically unassimilable within the current constitutional arrangements.

Fuel No. 9: EXTERNAL IMPOSITION

In 1974, Lord Denning referred to the impact of Britain's membership of the European Economic Community (EEC) in terms similar to those used by David Walker above: 'The Treaty [of Rome] is like an incoming tide. It flows into the estuaries and up the rivers. It cannot be held back.'[106] At the end of the century, the tide has encroached far further than even Lord Denning would have envisaged and there is every sign that the incursion will continue to increase in scale. The reference to a tidal force is particularly appropriate in this context because it conveys the sense of an external agency of change which any British government has only a very limited and indeterminate capacity to control. In contrast to David Walker's analogy which implies a changing political and administrative landscape through large-scale yet autonomous forces, Lord Denning's usage of expansive terms of reference gives emphasis to the sense of constitutional anxiety and disruption originating from without. The constitutional fuel of external imposition is attributable to a range of factors but by far the most potent source of such constitutional disarray is the EU. The origins, development and consequences of Britain's membership of the EU epitomise the anxieties of partial control and diminished responsibility that represent the key ingredients of this type of constitutional fuel. The effect of the EU in raising constitutional questions can be divided into three main categories.

First, is the sheer scale of the EU's penetration into British public life. It has been difficult for Britain to adapt not just to the magnitude of change but also to the significance of its membership which was prompted by the decline of the British Empire, the realisation that Britain was no longer a world power, the onset of severe economic problems, the changing pattern of world trade and the erosion of national confidence that had previously been based upon a detachment from, and a superiority over, what were seen to be the afflictions and excesses of continental Europe. With membership of the EEC came the need to assimilate a separate system of supra-national government. Even after a quarter of a century, European institutions, their powers and relationships to one another still amount to a baffling and alien set of structures to much of the British public. Just as the European Commission is widely perceived to be a remote and invasive bureaucracy, so Members of the European Parliament are afforded second class status compared to MPs because of the latter's traditional connection to the sovereign parliament of a sovereign nation.[107]

And yet, notwithstanding the misinformed and disparaging nature of public attitudes towards European institutions, the EU is recognised as having vast regulatory powers that cover large areas of social and economic policy (e.g. trade, agriculture, consumer protection, environmental standards, health and safety, industry, employment, immigration, education and housing).[108] The integration of Britain within Europe is especially evident within the legal sector, where the British judiciary and the ECJ have developed a close relationship with one another in support of the pre-eminent authority of European law. The ECJ will either decide cases itself ('direct actions'), or give rulings on EU law ('indirect actions') to guide national courts in the application of such law. Either way, British courts have to give expression to the primacy of European law even to the extent of supplanting parliamentary enactments where they conflict with European legislation.[109] The British government can be, and has been, taken to court and ordered not only to amend policy but to pay damages to aggrieved parties. As European law is paramount, there is no recourse to appeal. The only response seems necessarily to be one of compliance.

Following the passage of the Single Market Act (1986), the EEC became committed to an intensified process of 'harmonisation' to bring national regulations into line with one another, in order to create common competitive economic environment within the EEC. The Maastricht Treaty (1993) established the EU based upon economic co-operation, common security, open frontiers and comparable social and legal conditions. Maastricht set an agenda for the development of a European foreign policy, the creation of a common European citizenship and an enhanced economic and monetary union culminating in a single currency. Even though the Maastricht amendments to the original Treaty of Rome (1957) provide rich potential for further intervention from Brussels, the Maastricht 'process' should not overshadow the actual level of inter-connectedness between Britain and Europe that has already been achieved. For example, in March 1996, the EU responded to the scare over bovine spongiform encephalopathy (BSE) in British cattle by imposing an immediate and indefinite ban on all exports of British beef not just to the EU but to any outlet in the international market. This amounted to a direct threat to Britain's £4 billion beef industry and raised the prospect of wider costs to the British economy in the order of £20 billion.[110] Although John Major's government challenged the decision in the European Court of Justice, the British authorities were seen to be essentially powerless to protect an indigenous industry from the effects of such a severe measure. After extensive efforts to put political pressure upon the EU to relax its ban, the government had to resort to a damaging policy of dissident non-co-operation with the Union, which was in itself a reflection of the government's own impotence in the issue. After losing its case in the ECJ, the British government had to defer to a settlement based upon the compelling authority of the EU.

The *second* element of the EU's contribution to the fuel of external imposition relates to the manifold constitutional implications of membership. In some respects, the EU is clearly organised on the basis of its treaties which collectively provide a constitutional framework for the powers, procedures and dynamics of the EU's institutions and their relationship to the member states. In other respects, the EU is a rapidly evolving organisation whose development has arguably outpaced its own processes – prompting charges of a 'democratic deficit'. In both respects, the EU's position in relation to Britain's governing structures remains problematic to the spirit and the letter of Britain's constitutional culture. Notwithstanding the difficulties raised by the extent to which, and the pace by which, the EU is moving towards a federal organisation, the EU as things already stand disrupts the most fundamental precepts of the British constitution. While there is a conscious if occasionally reluctant recognition of the primacy of European law and directions in principle, this acknowledgement co-exists with a deep state of unease over the precise courses and future ramifications of the European dimension within the domestic context. For example, the EU's emphasis upon fully documented constitutional principles enshrined in the fundamental law of the treaties sits uneasily with the unwritten code of the British constitution in which the only fundamental rule is that Parliament is not constrained by any law of superior law of obligation. Parliamentary sovereignty is not just subverted by the existence of European treaties and a *de facto* constitutional court, it is directly confronted by the pre-eminence of European law which means that Parliament cannot enact or implement legislation which clashes with the EU's policy decisions.[111] The repercussions of such a change are clearly evident with the current disarray over the provision of political accountability inside the British system. As decision-making is increasingly transferred to specialised units of the EU, the opportunity of Parliament to hold ministers to account is commensurately reduced – even more so since the inception of qualified majority rule in the Council of Ministers which can mean that should a British minister be in a minority, he or she cannot be held responsible by Parliament for an ensuing decision.

The traditional working assumptions of the British constitution are strained in numerous other directions. The British executive, for example, is in many ways freer from constraints in the European context than it is at Westminster. The incorporation of small nations within the EU, together with the EU's support for regional economic development, has provided a significant stimulus for devolution and minority nationalism within the United Kingdom. Europe has created new cleavages within both the main British parties, thereby threatening the operational integrity of the two party system as a whole. The EU also functions on the basis of separate yet closely related and complementary powers, in contrast to Britain's unitary and centralised traditions. British politics is adversarial and dualistic in nature and therefore distinct from the more inclusive and co-operative style that characterises the looser weave of multi-party and multi-layered politics in Europe. According to Vernon Bogdanor, it is because of its different constitutional traditions that

> Britain finds it difficult to comprehend and operate a legislative division of powers between two levels of government. Instead, it seems natural to conceive of the Council of Ministers and the European Parliament as in *competition* with Parliament, rather than Parliament being complementary to Community institutions ... The consequence here is of two entirely separate political systems competing with each other; and on this view, the notion of a division of powers makes no sense.[112]

The disjunction is exemplified by the difficulties between Westminster and the European Parliament in which the former is geared to confrontational debate between government and opposition for political and electoral advantage, while the latter is characterised by coalition politics and legislative scrutiny. Bogdanor continues:

> Most Community legislation does not fit into the binary conception of politics dominant at Westminster; it departs from a normal pattern of a series of measures to which the government is committed and which it has an interest in defending. Community legislation, therefore, is bound to impose a strain upon the House of Commons as it struggles to assimilate an entirely different legislative process into its traditional procedures ... It is not surprising that the two Parliaments find it difficult to communicate with and understand each other. Their attempt to do so resembles a dialogue between two incompatible computers.[113]

The old imperturbability of a British constitution, therefore, is continually being assaulted by questions and ambiguities generated from Europe. The extent to which the EU can be said to be developing a parallel constitution to the British constitution, or else instituting a gradual metamorphosis of the British polity, amounts to the most searching constitutional question of all.

The *third* way in which the EU confronts the British constitution relates to the widely held perception that progressive integration is irresistible and inevitable.[114] The mutable and open-ended nature of the EU is seen in many quarters as concealing an unremitting process in favour of European federalism. To object to the logic and pace of further integration carries the risk of being marginalised and consigned to a notional second division in a two-speed Europe. Even though Britain is the least European-minded nation within the EU and maintains a distinct cultural suspicion both of continental state systems and of the motives behind European integration, it is generally assumed that the submergence of the British state within the European dimension is an unavoidable fact of late twentieth century conditions. Such a trend is treated as part of an ineluctable process in which economic security is driving, and will continue to drive, a progressive diminution of national identity, societal variation and political sovereignty across Europe.

The traditional inter-dependency in Britain between national identity and constitutional integrity can lead to impulsive backlashes against an alleged European 'super-state', but such populist gestures are invariably conditioned by a fatalistic realism over Britain's ultimate need to be part of the European project. Even Margaret Thatcher's Euroscepticism had to submit to a European timetable for closer harmony (e.g. the single market, European Exchange Rate Mechanism). Moreover, the end of her premiership was precipitated by her resistance to any further integration. And yet in spite of the ferment of disaffection surrounding the issue which divided both main parties, Parliament felt compelled to consent to the Maastricht Treaty. The problem for the British constitution is that because of its benignly uncodified nature, it is especially susceptible to being altered fundamentally and subconsciously in response to political forces and changing conditions. On the one hand, its porous nature accommodates 'Europeanisation'. On the other hand, it is precisely this traditional adaptability which brings into question whether the British constitution is being subverted from without and surreptitiously transformed into a European state, in which the present disjunctions between the constitutional traditions of Britain and those of Europe are being resolved in favour of the latter.

The underlying theme is ultimately one of an absence of choice over the progressive 'Europeanisation' of the British state and a recognition that 'the drive to political union in Europe is relentless'.[115] Whether the lack of a plausible alternative is couched in terms of a conscious and rational choice based upon the benefits of integration, or as a form of inertia derived from an original decision on membership – albeit 'by a process of deception'[116] designed to postpone the long-term consequences – the net effect is now widely perceived to be one of an unavoidable ratchet movement. The only plausible alternative to such an apparently irreversible dynamic is British withdrawal from the collective process but this would not amount to a real choice. It would lead to only the impression of autonomy. An ostracised Britain would become isolated from the economic advantages of EU trade and detached from the political potential of the EU as a world power in international relations. There may be mixed responses and dire anxieties about European integration, but there is little doubt that it exists and that Britain is part of a dynamic process over which it has only marginal control. It is this concern over the presumptive necessity of responding to European organisations and timetables, and the indeterminate nature of the constitutional implications for Britain, which gives the constitutional fuel of external imposition its peculiar property of graduated impotence.

Fuel No.10: TRADITIONAL ANOMALIES

One major premise of the British constitution is that the system has in the main provided responsive, representative and effective government. Another premise is that the constitution is an unwritten and incoherent assemblage of institutions and powers, whose relationships between and amongst one another remain fluid and inexact and, therefore, open to constant interpretation. A third defining premise is that the first two premises are reconcilable with one another by way of an intuitive code of conduct by which ambiguities and even disjunctions are sufficiently accommodated to maintain the constitution's workability. The absence of a definitive constitutional settlement has left the British system with a host of unresolved issues in the fabric of a constitution acknowledged to be necessarily developmental in nature. Many of these issues are trivial and do not warrant the expenditure of available resources to rectify; they are simply tolerated on the understanding that they will not be unduly exploited for political gain. Other issues are far more fundamental and have in effect to be regarded as condoned anomalies which means they become working anomalies within the constitution. Some disjunctions are lodged so deeply in the constitution that they can only be assimilated by an instinctive social acquiescence in the incompleteness or incoherence of the constitution's structure.[117]

Critical inquiries or direct challenges in such areas are usually curtailed by a protective self-discipline drawn from a collective self-interest in avoiding the serious political disruption that would accompany the transformation of such a normally dormant issue into open and unrestrained controversy. Such constitutional questions are not normally regarded as political issues so much as abstract problems that are amenable to practical management in a co-operative constitutional culture. When a major constitutional anomaly becomes the subject of aroused interest, political conflict and unaccustomed analysis, it is not merely accompanied by a constitutional crisis; the full exposure of such an anomaly represents the essence of such a crisis. This is because it marks the end of the implicit truce that had previously sustained the anomaly. Just as the prior existence of a managed disjunction could be taken as a sign of a constitutional community with the aptitude and disposition to assimilate the problematic nature of constitutional anomalies, so the refusal any longer to disguise, or to defer consideration of, such anomalies indicates the absence of a social order capable of supporting even the most traditional of the constitution's areas of wilful neglect. The most prominent, long-standing and potentially disruptive of the British constitution's traditional anomalies are without doubt the position of the House of Lords and the monarchy in what is a parliamentary democracy. The continued presence of these institutions, in addition to the status accorded to them in the political system, constitutes a standing challenge to the liberal democratic precepts that in so many other respects provide the organising principles of the constitution.

Even with the introduction of life peers (1958), the House of Lords remains an overtly feudal institution based upon the principles of inherited wealth and established social station. The large preponderance of hereditary peers[118] ensures the presence of a permanent conservative majority in the nation's second chamber – so much so that the bulk of the hereditary peerage is not actively encouraged to attend by the whips for fear of highlighting the inequity of the constituent membership. It is not simply that there exists an element of an *ancien régime* within government, it is that the peerage's culture of birth, rank, hierarchy, lineage and hereditary succession is openly responsible for the identity and authority of one half of the legislative process. It is true that the powers of the House of Lords have been circumscribed and that the institution's remaining powers have to be used with a caution conditioned by the knowledge that the source of overriding democratic authority remains the House of Commons. It is also true that much of the House of Lords' energy and work is attributable to the life peers, whose presence in the chamber is based upon a record of public achievement. In similar view, it is often claimed that the Lords perform a series of valuable functions by revising and correcting legislation, allowing time for second thoughts, scrutinising statutory instruments, providing a more discursive examination of new policy, and occasionally frustrating the government by rejecting controversial measures.[119]

Notwithstanding the merits of a countervailing power against a pre-eminent executive, the House of Lords remains an anomaly because of the questionable legitimacy of its authority to perform such a role. Either it does not really possess an effective authority in which case it does not constitute a reliable check and balance, or else it does have an alternative locus of authority in which case it is palpably and provocatively undemocratic in substance – if not always in effect. The conundrums posed by the House of Lords are similar to those raised by any second chamber in a system based upon democratic consent, but they are compounded by a body whose membership is the product of past and present patronage.[120] The very presence of the House of Lords casts doubt on the extent to which the system has been democratically transformed. The rituals, titles and roles of the Lords evoke a separate social order not only prior in time to contemporary party democracy but expressing the retention of much of that hierarchy's social, political, cultural and constitutional influence. It is for this reason that the House of Lords can be become the subject of radical reform proposals – most significantly in 1994 when the Labour party revealed its intention to abolish the voting rights of hereditary peers.

The democratic and systemic ambiguities generated by an aristocracy are deepened by the presence of a monarchy – albeit a constitutional monarchy. Like the House of Lords, the monarchy is in one sense non-controversial. Its powers have been eroded, the level of individual discretion in the use of the remaining powers is minimal and the office performs the valuable function of providing a focus for national pride, patriotic commitment and common effort. It also sponsors the arts, supports charities, promotes British interests abroad and provides the tourist industry with one of its biggest attractions. Because of the singular nature, the public prominence and the constitutional centrality of the position, the monarch is more protected from political controversy than the House of Lords. Under normal circumstances, a set of conventions and protocols sustain the monarchy's involvement in government without putting at risk the monarch's role as head of state. At its most benign, the monarchy can be seen as being confined to a vestigial role in government – defined by Bagehot as 'the right to be consulted, the right to encourage, the right to warn'.[121] This leaves the monarch free to generate a dimension of public life that is above party politics and is characterised by an ethos of public service, historical continuity, personal dignity and a sense of national identity.[122]

A more critical construction of the monarchy identifies it as a malign influence from several perspectives.[123] For example, it is seen as the supreme embodiment of a class society which symbolises landed wealth and social distinction, while at the same time providing popular distraction from the oppressive implications of such an ideology of social exclusiveness. The privileges and immunities of the crown are said to signify a culture that 'penetrates everywhere through the desire for peerages, the honours system, snobbery, social connections and deference'[124] The monarchy is also accused of being a recidivist institution that retards the modernisation of Britain by radiating a sentimental attachment to an idealised past. Tom Nairn refers to the monarchy's 'glamour of backwardness'[125] in which royalty's 'formidable ascendancy over the public's imagination.[126] is used to provide 'icons of continuity and reassurance'[127] to confront the 'tensions of a polity in disintegration'.[128] Monarchy's attachment to the imperial past, the contemporary Commonwealth and the Church of England is seen to be at variance with the current need for Britain to come terms with being a multi-cultural and multi-faith society.

Other concerns centre upon the monarchy's pivotal position in the British system of government. The ubiquity of the crown in the language and forms of governmental authority forecloses debate over the precise allocation and relationships of power within the system. The legal entity of the crown means that ministers are formally acting on behalf of the crown and that, as ministers of the crown, they are regarded as responsible for their departments in order to protect the monarchy from controversy and dissent. The blanket term of ministerial responsibility, therefore, originates from ministers' relationships with the crown rather than with the parliament. Ministers, and especially the prime minister, have also inherited the power of the crown prerogative which continues to be largely immune from statutory definition. The royal prerogative remains the 'well-spring ... where monarchical authority still pours into the world ... like glittering silver tributaries'.[129] As a result, 'it is not easy to discover and decide the law regarding the royal prerogative and the consequences of its exercise'.[130] Parliament's general avoidance of even a minimal supervision of prerogative powers has had the effect of transferring the mystique and proprietorship of the crown prerogative to the prime minister and cabinet. The device of the crown, and the progress of democracy to the point of co-opting its expansive, indefinable and unaccountable authority, has helped to underwrite a highly elusive constitution in which, for example, the criteria for dissolving Parliament and appointing a prime minister remain imprecise. The status and usage of the crown has ensured that the British system has remained 'a "great ghost" of a constitution',[131] leading to a concomitant 'frustration at the precariousness, the incompleteness, the haphazardness of it all'.[132]

Although there have been periods when the monarchy has engendered a mood of public scepticism (e.g. Sir Charles Dilke's movement in 1870–71 opposing state expenditure on the monarchy; the crisis surrounding the abdication of Edward VIII in 1936), the anomalies surrounding the sovereign in an increasingly libertarian and secular society have for the most part been effectively accommodated. Under normal circumstances, the potential for conflict has been successfully reduced to a minimum through an interior culture of social convention and reciprocal obligation, and through an exterior mass culture of a monarchy disarmingly portrayed as a dignified and charitable family on the throne. But during the 1992–96 period, a succession of personal and highly publicised misfortunes within the royal family, culminating in the formal separation of both the Duke and Duchess of York and the Prince and Princess of Wales, led to an altogether less compliant attitude towards the monarchy. The sheer scale of revelation in respect to the private lives and finances of the royal family, in conjunction with the sheer intensity of media interest in their marital fidelity and personal problems, created an atmosphere of siege in which individual family members made public appeals in support of their respective positions (e.g. BBC's *Charles: The Private Man, The Public Role*, broadcast on 29 June 1994; Princess Diana's *Panorama* interview, broadcast on 20 November 1995). Once the previously closed ranks had been breached, the monarchy itself seemed less magisterial or mystical in nature. The multiplicity of royal crises prompted a profusion of questions and debates, comparisons and speculations, and even a willingness to think of republican alternatives. With a monarchy now beset by tabloid exposures, opinion poll surveys, irreverent satire and the need for the Palace to engage in public relations campaigns of counter-information, the idiosyncrasies of the institution and, with it, the constitution itself were unremittingly revealed.[133]

In the turmoil, the level of reasoning and argument was often poor. Experience in subjecting the monarchy to critical review was demonstrably limited as the categories of analysis slipped repeatedly from the individual to the institution and, thence, to the entire role of the contemporary monarchy. Discussions were also marked by inductive leaps that would falsely assert causal links between the presence of monarchy and the weakness of Britain's industrial economy, or between a reformed monarchy and the need for a written constitution. This type of discourse served only to contribute to the sensationalism generated elsewhere by investigative journalism. For an institution that has traditionally depended so much upon the lure of distance and exclusivity, the monarchy was unable to resist the intrusive attention of an aggressive popular press locked in a bitter circulation war. It was not so much that members of the public were surprised by the content of royal lives, it was more that they were disillusioned by the prosaic aspects of royalty and by the realisation that the effectiveness of royalty depended upon a general complicity to suspend inquiry and evaluation. The spectacle of royal exposure provided an unaccustomed insight into monarchy, but in doing so it threw into high relief the scale of the constitutional anomalies surrounding the crown and the level of tolerance previously required to accommodate it in a democratic polity. Even to question the legitimacy of such an institution was in itself either to undermine it or to recognise that it had already been subverted.

The formal and institutional pressures against any public examination of the monarchy remained in place, supported in particular by the various conventions and rulings preventing the House of Commons from even discussing the sovereign.[134] The print and electronic media, however, were far less constrained and broke a series of previous 'understandings' in conducting their own forms of public discussion. In May 1993, *The Times* and Charter 88 jointly sponsored a grand debate with the intention of providing the 'most comprehensive forum on the subject of the monarchy since the 17th century'.[135] The event was attended by 90 speakers and was covered by an extensive corps of domestic and international journalists. But the debate, which was said to have 'ended a 40-year taboo'[136] on the subject, turned out to be a just prelude to Carlton Television's programme of *Monarchy: The Nation Decides* which took place in January 1997. In front of what was claimed to be the largest studio audience (i.e. 3000) ever gathered for a television debate, the programme discussed the costs, benefits and scandals of the royal family. The conduct of the debate and the organisation of the studio and viewer polls may have left much to be desired and the chief significance of the exercise may be said to have been in the fact that such an event had taken place at all; nevertheless, the programme did reveal that 66 per cent of over 2 million respondents in the 'television referendum' wanted the monarchy retained. This public defence of the monarchy was, however, qualified by a belief from 56 per cent in the programme's MORI poll that the institution would probably not survive the next 100 years.

This combination of criticism, affirmation and resignation reflects the findings of many other opinion surveys. While polls regularly record widespread complaints against the royal family on grounds of privilege, morality, extravagance, irresponsibility, lack of respect and concern for the common people etc., they also record support levels as high as 75 per cent against abolition.[137] And yet, the same fatalism in respect to the long-term future of the institution has grown conspicuously during the period of crisis.

In 1990, 12 per cent of the public did not think that Britain would still have a monarchy in 50 years, time. In 1996, that level of scepticism had grown to 43 per cent while those who believed the institution would survive slumped from 70 per cent to a third during the same period.[138] The Queen and the institution of monarchy attracted respect but the wider grasp of the anomalies surrounding the monarchy and its position in the constitution evoked a sense of unsustainability. The vulnerable nature of the institution was further underlined by the death of Diana, Princess of Wales in 1997 which not only precipitated a period of acute national grief, but generated an unprecedented public reaction against the Windsors and a general belief that the monarchy would need to reform itself in order to remain a viable institution. During this period, an NOP survey revealed that a third of the public (i.e. 35 per cent) believed that the monarchy would only survive for another 30 years, 72 per cent thought that the Queen was remote and out of touch, and 53 per cent believed she should abdicate either immediately or when she reached the age of 75 in 2000.[139] A Gallup poll revealed that over half the public (i.e. 53 per cent) believed the events surrounding Diana's death had damaged the Queen and the Royal Family, and that, as a result, 51 per cent thought that Prince William should be the heir to the throne rather than Prince Charles.[140]

As a constitutional fuel, the monarchy and the House of Lords have close similarities in that they can both arouse strong democratically based objections which in their turn produce a response in their favour founded upon historical sentiment, functional value and political stability. They both evoke systemic complaint and ideas for overall reform but it is precisely the difficulties and the problematic consequences of concerted change which inhibit structural alteration in such a densely packed but informal constitution. Uncomfortable discussion rather than open debate still characterises the way in which such issues are addressed. The problematic nature of the monarchy's role and performance in a modern democracy, together with the personal difficulties of allocating substantive power to a second chamber in a way that does not detract from the popularly elected chamber, remain central challenges to the system. The monarchy and the House of Lords are acknowledged to be anomalies and, as such, continue to be a constant source of constitutional inhibition and self-restraint, punctuated by periods of fevered speculation and ramifying social and political critique. The monarchy in particular is seen as epitomising both the nature of the constitution and the difficulty of revising it. The monarchy is portrayed as the 'pinnacle of a constitutional system'[141] in that its rationale permeates a multiplicity of other constitutional sectors and issues, but because its 'constitutional functions remain as misty and misunderstood as ever'[142], it serves to characterise the ambiguity that surrounds the concerted attempts to re-examine and reappraise the constitution.

CONCLUSION

All the themes addressed in this chapter have a common factor. They are, in the terms employed by this study, constitutional fuels in that they all provoke controversy over the state of the constitution; they all lead to an enhanced realisation of the problematic properties within the constitution; and they all provoke ideas and impulses for reform that translate into the currency, language and calculations of contemporary politics. Even though they all possess these common properties, this does not mean that such fuels are an undifferentiated stimulus to constitutional speculation. On the contrary, as has been demonstrated, these fuels are varied in origin and outcome. They have a diverse range of characteristics, contexts and implications. So much so that they can give the appearance of being wholly discrete inducements to constitutional anxiety and analysis. In many respects, they are qualitatively and quantitatively separate from each other, but it is possible to break down each fuel according to a set of criteria that will provide not only a framework for comparison but a means of identifying the main component properties of every one of the individual fuels. From an examination of the different constitutional fuels, six criteria emerge to provide the organising principles of a table of contents and ultimately a typology of fuels. The criteria are:

1 Problem recognition (a) Nature
2 Problem recognition (b) Dynamics
3 Dimension of response
4 Ignition opportunity
5 Form of controversy
6 Costs

The first two categories relate to how constitutional problems are conceived and defined. While category 1 addresses the extent to which a problem is behavioural or structural in nature, category 2 assesses whether such problems have stable and unchanging characteristics, or whether they are progressive and developmental features in the constitution. The dimension of response provides the third category which separates issues into those that generate discrete reactions and reform impulses (micro), and those that provoke more systemic critiques requiring integrated and strategic changes in the constitutional structure (macro). Constitutional problems do not become political issues unless and until they arouse sufficient public concern to become part of the agenda of political discourse and calculation. Category 4 relates to the ignition properties of the different constitutional fuels and in particular the degree to which the energy transfer is occasioned more by specific incidents or by general conditions. While category 5 traces the frequency and intensity of ensuing constitutional controversies, category 6 estimates the political and constitutional costs of the reform proposals generated by each fuel. The twin sub-classes within each category are not mutually exclusive zero-sum entities. For example, it is possible for a particular constitutional fuel to evoke both a micro and a macro response in category 3. While the political costs and constitutional costs of resolving problems in category 6 can both be high, so it is feasible for a problem to be not only behavioural but also structural in nature.

The six analytical categories derived from the overview of constitutional fuels are not susceptible to precise quantitative measurement. Nevertheless, an estimation of their relative strengths and weaknesses is possible through the attribution of a scale of designated values – in this case: (i) very high; (ii) high; (iii) medium; (iv) low; and (v) very low. Such values may be qualitative in nature and ultimately subjective in character, but they are an effective means of providing a series of approximate profiles that allow the differences and similarities in the several fuels to be elicited and assessed. The results of this exercise are given in Figure 3:1.

It is immediately evident from this figure that constitutional fuels vary widely from one another. The profile of an issue like *electoral inequity*, for example, differs visibly from an issue like *personal misconduct*. Similarly, a fuel such as *governmental misuse* differs markedly in characteristics from a fuel with the properties of *systemic dysfunction*. It is clear from such a figure which fuels are preponderantly structural in nature (e.g. *electoral inequity, traditional anomalies, systemic dysfunction*) and which fuels are based more on behavioural characteristics (e.g. *governmental misuse, personal misconduct*). It is also evident that no consistent pattern exists within such sub-classes. Even though fuels like *centralisation, secrecy, systemic dysfunction, traditional anomalies, and external imposition* have pronounced structural features, these do not lead to a uniform distribution of other characteristics. *Secrecy* and *traditional anomalies*, for example, are more incident-driven and tend to evoke micro dimensional responses. *Centralisation* and *systemic dysfunction*, on the other hand, tend to be condition-driven and to produce reactions on a macro dimensional scale. It is true that there is a close correlation between those fuels which are structural in character and those which are seen to have a progressive quality. Nevertheless, the correlation is not an absolute one. The fuel of *traditional anomalies* is structural but it is also in essence static because the monarchy and the House of Lords possess an antiquarian reputation in the British constitution.

Although a clear majority of the fuels are structural, progressive, condition-driven and macro dimensional in response, other fuels are conspicuous for their behavioural, static, incident-driven and micro level reactions (e.g. *personal misconduct, traditional anomalies*). While most fuels are assessed to be costly to address in political and constitutional terms, it is evident that the structural/progressive fuels are deemed to be generally more likely to carry higher costs than the behavioural/static fuels. But perhaps the most informative category is the fifth column which estimates the frequency and intensity of the controversies ensuing from each fuel. Given that the significance of any fuel lies at the point at which potential energy is converted into actual energy, an assessment of the incidence and force of actual political controversy is especially pertinent to the concept of constitutional fuel. The frequency and intensity categories reveal a wide variety of permutations ranging from fuels with high values in both characteristics (e.g. *external imposition*) to those fuels that can cause intense controversies but over limited periods of time (e.g. *electoral inequity, governmental misuse*). The inability of certain fuels to sustain political agitation is a weakness and demonstrates the difficulty of translating even intense controversy into durable pressure for constitutional reform. The relative strengths and weaknesses of the ten fuels in this respect is given schematic expression in Figure 3:2.

It is clear from the different rates of intensity and frequency that nearly every fuel has a different profile in the type of controversies it generates in the constitutional debate. All of them are rated medium or over in the intensity category, which is only to be expected given that they are designated fuels to constitutional controversy. Nevertheless, the variation is significant, with issues such as *governmental excess, governmental misuse* and *centralisation* having the capacity to provoke very intense pressure for change. A fuel like *traditional anomalies* on the other hand, which at first sight might be thought to have the capacity to raise serious democratic challenges to current constitutional arrangements, almost invariably fails to provoke the kind of reaction that might be expected from the presentation of such apparent inconsistencies within the prevailing democratic order. While differences in intensity are significant, they are not as great as the variation in frequency which ranges from very low (e.g. *electoral inequity, governmental misuse*) to high (e.g. *centralisation, external imposition*). The frequency ratings are without exception lower than the intensity ratings which in many respects is a logical outcome. This is so because a high frequency fuel would with repetition be likely to lose whatever shock value it initially possessed and quickly become a low intensity issue. Secondly, it is a logical consequence because the higher the intensity of a fuel, the more probable it is that the frequency will be commensurately lower, reflecting the magnitude of energy, the degree of reaction and the needs of assimilation. But notwithstanding the logic of the general pattern, each fuel has separate characteristics. Some produce sudden pulses of high energy controversy (e.g. *electoral inequity, governmental misuse*) which diminish quickly in effect as the circumstances that give rise to such issues are normally specific, discrete and limited in duration. Other fuels rumble through the constitutional debate but are difficult to ignite. Fuels like *traditional anomalies, secrecy* and *transcendent innovation* help to condition the movement for constitutional

Figure 3.1 *Constitutional fuels categorised according to selected typological criteria*

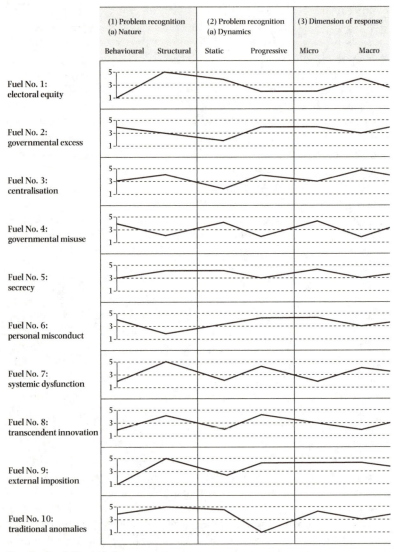

Key: Very low, 1–Very high, 5

(4) Ingnition opportunity		(5) Form of controversy		(6) Costs	
Incident	Condition	Frequency	Intensity	Political	Constitutional

Table 3.1 *Constitutional fuels ranked by 'controversy quotient' (CQ)*

Constitutional fuels		IR	FR	CQ
Fuel No. 3:	centralisation	5	4	20
Fuel No. 2:	governmental excess	5	3	15
Fuel No. 6:	personal misconduct	4	3	12
Fuel No. 7:	systemic dysfunction	4	3	12
Fuel No. 9:	external imposition	4	3	12
Fuel No. 10:	traditional anaomalies	3	3	9
Fuel No. 5;	secrecy	3	2	6
Fuel No. 8:	transcendent innovation	3	2	6
Fuel No. 1:	electoral inequity	5	1	5
Fuel No. 4:	governmental misuse	5	1	5

change but mostly lack the dramatic appeal of the more inflammable fuels. They make up in duration what they lack in intensity but they do not have the accessibility and palpable incitement to constitutional criticism of those fuels with higher ignition properties.

Measures like those used in this analysis are, of course, imprecise. While it is always possible to give the appearance of greater precision, such devices will not resolve the problem of qualitative difference. For example, by assigning a numeric value to the categories of (i) very high = 5; (ii) high = 4; (iii) medium = 3; (iv) low = 2; and (v) very low = 1, it is possible to acquire a general estimate of each fuel's contribution to constitutional controversy. By multiplying the intensity ratings (IR) by the frequency ratings (FR), an aggregate controversy quotient (CQ) could be produced giving the results presented in Table 3.1

Such a notional quotient may be plausible in a number of respects. For example, the prominence of such fuels as *governmental excess* and *centralisation*, and to a lesser extent *personal misconduct* and *systemic dysfunction*, would be in accord with the types of issue most likely to cause consternation in a constitution under critical review. Nevertheless, the assignment of a 5 to the fuels of *governmental misuse* and *electoral inequity* would amount to an under-valuation because it would fail to take into account the possible long-term conditioning effects, or the short-term catalytic effects, of such discrete incident-driven influences. It is quite conceivable that a single crisis could become a cause célèbre and, ultimately, the strongest stimulus of all for constitutional reconstruction.

Figure 3.2 *The location of constitutional fuels in relation to frequency and intensity rankings*

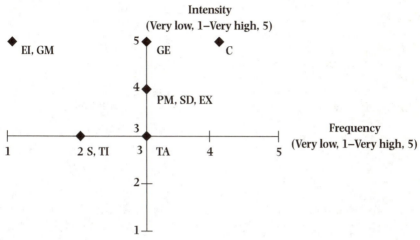

Key:

Fuel No. 1: electoral inequity (EI)
Fuel No. 2: governmental excess (GE)
Fuel No. 3: centralisation (C)
Fuel No. 4: governmental misuse (GM)
Fuel No. 5: secrecy (S)
Fuel No. 6: personal misconduct (PM)
Fuel No. 7: systemic dysfunction (SD)
Fuel No. 8: transcendent innovation (TI)
Fuel No. 9: external imposition (EX)
Fuel No. 10: traditional anomalies (TA)

This chapter has examined the varying properties of those issues that arouse constitutional concern and debate in a political culture not ordinarily noted for any developed sense of constitutional consciousness either amongst political participants or within the citizenry as a whole. Such constitutional fuels are potent sources of political speculation, radical criticism and defensive reaction. They fuel a sense of systemic flux to be recognised, or justified, or channelled, or condemned. They provoke a need for change and a need to resist change. They give rise to empirical arguments over current conditions and to normative prescriptions over responses and requirements. They generate a diagnostic uncertainty not only over the British constitution but over the British conception of what a constitution entails. Given that such fuels account for the immediate causes of constitutional disarray in a previously settled political process, it is now necessary to turn to their wider effects and, in particular, to the nature of the reformist energies released into the British political system.

Notes

1 Vernon Bogdanor, *Power and the People: A Guide to Constitutional Reform* (London: Victor Gollanz, 1997), p. 57.

2 *Ibid.* pp.58–9.

3 See Dennis Kavanagh (ed.), *Electoral Systems* (Oxford: Clarendon, 1992) *passim*; Vernon Bogdanor and David Butler (eds), *Democracy and Elections* (Cambridge: Cambridge University Press, 1983), *passim*; Neil T. Gavin, 'Proportional Representation and the Calculation of Party Political Advantage in Britain', *Representation: Journal of Representative Democracy*, vol. 33, no. 3 (Winter 1995/96), pp. 91–100; Philip Norton, 'Does Britain Need Proportional Representation?' in Robert Blackburn (ed.), *Constitutional Studies: Contemporary Issues and Controversies* (London: Mansell, 1992), pp. 136–47.

4 Peter Kellner, 'Electoral Reform': Principle or Self-Interest?', *Representation: Journal of Electoral Reform and Comment*, vol. 33, no. 2 (Summer/Autumn 1995), p. 27.

5 See David Marquand, *The Unprincipled Society: New Demands and Old Politics* (London: Fontana, 1988).

6 Rodney Brazier, *Constitutional Reform: Re-shaping the British Political System* (Oxford: Clarendon, 1991), p. 126.

7 Ronald Dworkin, *A Bill of Rights for Britain* (London: Chatto and Windus, 1990), p. 2.

8 Bogdanor, *Power and the People*, p. 136.

9 See David Farnham, 'Trade Union Policy 1979–89: Restriction or Reform?' in Stephen P. Savage and Lynton Robins (eds), *Public Policy Under Thatcher* (Houndmills: Macmillan, 1990), pp. 60–74. B. C. Roberts' 'Trade Unions' in Dennis Kavanagh and Anthony Seldon (eds), *The Thatcher Effect: A Decade of Change* (Oxford: Oxford University Press, 1989), pp. 64–79.

10 K. D. Ewing and C. A. Gearty, *Freedom Under Thatcher* (Oxford: Clarendon, 1990); Patrick McAuslan and John F. McEldowney, 'Legitimacy and the Constitution: The Dissonance Between Theory and Practice' in Patrick McAuslan and John F. McEldowney (eds), *Law, Legitimacy and the Constitution: Essays marking the Centenary of Dicey's Law of the Constitution* (London: Sweet and Maxwell, 1985), pp. 1–38; P. Thornton, *Decade of Decline: Civil Liberties in the Thatcher Years* (London: National Council for Civil Liberties, 1989).

11 Paul Sieghart, 'Foreword' in Paul Sieghart (ed) *Human Rights in the United Kingdom* (London: Pinter, 1988), p. 4.

12 Ewing and Gearty, *Freedom Under Thatcher*, p. 255.

13 McAuslan and McEldowney, 'Legitimacy and the Constitution' in McAuslan and McEldowney (eds), *Law, Legitimacy and the Constitution*, p. 32.

14 Ewing and Gearty, *Freedom Under Thatcher*, p. 106.

15 an Harden and Norman Lewis, *The Noble Lie: The British Constitution and the Rule of Law* (London: Hutchinson, 1986), p. 11.

16 See Joshua Rozenberg, *Trial of Strength: The Battle Between Ministers and Judges Over Who Makes the Law* (London: Richard Cohen, 1997); Michael Superstone and James Goudie, *Judicial Review* (London: Butterworths, 1992); *Richard Gordon, Judicial Review: Law and Procedure* (London: Sweet and Maxwell, 1996); Dawn Oliver, 'Politicians and Judges: A Conflict of Interest', *Parliamentary Affairs*, vol. 49, no. 3 (July 1996), pp. 423–40.

17 See Francesca Klug, Keir Starmer and Stuart Weir, *The Three Pillars of Liberty: Political Rights and Freedoms in the United Kingdom* (London: Routledge, 1996).

18 For example, see Dawn Oliver, *The Government of the United Kingdom: The Search of Accountability, Effectiveness and Citizenship* (Milton Keynes: The Open University Press, 1991); Geoff Andrews (ed.), *Citizenship* (London: Lawrence and Wishart, 1991).

19 'Why Britain Needs a Bill of Rights', *The Economist*, 21 October 1995.

20 Michael Mansfield, 'The Bounds of Silence' in *Taking Liberties: Civil Liberties and the Criminal Justice Act* (London: New Statesman and Society, 1995), p. 16.

21 See Lord Jenkins of Hillhead, 'Argument: The Case for a People's Bill of Rights' in William L. Miller (ed.), *Alternatives to Freedom: Arguments and Opinions* (London: Longman, 1995), pp. 21–30; Anthony Lester, 'A Bill of Rights for Britain' in Anthony Barnett, Caroline Ellis and Paul Hirst (eds), *Debating the Constitution: New Perspectives on Constitutional Reform* (Cambridge: Polity, 1993), pp.39-43; Francesca Klug, 'The Role of a Bill of Rights in a Democratic Constitution' in Barnett *et al.*, *Debating the Constitution*, pp. 44–54; Richard Gordon and Richard Wilmot-Smith, *Human Rights in the United Kingdom* (Oxford, Clarendon, 1997), *passim*.

22 Richard Rose, *Politics in England*, 5th edn (Glenview, Illi: Scott, Foresman, 1989), p. 64.

23 Ian Budge and Derek W. Urwin, *Scottish Political Behaviour: A Case Study in British Homogeneity* (London: Longman, 1966), p. 48.

24 See Simon Jenkins, *Accountable to None: The Tory Nationalization of Britain* (London: Penguin, 1995); Bob Jessop, Kevin Bonnett, Simon Bromley and Tom Ling, *Thatcherism: A Tale of Two Nations* (Cambridge: Polity, 1988).

25 Samuel Brittan, 'The Thatcher Government's Economic Policy' in Kavanagh and Seldon (eds), *The Thatcher Effect* p. 4.

26 *Ibid.*

27 See G. W. Jones and James Stewart, *The Case for Local Government* (London: George Allen and Unwin, 1985); Martin Loughlin, *Local Government in the Modern State* (London: Sweet and Maxwell, 1986); J. Stewart and Gerry Stoker, *The Future of Local Government* (London: Unwin-Hyman, 1989); Steve Leach and Gerry Stoker, 'The Transformation of Central–Local Government Relationships' in Cosmo Graham and Tony Prosser (eds), *Waiving the Rules: The Constitution Under Thatcherism* (Milton Keynes: Open University Press, 1988), pp. 95–115; Vernon Bogdanor, 'Local Government and the Constitution' in Vernon Bogdanor (ed.), *Politics and the British Constitution* (Aldershot: Dartmouth, 1996), pp. 163–82.

28 See K. Ascher, *The Politics of Privatisation: Contracting Out Public Services* (Houndsmills: Macmillan, 1987); Stuart Weir and W. Hall (eds), EGO TRIP: *Extra-Governmental Organisations in the United Kingdom and Their Accountability*

(Colchester: Human Rights Centre/Charter 88, 1994).

29 Jenkins, *Accountable to None*, pp. 266–7.

30 Dennis Kavanagh and Anthony Seldon (eds), *The Major Effect* (London: Macmillan, 1994), *passim*; Dennis Kavanagh, *The Reordering of British Politics: Politics After Thatcher* (Oxford: Oxford University Press, 1997), ch. 9.

31 Will Hutton, *The State We're In* (London: Jonathan Cape, 1995), p. 22.

32 *Ibid.*

33 Anthony Sampson, *The Essential Anatomy of Britain: Democracy in Crisis* (London: Hodder and Stoughton, 1992), p. 154.

34 *Ibid.*

35 John Gray, *Beyond the New Right: Markets, Government and the Common Environment* (London: Routledge, 1993), p. 2

36 *Ibid.*

37 Vernon Bogdanor, 'Bringing Power Back Home', *New Statesman*, 6 December 1996.

38 Arthur M. Schlesinger, Jr, *The Imperial Presidency* (London: André Deutsch, 1974) p.377.

39 Quoted in David Hencke, 'MPs Attack "Surprising" Pergau Deal', *The Guardian*, 31 March 1994.

40 Quoted in Christopher Elliot and Angela Macray, 'Was Overseas Aid the Quid Pro Quo for Billion-Pound Arms Deal?', *The Times*, 5 February 1994.

41 Quoted in Ben Jackson, 'Such Dams Will Not Drain Our Aid Again', *The Independent*, 11 November 1994.

42 Quoted in 'Pergau Deal Turned Recurring Nightmare', Will Bennett, *The Independent*, 11 November 1994.

43 Quoted in 'Ministers, Officials and an Imprisoned Malaysian Banker', *The Guardian*, 5 February 1994.

44 Quoted in 'That Dam Affair Returns', *The Economist* , 5 November 1994.

45 Quoted in Will Bennett, 'UK's £234m Aid for Pergau Dam Ruled Illegal', *The Independent*, 11 November 1995.

46 *Report of the Inquiry into the Export of Defence Equipment and Dual-Use Goods to Iraq and Related Prosecutions*, HC 115 (London: Stationery Office, 1996).

47 Marcus Linklater and David Leigh, *Not Without Honour: The Inside Story of the Westland Scandal* (London: Sphere, 1986).

48 Michael Foley, *The Rise of the British Presidency* (Manchester: Manchester University Press, 1993), p. 168.

49 Quoted in Peter Hennessy, *Cabinet* (Oxford: Blackwell, 1986), p. 106.

50 Peter Jenkins, *Mrs Thatcher's Revolution: The Ending of the Socialist Era* (London: Pan, 1989), p. 18.

51 See Peter Hennessy, 'Helicopter Crashes into Cabinet: Prime Minister and Constitution', *Journal of Law and Society*, vol. 13, no. 3 (Autumn 1986), pp. 423–32; Dawn Oliver and Rodney Austin, 'Political and Constitutional Aspects of Westland', *Parliamentary Affairs*, vol. 40, no. 1 (January 1987), pp. 20–40.

52 Margaret Thatcher, *The Downing Street Years* (London: HarperCollins, 1993), p. 43.

53 Hennessy, *Cabinet*, p. 106.

54 Tony Wright, *Citizens and Subjects: An Essay on British Politics* (London: Rout-

ledge, 1994), p. 113.

55 Rodney Austin, 'Freedom of Information: The Constitutional Impact' in Jeffrey Jowell and Dawn Oliver (eds), *The Changing Constitution*, 3rd edn (Oxford: Clarendon, 1994), p. 395

56 See James Michael, *The Politics of Secrecy* (Harmondsworth: Penguin, 1982); Klug, Starmer and Weir, *The Three Pillars of Liberty*, ch. 8; Maurice Frankel, 'Parliamentary Accountability and Government Control of Information' in Norman Lewis, Cosmo Graham and Deryck Beyleveld (eds), *Happy and Glorious: The Constitution in Transition* (Milton Keynes: The Open University Press, 1990), pp. 32–43.

57 Clive Ponting, *Secrecy in Britain* (Oxford: Basil Blackwell, 1990), p. 1.

58 Austin, 'Freedom of Information' p. 411.

59 Diana Woodhouse, *Ministers and Parliament: Accountability in Theory and Practice* (Oxford: Clarendon, 1994). Geoffrey Marshall (ed.), *Ministerial Responsibility* (Oxford: Oxford University Press, 1989).

60 Rodney Brazier, *Constitutional Practice*, 2nd edn (Oxford: Clarendon, 1994), p. 150.

61 Lord Armstrong of Ilminster, 'Argument: The Case for Confidentiality in Government' in Miller, *Alternatives to Freedom*, p. 59.

62 *Ibid.*

63 Peter Hennessy, *Whitehall* (London: Fontana, 1990), p. 350.

64 *Ibid.*, p. 346.

65 Clive Ponting, *The Right To Know: The Inside Story of the Belgrano Affair* (London: Sphere, 1985), pp. 38–9.

66 Quoted in Hennessy, *Cabinet* p. 12.

67 Quoted in Hennessy, *Cabinet* p. 12.

68 Quoted in Hennessy, *Cabinet* p. 13.

69 James Cornford, 'Official Secrecy and Freedom of Information' in Richard Holme and Michael Elliot (eds), *1688–1988: Time for a New Constitution* (Houndmills: Macmillan, 1988), p. 145.

70 *Report of the Inquiry into the Export of Defence Equipment and Dual-Use Goods to Iraq and Related Prosecutions*, HC 115. See 'Under the Scott-Light: British Government Seen Through the Scott Report', *Parliamentary Affairs*, vol. 50, no. 1 (Special Issue, January 1997).

71 Wright, *Citizens and Subjects* p. 118. See also Richard Norton-Taylor, *Truth is a Difficult Concept: Inside the Scott Inquiry* (London: Fourth Estate, 1995); Anthony Barnett, *This Time: Our Constitutional Revolution* (London: Vintage, 1997), pp. 230–50.

72 See *The State of the Nation Report*, MORI/Joseph Rowntree Trust Ltd, 1991; *The State of the Nation Report*, MORI/Joseph Rowntree Trust Ltd, 1995.

73 See Richard A. Chapman and Michael Hunt (eds), *Open Government* (London: Croom Helm, 1987).

74 Anthony Barnett, 'The Right to Know', *New Statesman and Society*, 1 March 1996.

75 Judith Cook, *The Sleaze File and How to Clean Up British Politics* (London: Bloomsbury, 1995), pp. viii–ix. See also Alan Doig and John Wilson, 'Untangling the Threads of Sleaze: The Slide into Nolan', *Parliamentary Affairs*, vol.

48, no. 4 (October 1995), pp. 562–78.

76 Lord Nolan quoted in Peter Riddell, 'How Nolan's Successor Can Keep Up the Good Work', *The Times*, 6 November 1997.

77 See David Leigh and Ed Vulliamy, *Sleaze: The Corruption of Parliament* (London: Fourth Estate, 1997).

78 'Revealed: MPs Who Accept £1,000 to Ask a Parliamentary Question', *Sunday Times*, 10 July 1994; 'Dishonourable Members?', *Sunday Times*, 17 July 1994.

79 *First Report of the Committee on Standards in Public Life, Volume 1: Report*, Cm 2850–1 (London: HMSO, 1995), p. 16.

80 *Ibid.*, p. 106.

81 See Roger Mortimore, 'Public Perception of Sleaze in Britain', *Parliamentary Affairs*, vol. 48, no. 4 (October 1995), pp. 579–89; Alan Doig, *Corruption and Misconduct in Contemporary British Politics* (Harmondsworth: Penguin, 1984).

82 *First Report of the Committee on Standards in Public Life, Volume 1: Report*, p. 15.

83 *Ibid.*, p. 20. See also Anthony King, 'Voters Pass Severe Judgement on Politicians' Moral Standards', *Daily Telegraph*, 4 November 1994; Anthony King, 'What Did They Expect?', *Daily Telegraph*, 20 May 1995.

84 *First Report of the Committee on Standards in Public Life, Volume 1: Report*, p. 3. See also Dawn Oliver, 'The Committee on Standards in Public Life: Regulating the Conduct of Members of Parliament', *Parliamentary Affairs*, vol. 48, no. 4 (October 1995), pp. 590–601; Dawn Oliver, 'Regulating the Conduct of MPs: The British Experience of Combating Corruption, *Political Studies*, vol. 45, no. 3 (Special Issue 1997), pp. 539–58.

85 Simon Jenkins, 'Is Nolan Just a Paper Tiger?', *The Times*, 18 January 1995.

86 Peter Hennessy, 'Goodbye to the "Good Chaps"', *The Independent*, 12 May 1995.

87 Peter Hennessy, *The Hidden Wiring: Unearthing the British Constitution* (London: Victor Gollanz, 1995), p. 199.

88 Paul Hirst and Anthony Barnett, 'Introduction in Barnett *et al.*, *Debating the Constitution*, p. 5.

89 See *Making the Law: The Report of the Hansard Society Commission on the Legislative Process* (London: Hansard Society, 1993).

90 Quoted in Celia Hadden, 'Mad Law and English Dogs', *Daily Telegraph*, 2 December 1995.

91 David Butler, Andrew Adonis and Tony Travers, *Failure in British Government: The Politics of the Poll Tax* (Oxford: Oxford University Press, 1994), p. 1.

92 David Judge, *The Parliamentary State* (London: Sage, 1993), 215.

93 Butler, Adonis and Travers, *Poll Tax* (Oxford: Oxford University Press, 1994), p. 303.

94 *Ibid.*, p. 302.

95 Dawn Oliver, 'The Judge Over Your Shoulder', *Parliamentary Affairs*, vol. 42, no. 3 (July 1989), pp. 302–16; Diana Woodhouse, 'Politicians and the Judiciary: A Changing Relationship', *Parliamentary Affairs*, vol. 48, no. 3 (July 1995), pp. 401–17; Diana Woodhouse, *In Pursuit of Good Administration: Ministers, Civil Servants and Judges* (Oxford: Clarendon, 1997); Andre P. Le Sueur and Maurice Sunkin, *Public Law* (London: Longman 1997), chs 24–6; Stephen Sedley, 'The Common Law and the Constitution', *London Review of Books*, 8 May 1997.

96   Robert Stevens, 'Justice vs the State', *The Guardian* 21 May 1996.

97   See Lord Lester of Herne Hill QC, 'European Human Rights and the British Constitution' in Jowell and Oliver *The Changing Constitution*, pp. 33–56; Brice Dickson (ed.), *Human Rights and the European Convention* (London: Sweet and Maxwell, 1997; Elizabeth Meehan, *Citizenship and the European Community* (London: Sage, 1993); Colin Turpin, *British Government and the Constitution: Text, Cases and Materials*, 3rd edn (London: Butterworths, 1995), ch. 5; Lord Browne-Wilkinson, 'The Infiltration of a Bill of Rights', *Public Law* (Autumn 1997), pp. 375–84.

98   *D.I.Y. Politics: A-Z Campaign Guide to the New Opposition* (New Statesman and Society Pamphlet).

99   'A Nation of Groupies, *The Economist*, 13 August 1994.

100 Andrew Marr, 'The Rise of Do-It-Yourself Democracy', *The Independent*, 18 January 1996. See also Andrew Marr, *Ruling Britannia: The Failure and Future of British Democracy* (London: Penguin, 1996), pp. 99–104.

101 See Robert Pyper, 'Accountability in the Utilities' in Robert Pyper (ed.), *Aspects of Accountability in the British System of Government* (Eastham: Tudor, 1996), pp. 158–90; Norman Lewis, 'If You See Dicey Will You Tell Him?: Regulatory Problems in British Constitutional Law', *The Political Quarterly*, vol. 59, no. 1 (January–March 1988), pp. 6–19; Peter Riddell, 'Where Do We Point the Finger?', *The Times*, 16 January 1995; Peter Riddell, *Parliament Under Pressure* (London: Victor Gollancz, 1998), pp. 87–92.

102 See J. Stewart and Kieron Walsh, 'Change in the Management of Public Services', *Public Administration*, vol. 70, no. 4 (Winter 1992), pp. 499–518; Patrick Dunleavy, 'The Architecture of the British Central State Part 1', *Public Administration*, vol. 67, no. 3 (Autumn 1989), pp. 249–75; Patrick Dunleavy, 'The Architecture of the British Central State, Part 2', *Public Administration*, vol. 67, no. 4 (Winter 1989), pp. 391–417; Norman Lewis, 'The Citizen's Charter and Next Steps: A New Way of Governing?', *Political Quarterly*, vol. 64, no. 3 (July–September 1993), pp. 316–26; Gavin Drury, 'Revolution in Whitehall: The Next Steps and Beyond' in Jowell and Oliver *The Changing Constitution*, pp. 155–74; Philip Giddings (ed.), *Parliamentary Accountability: A Study of Parliament and Executive Agencies* (Houndmills: Macmillan, 1995); Riddell, *Parliament Under Pressure*, pp. 92–4.

103 G. Kaufman, 'The Blank Checks of Government', *The Guardian*, 30 December 1994.

104 David Wilson, 'Quangos in the Skeletal State', *Parliamentary Affairs*, vol. 48 no. 2 (April 1995), pp. 181–91; Brian W. Hogwod, 'The Growth of Quangos: Evidence and Explanations, *Parliamentary Affairs*, vol. 48 no. 2 (April 1995), pp. 207–25; Stuart Weir, 'Quangos: Question of Democratic Accountability', *Parliamentary Affairs*, vol. 48 no. 2 (April 1995), pp. 306–22; Paul Hirst, 'Quangos and Democratic Government', *Parliamentary Affairs*, vol. 48 no. 2 (April 1995), pp. 341–59.

105 David Walker, *The New British State: The Government Machine in the 1990s* (London: Times Books, 1995), p. 7.

106 Quoted in Ferdinand Mount, *The British Constitution Now: Recovery or Decline?* (London: Mandarin, 1993), p. 219.

107 Stephen George (ed.), *Britain and the European Community: The Politics of Semi-Detachment* (Oxford: Clarendon, 1992); *Stephen George, An Awkward Partner: Britain in the European Community* (Oxford: Oxford University Press, 1994).

108 See Stephen Weatherill, *EC Law*, 2nd edn (London: Penguin, 1995); Simon Bulmer, Stephen George and Andrew Scott, *The United Kingdom and EC Membership Evaluated* (London: Pinter, 1991).

109 Vernon Bogdanor, 'Britain and the European Community' in Jowell and Oliver *The Changing Constitution*, pp. 3–32; Peter Madgwick and Diana Woodhouse, *The Law and Politics of the Constitution of the United Kingdom* (Hemel Hempstead: Harvester Wheatsheaf, 1995), ch. 3; Philip Giddings and Gavin Drewry (eds), *Westminster and Europe: The Impact of the European Union on the Westminster Parliament* (Houndmills: Macmillan, 1996).

110 'Cash For Cows', *The Economist*, 30 March 1996.

111 See Vernon Bogdanor, 'Britain and Europe: The Myth of Sovereignty' in Richard Holme and Michael Elliot (eds), *1688–1988: Time for a New Constitution* (Houndmills: Macmillan, 1988), pp. 81–99; J. Enoch Powell, 'Parliamentary Sovereignty in the 1990s' in Philip Norton ed., *New Directions in British Politics? Essays on the Evolving Constitution* (Aldershot: Edward Elgar, 1991), pp. 133–44; David Judge, 'Incomplete Sovereignty: The British House of Commons and the Completion of the Internal Market in the European Communities', *Parliamentary Affairs*, vol. 41, no. 4 (October 1988), pp. 441–55.

112 Vernon Bogdanor, 'Britain and the European Community', p. 6.

113 *Ibid.* p. 9.

114 See William Wallace (ed.), *The Dynamics of European Integration* (London: Pinter, 1990); William Wallace, *Regional Integration: The West European Experience* (Washington D.C.: Brookings Institution, 1994).

115 Taken from David Heathcoat-Amory's resignation letter, *The Guardian*, 23 July 1996.

116 Sampson, *The Essential Anatomy of Britain*, p. 157.

117 Michael Foley, *The Silence of Constitutions: Gaps, 'Abeyances' and Political Temperament in the Maintenance of Government* (London: Routledge, 1989).

118 Of those peers who were eligible to attend the House of Lords on 1 July 1998, 486 were created peers and 623 were peers by hereditary succession.

119 Donald Shell, *The House of Lords*, 2nd edn (New York: Harvester Wheatsheaf, 1992); Andrew Adonis, 'The House of Lords in the 1980s', *Parliamentary Affairs*, vol. 41, no. 3 (July 1988), pp. 380–401; Philip Norton, *The Constitution in Flux* (Oxford: Martin Robertson, 1982), ch. 6.

120 See Rodney Brazier, *Constitutional Reform: Re-shaping the British Political System* (Oxford: Clarendon, 1991), ch. 4; Donald Shell, The House of Lords: Time for a Change?', *Parliamentary Affairs*, vol. 47, no. 4 (October 1994), pp. 721–37; Robert Alexander, *The Voice of the People: A Constitution for Tomorrow* (London: Weidenfeld and Nicolson, 1997), ch. 4; Leonard Tivey, 'Constitutional Reform: A Modest Proposal', *The Political Quarterly*, vol. 66, no. 4 (October–December 1995), pp. 278–86; Dick Leonard, 'Replacing the Lords', *The Political Quarterly*, vol. 66, no. 4 (October–December 1995), pp. 287–98.

121 Walter Bagehot, *The English Constitution*, intro. R. H. S. Crossman, (London: Fontana, 1963), ch. 3.

122 See Vernon Bogdanor, *The Monarchy and the Constitution* (Oxford: Oxford University Press 1995); Ben Pimlott, *The Queen* (London: HarperCollins, 1996).

123 See Anthony Barnett (ed.), *Power and the Throne* (London: Vintage, 1994).

124 Anthony Barnett, 'Introduction' in Barnett, *Power and the Throne*, p. 5.

125 Tom Nairn, *The Enchanted Glass: Britain and its Monarchy* (London: Vintage, 1994), ch. 3.

126 *Ibid.*, p. 89.

127 *Ibid.*, p. 215 .

128 *Ibid.*, p. 215.

129 Andrew Marr, 'The Tale of Diana's Revenge', *The Independent*, 21 November 1995.

130 *Burmah Oil Co.* v. *Lord Advocate* 1965 AC 75 at 99.

131 Hennessy, *The Hidden Wiring*, p. 33.

132 *Ibid.*, p. 29.

133 See, for example, NOP surveys on the state of the monarchy published in *Today*, 24–25 January 1994, 9 January 1995. See also James Whitaker, Diana v. Charles (London: Viking 1993); Stephen Haseler, *The End of the House of Windsor* (London: B. Taurus, 1993); Anthony Holden, *The Tarnished Crown* (London: Bantam, 1993); Jonathan Dimbleby, *The Prince of Wales* (London: Little, Brown, 1994); Sarah Ferguson with Jeff Coplon, *My Story: Sarah the Duchess of York* (London: Simon and Schuster, 1996).

134 For example, no parliamentary question can be asked about the sovereign or a decision made in the sovereign's name (e.g. the allocation of honours) unless it concerns the Queen's *public* duties. Adjournment debates on the monarchy have been refused because the subject does not fall under an area of ministerial responsibility. Such limitations are derived from the royal prerogative itself. The traditional position is that Parliament cannot debate the monarchy - or more specifically any proposed legislation affecting the royal family - without the sovereign's consent in advance. On 4 March 1996, this tradition was qualified when the Speaker (Betty Boothroyd) ruled that the House of Commons could debate the issue if the two front benches collectively chose to do so. See Michael White and Ed Pilkington, 'Crowning glory for the Commons Touch', *The Guardian*, 5 March 1996.

135 Matthew d'Ancona, 'Forum that Buried a 40-year Taboo', *The Times* 24 May 1993.

136 *Ibid.*

137 NOP/*Daily Mail* poll, Daily Mail, 5 December 1993.

138 MORI/*Independent on Sunday* poll, *Independent on Sunday*, 18 February 1996.

139 NOP poll for the *Sunday Times*, 14 September 1997.

140 Gallup poll for the *Daily Telegraph*, 11 September 1997.

141 Anthony Sampson 'The old order changeth yielding place to news', *Daily Telegraph*, 20 January 1993.

142 Peter Hennessy, 'Let Some Daylight in on the monarchy' (review of Kenneth Harris, *The Queen), The Independent*, 21 April 1994.

4

Constitutional reform: ideas, advocates and techniques

Over the past 25 years, but especially since the mid-1980s, the issue of constitutional reform has become an established item on the British political agenda. The period has witnessed an intensification of interest in the principles and operation of the constitution leading to a sharper sense of critical realism over its unresolved problems and functional weaknesses. Such scepticism has fostered an increase in the currency and incidence of reformist ideas and language. The effect of constitutional fuels, both at an individual level and in aggregate form, has generated a profusion of reform proposals. Over time these have evolved into a well-defined series of reform objectives that have become the centre-piece of the constitutional debate. These highly publicised items of prospective govermental improvement have structured the nature of political argument and dispute; they have conditioned the strategies and calculations of the political parties; and they have geared the political agenda to a consideration of means rather than merely ends in the conduct of politics. The contemporary political salience of constitutional reform was particularly evident in the 1997 general election when the theme of the constitution was not only regarded as an issue which divided the two main parties, but was widely considered to be the only substantive point of contention between them.

   The purpose of this chapter is to demonstrate the dynamics of constitutional reform by examining the motive forces behind the construction of a reform agenda; by reviewing the ideas deployed to rationalise separate complaints and to pool plural dissent into a programme for change; and by studying the techniques of advocacy by which reform ideas are publicised and reform pressure is operationalised to maximise its political effect. The first section will specify the sources and composition of the constitutional reform agenda. The second section will analyse the different rationales used to systematise constitutional critiques not only into general indictments of the British constitution but into organising principles of reform. While section three will provide an overview of those organisations that have been instrumental in pressing the issue of constitutional reform, section 4 will examine the ways in which such organisations have generated public concern over the constitution and have worked to force the issue on to the political agenda.

The agenda of reform ideas

Even though its component parts may be diffuse and even incoherent, and despite the fact that each element of reform carries different implications, an agenda of constitutional reform now exists in British politics. The delineation of its outer margins may remain imprecise but there is little doubt that the main features of the project to restructure the British constitution have become established as a stable and prominent aggregate of reforms. They have acquired a collective identity through osmosis. When separate items are placed in a matrix of association where they are repeatedly linked together, it leads to an intuitive assumption that they are logically, materially and politically related to one another. Constitutional reform may have become a portmanteau term in British politics, but it is not a wholly open-ended or arbitrary repository of just any impulse for change. On the contrary, it has become a well-understood expression of a set of now familiar proposals which have become the thematic focus to the entire issue of constitutional reconstruction.

Any examination of the positions advanced by those organisations most directly associated with constitutional reform will reveal a close correspondence between their respective agendas for constitutional action. Some organisations may give a different emphasis or priority to selected items (e.g. The Electoral Reform Society's support for proportional representation; Liberty's interest in a bill of rights) but they all help to contribute towards an aggregate programme of reform with remarkably similar features. A review of the constitutional objectives of organisations like Charter 88, Justice, the Campaign for Freedom of Information, the Voting Reform Group, Liberty, the Electoral Reform Society of Great Britain and Ireland, the Constitutional Reform Centre and the People's Trust reveals a cumulative pattern of support for a set of inter-related innovative measures. Over time, the separate proposals have assumed the corporate identity of a reform agenda.[1] The core elements are as follows:

- a bill of rights
- proportional representation
- a reformed second chamber
- open government
- freedom of information
- Scottish and Welsh devolution

- de-centralised decision-making at local and regional levels
- increased democratic and legal controls upon executive power
- a written constitution

Over an extended period of political complaint and critical analysis, these items have risen to prominence as the most likely, or the most acceptable, means by which to achieve the optimum political resolution to the problems identified in the structure and operation of the British constitution. The radical nature of such proposals is itself a measure of the perceived severity of the constitution's defects. The political salience of such a reform agenda is also a reflection of the urgent need for change. On both these counts of radicalism and salience, the influence of the constitutional fuels surveyed in chapter 3 is evident. Each reform in the composite agenda is a direct effect of a mixture of fuels. The purpose of Table 4:1 is to give a schematic representation of the links between different fuels and different reforms. The attribution of estimated influence is divided into primary and secondary categories.

The table shows the varied roots and motive forces associated with each reform proposal. While some reform proposals like a bill of rights and a new second chamber tend to be generated by broad-scale constitutional concerns (e.g. *governmental excess, centralisation*), other parts of the reform agenda, such as proportional representation (PR) and freedom of information, are fuelled in the main by more specific and defined complaints (e.g. *electoral inequity* and *secrecy* respectively). It is also noteworthy that no two reforms are prompted and sustained by the same profile of primary and secondary fuels. For example, while it is estimated that the reaction to *governmental excess, governmental misuse* and *secrecy* provide the main drives to the campaign for a bill of rights, *electoral inequity, centralisation* and *systemic dysfunction* constitute the major fuels behind the campaign to introduce some form of PR into the electoral system. Some fuels clearly have a higher octane than others in that they are more likely to feed controversies and to stimulate reform measures. But even though there is a relatively high incidence of fuels like *centralisation, governmental excess* and *governmental misuse* in the primary categories, the influence of the slower burning fuels should not be underestimated. In many instances, these fuels are significant less for any direct connection to specific reform proposals than for their general contribution in creating a political context for constitutional criticism and the need to address the constitution as a cause for concern. *Transcendent innovation, external imposition, traditional anomalies* and *personal misconduct* are probably the most conspicuous examples of fuels that provide a generalised sub-text of constitutional disarray which in one form or another influence the shape and urgency of all the main reforms presented to improve the constitution.

Table 4.1 *The dependency relationship of constitutional reforms upon constitutional fuels, categorised by primary and secondary influences*

Bill of rights

Primary	Secondary
Governmental excess	Centralisation
Governmental misuse	External imposition
Secrecy	Transcendent innovation

Devolution

Primary	Secondary
Centralisation	Transcendent innovation
Electoral ineqity	External imposition
Governmental excess	Systemic dysfunction

Electoral reform

Primary	Secondary
Electoral inequity	Governmental excess
Centralisation	Governmental misuse
Systematic dysfunction	Traditional anomalies

Freedom of information

Primary	Secondary
Secrecy	Centralisation
Governmental excess	Personal misconduct
Governmental misuse	Traditional anomalies

House of Lords reform

Primary	Secondary
Traditional anomalies	Centralisation
Systemic dysfunction	Governmental misuse
Governmental excess	Secrecy

Written constitution

Primary	Secondary
Governmental excess	Centralisation
Governmental misuse	Transcendent innovation
Traditional anaomalies	External imposition

The agenda of constitutional reform has become an assemblage that has acquired a notional coherence out of repetition and familiarity. The roster of reforms has the initial appearance of systemic integrity because the reforms are almost invariably mentioned together and because they have a common link to the constitution. Nevertheless, there are limits to the social construction of reform coherence, not least because 'the constitution' in the British context has no history of being a singular entity with an objective and corporate existence. At a technical level, the constitutional debate in Britain has been marked by the same multiple improvisation as the British constitution itself, with little acknowledgement of the disparate nature both of the fuels energising constitutional controversy and of the reforms presented to resolve the deficiencies attributed to the constitution. As a consequence, little consideration has been given during the construction of the agenda to the complexity of the connections between the different reforms. This was recognised by the Constitution Unit prior to the 1997 general election when it arrived at the following conclusion: 'Jostling for position in the debate about constitutional reform are many possible measures. But no thought has been given to ranking them in terms of the order in which they might sensibly be brought forward in a legislative programme ... They are viewed by the supporters as a shopping list which can be given to the civil service to sort out.'[2] But such a composite of reforms will not be easily sorted out at the legislative level because of the need to establish priorities, to resolve procedural and timing problems, and to prevent the political movement for one reform disrupting the political coalitions in support of other reforms.

At a more substantive level, Table 4:1 demonstrates the range of critical principles informing the reform agenda. The eclectic nature of such principles leaves the constitutional agenda in a position of both strength and weakness. The breadth and depth of constitutional dissent enriches the agenda into a plurality of accessible causes and solutions which have served to animate a political movement in support of constitutional change. On the other hand, the underlying range of principles addressed in such an agenda are not readily reduced to any controlling theme giving definition to an integrated ideal of governance to which all reforms can be clearly related. On the contrary, the constitutional agenda evolved as an *ad hoc* compilation of reactive measures from which any over-arching principles of organisation needed to be actively fashioned from the several components.

Systems of advocacy

Given that constitutional critique is necessarily rational and analytical in content and style, and given that the advocates of reform have a political need to reduce the multiplicity of demands to a coherent and intelligible theme, over and above that of mere party advantage, the arguments for constitutional reform have been characterised by a drive to acquire a unifying organisation. At its most fundamental level, this need to simplify the complexity of the constitutional issue and to protect the flanks of constitutional reform from charges of inconsistency and contradiction, has led to two main types of strategy for reaching an operational rationale. At this level, the techniques may not be a matter of conscious design so much as an intuitive process to fathom out an underlying theme. Neither need they

114

be mutually exclusive in nature. Nevertheless, they remain quite separate methodologies.

One approach concentrates on examining the constituent properties and values of the several reform proposals with the objective of identifying one common characteristic, or a single set of common factors. Such an inductive approach aims at locating a central point of consistency from an empirical examination of the constituent features of the reforms, together with their logical and substantive inter-relationships with one another. The other approach is more deductive and instrumental in nature. It proceeds on the basis that irrespective of whether or not a point of convergence exists between the composition of the several proposals for reform, a unifying theme is assumed to exist based upon the aggregate contribution of the reforms in achieving a state of constitutional improvement. Different reforms may carry different weight and make different contributions but they are taken as being consistent with one another because of their demonstrable relationship to a single valued objective and because of their functional effect in collectively achieving such an end. Whereas the first method is more passive and analytical, the second is a more active construction in which the consistency of reforms is derived from their relationship to a general development and an overall end. As mentioned above, these two strategies of coherence can overlap and feed off one another as reformers seek to locate a rationale in their segmented agenda. These two devices constantly inform and condition the corporate themes adopted by reformers to weave together the separate threads of reform into an intelligible whole. It is now necessary to turn from how such rationales are formed to the nature of the unifying themes themselves.

The first rationale which is evident in the literature on constitutional reform is centred upon the theme of *prevention*. This minimalist conception is based upon a reaction to what is seen to be the negative properties of the current constitution. The thrust of this rationale is the use of reforms to prevent any further deterioration in the structure and processes of British government. The rationale of prevention is firmly centred upon a controlling preoccupation with governmental pathology, in which the weaknesses, and even failures, of the constitution motivate the drive towards measures whose radicalism is necessarily commensurate with the scale and gravity of the problem. The preventative rationale lays particular emphasis upon the alleged imbalance of constitutional forces, the increased scale and remit of centralised executive power and the erosion of traditional norms of political conduct. 'As concerns about the accretion of governmental power have grown, the shortcomings of other institutions and the absence of countervailing safeguards have become more apparent.'[3] As a consequence, the preventative rationale of the constitutional reform agenda is primarily defensive in nature, drawing attention to defects and abuses and to the need not only to value what is being lost but to preserve what remains through a series of emergency measures. Changes are advocated to prevent further changes to the detriment of the constitution. Indeed, without reform, the risk presented is one which questions the future viability not only of the constitution but also of the United Kingdom as a national entity.

According to this perspective, the crisis in the British political system is no longer one of ungovernability as that of 'over-governability'[4] and excessive centralisation. '[B]y the exercise of patronage, the executive has learnt to control parliament. Having learnt to control the power responsible for controlling it, it is perhaps the most arbitrary government in the world.'[5] The preventative rationale views government as the chief danger to civil society. This outlook is well captured in Anthony Barnett's indictment of what he describes as a 'group of constitutional subversives' who were instrumental in *de facto* constitutional change during the 1979–97 period of Conservative hegemony:

> They are the ones who have rolled over Britain's constitution, knee-capping local government, undermining the rule of law, abusing office, demeaning parliament ... Instead of tolerance, prejudice. Instead of world standing, little Englandism. Instead of rights, charters. Instead of democracy, centralisation, Instead of probity, sleaze. Instead of honesty, corruption. Instead of parliamentary sovereignty, quangos and Next Steps agencies. They have made a shambles of our constitution and called it open government.[6]

Whether it is the 'new magistracy' of the patronage state, or the secrecy shrouding the unaccountable exercise of prerogative powers, or the lack of recognition at the centre of the national aspirations to devolved government in Scotland and Wales, the conclusion drawn is the same – namely, that 'British democracy is fragile and under threat'.[7] A constitution corrupted by such means can only be resisted by extraordinary counter-measures designed to prevent any further expansion of the state's discretionary powers and any further deterioration in civil liberties. The exact nature and thematic coherence of the different constitutional reform proposals are probably less important in this rationale than the effect of such a raft of radical measures in underlining the urgency of the threat to the constitution and its public authority.

In contrast to the alarmist diagnoses associated with the preventative rationale is a more positive approach to constitutional reform that lays the emphasis upon the general theme of correction. Instead of the palliative defences of the preventative strategy, the remedial rationale seeks to build upon the acknowledged deficiencies of the existing constitution by offering reform as a means of acquiring a new condition of governance. The objective of reform according to such a rationale is one not merely of response but of solution by which the constitution is purposefully changed to achieve a range of consciously stipulated benefits. Corrective approaches to the constitutional agenda can be divided into two main classes that are distinguished by different forms of argument, appeal and guidance. They are sufficiently distinct in design and motivation to constitute two separate items in the present study of constitutional rationales. As such, they will be referred to as the second and third methods of agenda unification.

The rationale of *restoration* is a corrective device which uses the past as a frame of reference not just to make empirical and normative comparisons with the present but to establish a standard of constitutionalism to which reform should be directed and assessed. Correction in this guise is legitimised because it is aimed at regenerating the present in terms of a benign past. Such a rationale always runs the risk of becoming a tautology. Just as contemporary problems are used to enhance the appeal of the past, so the past becomes a means of validating the existence of present-day ills and, thereupon, a device by which to escape from them. The elevation of a past constitutional condition can animate and legitimate an agenda of constitutional reform by casting it in the role of a regenerative process. The projection of the past into a central and fixed criterion of constitutional value can be short term or long term in scope. It can be limited to the consensual placidity and 'club government'[8] of the post-war settlement era prior to the iconoclasm of the Thatcherite project when 'the subtle balance of powers in the constitution was totally thrown out by her imperious premiership'.[9] The time scale in a restorative rationale, however, can be much longer and more indeterminate. Accordingly, it can be said that the more imprecise the time scale, the greater the opportunity for idealising the historical point of emulation. Similarly, as the following passage from *The Economist* illustrates, the longer the suggestion of decline, the more urgent is the inferred need for reform.

> Britain must reclaim its constitution. Why 'reclaim'? Because ... the greatest virtues of the British constitution have been the very ones which time, and successive governments, have diminished. Traditionalists are fond of saying that the British constitution has been the country's most successful export: how can principles that have been so widely imitated require revision? Unfortunately, the ideas that Britain pioneered and others adopted are precisely those which the British constitution, as it evolved, failed to embody. Other systems copied the best things in the British tradition; Britain let them wither.[10]

Time can induce a narcosis in constitutional thought, but it can also be used to draw attention to a torpid sub-text of relative degeneration beneath the apparent continuity of a traditional constitutional settlement. Extrapolating a historical trend into a future state of anxiety over the constitution merely reinforces the impulse to engage in creating a restorative rationale to the agenda of reform. According to Ferdinand Mount, for example, it is the entrenched orthodoxy of the traditional and simplistic constructions of the British constitution which have fostered the atrophy of constitutional thought and effectively prevented an understanding of the constitution's foundations and the value of its original foundations. '[W]e need to become aware of the old parts of our constitutional machinery which have been left to lie rusting in disuse in the corner of the field ... If we are to rebuild the structure, if we are to restore some of its old complexities, get some of the old checks and balances back into working order, we need to start without delay.'[11] Mount is aware that constitutional reclamation is a form of tactical political language but regards its usage as historically justifiable, in order to facilitate the reintroduction of those basic principles that 'might enable us to repair the damage of the last century'.[12] He concludes:

> To talk of 'rebuilding' and 'restoring' has, of course, a certain political charm. It is the way reformers in this country have traditionally reassured those who were suspicious of reform; at all costs, the new measures had to be depicted, however improbably, as old-fangled. Yet, in the present case, there is a little more to be said for going about matters in this way. For there really are elements which we have lost and which other modern constitutions have discovered or conserved.[13]

The potential of historical consciousness for constitutional reform is also a theme examined by John Gray. He believes that the way in which the Conservative governments of Margaret Thatcher and John Major pursued their policy objectives led to an unprecedented degree of centralisation, which politicised previously neutral or impartial institutions and effectively unbalanced the constitution in favour of the government. As the British state became more synonymous with the interests of the Conservative party and its need to retain power, the more it became evident that the process represented 'a serious deformation of the constitutional settlement which the Conservatives inherited in 1979'.[14] In Gray's view, the Conservative ascendancy had rendered the political system unstable and, as a result, had affronted Britain's traditional conservatism on the constitution. Speaking in 1994, Gray concluded that the backlash in the shape of constitutional reform was an expression of a radical movement to retrieve the past: 'The demand for constitutional reform which is now being expressed in Britain is an expression of the genuinely conservative instincts of the British people. They perceive that the stability they enjoyed in the past has been destroyed.'[15] According to Gray, it was this traditional allegiance to the constitution which was proving to be instrumental in arousing dissent over the current state of the constitution. Paradoxically, therefore, the instinctive conservatism of the British towards the constitution was in fact capable of being harnessed to radical constitutional reform in the pursuit of a lost stability.

The restorative rationale raises a host of conceptual and operational questions such as the relationship between principles and their content, or expression, in different contexts of time; the possible disjunction between a principle in form and a principle in spirit; and the difficulty of converting the language of disequilibrium into calculable action to restore the constitution to a determinable condition of balance. Notwithstanding these difficulties, the rationale of restoration has proved to be a very effective device not only in projecting cohesion on to the reform agenda, but in acquiring a unified legitimacy for its varied measures. By engaging in 'an honourable groping towards tradition',[16] reformers have discovered the force of the argument that '[a]genda setting is in many ways the art of doing something new so that it looks old'.[17] In a society in which there exists a close interdependency between history, the constitution and national identity, the theme of reclamation both draws upon, and contributes to, such a nexus.

The other main corrective strategy is that of *modernisation* where the emphasis is on an escape from the past and the acquisition of a qualitatively different condition to current circumstances. Such a rationale to constitutional reform often proceeds on the basis that a close adherence to history is part of the problem of the British constitution. In this view, constitutional traditionalism has not only failed to prevent radical governments from drastically re-engineering the forms and functions of the state, but has denied a proper understanding of constitutional history itself and, in particular, the lack of substance in Britain's ancient heritage of limited government and individual rights. This jaundiced outlook upon British constitutional history coincides with a desire to escape from the constraints of historical debate and to emancipate the reform agenda from the credentials of past authority. But such a view also signifies something much deeper.

Constitutional reformers flying under the flag of modernisation do so because they believe that the current condition of the British constitution emphatically and conclusively reveals the fraudulent nature of the ideals that have served to animate the constitution since the settlement of 1688. Whether the principles of the Glorious Revolution are seen as inherently flawed or as having been successively corrupted, the net effect is to interpret constitutional history as a continuous process of unfulfilment where the past demonstrates just 'how vulnerable Britain has always been to elective dictatorship'.[18] This view of history is prominent in the preamble to Charter 88's agenda of constitutional reform:

[T]he inbuilt powers of the 1688 settlement have enabled the government to discipline British society to its ends ... The break with the immediate past shows how vulnerable Britain has always been to elective dictatorship. The consequence is that today the British have fewer rights and less democracy than many other West Europeans. The intensification of authoritarian rule in the United Kingdom has only recently begun. *The time to reverse the process is now, but it cannot be reversed by an appeal to the past.* Three hundred years of unwritten rule from above are enough.[19]

The same combination of historical consciousness and constitutional critique is evident elsewhere and leads to similar conclusions over the persistence of hierarchical and enclosed government at the expense of a fully functioning democracy. 'In reality, our constitution is an untidy and developing collection of compromises, the consequence of sullen responses to pressure; pressure which reflects the relative strength of wealth versus collective action at different periods of history ... The superiority of our constitutional methods is illusory'.[20] An awareness of this type of critical history underlines both the chronic incompleteness of previous reform and the urgent need to break traditional continuity and to remedy the inherently corruptible nature of the present settlement by breaking free from its terms of reference and rules of engagement. Constitutional history in this perspective is equated with the need to modernise the constitution by breaking the continuity with the past.

Even though those who employ the language of modernisation wish to establish a disjunction with the past as their justification for reform, they cannot always resist using the capacious nature of the British constitution's historical flexibility for their own ends. The usage of historical means to break historically sanctioned forms in the cause of modernisation is evident in the following statement drawn from *Here We Stand: Liberal Democrat Policies for Modernising Britain's Democracy*: 'For Liberal Democrats constitutional reform and a written constitution are neither breaches of British tradition nor ends in themselves. Rather, they represent a revival of the British tradition of institutional flexibility which long made the United Kingdom the envy of other would-be democracies.'[21]

Notwithstanding such digressions, the modernisation rationale normally concentrates upon the relationship between the separate reform items and the proposed establishment of a new regime in which power is effectively redistributed and the relationship between the citizen and the state is accordingly redefined. The theme animating the modernisation rationale is one in which new political forces are recognised and accommodated; new constraints upon government are imposed; new constructions of permissible governmental activity and processes of accountability are designed; new forms of open government are brought into existence; and new initiatives 'to decentralise power throughout Britain'[22] are adopted. The defining essence is one innovation rather than of restoration. In *Why Vote Labour?* published prior to the 1997 general election, Tony Wright described the party's 'bold and daunting programme of political reform ... not as a shopping list of separate items but as an interlocking and coherent process of political renewal'.[23]

The agenda of constitutional reform thus becomes the instrument of modernisation through which a more developed democracy can be finally realised and a more active, participatory and rights-based citizenship can be established. The objective of constitutional reform according to such a rationale is to 'give government back to the people'.[24] Despite the historical allusion to an ancient condition, those who employ the rationale of modernisation see the constitutional reform agenda as a means of moving towards a state of popular sovereignty – i.e. not a feature in British history so much as a theoretical point of origin in the theory of the state. Constitutional reform in this sense is a means not only of relating the constitution to contemporary conditions, but of actively shaping the future of British politics. 'Of course we have to change the Government if we are to turn the country around,' remarked Tony Blair in February 1996, 'but we also have to change the way things are run so that people exercise more power over those they elect and what is done in their name – not just a new set of politicians but a new politics.' Blair explicitly equated constitutional reform with the evocation of a new politics, allowing people to have more power in the political decisions that affect them. 'After all, politicians are there to serve the public, so why should the public not have more control over what they do? ... Power to the people is not a slogan but a necessity if we are to reconnect politics with the majority and create the new politics on which a new Britain will, in part, be built.'[25]

The final type of rationale used to systematise constitutional reform is corrective in basis but is *instrumental* in content and strategy. It recognises the need for, and the importance of, reform but it looks beyond the benefits within the immediate political sphere and outwards to the gains to be accrued in the wider dimensions of social and economic life. According to this perspective, the deficiencies of the political system will, in the absence of constitutional change, spread and create a general deterioration in the condition of the nation as a whole. If we do not rise to the challenge of such systemic reform, then in the view of Andrew Marr: 'we will feel less secure, less confident about our country. We will become shabbier and grumpier and these islands will slowly become a less pleasant place to live.'[26] Such pessimistic projections are the obverse of the more customary linkage between the prospect of constitutional reform and the achievement of other advantages. The nature of these benefits can vary from constructions of social justice and individual freedoms to improvements in the morality of public life and personal conduct.

But the linkage given most prominence in such instrumental rationales is that between the condition of the constitution and the state of the national economy. Working on the premise of a discernible 'association between Britain's relatively poor economic performance and its form of government',[27] then, other things being equal, an improvement in the operation of government should contribute towards an improvement in the country's economy and in the services provided by such resources. The message of an instrumental rationale is clear from the following prescription taken from the Liberal Democrats' document on constitutional reform: 'After centuries of piecemeal tinkering, it is time Britain tackled the root problem of its outmoded political institutions. Only by changing not just the things we do, but also the way in which do them, will we set the framework for Britain's future success and prosperity.'[28] In his conclusion to *The State We're In*, Will Hutton echoes such sentiments by referring to a 'written constitution [and] the democratisation of civil society' as 'reforms [that] must be accomplished if the dynamism of capitalism is to be harnessed to the common good'.[29] In effect, constitutional reform comes with social and economic payoffs. In Hutton's view, a successful economic and social policy is continually frustrated by the inequity of the 'first-past-the-post' system and the monopoly privileges of parliamentary sovereignty. As a result, '[m]easures which have longer-term pay-backs always struggle to win political priority over the governing party's pet projects and the interests of its supporters'.[30] By accepting that the 'British constitution is at the root of the problem',[31] then the reform of the constitution's machinery will necessarily lead to other and more diversified improvements. Because of the existence of a 'direct link ...   between constitutional measures and the daily lives of people and their families', then in the words of Jeff Rooker constitutional reform 'is the ultimate "bread and butter" issue'.[32] Even though the linkage between constitutional reform and economic benefits is normally based upon notions of democratic modernisation and communitarian purpose, it can be construed as a libertarian enterprise and, therefore, be attractive to an organisation like the Institute of Economic Affairs. It sees constitutional change as a device by which to liberalise the market economy through the entrenchment of freedom of contract and unlimited property rights, and the privatisation of education, medical care and other social provision.[33]

In some respects, the instrumental rationale can seem to be a poor unifying theme as it distracts attention away from an exclusive interest in constitutional reform. On the other hand, what it lacks in concentration it makes up for in scale by integrating a range of different, and arguably more potent and coherent, motives and interests in support of constitutional change. Even though the inference of a direct connection between constitutional reform and socio-economic utility may be empirically and even ethically open to question, the notion of a wider polity intrinsically connected to a civil society and political culture is not only rooted in the traditions of constitutionalism, but remains a serviceable source of unity to a society which is sufficiently lacking in cohesion to be giving serious consideration to constitutional reform.

Agents of advocacy

Constitutional adaptation is an ever-present feature of the British system of government. Moreover, the system is widely regarded as being dependent upon the continuity of rolling change and responsive accommodation. The advocacy of constitutional reform by design, therefore, is relatively unconventional and novel in nature. The emphasis here is on the term 'relative' since constitutional reform is both old and new. In one respect it has a long pedigree, in another it is thoroughly contemporary in character. Clearly, concerted constitutional change and in particular the reform of the franchise, was a distinguishing feature of British political development in the nineteenth century. The movement to extend the franchise continued into the twentieth century with the pressure for women's suffrage. This coincided with the radical assault by the administrations of Sir Henry Campbell-Bannerman and Herbert Asquith upon the institutional structure of government, followed after World War I by a serious attempt first by the Labour party and then by the Liberals to transform the electoral system in accordance with the principle of PR. Pressure for such sweeping reform diminished during the middle of the century as the system stabilised around a solid two-party system of alternating governments with their respective programmes of socio-economic reform and their mutual self-interest in exploiting, rather than questioning, the system's provision and distribution of power.

The subversion of the two-party symmetry, especially following the general elections of February and October 1974, together with the contemporary challenges to the prevailing social, economic and political order, and with the accompanying disruption to the government's authority, brought in its wake the first substantial revival of the issue of constitutional reform for half a century. Prior to the mid- and late 1970s, constitutional reform had been associated primarily with the Liberal party and, as such, had generally been seen as a minority interest that only had relevance to those parties that were unable to break into the established two-party system. But after 1974 even this premise was open to question as both the Liberals and the nationalist parties in Scotland and Wales made sufficient electoral advances to cast doubt upon the legitimacy or viability of such a centralised duopoly. The state of the British constitution and with it the issue of constitutional reform received a further, and arguably more substantial, injection of critical analysis when a senior figure in the Conservative party rediscovered the political leverage of the constitution in opposing an incumbent Labour government. Lord Hailsham's celebrated indictment of the British system as an 'elective dictatorship' assembled a range of pre-existing concerns and provided them with a focus of exposition which culminated in a highly publicised call for a fully codified written constitution that would limit Parliament both by law and by a system of checks and balances.[34] Lord Hailsham's call for a bill of rights to be constitutionally entrenched and made applicable to Parliament was echoed by senior judicial figures such as Lord Scarman and Lord Denning. Even though Hailsham's analysis was ostensibly party-neutral in its aim to demonstrate how the constitution was 'wearing out', its effect could not be anything other than critical of the Labour government. Given the conventional construction of the British system as a political constitution, reducible ultimately to the agencies of electoral competition, public tolerance and political prudence, it was difficult for Lord Hailsham's analysis and prescriptive solutions to be taken as purely objective and non-partisan excursions into constitutional theory. It was even more difficult after 1979 when he appeared to conform to the classic model of the political constitution by jettisoning his call for a written constitution and a bill of rights – even though his role as Lord Chancellor gave him the best position from which to advance such reforms. A new Conservative government had provided a political solution to the alleged excesses and anxieties of a Labour government and, as such, the once flamboyant calls for constitutional reform by Hailsham and other conservatives became muted to the point where they corresponded to Margaret Thatcher's own 'lack of radical resolve in constitutional matters'.[35] The Hailsham episode served to reaffirm the statism of both the main party contenders for power and to demonstrate yet again the absence of a unifying faith in the content, authority and agency of a politically neutral constitution that would allow British politics to be safely accommodated within a standard medium of constitutional principle.[36]

Notwithstanding the political reductionism of the constitutional dispute in Britain, it was the sheer iconoclasm of the 'Thatcher revolution', combined with the methods used to achieve it and the lengthy ascendancy of the Thatcher and Major administrations, that led to the issue of constitutional reform being transformed from a minority interest into a highly influential political movement able to place the need for sweeping reconstruction firmly on the political agenda. During the Thatcher and Major administrations, the proliferation and explosive properties of the constitutional fuels which have occupied much of the preceding analysis led to an upsurge of public interest in the weaknesses of the British constitution and in the professed need for change. References to the incidence of constitutional transgressions, to the decline of constitutional standards and to the desirability of a new constitutional settlement became commonplace as constitutional criteria and the language of constitutional analysis impregnated the terms of political debate. It was in this period that the idea of the constitution as a legitimate and effective instrument of political dissent and mobilisation was firmly re-established. It would be no exaggeration to say that the issue of the British constitution was not only reintroduced, but achieved a position of such central significance by the end of the Conservative hegemony that the projected reform agenda had acquired such porportions as to make it comparable only to the reform period of 1832 or 1911.

It can be claimed that in accordance with the precepts of a political constitution, the pressure for constitutional reform is merely the extension of normal party conflict by other means – i.e. an unconventional outlet for conventional political differences. In some respects, there is necessarily some substance to such a proposition. Constitutionalism did present an alternative form of political dissent for an opposition dispirited and demoralised by successive electoral defeats that appeared to deny even the prospect of imminent power through the two-party system. Given the concurrent collapse of the socialist alternative at an international level, and the accompanying assumption of an end to ideological politics by way of the all-embracing inclusiveness of a pre-eminent liberalism, the movement to reform the British constitution undoubtedly represented an alternative means of challenging an apparently impregnable government. It is an entirely plausible contention to argue that to a significant extent constitutional reform was for a sustained period the only satisfactory form of opposition capable of making a concerted impression upon the prevailing style and programme of Conservative governments.

Relevant though such propositions may be, they overlook one central and overriding factor. Constitutional analysis and constitutional reform may well have been used to counter the claims of a government confident both in its programme and in its capacity to secure such a programme over opposition. Furthermore, constitutionalism may well have been deployed as an alternative source of populism, through which Margaret Thatcher's own populist assaults upon the institutional and operational character of government could be contested as a challenge to the conventional morality of power in the British system. But notwithstanding the validity of such observations, they do not explain how the constitutional dimension in British politics was activated; how the latent potential of the constitution issue was realised; how the groundswell for change was harnessed in a system renowned for pragmatic politics and policy outcomes to a call for changes in the processes, structures and principles of governance; how arguments for reform were mobilised and sustained to channel dissent into a political movement for a full programme of constitutional reform. In effect, assertions of the constitutional issue being merely an alternative expression of traditional politics do not account for how the issue of the constitution became a political priority to all the main parties. It is one thing to create a reform agenda; it is quite another to succeed in placing it on the national agenda for political action. A host of reasons exist for the rise of constitutional reform as a high-priority political issue. This entire study bears witness to the complexity of the theme's salience as an issue in British politics.

Nonetheless, it seems clear that the main impetus for change came as a result of a process of insurgency in which the main driving forces of reform were not initially the large political organisations normally associated with institutional critique (e.g. Labour party, trade unions) but a set of smaller centres of advocacy which ultimately succeeded in giving direction and coherence to a broad social impulse for political improvement. It was a movement which culminated in the emergence of a nationally recognised programme for constitutional reform reflected in the priority given to the issue in the 1997 manifesto of the Labour party – the one organisation with the electoral and political potential for securing such reforms.

Agents of advocacy can be broken down into a number of sub-categories. *First,* are those external pressure groups that have had a long-term interest in reforming specific areas of the constitutional activity. The Electoral Reform Society, for example, has long been in the forefront of the campaign to change the electoral system to one that incorporates the principle of proportional representation. What used to be termed the National Council of Civil Liberties, and is now called Liberty, has become synonymous with publicising miscarriages of justice, promoting the extension of civil and political rights, and campaigning for the adoption of a bill of rights. The Radical Society provides another example of specific advocacy through its close association with the republican cause of drastically reducing the role of the monarchy and the House of Lords within the British constitution.

A second type of advocacy has been provided by professional organisations like the Association of First Division Civil Servants, the Association of District Councils, the Association of Metropolitan Authorities and the Royal Institute of Public Administration, which can and have used their positions within the structure of government to draw public attention to the inefficiencies, deficiencies, imbalances and abuses of governmental operations and to offer constitutional remedies to the problems identified in the machinery. Because of the constitutional doctrine of parliamentary sovereignty, professional organisations are normally inhibited from explicitly promoting a tranche of constitutional reforms, but by responding to specific professionally related concerns, they are in a position to engage in constitutionally related issues which have a public impact on both the need for, and the requirements of, structural reform.

With the notable exception of Scotland, where trade unions working in close conjunction with the Scottish Trade Union Congress were a major force behind the Scottish Constitutional Convention, the union movement in general has not been in the forefront of the campaign for constitutional reform.[37] In many respects, the unions have had a record of opposing change that might jeopardise the traditional adversarial framework of British politics, with its electoral and systemic opportunities for the Labour party to acquire a monopoly of government power. Their antipathy towards

PR, for example, has been a significant restraint upon the reform lobby's attempts to shift the Labour party more decisively to the cause of constitutional change. While prominent individuals within the trade union movement (e.g. Bill Morris of the Transport and General Workers Union, Richard Rosser of the Transport Salaried Staffs' Association, Alan Johnson of the Communications Workers Union, David Triesman of the Association of University Lecturers and Nigel Stanley at the Trade Union Congress) have publicly associated themselves with constitutional reform and have used their position to publicise the issue and to press for collective endorsement, the unions in general have been reactive or neutral rather than proactively on the cutting edge of the constitutional debate.[38] Their caution on the wider themes, however, has been punctuated by their intervention in some specific areas which has had an effect on the context within which the campaign for constitutional reform has developed. The opposition of individual unions to various elements of Conservative government policy helped raise public awareness of the wider issues of governmental power and legitimacy (e.g. the campaign conducted by the Council of Civil Service Unions against the Thatcher government's 1984 ban on trade unions operating in the Government Communications Headquarters) which have had long-term consequences for the penetration of the constitution as a political issue. In attending to the interests of its members, unions have funded litigation both in Britain and in the European Court of Human Rights, in order to pursue test cases relating to social and economic rights and to civil liberties. Apart from clarifying the law, such cases have helped infuse individual grievances with a language and process of fundamental rights, and have contributed to the groundswell of interest in the constitutional recognition and entrenchment of such rights. More recently, unions have increasingly been prepared to address the possible implications of constitutional reform for social and economic policy, and they have taken an active role in considering specific items of constitutional change or development which might have a direct bearing upon the interests or working arrangements of their members – ranging from the economic potential of regionally based government for local redevelopment to the efforts made by the Association of First Division Civil Servants to protect civil servants from the disciplinary consequences of 'whistle-blowing', or from any graduated transfer of accountability from ministers to executive professionals. A related kind of advocacy comes from those bodies that are explicitly party-based but which draw upon their professional position within government for their organisational focus and leverage. The Association of Liberal Democrat Councillors, for example, which is based upon its members' first-hand experience of the problems of local democracy and government services, has been highly active in exchanging information on, and in mobilising support for, constitutional reform.

127

A *third* category of advocacy is provided by think tanks like the Institute for Public Policy Research (IPPR), the Fabian Society, Demos, the Institute for Citizenship Studies, and the Institute of Economic Affairs (IEA). Although constitutional reform represents only a part of their respective remits of policy innovation, these types of organisation have helped create a climate of radical speculation in which proposals for broad constitutional reform are incorporated into ideologically coherent schemes of socio-economic change. Notwithstanding the contrast in the philosophical motivations and objectives of organisations like the IEA and the IPPR, they have both been closely associated with the issue of constitutional reform in the 1990s.

A *fourth* category of advocacy is a less conspicuous and more indirect form of advocacy that emerges from those supportive organisations that help to fund projects and movements related to constitutional reform. For example, the general cause of constitutional reform has been advanced by the corporate policies of companies like Sainsburys and The Body Shop to offer donations and sponsorship to further the renovation of the British democratic system. The research priorities of bodies like the Nuffield Foundation, the Joseph Rowntree Reform Trust (JRRT) and the Scarman Trust have all reflected the shift in interest towards the organisation and performance of government. The agenda of constitutional reform has been advanced in many different ways by the financial contribution of such trusts and foundations. The Constitution Unit, for example, was established and funded by six organisations[39] with the sole purpose of making detailed inquiries into how the agenda of constitutional reform could be brought to fruition. The Constitution Unit's terms of reference notes that debate on constitutional change has tended to 'focus on the substance of reform rather than the means of achieving it'.[40] The working assumption of the Unit's brief, therefore, was that an agenda of reform had already been established. Working on this basis, the Unit's objective has been to 'identify the practical steps involved in implementing reform'.[41]

Of all the organisations that have helped to fund the campaign for constitutional reform, the JRRT has been by far the most significant, not just because of the scale of its financial sponsorship but because of its explicitly proactive agenda of targeted political support. The JRRT has had a long history of endorsing radical reform within the framework of liberal democracy and in the late 1980s and 1990s it embarked upon a concerted plan of action to support an agenda of constitutional reform. The backing which the JRRT gave to the campaign was prodigious and touched every part of what was a diverse set of pressure points. The object was one of 'developing a counter-consensus based upon a perceived popular desire for constitutional and electoral reform'.[42] With this in mind, the JRRT helped to found the Common Voice organisation which analysed key battleground seats where Conservative MPs might be vulnerable to campaigns of tactical voting. It was instrumental in setting up *Samizdat* magazine, and in first saving the *New Society* magazine and then in brokering a merger with the *New Statesman* in 1988 to ensure the survival of at least one left of centre weekly in Britain. Both *Samizdat* and the *New Statesman* and *Society* were to give constitutional reform a strong emphasis in their editorial priorities. The JRRT was also central in the formation of Charter 88 and in the launch of Demos in 1993. Many other organisations connected to the constitutional reform issue received JRRT backing, including the Campaign for a Scottish Assembly, Plaid Cymru, the Labour Campaign for Electoral Reform, the Labour Working Party on Electoral Mechanisms, the Association of Liberal Democrat Councillors, the Institute for Citizenship Studies, the Voting Reform Information Service, the Campaign for Press and Broadcasting Freedom, the Campaign Against the Asylum and Immigration Bill, and the Lesbian and Gay Christian Movement. The trustees were committed to encouraging political pluralism, democratic citizenship, de-centralised decision-making and inter-party co-operation between Labour and the Liberal Democrats. They were also keen both to measure and to mobilise public opinion through social surveys. To this end, they funded the *The State of the Nation* reports conducted by MORI in 1991 and 1995, which made a major contribution to the debate on the constitution by demonstrating broad-based voter support for structural reform. Following the Conservative party's fourth consecutive election victory in 1992, the JRRT felt constrained to increase still further its commitment to constitutional reform. The shift in emphasis is described by the JRRT's own analysis of its reforming activities.

> Throughout the 1992–97 Parliament, the Trust's work was a coherent story of sustained and deliberate concentration on constitutional issues: focusing on getting the Labour Party to commit to constitutional reform and equipping shadow ministers with research assistants working on the issues; backing to the hilt the principal pressure group, Charter 88, in its attempts to force constitutional reform up the agenda, funding numerous other bodies working in the field, and helping to keep the Liberal Democrats afloat. Having made the judgement that an improved performance at the polls by the Liberal Democrats would improve the prospects of constitutional reform, the Trust offered the Party significant financial support at this time ... Throughout the 1990s, the nature of [the] agenda was clearly reflected in the accounts. Of almost £3 million which the Trust distributed in grants in the 1992–97 Parliament, at least two thirds was specifically given for the cause of constitutional reform, and almost all the remainder was in some way related to constitutional issues.[43]

Included in this figure of £2 million was £1 million given to political parties for activities related to constitutional reform, £0.75 million given to individuals and organisations engaged in the campaign for constitutional change, and nearly £0.25 million on opinion polling. According to an independent study by Michael Pinto-Duchinsky, the 'Trust's political gifts across the parties of almost £1.5 million in the 1990s were as large as the combined political payments of the ten largest company donors to the Conservatives. The Trust's political giving was not only of a different scale ... it was also different in kind, being almost wholly devoted to the cause of constitutional reform.'[44]

Research into the functioning of the British constitution and inquiries into the implications of its identified deficiencies have also been assisted by combinations of private and public support. The work of the Democratic Audit,[45] for example, which includes the publication of a series of in-depth reports on democratic and human rights issues (e.g. civil liberties in Britain, quangos, parliamentary reform, electoral systems) has been variously supported by the Joseph Rowntree Charitable Trust, the Scarman Trust, the Human Rights Centre at the University of Essex and on occasion by the Nolan Committee on Standards in Public Life. The government's own Economic and Social Research Council (ERSC) has acknowledged the need for the institution to have a 'greater public engagement and legitimacy'[46] and, as a consequence, has determined that one of its key research priorities should be in the area of governance and regulation. In 1995, the ESRC recognised the 'changing nature of governance in the UK';[47] the impact of 'more autonomous institutions ... free from traditional lines of control';[48] the restructuring of government service and delivery; and the onset of a 'transformation ... in the relationship between central government and the regions (Northern Ireland, Scotland, Wales) which may bring constitutional changes'.[49] The stated purpose of the ESRC in this context was to 'to assist in establishing forms of governance and a regulatory framework which adequately balance economic incentives with the protection of the wider public interest'.[50] Whether the support of such organisations is public or private, whether it is oriented to the provision or usage of research, and whether it is directed towards pure social inquiry or to achieving part of a larger objective of social reform, the aggregate effect of these trusts, foundations and research establishments has been to provide the resources of information, analysis and evaluation upon which constitutional reformers have come to depend to substantiate and disseminate their message for change.

A *fifth* category is accounted for by the judiciary. In his Hamlyn Lectures, *English Law – The New Dimension*, Lord Scarman identified a 'basic imbalance in our constitution'[51] and called for a new constitutional settlement to 'protect the individual citizen from instant legislation, conceived in fear or prejudice, and enacted in breach of human rights'.[52] That controversial call in 1974 for the establishment of a bill of rights has been repeated on numerous public occasions by Lord Scarman. The publicity surrounding such interventions into constitutional debate has not only helped establish the political and intellectual case for the entrenchment of private freedoms, but has contributed towards the widespread assimilation of judges acting as possible tribunes of the public interest during a period of rapid constitutional change. From its institutional vantage point, the judiciary has helped raise the level of constitutional consciousness by enlarging the scope and volume of judicial review in respect to government decisions and by issuing public reminders of the constant need to ensure that government actions remain lawful. Whether the recent injection of judicial activism orginates from judges incorporating European techniques of drawing judicial solutions from broad principles, or from the inadequacies of other checks and arenas of political debate, or from an insensitivity over civil liberties by a party which had been in office for such extended period of government, the end result has been that judges have amended the position of the judiciary within the British constitution. The judges have relaxed the restrictions upon gaining access to the courts; they have become more professionally oriented to issues of fairness, justice and human rights; and they have transformed judicial review from a pragmatic exercise into an altogether more principled and open-textured rule of law within the formal structure of parliamentary sovereignty. The increased incidence of cases involving public bodies and government decisions, the arguments used in adjudication, and the rising prominence of the judiciary in the British political system' have all made an indirect contribution to constitutional reform. Such levels of judicial activity are seen not merely as a sign of traditional *de facto* constitutional adaptation, but as an indication of the necessity for a more regulated and concerted revision of the constitution. The centrality of the judiciary to the promotion of a constitutional culture was conspicuously reaffirmed during John Major's second administration (1992–97) by the incidence of several high-profile cases in which ministers were embarrassed by the reversal of government decisions; by the judicial character of the highly charged inquiry into the export of defence equipment to Iraq conducted by Lord Justice Scott; and by the personal opposition of senior judges such as Lord Donaldson, Lord Denning, Lord Scarman, Lord Woolf, Lord Taylor and Lord Bingham to controversial government proposals such as the curtailment of the right to silence, the imposition of mandatory custodial sentences, the restriction of jury trials, the introduction of tougher penal regimes and the refusal to establish a review body into miscarriages of justice.

A *sixth* and more diffuse category of advocacy is that of mass dissemination through which constitutional dissent and ideas for corrective action are conveyed to audiences larger than those previously attentive to such issues. Centres of news gathering and analysis do not simply report constitutional problems as and when they arise. Over time, their choices and activities disclose an agenda in which constitutional reform is given sufficient editorial priority to ensure that news and events are consistently interpreted in terms of constitutional problems and the availability of solutions. *The Independent,* *The Guardian, The Observer* and the *New Statesman* (now the *New Stateman and Society*), for example, are four cases in point where the constitution is regularly featured in depth and where social and economic issues are directly related to the constitutional debate. This is not to say that the motivations of different news organisations do not vary. *The Independent, The Guardian, The Observer* and the *New Statesman* have regularly supported moves to increase scrutiny, improve accountability, enhance the constitution's checks and balances, and establish a more pluralist and de-centralised state. The *Sunday Times* has placed itself in the vanguard of democratic renewal, but is more prompted by the values of the market economy and aggressive individualism than by the inclusive pluralism of the *The Guardian* or *The Observer*'s social democracy. Anthony Barnett draws out the contrast:

> The *Sunday Times* ... campaigned harder and earlier for a Freedom of Information Act and a Bill of Rights than any other paper in Britain ... The Murdoch media have assaulted the pomposity, paternalism and incompetence of the Establishment with vigour and elan, and gained enormously in the process in the democracy of the market place. This *is* its definition of democracy. The underclass, those who cannot enter the marketplace, are seen as 'not like us', as non citizens, while the inscription of a set of values for our society as a whole is regarded as antiquated egalitarianism.[53]

The Economist has been another force in the propagation of the faith but it has avoided the strident tone of the *Sunday Times* in its quest for the liberalisation of British society and government. It has occupied an intermediate position, stressing the reform agenda while maintaining a realistic assessment of problems and being aware that a reform like a bill of rights can only 'nurture a culture of liberty in a society which already recognises its value'.[54] Despite the variation in style and strategy among the different outlets, the net effect of such sustained interest in the issue of the constitution has helped create and sustain a critical awareness among the public of the important ethical and practical ramifications of how the government is governed.

The extent to which the British constitution has become the subject of deepening news interest over the period of agenda formation and consolidation is reflected in the citation measures of news stories and analyses related to the constitution. Figure 4.1 reveals a sharp rise in press interest from 1990 to 1992, reflecting both a growing concern for the state of political constraint after a prolonged period of Conservative hegemony and a need to consider the possible imminence of constitutional reform in the event of a hung parliament or a Labour victory in the 1992 general election. Even though the volume of entries suffers a relative decline after 1992, the issue of reform remains conspicuously high compared to the 1980s and by 1996 resumes about the same level as that acquired in 1992. A more marked pattern of rising salience is revealed in the increased incidence of opinion polls surveying public attitudes towards constitutional problems and proposed solutions. The growing frequency of such polls, most of which are conducted for newspaper clients, reaffirm the rising salience of issues and responses related to constitutional questions (see Figure 4.2). These two figures reveal the issue's capacity both to make a deep impression upon editorial priorities and to attract the kind of public interest that gives constitutional reform a degree of populist resonance.

The contribution of the electronic media has been primarily one of registering the effects of the behaviour of government and the activities of the reformers in shaping the political agenda. Although its influence has largely been to reflect the increased salience of the constitutional dimension in its news values and editorial priorities, the electronic media has not been entirely passive in its contribution to the constitutional debate. In addition

Figure 4.1 *Newspaper citation count*

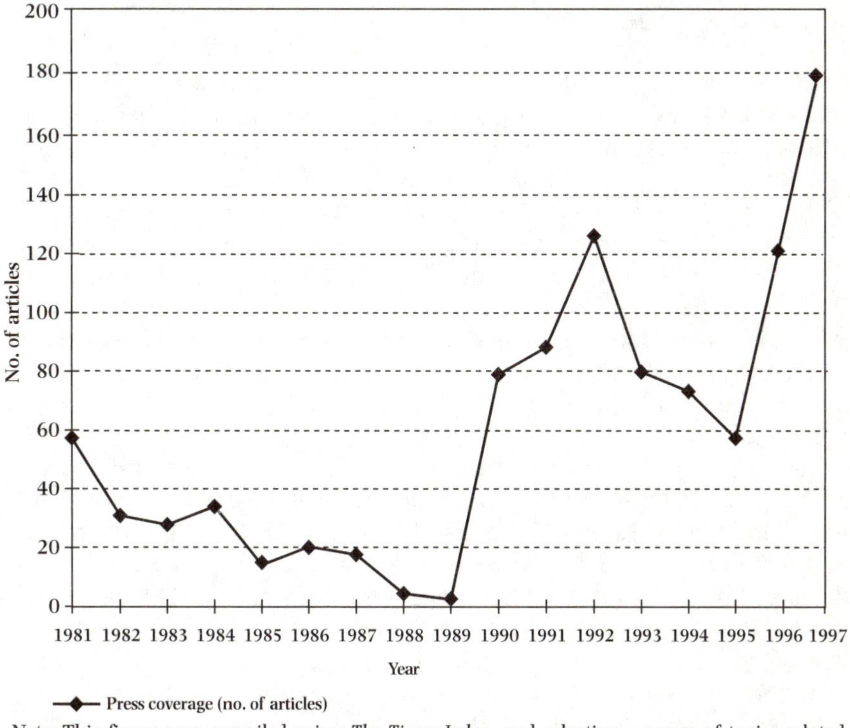

◆ Press coverage (no. of articles)

Note: This figure was compiled using *The Times Index*, and selecting a range of topics related to constitutional reform, including reform of the electoral system, devolution, open government, freedom of information, Bill of Rights, House of Lords reform and the general heading of constitutional reform. The *Index* was then analysed to determine the amount of coverage in each year.

Figure 4.2 *Opinion polls conducted on constitutional reform*

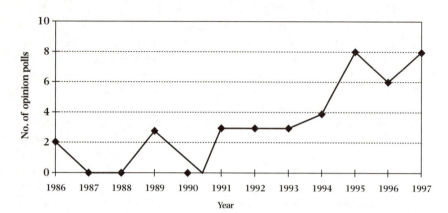

Note: This figure was compiled using the MORI Index to British Public Opinion, and identified opinion polls where topics related to constitutional reform e.g. freedom of information, Bill of Rights, electoral reform and devolution were included.

to the discrete pieces of investigative reporting and analytical features provided by such programmes as BBC's *Newsnight, Panorama and Rough Justice,* BBC Radio's *File on Four, Analysis* and *Call Nick Ross,* ITV's *World in Action* and Channel 4's *Dispatches,* the broadcasting organisations have made some concerted efforts to raise the public's awareness of the issue of the constitution. They have done this either by means of sustained in-depth studies, or through prime-time examinations of a particular constitutional theme. The BBC's *The State of Democracy*[55] was a pioneering series that investigated the various dimensions of the developing critique of the British constitution. Carlton Television's *Monarchy: The Nation Decides*[56] examined the contemporary state of the monarchy through a live debate in front of a 3-000 strong studio audience which voted on a series of questions relating to the royal family. The programme ended with the result of a telephone poll conducted in response to the issues raised in the studio discussion. A television audience of 8.3 million viewers generated 2.6 million calls which more than doubled the previous record for a television phone-in. The potential of this type of interactive and populist dimension of opinion presentation was explored most vigorously by Channel 4 in its series *The People's Parliament.* In conjunction with its fellow sponsor, *The Observer,* the programme examined the arguments for and against a particular motion on an issue of public concern. Viewers and readers could then call and register their votes. Apart from the fact that *The People's Parliament* included constitutionally related issues in their range of selected motions for popular consideration, the whole format of the programme was explicitly premised upon the inadequacy of Britain's constitutional arrangements. This was made evident in the stated rationale of the programme-makers: 'Do you ever feel that the Government – and indeed the whole parliamentary system – is out of touch with ordinary people? ... Is democracy working, or has Parliament grown complacent? ... [O]ver the next two months Channel 4 will be rattling the democratic cage by giving ordinary people the chance to have their say in a series of programmes – *The People's Parliament*.'[57]

The implicit empirical, ethical and prescriptive themes that inform the press, radio and television have received their fullest and most explicit exposition in a number of popular full-length inquiries into the overall performance of government. Andrew Marr's *Ruling Britannia: The Failure and Future of British Democracy* (1995)[58] Peter Hennessy's *The Hidden Wiring: Unearthing the British Constitution* (1995)[59] Simon Jenkins's *Accountable to None: The Tory Nationalization of Britain* (1995)[60] and Will Hutton's, *The State We're In* (1995)[61] have all been conspicuous not just by the cogency and accessibility of the presented arguments but by their very popularity. Explorations into the British constitution used to be very much a minority interest but by the middle of the 1990s the subject had become modish with these types of publications becoming prominent in political discussion and in the listings of book sales and book clubs. One of the authors, Andrew Marr, observed that the success of publications like his own signified that 'constitutional argument had finally tumbled into the political mainstream'.[62] He noted how a 'stream of articles, programmes and interviews grappling with the theme of political decadence [reflected] a mood of determined interest in political reform'.[63]

A *seventh* agency in the propagation of constitutional reform is provided by the 'minor parties' within the context of the British two-party system. It is the threat of being more than minor that has given the Liberals, the Social Democrats, the Liberal Democrats and the Scottish and Welsh nationalist parties the periodic political and electoral leverage to press their policy agendas upon the two main parties. For the Liberal Democrats, constitutional reform has remained at the core of the party's ethos as the embodiment of a genuinely third force in national politics. The issue is integrally connected to its identity and strategy as a radical alternative to both the Labour and Conservative parties. In many respects the nationalist forces in Wales and Scotland are more influential than the Liberal Democrats because of the geographically concentrated nature of their support in what increasingly have become Labour strongholds. Nationalist voters can have a disproportionate effect upon the political calculations of both the major parties, especially when the electorate has become more unpredictable owing to the effects of progressive partisan de-alignment. The threat to Labour from nationalist parties is, however, more acute because of its greater dependence upon Welsh and Scottish seats in acquiring an overall majority of seats at

Westminster. The inroads made by nationalists either into Labour territory, like the by-election victories in Hamilton (1967), Govan (1973), and Govan again in 1988, or into seats that might otherwise have been susceptible to Labour advances, like Carmarthen in 1966, and Perth and Kinross in 1995, assumed enormous significance and alarmed the Labour leadership into reviewing its position on the issue of devolution. The suggestive nature of such reversals, combined with the periodic surges of nationalist support (e.g the capture by the Scottish National Party (SNP) of 32 per cent of the Scottish vote in the 1994 European elections) and the key precedent of the October 1974 general election when Plaid Cymru won 11 per cent of the Welsh vote and the SNP achieved a 30 per cent share of the Scottish vote, have produced a general acknowledgement by Labour of the need both to respond to nationalist opinion and to co-opt the pivotal issues for itself, in order to pre-empt any further loss of support.

But the role of the nationalist parties in the pressure for constitutional reform has not been limited to devolution. During the 18 years of continuous Conservative government, both Plaid Cymru and the SNP provided not only an expression of geographical and moral detachment from a government to which their respective national electorates had not given their consent, but embodied the sense of disfranchisement and alienation experienced by many sectors of English society which were coming to question the merits and ethics of the political system as a whole. Bernard Crick, for example, observed in 1990 that 'the English constitution' had traditionally been seen as a 'barrier to Scottish rights. But it is now widely canvassed as never before that the constitution is an obstacle to all our British civil liberties.'[64] In this respect, the SNP was not merely an introverted response to Westminster: it could be construed as a litmus test on the overall viability of the British constitution and a generic sign of the need for it to be fundamentally renewed. Far from seeking to replicate the Westminster system for their own national interests, both the Welsh and Scottish nationalist parties have sought to link the nature of aroused national cultures and identities with comprehensive programmes of constitutional reform. Plaid Cymru's 1997 party manifesto, for example, explicitly equated national self-government with popular sovereignty and localised decision-making: 'At every level and for every aspect of Welsh life, Plaid Cymru believes that the principle of subsidiarity should prevail ... [I]n our view sovereignty rests with the citizens and is only vested with local, national and international government in so far as it is necessary to achieve effective government at every level ... A fully self-governing Wales would ... have a written constitution and a Bill of Rights.'[65] The nationalist parties, therefore, have provided arenas of constitutional radicalism in which political mobilisation has been explicitly organised around programmes of structural change. During the years of Tory hegemony, they also served as a counterpoint to the Labour party's status as the official opposition. They have done so by acting as a reminder of Labour's past failures in converting Scottish and Welsh support into changes of government in London, and by remaining watchful of New Labour's commitment to translating pledges of constitutional change into legislative action. The alternative opposition of the nationalist parties has rested heavily upon the idea of an alternative politics through constitutional change. Given New Labour's reputation as the 'the most centralised and disciplined force in Britain's democratic history',[66] it is likely that Plaid Cymru and the SNP will continue to press for the development of constitutional reform beyond any nominated settlement issuing from Westminster.

The *final* category belongs entirely to the one organisation that has done most to bring the issue of the constitution to the attention of the public and to place constitutional reform in the mainstream of British political debate. Charter 88 adopted a comprehensive ten-point reform package for a thorough overhaul of the constitutional structure with the aim of establishing a modern pluralist constitution based upon the concept of popular sovereignty and a culture of active citizenship. Its key theme of a charter of principles and reforms and its main strategy of a rolling petition have provided the core elements of a highly effective campaign in publicising complaint, in mobilising dissent and in organising pressure for remedial action. Charter 88 has remained an insurgency movement whose activities have not only acted as a catalyst to reformist energies, but have in themselves provided an expression of the level of public dismay in the conventional conduct of politics. Charter 88 has combined a high-profile leadership networked into many of the strategic centres of political communications with an open reliance upon public support, voluntary action and local participation. The prominence of Charter 88 owes much to the penetrative force of its simple theorem about the organisation of political authority. 'We believe that major reforms of the structures of rule are necessary. Simply that. With them Britain has a real chance of freeing the energy and qualities of its people. Without them, nothing will go right and there can be little or no hope.'[67] The focus of Charter 88 has provided an effective outlet of discontent in a society with an increasing distrust of politics and politicians. It has succeeded in popularising the message of a connection between political alienation and government failure with the need for constitutional reform. And it has familiarised the British public with the concept of constitutionalism by popular demand as an alternative to conventional party politics and as a source of hope for a more equitable distribution of power through a different kind of politics. By 1997, Charter 88 could justifiably claim that '[all] the main parties have now had to acknowledge the people care – and care deeply – about how we are governed. A whole range of constitutional issues are now the subject of serious debate.'[68] It is a testament to Charter 88 that much of the pressure, direction and salience of the constitutional debate has been attributable to the presence of such a vigorous non-party organisation in the development of the constitution as a political issue.

Techniques of advocacy

The techniques of raising constitutional consciousness and generating a reform agenda are as varied as the different agencies of advocacy. In some respects, techniques of advocacy can be dissociated from conscious design in that individuals, groups or organisations can through their statements or actions unwittingly add to a political environment of constitutional scepticism and speculation. The Conservative governments of Margaret Thatcher and John Major represent the clearest example of unintentional advocacy by being so closely associated with all ten of the constitutional fuels (see Chapter 3) which have propelled disquiet over the style of government into a general acceptance of the need for constitutional change. 'It is a paradox that a government so determined to resist constitutional change has made the constitution itself a political issue.'[69] Vernon Bogdanor's observation was directed to Margaret Thatcher's administration but it was equally applicable to John Major's period in office. While acknowledging the significance of such unintended contributions to the constitutional debate, it is more appropriate to concentrate on the techniques of intentional advocacy, not only because it is the latter which translate the former into the currency of constitutional argument, but because it is the methods of those purposeful advocates of constitutional reform that have been primarily responsible for turning negative constructions of government into politically viable alternatives.

One particularly potent method of raising the constitutional dimension has been to publicise repeatedly and consistently cases of governmental misconduct, misjudgement or failure. The employment of the marketing strategy of repetition has the effect of implanting a focused message within the contemporary framework of political perception that transcends simple party allegiance and conventional party solutions. The inductive technique of persistently presenting a set of particular government offences fosters the realisation of a profusion of other defects which can then be incorporated as part of an attributed pattern of decay. This leap to deductive suggestion, in which all governmental ailments can be assigned to a chronic systemic condition, can lead to an indiscriminate assault upon the institutional arrangements of government. Even though the process can become circular in nature – with generalised indictments conditioning the reaction to particular political deficiencies at the same time that the latter are taken as proof positive of a systematic breakdown – its effect is to underline both the possibility and the desirability of eliciting a separate dimension of constitutional ethics from the superstructure of political engagement. Charter 88 has been particularly effective in generating such a dynamic in its diagnoses of government. Its ten-point programme fuses prescriptions to inferred empirical conditions of constitutional failure. For example, the Charter draws attention to the need to 'create a fair electoral system ... to place the Executive ... and all the agencies of the state under the rule of law ... [and] to provide legal remedies for all abuses of power by the state'.[70] The organisation's strategy of reducing political problems to the focused terms of its charter has helped encourage the formation of a constitutional perspective to the problem of the British constitution. The repeated indictments and prescriptions of Charter 88 have provided a continuous demonstration of an approach to government that is based upon permanent and identifiable principles of operation by which governments can be assessed, evaluated and held to account. This is not to say that such a technique is sufficient to create a constitutional culture, or that Charter 88 and other organisations using such techniques have lifted constitutional reform to the top of the political agenda. What can be concluded is that the method of repeated reference to constitutional problems and constitutional solutions can be very influential in affecting the way government performance and political alternatives are perceived, especially during a period when a government has been in office for so long that the limitations of a 'political constitution' give pause for critical reflection.

Another technique in highlighting the constitutional issue is that of offering alternatives. It is often said of constitutional reformers that they engage in negative campaigning and that their critical faculties are too highly developed to consider the problems and contingencies of practical improvements, or comprehensive reconstruction. To counter these accusations of dilettantism and to provide their supporters with a rallying point of purposive action, reformers have deployed their forces in the promotion of a variety of remedial measures. The most evident expression of such objectives are those listed in Charter 88 but they do not exhaust the reformist agenda for action. The Charter lists a series of umbrella principles for change but the exact application of such axioms remains open to interpretation. Constitutional reformers have shown that they can turn from criticism to construction by giving their support to measures which may not satisfy all their requirements, but which can be construed and defended as practical derivatives of their central principles. Thus, reformist organisations such as Charter 88 and the Campaign for the Freedom of Information formed a cross-party Right to Know Campaign in 1993 to lobby for the passage of Mark Fisher's 'Right to Know' private member's bill. The importance of adapting the constitutional reform movement to new issues and to new practicable applications of constitutional principle was also clear in the response to the issue of sleaze.

The revelations and accusations of personal misconduct by MPs, which in 1995 led to the establishment of the Nolan Committee on Standards in Public Life, was expected to result in a classic exercise of establishment reformism. The issue would be neutralised by a prolonged inquiry that would ultimately propose minimal remedies in an attempt to reassure the public of the presence of high standards in political life. But when Lord Nolan appeared to extend the brief of his committee and proposed more far-reaching reforms than was previously thought likely, there was a backlash within the Conservative party over the regulations and limitations relating to MPs' outside earnings. The supporters of constitutional reform felt the Nolan recommendations were insufficient. The radical position would have imposed severer restrictions on outside income and employment, and would have given the parliamentary rules of conduct a legal basis, thereby allowing disputes and transgressions to be resolved by an independent commission or the civil courts. Nolan's recommendation of a full disclosure of MPs' contracts and earnings, together with the establishment of a Parliamentary Commissioner for Standards to address complaints, was greeted with alarm by many traditionalists. It prompted the *Daily Telegraph* to declare that a watershed in parliamentary history was in prospect: 'For the first time in its 700-year history the behaviour of MPs and ministers is to be subject to independent scrutiny to counter allegations of sleaze and corruption in public life.'[71] The reformist outlook regarded this as a technical transformation in that the self-regulation by MPs on the basis of individual trust had only been replaced by the collective self-regulation by Parliament on the basis of the institution's own rules of disclosure and the installation of a Parliamentary Commissioner to enforce them. Nevertheless, the reform lobby acknowledged the constitutional value both of Nolan's proposals and of the rolling prospectus of subjects (e.g. party funding) for future Nolan inquiries. Pressure from constitutional reformers helped prevent the misgivings within the Conservative party from slipping into a rejection of the Nolan proposals. Reformers would have questioned Lord Nolan's premise that 'if standards of conduct in Parliament command public confidence, nothing much can go wrong'.[72] But they would have sympathised with his conclusion that: 'Unless corrective measures are promptly taken, there is a danger that anxiety and suspicion will give way to disillusion and growing cynicism.'[73] The Nolan inquiry may not have recommended the most radical of corrective measures but the very fact of the Committee's existence, along with the critical nature of its report, demonstrated the extent to which public pressure could lead to constitutional experimentation and to new departures in openness and accountability which reformers could endorse as an initial and practical step in establishing a general structure of enforceable constitutional principle.

Probably the most emphatic technique of offering constitutional alternatives to stated problems has been the construction of large-scale plans for a new constitutional settlement. Since constitutional reformers operate from the premise that the contemporary problems of British government are systemic in nature, the logical conclusion of such a position is that of providing a holistic solution in the form of comprehensive schemes of reformed governance. The IPPR, for example, produced an 18-article bill of rights in draft form not merely in order to highlight the precarious nature of individual rights and liberties in a system of parliamentary sovereignty, but to demonstrate the feasibility of producing a legally workable charter of entrenched freedoms.[74] In the words of the IPPR's supportive document A *Bill of Rights*, the proposal would 'help to make a reality of rights' by acting as a 'rallying point for all who care about human freedom'.[75] The organisation Liberty also produced its own bill of rights as a discussion document.[76] A similar educative device was supplied by Tony Benn's Commonwealth of Britain Bill which was prompted by a desire to redesign the British constitution, in order to sweep away the remnants of hereditary and monarchical power in favour of a fully democratic, de-centralised and accountable system of government. Even though the bill may have been more of a thought experiment than a genuine attempt at constitutional change, Benn's proposal did provide an illustration of how a constitution of unassembled parts might be integrated into a corporate and documentary form. The Commonwealth of Britain Bill was 'an appeal for a great public debate about the future'[77] but its function was not limited to revolutionary polemics. It supported a wider contention that serious alternatives in government structure are feasible and that a 'set of human aspirations in a constitution is a plausible proposition'.[78] It was the Liberal Democrats' document *We, The People ... Towards a Written Constitution*,[79] and the IPPR's *The Constitution of the United Kingdom*,[80] however, that probably rank as the most extensive exercises in constitutional formulation during the construction of the constitutional reform agenda. They both proposed a coherently designed structure of government, defined a set of dynamics between the institutions of state, enumerated the rights and freedoms of citizens and established the principle of the constitutional supremacy in law. The intention was to show that a written constitution in Britain could be succinct, coherent and comprehensible while achieving a status of fundamental law based upon the consent of a sovereign people. The production of a ready-made constitution drawn *de novo* from first principles was designed to give an ultimate or ideal form to the reform agenda, which would provide a frame of reference to the myriad proposals for change, give a sense of direction to the objectives and consequences of constitutional revision, and stimulate the reform process itself by implying the viability, and even the likelihood, of a fully codified written constitution from the current democratic activity for change.[81]

The Scottish Constitutional Convention succeeded in combining the provision of a constitutional corrective with the active generation of political support in favour of the measure. This extraordinary experiment in co-operative politics originated in March 1989 with the presentation of 'A Claim of Right for Scotland' by the Campaign for a Scottish Assembly. It argued a position of popular sovereignty for Scotland. Parliamentary sovereignty was declared to be a feature of English law that had been established prior to the Act of Union and had never, therefore, been approved by the representatives of the Scottish people through the parliamentary process. As a consequence, the Scottish people should reassert its implicit right of sovereignty and determine for itself how the nation should be governed. The 'Claim of Right' called for representatives to gather in a constitutional convention to draw up proposals for future self-government. The Conservative party declined the offer and the SNP withdrew from the convention because national independence was not included on the agenda. Nevertheless, the assemblage of Labour and Liberal Democrat figures, together with representatives from the churches and organisations like the Scottish Confederation of British Industry and Trades Union Congress, succeeded both in formulating an agreed package of constitutional reforms (i.e. *Scotland's Parliament, Scotland's Right* published in November 1995) and in creating a broad based-structure of popular support for the outcome of such a deliberative process. The prior consulation and pooling of resources around a set of common demands were instrumental in creating a depth of consensus in favour of a Scottish government that would provide the basis of the successful 'Yes campaign' in the referendum on Scottish devolution in September 1997.

The technique of suggesting a groundswell of interest in the state of the constitution has been advanced by other means. For example, the reformist cause has benefited from the constitutional evangelism of high-profile supporters such as Helena Kennedy, Melvyn Bragg, Salman Rushdie, Martin Amis, Sir Simon Rattle and Dame Judi Dench. These and others have used their celebrity status to cast themselves in the role of articulators of common anxieties over the condition of governance. Their very prominence is used not merely to publicise the issue of reform but to convey an impression of the need for such voices to express an underlying public demand for radical action. The provenance of the issue has been further enhanced by the work of polemicists like Tom Nairn, Tony Benn and Peter Tatchell on aspects of the constitution and by the open association of experienced political figures with the objectives of reform (e.g. Lord Jenkins of Hillhead, David Marquand, Des Wilson, Anthony Lester). Useful though such prominent and articulate supporters may have been, they were insufficient to constitute a movement for reform. On the contrary, their very prominence helped to lend weight to the charge of their opponents that constitutional reform was an elitist and cerebral concern that was of interest only to the 'chattering classes'. Among such detractors, the issue was derided as a contrived distraction foisted by a single issue group intent upon subverting the majoritarian authority of an elected government in favour of a tiny and unrepresentative minority of political dissenters. The reformers themselves were aware of their own numerical limitations and sought to widen the outreach and, thereby, the political leverage of their position. It would have been difficult to argue for popular sovereignty in the absence of any apparent demand for it, or any attempt to engage with it. As a consequence, reformist organisations sought not only to reflect their ideals in the openness and responsiveness of their own structures but to evoke a public response to their constitutional diagnoses. No organisation was more intent upon generating public interest and engagement than Charter 88. Its rallies, demonstrations, pavement vigils and 'Democracy Days' reflected the organisation's conviction that the 'power of the Charter lies in linking its ideas with popular demand ... [which] must be rooted locally'.[82] Charter 88 carried the rationale of the case for constitutional reform to its logical conclusion by attempting to show, through forms of popular response, the substance of its own claims to represent the people's voice and to express widespread anxieties over liberties and rights.

But by far the most effective technique in substantiating claims to represent genuine public concerns has been the usage of survey research into social attitudes towards constitutional change. When reformers can refer to an actual state of public opinion, the arguments for change are appreciably strengthened because it adds popular legitimacy and political leverage to the analytical logic for reform. Nowhere has direct proof of the public interest in constitutional change been more significant than in the *The State of the Nation* reports commissioned by the JRRT and published in 1991 and 1995.[83] The reports were based upon a set of MORI polls, which were described as 'the most comprehensive yet undertaken on public attitudes on political and constitutional issues'.[84] When the Rowntree Trust commissioned the survey, it was hoped that the 'publication of the results ... would in itself be a contribution to the public debate on reform; it would help gauge the public impact of the various reformist interest groups and would further assist them in formulating their future policies'.[85] The outcome exceeded all expectations.

The first two Reports were published in 1991 and immediately attracted intense public interest because they revealed the existence of majority support for a bill of rights, devolution for Scotland, fixed-term parliaments, a freedom of information act and the usage of referendums for important issues. They also showed a preponderance of support over opposition in such areas as devolution for Wales, House of Lords reform and a system of PR for parliamentary elections. In some instances, the desire for change was emphatic, with the freedom of information, bill of rights and referenda items attracting support levels of 77 per cent, 75 per cent and 72 per cent respectively. The polling evidence countered the claim that constitutional change was a middle-class issue. It showed that support for electoral reform among working-class respondents (47 per cent in favour to 23 per cent opposed) was comparable to the pattern of support and opposition shown by middle-class respondents (55 per cent to 23 per cent). Among trade unionists, the pattern of support (59 per cent to 22 per cent) even exceeded the profile of middle class responses. On the bill of rights issue, working class respondents (76 per cent to 8 per cent), council tenants (78 per cent to 7 per cent) and trade unionists (79 per cent to 9 per cent) all revealed higher levels of support than those recorded from middle class respondents who favoured such a measure by 63 per cent to 19 per cent. The survey also confirmed the scale of disillusionment in the generic performance of government, with clear majorities believing that government is too centralised (60 per cent agreement to 18 per cent disagreement) that rights are too easily changed (54 per cent to 22 per cent) and that parliamentary control over government is insufficient (50 per cent to 23 per cent). The severity of the diagnoses was commensurate with the radicalism of the proposed changes. Even when the survey's designers tried to warn respondents of the possible costs of such reforms to the conventional virtues of two-party politics, it was evident that the support for structured change prevailed over traditional scepticism. Patrick Dunleavy concluded that:

> The traditional public support for two-party politics to which party leaders habitually appeal is no longer there ... . The Rowntree poll shows clearly that voters who want proportional representation appreciate that it may spell the end of strong, single-party governments able to act decisively with the backing of a loyal Commons majority. Most of them want at least that. The rules of the game are being changed, from below.[86]

The first and the second *The State of the Nation* reports allowed reformers to claim the existence of a real constituency in support of fundamental constitutional change. It was now possible to assert that 'the public is, in short, far more radical than most politicians, reform agencies and mediacrats when it comes to rights and liberties'.[87] With the assistance of this type of research, reform groups could depict themselves as the outward sign of a largely unmobilised, yet powerful, insurgency movement with enormous potential for shaping the direction and substance of political debate. Reformers not only felt vindicated in their analytical judgements and policy positions, but believed the survey evidence gave them the momentum and the authority to press home the case for change. Trevor Smith, the chairman of the JRRT, had no doubts that the survey armed the reform lobby with genuinely populist credentials: 'Politicians of all parties should listen to what the people are saying. MPs pay lip-service to democracy, but it is now obvious that the electorate strongly desires an updated system of government.'[88] The information generated by the poll could be, and was, projected to show not only that the two main parties were out of touch with the public on the issue of the constitution, but that they themselves were part of the problem of British government and were in part responsible for the public's declining confidence in its performance. On the other hand, the survey alerted the main parties to the political status of the reform issue and the need to take account of the pressures and arguments for change in the strategic and tactical calculations of their organisational self-interest.

Survey research illustrates a further technique in advocating constitutional change. Comparing opinions and attitudes across different periods of time allows inferences to be drawn concerning trends and projections. Comparisons can confirm the depth of public scepticism; they can trace the scale of deterioration in social confidence over the performance and integrity of government; and they can underline the urgency for remedial action. The third *The State of the Nation* report published in 1995 was able to demonstrate not only that opinions had remained consistent over four years, but that in selected key areas they had hardened, giving rise to concern that a prolonged postponement of reform might threaten social stability. Time has been a valuable commodity in the promotion of the reform agenda. Time allowed the reform groups to establish their agenda as the measure of political unresponsiveness, thereby contributing to the terms of their own validity as critical assessors. The longer the system remained constitutionally unreconstructed, the more it could be construed as verifying the proposition that it was chronically unresponsive to popular demands, thereby deepening public cynicism over conventional politics and fostering a higher regard for constitutional alternatives in the process. In effect, time could reveal the public's irritation over time itself – the time during which it was perceived that nothing substantive had changed apart from 'an accelerating dissatisfaction with the system of government'.[89] The 1995 *Report* demonstrated that the identity and intensity of public demands for constitutional change had changed little over four years, confirming that the original findings were not a temporary reaction to the Thatcherite era but were solid perceptions of government that stretched across administrations and had become firmly embedded in opinion structures (see Figure 4.3).[90]

The analogue of preferences for constitutional reform remained a deep dissatisfaction with how the system appeared to function. In 1973 48 per cent of the British public thought that the system of government worked well. In 1991 that level had dropped to 33 per cent and in 1995 it stood at 22 per cent. The proportion of those believing that the system needed to be improved rose from 49 per cent in 1973, to 63 per cent in 1991 and to 76 per cent in 1995. Judgements of the system were translated into assessments of the personnel, with sustained increases in the level of public cynicism towards politicians. In 1973, two-thirds agreed that 'most politicians

Figure 4.3 *British attitudes to constitutional reform*

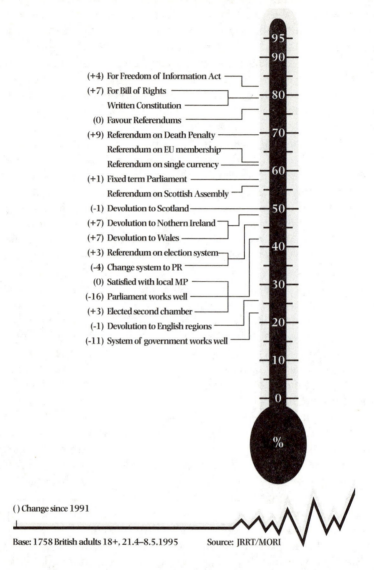

(+4) For Freedom of Information Act
(+7) For Bill of Rights
Written Constitution
(0) Favour Referendums
(+9) Referendum on Death Penalty
Referendum on EU membership
Referendum on single currency
(+1) Fixed term Parliament
Referendum on Scottish Assembly
(-1) Devolution to Scotland
(+7) Devolution to Nothern Ireland
(+7) Devolution to Wales
(+3) Referendum on election system
(-4) Change system to PR
(0) Satisfied with local MP
(-16) Parliament works well
(+3) Elected second chamber
(-1) Devolution to English regions
(-11) System of government works well

( ) Change since 1991

Base: 1758 British adults 18+, 21.4–8.5.1995   Source: JRRT/MORI

will promise anything to get votes' but by 1995 that level of agreement had risen to 81 per cent. The statement that 'politicians are in office for what they can get out of it' struck a chord with 39 per cent of respondents in 1973, but by 1995 two-thirds of the British public shared this view. The information garnered from the *The State of the Nation* surveys, and other polls examining the same phenomena, allowed reformers to add further substance to their allegations that the political elites were detached from public opinion and from the public interest. When the 1995 Rowntree report was compared with the 1991 reports, it enabled supporters of constitutional change to contest with even greater vigour those who would seek to dismiss the issue as ephemeral: '[P]ublic opinion on constitutional issues has been seen as shallowly based, expressing mainly the fleeting discontents of current opposition voters. Elites of both parties simply sat out or sat on demands for change, confident that only the "chattering classes" would remember them. Now ... the great mass of voters are insisting on change, and sticking to their guns.'[91]

The comparative technique has not been confined to the temporal dimension. Spatial comparisons between the British and other systems have been used by reformers to suggest that the reputed quality of British arrangements is not as well founded as is commonly thought. Unfavourable comparisons with the United States in areas like open government, executive checks, freedom of information and individual rights have been commonplace rhetorical devices for years, but increasingly European states have been used as the point of comparison, with numerous allusions to the superior constitutional guarantees and constraints of continental systems. An awareness of the capacity of the European Court of Justice and the European Court of Human Rights to make decisions against government has served to underline the status of the European dimension in the sphere of constitutional government – especially so when Britain is regularly accused of having more judgements declared against its position than any other signatory to the European Convention on Human Rights. Northern Ireland has also been used as a comparative frame of reference. The province's experience with religious discrimination, detention orders, internment, exclusion rules, altered trial procedures and the provisions of the Prevention of Terrorism Act can be used to provide a litmus test to the claim that civil liberties are highly vulnerable in a system of parliamentary sovereignty.[92] By the same token, the presence of PR in Northern Ireland elections, together with the proposals for imaginative quasi-federal solutions to the territorial organisation of the province's future relationship with Britain and the Irish Republic, can demonstrate the feasibility of such innovative arrangements within the British constitution. It can serve to highlight the fact that constitutional reform in the British system is conspicuously confined to a region regarded as chronically dysfunctional and, therefore, in need of extraordinary emergency measures. In effect, the Northern Ireland comparison can support the contention of a relative denial of constitutional innovation on the mainland.

In a political culture that has traditionally possessed a high level of constitutional self-esteem, any form of comparison with other states still ranks as a novel departure from the norm, but when the comparison is unfavourable the result is deeply unsettling as it suggests a severity of decline that relates to a loss of national identity. When Britain is featured in the *Index on Censorship*,[93] is cited in Amnesty International campaigns, is found to be 'in violation of the Convention [i.e. the European Convention on Human Rights] more than any other country',[94] and receives the same rankings as Botswana, Greece and Uruguay, and even lower rankings than Italy, Spain, Costa Rica and the Irish Republic in international indicators of freedom,[95] then the case supporting a national campaign of constitutional reform in response to a comparative deterioration of constitutional standards seems to be complete. Over a twenty-year period, the advocates of constitutional change had succeeded in projecting the issue of reform as an item of public concern. With increasing intensity, reformers had associated social, economic and political ills with the underlying condition of governance. They had consistently explained incidents of policy failure, government mismanagement, personal impropriety and miscarriages of justice in terms of structural dysfunction. Serious though such assertions were, they not only provided fundamental problems with a form of accessible explication, but offered the availability of clear solutions. At a time when public cynicism over the political process was rising to unexpected levels, when the social and ideological allegiance to political parties was being replaced by more fluid and de-aligned attachments and when the customary periodicity of power within the two-party system had apparently been suspended, constitutional reform offered an alternative frame of reference for political speculation and evaluation. At the very point when the limitations of Britain's traditional conceptions of constitutionalism had become more evident than ever, reformers advocated constitutional change, not merely as an appropriate reactive device but as the most apposite means to social and political renewal.

Confronted with charges that constitutional reform proposals were simplistic, or dangerous, or both, the reformers' persistent and reassuring promise of the remedial benefits of constitutional change began to condition the terms and substance of political debate. Time became the great ally of reform because it allowed the arguments for purposive change to ramify into the landscape of traditional modes of perception, thought and judgement. The reform position was essentially one of proposing an allegedly self-evident good that could not be falsified other than by the material consequences of constitutional reform. Just as the appeal of constitutional reform was based upon the varied experiences of a government that could be depicted as over-centralised and insensitive to civil liberties and standards of integrity, so the substance of constitutional change could only ever be determined by the actual experience of reform. Given this advantage of an untried and untested but increasingly credible panacea, the longer the message of constitutional reform remained a promise that could not be disproved, the more it acquired the appearance of being a self-evident and benevolent solution which would logically only be opposed by those with a vested interest in retaining the traditional structures of power. The longer the reform agenda could not be challenged on the basis of results, the more public space it acquired within which proposals for change were increasingly assimilated as plausible items of political attention. Time assisted the establishment of a reform agenda in another respect. After an extensive period of advocacy, reform ideas simply lose their capacity to shock. Serious arguments for a bill of rights, for example, had been advanced in the public realm by figures like Lord Scarman since 1974. By 1997 when the incoming Labour government announced legislation to incorporate the European Convention on Human Rights, the radicalism of such a measure had long since faded. Prolonged advocacy had so acclimatised the public to the merits of the case that the principle of entrenched positive rights had become almost conventional. The dynamic of such a process of de-radicalisation had received additional stimulus from the 18-year tenure of the Conservative government. In a period of radical change sponsored by government in so many areas of social and economic life, the intransigent rejection of any consideration of explicit constitutional change by successive Conservative administrations only succeeded in raising the profile of constitutional reform as an increasingly and conspicuously belated response to the scale of change incurred elsewhere. In many respects, the prolonged and implacable opposition of a progressively discomforted government helped to compromise the arguments against constitutional innovation and to enhance the authority and leverage of those using the issue of the constitution as an instrument of opposition critique. The depth and length of the administration's unpopularity between 1992 and 1997 not only highlighted the constitutional anomalies of minority government, but culminated in the electorate's conjunction of a 'time for a change' of government with a 'time for a change' in the constitution.

Messages of the deepening need and widening demand for renovation echo insistently through the literature on constitutional reform. 'The democratic agenda may well have been inspired by Charter 88 and "chattering classes"', but according to one advocate of change it had now become the 'unifying theme among the population as a whole.'[96] Another leading supporter of change concurred: 'Aggregating the results from all the polls suggests that the weight of evidence reveals a widespread desire for constitutional reform on the part of the public.'[97] The reason for such a desire is claimed to be rooted in a general disillusionment with politics leading to an increasing alienation and a concomitant decline in the legitimacy afforded to the political system and its component institutions. It is alleged that a 'political and constitutional crisis is now widely recognised'[98] as the political system is 'disoriented, deficient and out of sorts with itself'.[99] As a consequence, 'British politics is in a very neurotic state: there is widespread acceptance that a critical systemic condition exists that needs remedying'.[100] Occasionally the claims made by and on behalf of constitutional reformers can appear to be extravagant and even triumphalist. It is necessary to recall that the pressure for constitutional reform has never achieved the status of a mass movement. Constitutional reform has never reached the highest ranking in the issues that are of most concern to the public. Even in the 1997 general election, when the theme of constitutional reform was particularly salient, it did not figure as a decisive issue in the determination of choice.[101] Nevertheless, the construction and promotion of the constitutional reform agenda represented a major achievement in the mobilisation of a programme for political change. The reform movement may not have been exclusively responsible for the currency and penetration of their proposals. Furthermore, the movement was far from being the sole factor in the creation of a political environment amenable to the arguments for change. The issue of constitutional reform fed just as readily from the context of a heightened interest in the condition of civil society as it contributed to an enhanced interest in the meaning and value of citizenship and participation.

Notwithstanding the co-existence of contributory causes and effects, the advocates of constitutional change were instrumental in capitalising upon diffuse social anxieties over government to gear public attention to the mechanics of the state. The agenda of constitutional reform gave direction and coherence to the dissident energy of the constitutional fuels. The reformers maximised the opportunities and techniques for presenting their arguments for change in arenas of public debate and mass dissemination. They reaffirmed the importance of establishing an issue on the agenda of media attention, in order for that issue to acquire a place of priority on the national political agenda. The reformers were highly adept at presenting their diagnoses, prognoses and plans for remedial treatment. They used the ideas of constitutional decline and constitutional renovation to make sense of contemporary political experience, to arouse a sense of awareness over the need for change, to provide objectives to be sought and to prompt action in their pursuit. The advocates for change understood and used the issue's populist edge to radiate a sense of unjustified exclusion from the decision-making process and to provoke a democratic backlash against the organisation of the political system. In effect, the reform agencies succeeded in using the language of rights to establish a series of compulsive links between contemporary social conditions and governing structures, and between the project of constitutional reform and the availability of generalised improvement. It was a considerable achievement in a system noted for its pragmatic and empiricist constitutional culture for such an abstract, systemic and idealised conception of constitutional potential to be given such extensive political consideration.

And yet in spite of the reformers' best efforts at generating a campaign of direct democracy against established structures to elicit a genuine constitutional dimension within British politics, the reform agenda was ultimately dependent upon the position of one of the most established and centralised intermediary structures in the system. The Labour party was the only organisation with both the capacity and the likely disposition to transform constitutional reform from a set of ideas to a material reality. The reform movement may have been able to assemble a publicly recognisable and approved agenda for constitutional change. The movement may have been able to explain why it should not have been in a position of dependency upon any political party – let alone a party which had never shown much attachment to the virtues of constitutional reform. But the campaign for constitutional reform could not succeed without first converting the Labour party to the advantage of reform ands second, ensuring that its endorsement was translated into commitment. The catalytic process by which this was achieved will be the subject of chapter 6, but first in order to understand the configuration of constitutional debate and, therefore, the nature of the political incentives and constraints peculiar to it, it is necessary to examine the positions and arguments of those opposed to constitutional reform.

Notes

1 The Labour party's measure to create an elected authority and mayor for London was never an established component of the constitutional reform agenda before 1997 when it was included in the Labour manifesto and subsequently became a priority issue for the Labour government following the general election. It had not featured in Labour's constitutional reform programme until after Tony Blair became leader in 1994 when he gave the idea his personal backing.

2 The Constitution Unit, *Prospects for Constitutional Reform in the UK*, http://www.ucl.ac.uk.

3 Rodney Brazier, *Constitutional Reform: Re-shaping the British Political System* (Oxford: Clarendon, 1991), p. 10.

4 See K. D. Ewing and C. A. Gearty, *Freedom Under Thatcher* (Oxford: Clarendon, 1990), *passim*.

5 Conrad Russell, 'Time for Parliament to Regain the Upper Hand', *Daily Telegraph*, 16 July 1991.

6 'Changing the Rules', *New Statesman*, 16 February 1996.

7 Tony Benn and Andrew Hood, *Common Sense: A New Constitution for Britain* (London: Hutchinson, 1993), p. 73.

8 David Marquand, *The Unprincipled Society: New Demands and Old Politics* (London: Fontana, 1988), pp. 175–206.

9 Brazier, *Constitutional Reform*, p. 7.

10 'Reclaiming Britain's Constitution', *The Economist*, 14 October 1995.

11 Ferdinand Mount, *The British Constitution Now: Recovery or Decline?* (London: Mandarin, 1993), pp. 29, 35.

12 *Ibid.*, p. 28.
13 *Ibid.*, pp. 35–6.
14 John Gray, BBC Radio 4, *The World This Weekend*, 30 October 1994.
15 *Ibid.*
16 Mount, *The British Constitution Now*, p. 36.
17 B. Guy Peters, *American Public Policy: Promise and Performance*, 2nd edn (Houndmills: Macmillan, 1986), p. 61.
18 Preamble to Charter 88's statement of demands for a new constitutional settlement.
19 *Ibid.*.
20 Benn and Hood, *Common Sense*, p. 25.
21 *We, The People ... Towards a Written Constitution, Federal Green Paper No. 13* (Hebden Bridge: Hebden Royd, 1990), p. 8.
22 *New Labour Because Wales Deserves Better, Labour Party Manifesto 1997*, p. 32.
23 Tony Wright, *Why Vote Labour?* (London: Penguin, 1997), pp. 87–8.
24 *Make the Difference: The Liberal Democrat Manifesto 1997*, p. 43.
25 Tony Blair, 'Power to the People Must Be Our Aim', *The Independent*, 7 February 1996.
26 Andrew Marr, *Ruling Britannia: The Failure and Future of British Democracy* (London: Penguin, 1996), p.349.
27 Frank Vibert, 'Constitutional Reform in the United Kingdom: An Incremental Agenda', *IEA Inquiry*, September 1990, pp. 3-4.
28 *Here We Stand: Liberal Democrat Policies for Modernising Britain's Democracy, Federal White Paper 6* (London: Liberal Democrat Publications, 1993), p. 4.
29 Will Hutton, *The State We're In* (London: Jonathan Cape, 1995), p. 326.
30 Will Hutton, *The State To Come* (London: *Oberserver*/Vintage, 1997), p. 39.
31 *Ibid.*, p. 39.
32 Jeff Rooker, 'Change of heart', *The Guardian*, 16 July 1996.
33 See also Frank Vibert, 'A Free Market Approach to Constitutional Change' in Anthony Barnett, Caroline Ellis and Paul Hirst (eds), *Debating the Constitution: New Perspectives on Constitutional Reform* (Cambridge: Polity Press, 1993), pp. 30–6.
34 Lord Hailsham, *The Dilemma of Democracy: Diagnosis and Prescription* (London: Collins, 1978).
35 'Time to Break the Spell', *The Times*, 15 August 1988.
36 Michael Foley, *The Silence of Constitutions: Gaps, 'Abeyances' and Political Temperament in the Maintenance of Government* (London: Routledge, 1989), p. 108.
37 There have been individual exceptions to this general rule. Manufacturing Science Finance (MSF) and the Fire Brigades Union are notable examples of unions that have taken up public positions in support of almost the entire reform agenda.
38 I am particularly indebted to Greg Power of Charter 88 for these insights.
39 The Nuffield Foundation, the Joseph Rowntree Charitable Trust, the Esmée Fairbairn Charitable Trust, the Joseph Rowntree Foundation, the Barrow Cadbury Trust and the Pilgrim Trust.
40 The Constitution Unit, *Delivering Constitutional Reform*, http://www.ucl.ac.uk.
41 The Constitutional Unit, *Blueprint For Reform*, http://www.ucl.ac.uk.

42 *Trusting in Change*, 2nd edn (York: The Joseph Rowntree Reform Trust 1998), p. 16.

43 *Ibid.*, pp. 20–2.

44 Quoted in *ibid.*, p. 25.

45 See Francesca Klug, Keir Starmer and Stuart Weir, *The Three Pillars of Liberty: Political Rights and Freedoms in the United Kingdom* (London: Routledge, 1996).

46 *Thematic Priorities ESRC*, 1995, Section I.

47 *Ibid.*, Section 4.

48 *Ibid.*, Section 4.

49 *Ibid.*, Section 4.

50 *Ibid.*, Section 4.

51 Leslie Scarman, *English Law – The New Dimension* (London: Stevens and Sons, 1974), p. 69.

52 *Ibid.*, p. 20. See also Lord Scarman, 'Human Rights – Can They Be Protected Without a Written Constitution?' (Swansea: University of Swansea, 1986); Lord Scarman, 'Why Britain Needs a Written Constitution' (London: Charter 88, 1992).

53 Anthony Barnett, *The Power and the Throne* (London: Vintage, 1994), p. 47.

54 'Why Britain Needs a Bill of Rights', *The Economist*, 21 October 1995.

55 The series of five programmes were broadcast over a period from 4 to 8 July 1989.

56 Carlton Television, *Monarchy: The Nation Decides*, 8 January 1997.

57 'The Observer Debate', *The Observer*, 24 July 1994.

58 Andrew Marr, *Ruling Britannia: The Failure and Future of British Democracy* (London: Penguin, 1996).

59 Peter Hennessy, *The Hidden Wiring: Unearthing the British Constitution* (London: Victor Gollanz, 1995).

60 Simon Jenkins, *Accountable to None: The Tory Nationalization of Britain* (London: Penguin, 1995).

61 Will Hutton, *The State We're In*.

62 Marr, *Ruling Britannia*, p. 350.

63 *Ibid.*, pp. 350–51.

64 Bernard Crick, 'The Sovereignty Question and the Scottish Question' in Norman Lewis, Cosmo Graham and Deryck Beyleveld (eds), *Happy and Glorious: The Constitution in Transition* (Milton Keynes: Open University Press, 1990), p. 58.

65 *The Best for Wales: Plaid Cymru's Programme for the New Millennium*, pp. 10–11.

66 Brian Groom, 'Flowers of Scotland', *New Statesman*, 1 August 1997.

67 Charter 88, An Idea Whose Time Has Come (London: Charter 88, 1993), p. 10.

68 Charter 88, The Parties Are Not The Problem (London: Charter 88, 1997).

69 Vernon Bogdanor, 'The Constitution' in Dennis Kavanagh and Anthony Seldon (eds), *The Thatcher Effect: A Decade of Change*, (Oxford: Oxford University Press, 1989), p. 139.

70 Taken from Charter 88's ten-point list of demands for a new constitutional settlement.

71 George Jones and Sonia Purnell, 'Public Watchdog to Curb Sleaze in Parlia-

ment', *Daily Telegraph*, 12 May 1995.

72 Quoted in *ibid*.

73 Quoted in *ibid*.

74 Anthony Lester, James Cornford, Ronald Dworking, William Goodhart, Patricia Hewitt, Jeffrey Jowell, Nicola Lacey, Keith Patchett and Sarah Spencer, *A Bill of Rights, Constitution Paper No. 1* (London: IPPR, 1990).

75 *Ibid.*, p. 23.

76 Liberty, *A People's Charter: Liberty's Bill of Rights* (London: Civil Liberties Trust, 1991).

77 Benn and Hood, *Common Sense*, Foreword.

78 *Ibid.*, p. 92.

79 *We the People ... Towards a Written Constitution* (Hebden Bridge: Hebden Royd, 1990).

80 *The Constitution of the United Kingdom* (London: IPPR, 1991).

81 James Cornford, 'On Writing a Constitution', *Parliamentary Affairs* , vol. 44, no. 4 (October 1991), pp. 558–71; Geoffrey Robertson, 'What Kind of Constitution?' (London: Charter 88, 1991).

82 Charter 88, *An Idea Whose Time Has Come*, p. 5.

83 *The State of the Nation Report*, MORI/Joseph Rowntree Trust, 1991 (in two parts); *The State of the Nation Report*, MORI/Joseph Rowntree Trust 1995.

84 Trevor Smith, 'Citizenship and the British Constitution', *Parliamentary Affairs*, vol. 44, no. 4 (October 1991), p. 432.

85 *Ibid.*, p. 432.

86 Patrick Dunleavy and Stuart Weir, 'Ignore the People at Your Peril', *The Independent*, 25 April 1991.

87 Patrick Dunleavy and Stuart Weir, 'They Want to See It in Writing', *The Independent*, 2 October 1991.

88 Quoted in 'Poll Shows Support for Reform', *Constitutional Reform: The Quarterly Review*, vol. 6, no. 2 (Summer 1991), p. 1.

89 Robert Worcester, 'The People and the System', *Political Quarterly*, vol. 66, no. 4 (October–December 1995), p. 337.

90 See Worcester, 'The People and the System', pp. 335–41; Patrick Dunleavy and Stuart Weir with Gita Subrahmanyam, 'Public Response and Constitutional Significance', *Parliamentary Affairs*, vol. 48, no. 4 (October 1995), pp. 602–16.

91 Dunleavy, Weir with Subrahmanyam, 'Public Response and Constitutional Significance', p. 614.

92 Liberty, *Broken Covenants: Violations of International Law in Northern Ireland* (London: Civil Liberties Trust, 1992).

93 See *Index on Censorship*, vol. 24, no. 2 (March-April 1995), pp. 22–73.

94 Klug, Starmer and Weir, *The Three Pillars of Liberty*, p. 47.

95 See R. Bruce McColm, 'The Comparative Survey of Freedom: 1991', *Freedom Review*, vol. 22, no. 1 (1991) p. 23. See also G. Sorensen, *Democracy and Democratization* (Boulder, Colo.: Westview, 1993), ch. 1. See also World Survey of Constitutional Rights, *New Statesman and Society*, Special Supplement, 30 April 1994; Stuart Weir, 'Democracy in the Balance', (University of Essex: The Democratic Audit, Human Rights Centre, 1996).

96 Stuart Weir and P. Dunleavy, 'The Nation in a State', *The Independent*, 23 September 1996.

97 Trevor Smith, 'Citizenship and the British Constitution', p. 439.

98 Trevor Smith, 'Citizenship, Community and Constitutionalism', *Parliamentary Affairs*, vol. 49, no. 2 (April 1996), p. 272.

99 Trevor Smith, 'Post-modern Politics and the Case for Constitutional Renewal', *Political Quarterly*, vol. 65, no. 2 (April–June 1994), p. 137.

100 *Ibid.*, p. 137.

101 See chapter 6.

5

Defending the constitution

The content and appeal of the British constitution has traditionally been suffused in ambiguity. As a summation of national and political experience, it has customarily embodied its own justification and has benefited from the circularity of its attributed merits. The standard impulse is to declare that it is what it is and it is right that it should be so. While other constitutions specifiy their substantive principles and underlying ethos, the British constitution has always been renowned for its emphasis upon due process, pragmatism and responsiveness. Just as its rationale is primarily functional in character, so the social allegiance to it is based upon what the constitution signifies and what it avoids rather than what it actually consists of in terms of a precise form. As a consequence, the viability of such a constitution has been grounded in its capacity both to express and to evoke a consensus of basic social values, an understanding of good political practice and a sense of trust between the rulers and the ruled. Given the intuitive and tacit properties of a system of government that invites questions over its very existence as a constitutional entity, direct and sustained criticism of the British constitution is unusual. Defenders of the constitution are not normally placed in a position of having to defend it. This is not only because its mercurial properties make it difficult to provide a definitive rationale, but because its chief virtue of experiental expression renders a substantive defence self-evident and, therefore, superfluous.

In spite of the unaccustomed position of having to defend the current constitutional arrangements and in spite of the instinctive prejudice against such an analytical exercise in the normally pragmatic medium of British politics, opponents of constitutional reform have had to assemble a defensible set of defensive positions. Even if the main strategy is one of exploiting the many opportunities for maintaining the status quo – albeit in a constitution celebrated for its accommodating fluidity – arguments in support of the constitution are required to provide a counterweight to the reformers' indictments of the current system. The initial structural advantages in such an encounter lay predominantly with the defenders of the current structure who know the strategic and tactical problems of securing reform, and the costs in political capital that reform would incur for its supporters. But once the deterrent value of these difficulties has been undermined and the pressure for constitutional change reaches a point where reform becomes both plausible and possible, constitutional loyalists can no longer afford merely to depend upon the normal dynamics of deferment. They have to accept the discomforture of articulating a defence in an increasingly public exchange over the operation and value of the British constitution. A range of arguments have been deployed but it is clear that they are all variations upon a limited set of themes.

Positive defence

The first line of defence in the armoury against constitutional reform is the reaffirmation of the benefits and virtues of the British constitution as it stands. Far from conceding anything in the indictment of the constitution's principles and performance, the emphasis in such a response is one of positive and unqualified support for its past achievements and present advantages. It underlines the merits of the common law tradition in preserving individual liberties; the aggregated equilibrium of institutional and political checks; the pivotal significance of conventions, protocols and traditions of political conduct in the control of executive power; the presence of strong intermediary organisations affording an ameliorative and communicative medium between the citizen and the state; the fusion of personal freedoms with a central and protective government operating under the rule of law; and the advantages of an unwritten constitution in combining the flexibility of political response with a finality of authority. In answer to the reformist calls for change, the constitution's defenders draw attention to Britain's tradition of rolling constitutional change which reacts to the need for adjustment and assimilates the consequences of even radical adaptation. Unlike the United States which is alleged to be encumbered by the textual stasis of a written constitution and by the masochism of institutional gridlock, the British constitution is applauded for its proven capacity for fluent and even far-reaching change without having to squander resources in protracted disputes over formal constitutional amendments or tests of constitutionality. If the British constitution is a device for structural immobility, then it could be argued that this property would be most evident during periods of Conservative rule when, on the balance of probabilities, the government's interest in social continuity would correspond with the constitution's purported predisposition towards the established configuration of government. But 'constitutional drag' has not been noticeably more prominent during Conservative administrations. On the contrary, during the

Thatcher-Major era, the Conservatives acquired a reputation for constitutional innovation rather than constitutional preservation. As a consequence, it can be concluded that there is no *prima facie* case for reform on the basis of the constitution being resistant to change.

Change is intrinsic to the very ethos of the British constitution and, therefore, to claim that it needs to be consciousy transformed in order to improve its adaptability is to misunderstand its main strength. Opponents of constitutional reform point to the profusion of radical measures passed during the period of Conservative hegemony as proof positive of the constitution's capacity both to produce and to experience change through the normal political processes. Whether it is trade union reform, the restructuring of local government, the introduction of executive agencies, the transformation of the civil service, the growth of quangos, the onset of Citizen's Charters, the delegation of powers to school governors and hospital trusts, or the adjustment to Britain's membership of the European Union, they all give ample weight to the proposition that the 'constitution is not standing still'.[1] It can be contended that transformations on the scale of the 'hollowing out of the state' and the consequences of the Single European Act (1986) and the Maastrict Treaty (1992) 'amount to a rolling constitutional revolution'.[2] Under John Major, Conservative ministers even began to annex the language of constitutional reform in order to underline the responsiveness of an unreformed constitution. Freedom of information was equated with the provision of previously undisclosed or uncollected information (e.g. league tables). Similarly, references to open government were used to support a policy like the open enrolment of pupils in schools. In his defence of traditional constitutional arrangements, John Patten alludes to mutability as a decisive criterion of constitutional viability and one that is all too often overlooked by the constitution's critics:

> The leave-our-constitution-alone majority are normally patronised and characterised by wrtitten constitution-mongers as 'unthinking', 'complacent', or 'uninteresting'. We are none of these things. Sensible people view the constitution as akin to a well-built house of character. They view demands that it be torn down and replaced by some modern, pretentious edifice, the design for which exists only on paper, as unappealing. However, to defend our constitutional structure is not the same as saying 'leave well alone'. A solid structure only remains such by continual attention to its mortar. Even the best of houses will need occasional repair, and perhaps even structural modification.[3]

To those disposed towards reform, these types of contention illustrate precisely what is wrong with British constitution. First, it reveals an indiscriminate view of change as a form of constitutional efficiency in which reforms to enhance consumer choice in education or to increase competition in healthcare are indistinguishable from changes that would circumscribe the executive, increase its accountability and prevent it from possessing the coercive capacity of securing sweeping constitutional changes under the emollient guise of de-centralisation. Second, statements like those given above underline the extent to which the conventional strengths of the British constitution are defined in functional terms of policy ends and outputs, rather than being oriented towards the means or principles of constitutional action. The normal defence against such objections is to dismiss them as fine distinctions and to concentrate instead upon the *de facto* expansion of individual choice and government customer services that give greater material substance to liberty than any abstract schemes to immobilise the government that would only result in a poor end product, or no end product at all. According to this perspective, the absence of any distinction between the passage of ordinary statute law and a change in constitutional law is an advantage that allows the constitution to maintain its authority by responding decisively to social and economic change. In doing so, it prevents the growth of the kind of frustration that ensues when political demands remain unattended to the point where they constitute a threat to social stability.

Another strand to this positive defence of the British constitution is the assertion that change is balanced by continuity, complexity and security. While the British constitution may facilitate change more adeptly than other systems of constitutional government, its defenders offer a reminder that not everything is change; not all changes are cases of purposive change; and not all constitutional activity can be equated with the actions or self-interest of government. Notwithstanding the recent charges of centralisation, the British system is claimed to have remained highly pluralist in character, with a profusion of political centres capable of exerting countervailing power upon the government. Despite the most strenuous efforts by Conservative governments from 1979 to 1997 to confront and undermine the position and status of a variety of established interests, the outcome was by no means always in the government's favour. On the contrary, entrenched interests have for the most part remained in place. It is conceded that the trade unions were humbled but they were already a declining force in terms of economic strength and public support. Other organisations, it is contended, demonstrated significant powers of resistance even in the face of a determined 'conviction' government. When this level of pluralist defence is combined with the proliferation of new interest groups in an increasingly fluid political context of multiple access points to government, multiple media outlets and multicultural diversity, the net effect is a state of enhanced pluralism in which power is more dispersed than it was prior to the Thatcher era. The topography of the political landscape may have changed but the underlying dynamics of dispersal are claimed to have remained the same.

The presence of deep continuities of politics within a liberal democratic system is a theme which is pursued assiduously by Philip Norton in his erudite defence of the British constitution. He objects to the reformist theme of a progressive and oppressive trend towards a centralisation of power and thus to a failure of constitutional government. In addition to the enhanced pluralisation of British society, Norton alludes to the way that government is being increasingly squeezed both from the top and the bottom. Discretionary power at the centre is constrained by the legislative and judicial processes of the European Union and the conditioning forces of the European Court of Human Rights at Strasbourg. At the same time, the gravitational force of the centre is being weakened with the impact of new public management techniques, privatisation transfers of state assets, select committee inquiries, single issue lobbying, party indiscipline, entrenched policy communities and the judicial review of ministerial decisions. 'The policy-making process, then, is a far more complex and fragmented than a simple power-concentration model would suggest'.[4] Norton goes on to conclude with approval that: 'In so far as there is a predominant new direction in British politics it is this fragmenting of power'.[5] Such an avowal of existing de-centralisation flies in the face of the controlling assumption of the reform movement. On occasions, it also sits uneasily with conservative assertions of the continuing 'need to reduce the stranglehold of centralisation'.[6] Norton, however, is only too well aware of the significance of decentralisation for the defence of the constitution and is not prepared to be distracted from the main theme by surface features and political rhetoric. He pursues the logic of his assertion to its conclusion:

> To identify the persistence of pluralism in British politics and a leakage of policy-making power from the apex of government is, by itself, not sufficient to destroy the arguments advanced by proponents of Charter '88. Nor is it to suggest that there are not problems with the form and activity of government, especially particular agencies of government. It is, however, sufficient to undermine the central explanatory premiss on which the Charter is based. On the basic charge levelled against government, there is insufficient evidence to convict.[7]

The emphasis laid by constitutional loyalists upon power dispersal and pluralism within the matrix of the British constitution is not to say that political mistakes and incidents of miscalculation at the centre do not occur. The policy decision to introduce the poll tax over numerous objections both inside and outside government was a case where the government acknowledged it made a serious error of political judgement. But to supporters of the constitution such a case is atypical. It is not seen as being symptomatic of a general pattern of policy. The measure became notorious partly because it was so exceptional in acquiring legal status with so little evidence of public acceptability. More to the point, the case history of the poll tax does not constitute evidence that the system had failed to work properly, and that as a direct consequence the British constitution requires reform. It cannot be proved that any other constitutional arrangement would have prevented such a policy decision being made and subsequently implemented. Just as no constitutional structure can preclude acts of political misjudgement, so the incidence of political mistakes is a poor pretext for constitutional reform. Moreover, the poll tax episode was brought to an end by an array of forces mobilised against it. In a dispute reminiscent of the debate over whether the Vietnam War amounted to an indictment or a vindication of the United States constitution, the poll tax policy generated its own corrective of abandonment. The US constitution had not prevented the gradual enagement of American forces in Vietnam but the war policy did activate a series of constitutional counter measures which ultimately reversed America's involvement in the war and basically reaffirmed the established machinery of checks and balances. The poll tax policy can be construed in the same light. Constitutions do not suspend politics. The British constitution allowed the poll tax to be established in law. Equally, it facilitated its rapid abandonment. Such a life cycle can be interpreted as less of an indictment of the constitution and more of a sign of its effectiveness in reflecting social pressures and in allowing political resistance to be legitimately and effectively invoked.

Just as constitutions cannot prevent the incursion of political conflict, so pluralism cannot preclude errors in political decision-making. Initial mistakes and painful reversals can even be seen as the hallmarks of a vibrant system of constitutional government. A positive defence of the British constitution acknowledges its idiosyncrasies and anomalies. It concedes that it is not a coherent and codified whole where power relationships are precisely discernible and liberties are permanently entrenched. The constitution exemplifies the British antipathy to abstract theorising about the origin and meaning of the state. To its defenders, the chief virtue of the constitution lies precisely in the way that it is so dissimilar to other constitutional systems. It is characterised by the themes of adaptability, improvisation and utility. It values temperament over content, trust over suspicion, and policy ends over procedural disputes. It may operate in a highly politicised environment, but it can do so only by remaining as de-politicised as possible. The constitution's defenders regard this outlook as being thoroughly in the grain of British political culture and they draw attention to the traditional disinclination in Britain to translate political drives into constitutional argument. It is even claimed that British politics can be characterised by this missing constitutional dimension. Political discussion certainly reveals a basic discomfort with the language of constitutional dispute and an 'unfamiliarity with discussing the constitution in broad conceptual terms'.[8]

According to Gillian Peele, the way in which the British debate issues which elsewhere would be regarded as thorough-going constitutional issues 'displays the depth of the United Kingdom's attachment to *ad hoc* solutions and its lack of interest in general constitutional issues ... . Many examples could be given to bear out the assertion that the British are reluctant to treat what are manifestly constitutional issues in terms of general principles'.[9] The net effect, in the words of Ferdinand Mount, has been a social backwardness in constitutional affairs. 'The general standard of Constitutional argument in this country would barely scrape a GCSE pass in a poor year. We most of us rub along on a few inherited patches of wisdom. The greater part of the estate has been set aside; the traditional machinery lies, still visible to the gaze, but neglected and rusting in a corner of the field ... . It requires only a brief acquaintance with the vigour, the ferocity, the scholarship of debate on constitutional questions in the U.S. to come to the conclusion that we, to put it kindly, are a bit out of practice.'[10] The sense in which reform proposals have affronted the conventional British impulse to withdraw from constitutional matters is reflected in the defensive tone and stunning banality of the declaration by John Redwood: 'It is fashionable to decry Britain and the British constitution. Indeed, the public sport of knocking it all has led to a new consensus: that Britain does not have a written constitution.'[11]

It can be contended that far from being deficient or retarded in its development, the British constitution is in fact highly advanced in its understanding and acknowledgement not only of the restrictions upon legal rules to resolve political issues, but of the inherent limitations of any constitutional settlement. All constitutions are messy and it is a serious mistake to believe that they can ever successfully be transformed into coherently ordered designs. Constitutional loyalists do not regard such an outlook as submiting to tragic fatalism so much as recognising the opportunity of realistic optimism. It is the very existence of the British constitution's peculiar gaps and disjunctions which maximise the need for operational consensus and co-operative sensitivity. It is Britain's idiosyncratic history and sophisticated traditions in constitutional management which have allowed social, economic and national differences to be continually accommodated within a single system of political resolution.[12] The British constitution is different to the point of being atypical and even exceptional, but according to such a perspective constitutional difference is not in itself a cause for concern:

> We have had a different history from the countries of the Continent and that does give our constitution a different shape from theirs. But that is not evidence that it is wrong. Different countries with their own traditions can quite reasonably have different constitutional arrangements. That the German constitution works well for them is no reason for us to have it here.[13]

According to this particular defence, far from being wrong, the British constitution is not only utterly right for Britain but significantly better than other types of system, and preferable by far than any artificial reformist construction that would necessarily subvert Britain's exceptionalism in constitutional government.

Concessionary defence

This type of defence recognises the validity of constitutional evolution not just as an abstract characterisation but as a practical condition of a functioning government. The onus of proof may be laid upon those instigating change but as long as they can satisfy the criterion of necessary and specific change, then constitutional support and incremental revision can be reconciled. Those willing to concede the legitimacy of change to a basically sound constitution know that such change does not just occur spontaneously. Like evolutionary progression, it has to be sifted and selected from an environment replete with ideas and pressures for indiscriminate change. It has to be integrated on the basis of sustained equilibrium and constitutional stability. It is those who recognise both the value of adaptive continuity and the problematic properties which can accompany change who in effect provide the guardianship role of intermediaries between 'no change' and 'all change'.

Concessionary defences assume a variety of forms. For example, concessions to change may represent a genuine belief in the need for marginal alterations to fine-tune the constitutional machine. In such a case, the principles of change may be persuasive but caution is recommended, in order to assess the full ramifications of any new arrangement in such an inter-connected entity as a constitution. The basic position is one of accepting change on the merits of the arguments presented and the needs expressed but at the same time treating reform proposals with circumspection because of the threat of unforeseen and unimaginable consequences. For example, in his book *The Voice of the People: A Constitution for Tomorrow*,[14] Lord Alexander supports the principle of constitutional reform across a range of areas. But he also uses the issue of reform to give warnings over the problems of institutional change (e.g. the House of Lords) and the repercussions of altering the territorial structure of United Kingdom. The mix of ostensible radicalism and conservative caution is encapsulated in Alexander's rejection of a written constitution. Instead, he proposes the creation of a Constitutional Commission, drawn mainly from the House of Commons and the House of Lords, to determine the sense of the British constitution in relation to proposed or actual government actions. The logic of reform is conceded, therefore, but not to the extent of accepting the logical culmination of a reform agenda.

Another variant of concessionary defence is based upon an acknowledgement of the need for change, and even an acceptance of the general principles of a particular reform proposal, but questions how such change is to be achieved and by whom. It asks searching questions over the techniques of change, over the possible contradictions within change, over the timing of reform proposals and over the extent to which a reform project can actually be realised in practice. A bill of rights, for example, commands widespread support in principle but one of the best defences against such a measure is to highlight the problems inherent in defining and implementing such rights. A key objection to such a venture and one that raises profound doubts in a system so strongly conditioned by parliamentary sovereignty lies in the projected enhancement of the judiciary's role in subjecting the government to constitutional review. In his 1986 Reith Lectures, Lord McCluskey argued against the enactment of a bill of rights precisely on these grounds. He acknowledged the perception that individual rights and constitutional machinery were theoretically vulnerable to a sovereign parliament and that this fuelled demands for a new constitutional settlement and a bill of rights that would be resistant to incursions by temporary majorities. But Lord McCluskey warned that a bill of rights would necessarily lead to judges making policy decisions and political choices. He questioned their ability to perform such a role:

> Why it should be supposed that elderly lawyers with cautious and backward-looking habits of thought are qualified to overrule the judgements of democratically elected legislators as to what is, in the circumstances of the time, justitified, I do not profess to understand ... . If I am right in believing that such a change would make our judges perform tasks for which they are not equipped, and risk drawing them into the political arena in a way alien to the best traditions of the judiciary, we must before embarking upon it be satisfied that the change is reasonably necessary.[15]

In this type of concessionary defence, it is not always possible to discern whether the objections to the corollaries of a reform are fuelled by a genuine concern over the wider implications of change or by a surreptious antipathy towards the principle of the reform itself. But notwithstanding the question of motivation, the effect of such a guarded responsiveness is to keep the door open for the possibility of the kind of change that can be accommodated within the limits of practicaility, tradition and tolerance.

A concessionary defence, however, may be based upon quite different factors. The intermediary position can be occupied by those who recognise the weight of support for change and who duly respond to its political force by offering reformers the immediate gratification of marginal change. Such a concession may be couched as a decisive readjustment but it is more comon for it be portrayed as an initial response, thereby holding out the prospect of further concessions in an implied process of successive change. Such concessions are normally employed as techniques in political management.

They are designed to assuage reformers and to diminish the pressure for more radical measures. In the field of freedom of information, for example, the pressures for open government have led to periodic attempts in White-hall to make government information more freely available. The Croham Directive in 1977 was an initiative to establish practices within the civil ser-vice which would lead to the greater disclosure of information to the public. In Lord Croham's instructions, there was a 'reminder of pressures to bring in measures on the lines of the United States's Freedom of Information Act and a warning that "our prospects of being able to avoid such an expensive development here" might depend on results'[16] – i.e. 'a small change has to be made to avoid something worse'.[17] The Callaghan government at the time was being pressured into relaxing the restrictions of the Official Secrets Act and into honouring a Labour manifesto commitment to place the burden of witholding information upon the public authorities. The Croham Directive allowed Callaghan to drop such a commitment and to replace it with a gen-eralised undertaking to place more background and analytical material in the public domain. The overall impact of the Directive was minimal and demonstrated that 'voluntary, discretionary systems of public access to offi-cial information are variable in their implementation, vulnerable to policy changes or reductions in public expenditure, and unenforceable, having no independent systems of monitoring, review, complaint, or appeal'.[18] In April 1994, John Major also sought to 'deflect demands for a Freedom of Infor-mation Act'[19] by introducing a Code of Practice on Access to Government Information to be supervised by the Parliamentary Ombudsman. It gave individuals and organisations the right to *request* information from any gov-ernment department. Once again, it was a voluntary code that reserved the right of officials to refuse disclosure on public interest grounds. Even though it represented a genuine attempt to reduce the number of unnecessary statu-tory and administrative restrictions on the disclosure of information, the code remained flawed. It did not permit access to original documents and, given that in its first year of operation only £51,000 was spent on publicis-ing it, the code remained largely unknown and, therefore, unused.

Such pre-emptive accommodations are not always successful in displac-ing the pressure for further reform. But even though the reformers may win further arguments and extract additional concessions, the rationale of the defence remains the same. Arguments against reform may be lost but that does not mean the strategy of graduated response by concessionary defence is misplaced. On the contrary, the disposition against change ensures that the case for reform is rehearsed and re-examined at every stage. In many respects, concessionary defence is simply good politics in that it allows for a rearguard strategy which reduces the antagonism that would otherwise be generated by a stonewalling refusal even to consider the merits of the other side. Intransigence in such a sphere can lead to a waste of political resources

as the rejection of any alternatives has the countervailing effect of polaris-
ing opinion and of radicalising the reform programme. Relying solely upon
tradition, scepticism and reaction can make drastic reform more rather than
less likely. As a consequence, political prudence can coincide with constitutional prudence in that the optimal usage of political capital can result in
maximising the potential for change admissible within the limits of an
empirical constitutional tradition based upon the value of continuity and
assimilation. In terms of strategy and spirit, concessionary defences of the
constitution are closely associated with a conservative cast of mind. Given
the nature of constitutions in general and that of the British constitution in
particular, there would seem to be a logical connection between constitutional arrangements and the need to ensure their permanence and continuity. This outlook encompasses the Burkean principle of adaptation as a
necessary agent of institutional integrity. In terms of the contemporary conservative campaign against the state, it is even possible for a number of the
more radical items on Charter 88's agenda to receive conservative endorsement. An editorial in *The Times* prior to the 1997 general election bears witness to the connections of concessionary defence with conservative
interests:

> Reform would augment, not offend, the Conservative Party's principles. Fear of
> the intrusive state, and thus attraction to a Bill of Rights and Freedom of
> Information Act, should come naturally to those who profess a preference for
> smaller government. Similarly, suspicion of centralisation, and thus backing for
> stronger checks and balances, should rest comfortably with the Tories.'[20]

This is not to say that constitutional reform is necessarily analogous to
conservatism. Far from it. Those conservatives who either emphasise the
organic nature of the state or give priority to direct political action in the
movement to diminish the regulatory state remain suspicious of constitutional reform for contradictory reasons. The former fear the effects of change
upon the fragitlity of historical structures and authority, while the latter are
concerned that constitutional reform may be a Trojan horse concealing the
reimposition of the corporate state. But notwithstanding these reservations
and exceptions, conservatives have traditionally acknowledged the need for
graduated change and, consequently, have often adopted the strategy of
concessionary defence. The Conservative 2000 Foundation, for example,
recently issued a 20-point plan for constitutional reform based upon an
anlaysis that placed 'current constitutional issues into the context of constitutional history, and the Conservative's understanding of tradition, evolution and practical effectiveness'.[21] By openly relying upon custom and 'the
verdict of experience.',[22] the authors are able to claim that their agenda of
'incremental reform' will satisfy the conservative objective of providing a
means 'to restore the balance of our constitutional settlement'.[23]

In the debates over the British constitution, concessionary conservatives often find themselves in the company of left-of-centre reformers who have reservations over the scale of reform being advanced by some of their more iconoclastic colleagues. It is true that these two bedfellows approach the constitution from different perspectives. While the reformist role remains proactive and critical, the conservative outlook remains reactive and passive providing the response to the stimulus of proposed change. In the same way that concessionary conservatives qualify their opposition to change by recognising the ultimate need for some element of adaptation, so constitutional sceptics qualify their reformism to take account of the practical value of traditional structures and processes.

This fusion of left-of-centre constitutional critique with the need for reformist restraint is exemplified by a figure like Peter Hennessy. He is highly adept at exposing the concealed anomalies and anachronisms at the centre of the British state, but his ascerbic diagnoses do not act as the prelude for a sweeping agenda of remedial measures. On the contrary, it is his insight into the functioning of the British system which leads him to conclude that successful constitutional change will not be achieved by large-scale legislative excursions. It requires instead a 'philosophy of reforming-with-the-grain'.[24] He concedes that his proposals for reform are 'relatively modest but practically achievable'[25] and refers with approval to the working methods of the Nolan Committee: 'The first Nolan Report is written in exactly this kind of modern-within-the-ancient reformist spirit and promises to be all the more effective for that. For the proliferation of codes represents constitution-making by stealth disguised in a typically British fashion as something practical and informal and organically inseparable from the compost of tradition'.[26] Tradition is not merely a tiresome constraint to Hennessy, it possesses a positive value as the context within which constitutions necessarily reside. Inside, there is room for inventive manouevre by which practical yet significant reforms can be secured to great material effect. Hennessy's respect for tradition amounts to a concessionary defence of the constitution because by acknowledging the limits of reform he is conceding that the constitution is worth preserving. Hennessy's fellow constitutional sceptics take note of the dualism between his reformism and his conservatism. They observe that his 'prescriptions are not on the same scale as the ailments he diagnoses' and that his 'nudging and fudging forward [amounts to] a Burkean solution to a Burkean predicament'.[27] Walter Ellis asks 'is it enough?'.[28] David Cannadine replies that 'it is probably inadequate; it may, alas, turn out to be the best that can realistically be hoped for'.[29] Peter Hennessy's view would be that anything more should neither be envisaged nor hoped for in the interests of constitutional integrity.

Hennessy is critical of the constitution but his is an indictment limited by a sense of technical realism. Such conditional criticism may in this context be termed concessionary *offence*. Instances of concessionary offence are not, however, limited to Hennessy's concern for the necessary constraints of tradition. Other constitutional critics have sought to limit the scope of reform advocacy on the grounds that it is simply bad politics. By giving such emphasis to civil rights and the restraint of government, it is said to distract attention away from the more substantive agendas of social and economic reform. Ben Pimlott, for example, is sympathetic towards Charter 88 and has been instrumental in setting up journals like *Samizdat* and *Renewal* which have made important contributions to the propagation of the constitutional reform message. Nevertheless, he believes that 'even if a progressive government did set about clipping its own wings in the way that Charter 88 recommends, the lives of most citizens would barely be affected'.[30] As a consequence, 'a new Labour government should busy itself with more important things than constitutional reform'.[31] It is not simply that constitutional reform is an expensive project requiring prodigous amounts of political capital to secure large-scale change in a system resistant to such transformations. It is that it needlessly places at risk other aims and objectives which will make a more material difference to the constituencies of a left-of-centre government.

Concessionary offence can also be rooted in political and ethical objections to the projected repercussions of constitutional reform. Far from leading to an unqualified improvement in the preservation of liberties and in the standard of governance, constitutional reform can be seen as carrying an excessive risk of unintended consequences. A bill of rights, for example, is often cited as a means of striking a new balance between individual rights and state interests that will permit freedoms to be defined, codified and entrenched, thereby allowing individuals to challenge the constitutionality of government actions. But such an expansion in the capacity of individuals to seek a legal redress of grievances comes at too high a price for advocates of constitutional reform like K. D. Ewing and Conor Gearty. Despite co-authoring the best-known indictment of the state of civil liberties under Margaret Thatcher, Ewing and Gearty stop short of endorsing the bill of rights solution because of (i) the institutional difficulties of grounding such a measure within a system of parliamentary sovereignty, (ii) the technical difficulties of defining rights while incorporating discretionary exceptions, and (iii) the demarcation difficulties of allowing the judiciary a greatly enhanced role in a democratic polity. To Ewing and Gearty, a bill of rights would not be the holy grail of constitutional reform so much as a poisoned chalice.

> Judges ... [would be] given the power to disrupt decisions and adjustments made by the process of persuasion, compromise, and agreement in the political

arena. Difficult ethical, social, and political questions would be subject to judicial preference rather than the shared or compromised community morality. While politicians must account for these decisions, the judges would exercise this power without any such constraint. Personal policy preferences can thus be imposed on a nation in the manner of a feudal king.[32]

Ewing and Gearty strongly approve of constitutional reform that will 'redress the balance of political power'[33] (e.g. electoral reform, devolution, an elected second chamber, freedom of information) but they retain the left's traditional suspicion of the judiciary and are wary of any change – however radical in theory – whose practical outcome increases the role of judges in the political process. At a different level of objection, Gearty also alludes to an ethical problem with a bill of rights. He fears that in attaining such a reform, the pressure for other constitutional reforms will immediately dissipate because those 'who have been educated to feel anxious about the constitution will feel: "that's it – we've got human rights"'.[34] But a bill of rights requires an active level of citizenship to develop what needs to be a continuing process of popular engagement in the interpretation and apparatus of rights. Gearty fears that we would be 'guilty of a kind constitutional immaturity'[35] in allowing a bill of rights to become such a panacea of reform that our citizenship responsibilities could effectively be subcontracted to the courts. A bill of rights should not be treated as a substitute for the development of a democratic ethos. On the contrary, given that 'there never has been a democratic cuture in England',[36] such a measure could actively discourage the formation of such an ethos. To Gearty, the emphasis in constitutional reform should be upon substantive changes to energise democracy and active citizenship, rather than to depend upon the false prospectus of a bill of rights.

Other forms of concessionary offence on the left are based less on the scale or projected effects of constitutional change and more on the nature and motives of reform. For example, it is possible to acknowledge the legitimacy of a movement like Charter 88 and its objective in raising public awareness of the 'gulf between the complacent rhetoric ... and our constitutional poverty as citizens'.[37] But in giving emphasis to the traditional rights of liberal philosophy, constitutional reformers can be seen as placing at risk more substantive reforms pertaining to the distribution of power in society. Stephen Sedley poses the key question on the part of those who think that Charter 88 is 'trapped in a time-warp'.[38] 'How does Charter 88 ... envisage the actual protection and enforcement of substantive human rights in the face of the social distribution of power?'[39] By concentrating upon the state and the dissipation and limitation of its power, constitutional reformers are thought not only to ignore the protective benefits offered by the government, but to preclude any future development towards the establishment of social and economic rights that will turn on confronting deeper questions related to the location and deployment of power within the infrastructure of society. This type of concessionary offence concedes that there is a problem with a 'left conservatism which tends to cling to traditional oppositional forms'.[40] At the same time it is wary of excessive constitutional reform because of the risk of replacing one form of myopia with another, leading to the disintegration of the corporate capacity and collective identity of the positive state. By casting the state in the role of the enemy of personal freedoms, it draws attention away from the question of 'whether it is simply the state that the individual needs to be protected against'.[41] Such guarded responses generate elements of convergence with the constitutional conformity of High Toryism, which sees Charter 88 as a force of radical digression featuring 'the omnicompetent individual, divorced from duties, timelessly enjoying rights in a state which is to be devolved into a thousand voluntary communities'.[42]

Strategies of concessionary defence, or concessionary offence, tend to be adopted by those temperamentally in favour of reform but who feel that there are limits upon the feasibility and costs of large-scale constitutional reform by design. The net effect is an amalgam of arguments and ideas that revolves around the joint theme of the necessity of change and the necessity to restrain the process of change. It opens up the possibility of constitutional reform at the same time that it underlines an intuitive conservatism over the nature of constitutionalism in the British context and in particular over the utility value of a 'political constitution' – i.e. one that accommodates a political process but which, paradoxically, remains in the main outside the area of political disputation and which generates a low level of constitutional consciousness.

Negative defence

The third variant of constitutional defence concentrates more on playing the man rather than the ball. It seeks to counter the argument for constitutional reform by discrediting the capacities, motives and projected outcomes of the reform movement. Instead of looking to the merits of the constitution itself to form the basis of a defence, the negative counter-attack depends for its effect upon prompting a critical reconsideration of the reform programme by giving a negative colouration to the entire project of purposive constitutional change. According to this perspective, it is necessary to confront the opposition head on and to stop the reform movement in its tracks before it acquires a momentum that will quickly derail the entire constitution. The tone is alarmist and the strategy is confrontational because, to those who adopt this stance, the constitution is already in jeopardy and it is only through intransigent opposition that the mischief-making of the reformers will be exposed and, thereby, checked.

Changes to the constitution are acceptable when they are incidental to the normal processes of political accommodation and when they can be construed as the necessary concomitant of other transformations in the flow of societal development. But when large-scale changes are propelled by a process external to the customary agencies of incremental alteration, then it is seen as imperative on the part of the constitution's most resolute defenders to draw attention to the effrontery of reformers in seeking to substitute the product of evolutionary progression with a comprehensive prospectus of change guided only by political will and abstract reasoning. Such a focus upon both the constitution itself and the need to reconstruct it is regarded in the British context as tantamount to unconstitutional behaviour. In this light, constitutional change is not the same as changing the constitution. The former is largely unproblematic not just because the use of the adjective infers an integral legitimacy but because the phrase carries the implication of a spontaneous, discrete and self-contained derivative of the established framework of governance. The latter is suspect because it lays the emphasis upon the usage of politics to engage directly in a campaign to revise the structures and processes of government in a way that will deliberately transform all subsequent political exchanges in a large-scale yet surreptious pay-off. The British constitution has always been susceptible to this type of political manipulation and, as a result, has always been dependent upon a collective restraint and normative conservatism. During the present period when the pressure for transformative change has been at its most intense and when the arguments for reform have been at their most persuasive, the defence of this constitutional culture has been at its most robust. Working on the principle that the best form of defence is attack, the issue of constitutional reform has been taken to its proponents in an offensive operation based upon casting doubt upon the entire project. This form of negative campaigning derives its force from questioning the *intelligence, integrity* and *foresight* of the reformers and, with it, their programme for a consciously redesigned constitution.

Negative intelligence

Casting doubt upon the logic of an opponent's position and upon the ability of the other side even to engage in a rational argument have always been key components of any negative defence. The debate over the British constitution has proved to be no exception, with regular allusions being made to the limited intelligence of the reformers and in particular to their failure to comprehend the nature of constitutions or to grasp the full implications of their projected remedies. Constitutional reformers are regularly accused of failing to understand the flawed logic of their own position. For example, the principle of constitutional reform is dependent upon the idea of a functioning civil society that will provide the stabilising foundation for a transition to a new constitutional order. And yet, new constitutions are almost invariably associated with the type of extensive social dislocation drawn from conditions of war, or revolution, or newly acquired national independence. If a successful constitution is an epi-phenomenon of a settled social order, then a new constitutional framework cannot be unilaterally imposed upon a society in a top-down process by a set of legal theorists and institutional designers. If on the other other hand, the constitutional reformers claim that their call for change is being driven by the disarray within society, then a community under such a strain would be unlikely to agree upon a new constitutional arrangement or to sustain whatever constitutional reconstruction were to emerge from the old framework. It can even be contended that a new constitutional order might further diminish the rudiments of social consensus remaining after the displacement of a preceding constitution. In effect, constitutional reformers cannot expect to depend upon the traditions of an established constitutional order to maintain continuity through the iconoclasm of what amounts to a regime change. Refomers cannot have their cake and eat it. Either the reform project is a serious initiative in political and social renovation in which case it can be denounced for its 'ahistorical understanding of what a constitution is and what it can be made to do';[43] or it is merely the product of a pressure group which cynically overstates its case to maximise its political leverage but in doing so not only undermines political institutions in order to substantiate its own arguments, but raises public expectations to such unsustainable levels that the end result will be a backlash of increased public cynicism.

The illogical and contradictory nature of constitutional reform is a well-worked theme in the strategy of negative defence. For example, it is said that key reforms like a bill of rights are contrary to the controlling ethos of parliamentary sovereignty, and that measures to convert the 'democratic deficit' will only end up by re-creating it through PR-driven coalition governments and the expansion of judicial review. It is alleged that reform necessarily borrows from other systems and is, thereby, redundant on the grounds of the non-transferable nature of constitutional design. Constitutional reform also evokes complaints that the enhancement of constitutional limitations will lead to more, rather than fewer, issues over the remit, efficiency and accountability of government. Constitutional reform is said to display a 'dissonance ... between diagnosis and prescription' in that the 'medicine prescribed will not cure the supposed ills'.[44] To make matters worse, the ultimate objective of the constitutional reform agenda is 'unachievable because no formal means exist for its enactment'.[45] Critics complain that reformers not only seek the impossible but pursue objectives by means that will ensure precisely the opposite outcome to that intended. For example, constitutional reform is often advanced as a means by which to modernise the British state and as a consequence release the economic potential that is presumed to be repressed by outdated and anachronistic structures of government. But as John Patten points out, the British constitution's characteristic mobility through rolling development is far more consistent with the dynamics of a market economy than any protracted hiatus of constitutional reconstruction: 'The economic argument sinks because markets do not need constitutional change; indeed they fear it because of the uncertainty it brings. To markets, political economy, not the political constitution, is of overriding importance.'[46] Far from assisting the national economy, the distraction of constitutional unpredictability would increase the risk assessment within commercial, manufacturing and investment sectors. Moreover, given the fine margins of competitive advantage in an increasingly international market of fluid industrial location and capital liquidity, the diversion of political resources to a programme of constitutional change could well lead to damaging consequences for Britain's economy.

Another example of where reform ideas have been confronted by questioning the perspicacity of those advancing came with the Nolan Committee and its recommendations on the supervison of MPs' outside interests. The thrust of the negative defence lay in pointing out the implausibility of both the means and the ends of regulation in such a sphere. The methods designed to monitor influence were said to be inappropriate to the stated objective. Sir Edward Heath, for example, denounced the principle of an independent parliamentary commissioner for standards because an external bureaucratic organisation could not possibly understand the internal complexities of Westminster's interior social order. He complained that Lord Nolan seemed to 'lack a certain worldliness, of realising what goes on in this world of ours'.[47] Heath continued: 'We in this House know far more of what is going on with our fellow members than any bureaucrat brought in from outside. Of course we do. What can this gentleman do? He can't come into the smokeroom and say "By the way, have you heard so-and-so about so-and-so? Do you think I ought to look at that?" Of course not'.[48] Enoch Powell on the other hand complained that the entire exercise was logically flawed. It was not merely a matter of how it was implemented, it was more that such a constitutional device could never satisfactorily be turned into a workable system of review.

> The trouble about the Nolan committee is that it was established to define the indefinable and reduce to a set of rules that which cannot be so treated. The House of Commons expects its Members to behave as a gentleman would behave; but to sit down and draw up a schedule of how a gentleman will behave is in the nature of the case not possible. If it were, we could do without gentlemen … . If 'my honourable Friend' or 'the honourable Member' is not honourable, no amount of regulation or supervision will make him so.[49]

173

To Powell and to those who agreed with him, the Nolan recommendations were nonsensical and pointless. If the the aim was to restore public trust in Parliament, it could only be achieved by individual members earning it on the basis of their own integrity rather than through external contrivances to induce good behaviour by surveillance.

The defining property for this element of negative defence is one of an absence of insight and foresight on the part of the reformers. The reform agenda is criticised for not having been properly thought out or thought through. The proponents of negative defence identify the inconsistencies in the range of items on the reform agenda and translate them into glaring contradictions, which immediately de-legitimises the reform programme in its entirety. They pour scorn on the very idea of conceiving and designing something as materially practical as a constitution. The extract below typifies the genre:

> [T]here is a contradiction in the reformer's argument. On the one hand they say that our existing constitutional arrangements cannot be sustained because we are now a pluralist, multi-cultural society. Yet they also maintain that if only some miscellaneous group of retired politicians, political scientists and eminent lawyers got together they could write a constitution which would command widespread assent. Why should those experts command greater authority than our long-established and loved institutions?[50]

The rhetorical question virtually demands a negative answer because in a system based so much upon incremental and pragmatic developments the very notion of a preconceived and coherent alternative constitutional order appears suspect. An effective negative defence succeeds in fostering a circularity of suspicion between the competence of the reform agenda and the competence of the reformers themselves in such a way that doubts attached to one help to reinforce the doubts associated with the other. The resultant intenisification of scepticism leads inexorably to the motives and intentions of the reformers being brought into question.

Negative integrity

This next element of negative defence seeks to expose the reformers' high-minded altruism as nothing more than a cover for a much more prosaic set of impulses. The indictment in essence is that constitutional reform is simply traditional party politics through other channels. It is an integral part of the calculus of party competition and political leverage by which one set of political forces seeks to change the rules through which another set of interests have acquired the power to govern. In the context of the 1990s prior to the 1997 general election, when the dynamics of the party system had failed to produce a change of government in 18 years, then in the light of this jaundiced view of constitutional reform it was only to be expected that

174

those who found themselves excluded from power for such a protracted period would opt for the politics of last resort. They proceeded to question not so much themselves and their ideas but the integrity of a system which had excluded them from an effective role in public life. They could 'only conclude it [was] some deep failing in the British constitution which ha[d] allowed Conservative governments successfully to pursue their policies'.[51] The attempt to de-legitimise successive Conservative governments, by raising inflammatory questions over the constitutionality of their electoral authority and governing style, led in turn to an equally robust condemnation of the reformers' own standards of political ethics. Lord Beloff, for example, felt that the very use of the term Charter 88 was an indictable offence in its own right: 'There are participants whose stock in trade is to make our flesh creep with allegations about the erosion of human rights in Britain. How else to explain the disgusting use of "Charter 88" as the name of their pressure group, in mockery of "Charter 77", the heroic Czechoslovaks who fought a genuine tyranny?'[52] The accusation of self-serving exaggeration was further extended to embrace the idea of a delusional sense of conspiratorial exclusion from the policy process: 'Constitutional reformers seem united by a sense of being excluded from national affairs by some half-concealed elite and deprived of the knowledge they need to understand what is going on'.[53] Apart from attributing to constitutional reform a brand of narcissism reserved to those who necessarily equate a lack of influence with a pernicious form of unwarranted and illegitimate ostracism, the proponents of negative defence implied that constitutional reformers were themselves engaged in a form of conspiracy in order to conceal the inherent weaknesses of their own critical agenda.

In its benevolent guise, this view of the duplicitous nature of constitutional reform assigns no malicious intent to the theme itself. To Charles Moore, for example, the issue of constitutional reform came to prominence almost by default. Speaking prior to the 1997 general election, he observed that the Labour party had become 'more militantly moderate than at any time in its history'.[54] As a consequence, the party had 'given so much thought to avoiding radicalism in economic and social policy that it has almost accidentally committed itself to the most sweeping reforms of the constitution'.[55] According to this perspective, constitutional reform is simply a convenient means by which a demoralised opposition can divert attention from its political weaknesses and conceal the divisions within itself over more substantive areas of policy. For much of the 1990s, the issue provided a sense of purpose and identity to an otherwise disoriented and disordered set of opposition forces that needed a unifying theme to provide a source of critical leverage upon the government.

A less benign construction of the incidental usage of constitutional reform locates the theme more in the realm of ideas and in particular the collapse of the socialist alternative. The rise of the free market hegemony and the related decline in *dirigiste* state intervention divested the left of both an animating historical cause and a strategy of political mobilisation. The resultant vacuum in the intellectual landscape has been filled by a progressive process of substitution with the theme of constitutional reform embodying a new set of first principles from which to engage in a comprehensive critique of the state in the name of liberty. The constitution provides an alternative explanation of the retreat of the centre-left in British politics. Instead of a pathology connected to the collapse of Soviet communism and the related decline in the international and universal dimensions of socialist ideology, the constitution offers the prospect of localised relief from general trends in the form of the indigenous anachronisms, anomalies and injustices of the British system. Jonathan Clark describes this sudden interest in constitutional affairs on the part of the left in the following terms:

> We have certain groups of people with a philosophy of history, whether it is a liberal philosophy of history or a socialist philosophy of history, which told them history was evolving in a certain direction through a particular logic of events. They were therefore in the vanguard of progress. Things were going their way ... It looked credible until the late 1970s. When they find that things are no longer going their way, when they find that the results of several general elections are pointing in quite a different direction, they are stuck for an answer. They don't have an analysis, but what their philosophy has told them in both cases is that things must have been fixed; things must be rigged; things are going wrong ... things must have been taken out of their hands and something illegitimate must be going on.[56]

According to this perspective, the left of centre's accusation that Conservative governments had exploited the historical weaknesses of the constitution in illiberal and authoritarian ways was nothing more than a surreptious device by which to subvert the Conservatives' electoral mandate and to counteract the substance and direction of its policies. But in Clark's view, attempts to prove that the British constitution had in some way run its course could in no way compensate anaytically for the historical dead-end of socialism. On the contrary, Margaret Thatcher's governments were no different to any other in their usage of the power made available by the system. Speaking in 1989, he was adamant that the 'government is as illiberal as Atlee's socialist government was illiberal. Equally, it has a programme, equally it has a parliamentary majority, equally it has sought to implement that programme and largely it has succeeded. There is nothing more authoritarian about this government then there was about Atlee's or Wilson's.'[57]. Accordingly, the negative defence sees within constitutional reform an attempt by the left to discover a new *raison d'etre* through 'liberal rationalism and the belief that the rebuilding of institutions can transform the economic, social and political experience of the masses'.[58] But given that the logic of the Thatcherite programme was one of enhancing market forces, personal choice and individual liberty, then any assault upon the means of such a libertarian vision necessarily amounted to the fraudulent use of liberal principles to lever socialist values back into contention. If the British constitution was being criticised for the political ends acquired through it, then the negative defence reversed the analysis by equating the agenda of reforming the constitutional processes with the projected sub-stance of such changes -- namely, the restoration of state intervention, central direction, corporatist management and social democracy.

An even less benevolent interpretation of constitutional reform views the issue not as the surface projection of subterranean ideological movement but purely and simply as a weapon of power politics. Constitutional reform is depicted as a tried and tested device by which those excluded from power seek to undermine the provision of power itself. It is seen as cynical means by which to frighten individuals into thinking they are living in an author-itarian society where the government and the state are indistinguishable from one another and where both necessarily require reconstructive surgery as an obligation of citizenship. In this light, constitutional reform is simply a stratagem by a maladjusted opposition to maintain traditional priorities and agendas by alternative means. It is not about ideas so much as the management of power. Even though constitutional reform is portrayed as a new issue resting upon principle, it is in reality arguably nothing more than a disguise for something old and amoral – namely, the competitive manouevring to acquire or retain political power for the benefit of client constituencies. In the logic of such a negative defence, no other explanation can account for the allegedly misguided, frivolous, fallacious and contra-dictory nature of the reform proposals. Furthermore, there would arguably be no limit to the lengths that constitutional reformers will go to extract the maximum utility from the issue, however damaging the system or to the nation. Whether it is the technically flawed comparisons with the democ-ratic performance of other countries, or the use of 'skilful questionnaires designed to conceal the costs of what is on offer',[59] or the catch-all claims of a panacea within reach made on behalf of the proposal for a bill of rights, the objective of political maximisation remains the same. Thus the moti-vating spirit behind the Nolan Committee's call for the regulation of MPs' interests and activities was seen to be nothing other than a power grab by the Labour party. Alan Duncan, for example, opposed the reform because of what he perceived to be the partisan usage of the issue and the partisan implications of such a reform:

> We are in fact in the middle of the most vicious and artful political campaign ever seen in Britain, in which the Labour Party has quite brilliantly seized on discontent and dressed up party politics as a battle of principle. This is war by

other means, and they are winning it. They have successfully conveyed the impression that Conservative MPs and the private sector are all bad, and have escaped any comparable scrutiny of their own conduct. Mr Blair's ... objectives have little to do with standards, and have everything to do with destroying the nature of Conservative representation in Parliament, at whatever cost to the institution itself.[60]

In the view of David Willetts, the development of the Labour Party's position on devolution has also been guided exclusively by a conspiracy to draw as much political advantage from the issue as possible, irrespective of its effect upon the continued viability of the constitutional settlement or the state of the union. In his polemical assault upon the left of centre in British politics *Why Vote Conservative?* Willetts describes Labour's devolution proposals as 'among the most confused, unworkable policies ever put before the British electorate by a serious political party'.[61] Even at the cost of raising the 'West Lothian' question which lay at the 'the heart of the British constitutional settlement',[62] the Labour party was accused of seeking to use the issue to protect its power base in Scotland from any incursion by the Scottish National Party and in the process to increase its ideological leverage south of the border: 'After all, the general elections of 1964 and 1974 saw a Conservative majority in England which was offset by Labour majorities in Scotland and Wales. What Labour want to do is to keep those Scottish votes so that they can impose socialism in England whilst at the same time keeping the English out of all matters affecting Scotland. It is playing with fire.'[63] Such an attack draws upon the two elements of negative defence mentioned thus far. First, the plan is dismissed as fanciful and even nonsensical. Second, it is portrayed as a devious strategy that conceals its real motives. It typifies the reliance of the negative defence upon attributing to the reformers the vices of double-standards and duplicity. Constitutional reform, therefore, is always to be deplored because it must by necessity mean something other than what it appears. Its sponsors are not worthy of public trust because of the nature of their political motives which will lead to the abandonment of electoral commitments once in power, just as easily as it had prompted the initial adoption of radical measures for positional advantage when out of power.

Negative foresight

Lord Beloff once mused that where the advocates of constitutional reform are concerned it is 'hard to decide whether [they] ... are disingenuously seeking their own objectives, or are victims of their own ignorance'.[64] Those adopting a negative defence of the constitution would cite both these features as grounds for criticism. But they would add a third category to the list. Constitutional reformers are not merely stupid or deceitful; they are also positively dangerous. On occasions, constitutional conservatives are prepared to take a tolerant view of reformers in this field. They are seen as basically harmless dissenters who make a virtue of their self-imposed exclusion from the mainstream of political activity. By the same token, an organisation like Charter 88 is dismissed as an 'appealing home for political waifs and strays'[65] or as an 'escape route for those unwilling to tackle real problems',[66] or simply, in Neil Kinnock's succinct phrase, a group of 'whiners, whingers and wankers'.[67] According to Daniel Hannan, the signatories of Charter 88 are the most recent expression of an established tradition: 'Charter 88 attracts support from the kind of benign cranks who, in past generations, campaigned for Esperanto, pacifism, decimalisation and nudism.'[68] But this patronising fusion of constitutional reform with social maladjustment changes markedly when the agenda of constitutional change becomes the object of serious political consideration. As the unthinkable is openly thought and becomes a plausible possibility and even a probability, then the response changes to one of genuine alarm and impending disaster. If the response to constitutional reformers is initially one of questioning their seriousness of intent, the reaction to their evident impression upon the political agenda becomes one of questioning the seriousness of the consequences should the British constitution become hostage to the utopian amateurism of Charter 88 or the cynical professionalism of parties seeking power.

Constitutional reform is alleged to be dangerous for a profusion of reasons most of which have already been alluded to in this chapter, either directly or by implication. While concessionary defences are likely to regard many reforms to be acceptable risks because they are assumed to be balanced by a greater probability of positive gains, a negative defence is unlikely to allow such qualifications or counter-weights to soften the condemnation of sweeping constitutional adjustment. In such a perspective, constitutional reform is a euphemism for nothing other than constitutional destruction. There is no guarantee that reform would be a prelude to the attainment of an improved constitutional order. The only certainty is that a historically proven and reliable constitution would have been dismantled in the unlikely hope that a substitute constitution would immediately acquire not only a comparable level of viability but also an improved standard of performance.

The negative defence's trump card in the argument over constitutional change is that reform leads to a constitution *in extremis* – namely, a constitution precariously stripped of its traditional protections and immunities. Change is said to endanger not merely the structure of the constitution but the entire fabric of the traditions, norms and understandings that collectively constitute a civil society. Modifying such a complex and inter-related entity is necessarily fundamental in nature. Thus, the prospect of PR is defined as a threat to the coherence of the whole constitution. It would mean 'flattening the familiar contours of our political landscape in the name of abstract uniformity. It would have done to the constitution what the urban planners did to the inner cities.'[69] But the damage is not limited to aesthetics. Reform is also inherently unpredictable in its consequences. Those disposed to a negative defence are those who are predisposed to thinking that fundamental, and necessarily unforeseen, change in such a sphere as constitutional governance is always likely to be de-stabilising and dysfunctional. The role of negative defence in such circumstances is simply to point out the imminence of material disaster irrespective of the merits or principles of the reform drive. It proceeds on the premise that an organic entity like the British constitution cannot long withstand the necessarily disaggregative effects of radical constitutional change. The position is encapsulated by John Major:

> The British constitution is vibrant and robust. But it is not indestructible. People must realise that our constitution is not a piece of architecture that one can re-engineer by knocking down a wall here or adding an extension there. It's a living, breathing constitution. Its roots are ancient but it has evolved ... It embodies a set of values, a legacy of understandings, that have developed year by year over the centuries ... No one should lightly contemplate tampering with an institution that is so ancient and yet so alive.[70]

The negative defence responds in like manner to the negative critique of the British constitution by the reformist agencies. Those employing a negative defence point out the extent to which the reformers rely upon a strategy of unravelling the constitution by specific complaints which may be individually defensible as discrete charges, but which taken cumulatively amount to an unlimited licence for reform. Constitutional dissent, therefore, may be an understandable form of social and political frustration but it leads, however unintentionally, to the actual subversion of the constitutional order. In this light, constitutional reformers are dangerous because the project of constitutional reconstruction is seen as being overwhelmingly weighted on the side of negative critique, rather than towards a viable positive vision of an alternative constitutional entity. Indeed, the latter can be seen as merely the obverse of critical complaint as if constitutional construction were merely an analogue of constitutional dissent with a replacement constitution defined by the absence of its predecessor's flaws. According to this perspective, constitutional reformers are seriously deluded over the ease with which a revised constitution can brought into existence. Apart from the fact that the present constitution can in no way support the charges of pathological decline levelled against it, it is claimed that the lack of serious consideration given to the deeply problematic difficulties of reconstituting a constitution betrays a dangerous naïveté on the part of the reformers. As a consequence, the public requires protection from their cost-free panaceas by a strong dosage of hard-edged realism.

Reformers, for example, are accused of national and cultural disloyalty in their criticism of a constitution which is so closely tied to British identity:

> In a tradition stretching back to Lytton Strachey and the Bloomsbury writers, groups of *bien pensant* liberals have tried to demonstrate their sophistication by denigrating their country. It is an attitude which has led the Left into some unholy alliances, from Soviet Russia to Irish republicanism. It even motivates a minority of the supporters of European political union. Constitutional reform is a soft and fuzzy manifestation of the same tendency. It does not attract people who dislike Britain, so much as those who dislike all the things which make Britain different.[71]

The Anglophobia implied by the reformers' critique of the British constitution is seen as fuelling the incoherence and excess of their intemperate rush to emulate what amounts to a socially constructed model of an idealised European norm of rights provision. Constitutional loyalists point to the uncertain status of rights in the modern history of Europe, where the state has always assumed a greater role in society and where historical divisions have made the state into a much more volatile and dangerous entity in the memory of many European cultures. Critics also refer to the United States but in contrast to Europe. The American model is used to portray the nightmare of a traditional liberal society deranged by the reality of an extreme rights-based political culture. Where Europe is a false prospectus, the United States is an only too real projection of constitutional sovereignty, where entrenched rights generate so much litigation that it occupies 39 per cent of the world's lawyers, and where judges are required to substitute legal judgement for carefully constructed forms of political accommodation.

Advocates of constitutional change are also accused of sponsoring cruel delusions. They suggest that reform would produce a level of social and economic improvement far higher than any adjustment to the structure of a constitution could ever secure. They also claim that constitutional change would generate a modern state with a culture of participatory citizenship. The response of those adopting a negative defence is to assert the opposite. Far from introducing an advanced and open state of decision-making, the reform agenda would multiply the constitution's checks and balances to a point where they would begin to nullify effective government action. Disputes over inter-connected rights and jurisdictional remits would inflate political activity at the direct expense of governmental competence. Constitutional reform is often portrayed by its proponents as a resolution to a set of political problems. Working on this premise, a new constitutional settlement would necessarily reduce the differences over the structural biases of the present constitution. Constitutional loyalists believe the opposite to be the likely effect. A new constitutional arrangement would exacerbate old tensions and generate a host of new divisions in the rush of interests intent upon maximising the gains of any constitutional revision. The idea that the fulfilment of the constitutional agenda would de-politicise the constitution would be revealed as a hoax. A new constitution would not acquire a non-political status. It would be so riven with dispute that political resources would be progressively dissipated over the rights and consequences of constitutional interpretation. It would lead to institutional and interpretive gridlock that would erode the political parties' ability to deliver policy programmes and, thereby, reduce their capacity to offer effective electoral choice. A plurality of micro-responsiveness would bring in its wake a level of macro-*un*responsiveness that would fuel populist surges against normal political channels and intermediary organisations and, in the process, raise the threat of illiberalism and intolerance overwhelming the fledgling constitution. In this perspective, a constitutional transformation would be a pernicious delusion that would not only foster public cynicism and despair over the role of politics in society but encourage citizen apathy and passivity. Instead of resolving problems through constitutional mechanisms, an irreversible constitutional experiment would amount to a devastating anti-climax with profound social repercussions. The level of disillusionment would be directly proportional to the scale of anticipation preceding such an exercise. Prodigous amounts of political capital would have been wasted on a fruitless and damaging diversion. Opportunities for substantive reform in other areas of society would have been needlessly lost. Even if the constitutional changes were to be technically successful by being effectively established within the system, they would herald no tangible change in the lives of ordinary citizens. In the final analysis: 'Constitutional change will do little if anything to affect the roots of contemporary problems that impinge most upon citizens' lives. Electoral reform or frequent referendums will do nothing to ensure that blacks in Liverpool get jobs, or that the harassed housewife can make ends meet in providing for her family.'[72]Seen in this light, constitutional reform would have squandered the decisive use of governmental power for community purposes and replaced it with a political culture of perennial complaint over the multiple and continuous distractions of a system neutralised by its own countervailing powers into a condition of expensive stasis.

Other forms of negative defence accuse constitutional reformers of courting danger not so much of an envisaged scenario, but of something more serious – namely, a void of unpredictability in which any disaster might befall the political system and with it the nation state. With the fragility of civil society and the tragedy of history in the forefront of their minds, those who respond to constitutional reform in this manner seek to draw attention to the organic nature of any social order and to its limits of assimilation. Social organisations can adjust incrementally over time to necessary change, but they cannot simply be peremptorally transfomed without subverting the entire fabric of those inter-relationships upon which the viability of the overall structure depends. In Roger Scruton's view, that a constitution can be made has always been a fallacy, but it is a 'greater modern fallacy that a constitution can be endlessly and in every particular *reformed*'.[73] Because a constitution is so central to a society, it is concluded that constitutional reformers are in fact radicals intent upon placing the entire social order in jeopardy, not simply because of the strain likely to be incurred by such anticipated alteration, but because change to such a structure is seen to be wholly indeterminate in effect. This type of negative defence is not concerned therefore with defining a prospective state of altered constitutional arrangements. This is regarded as simply falling into the trap set by the reformers, in which the response to proposals for change is confined to disputing the relative gains and losses of change in the terms established by the reform agenda. The negative outlook is not simply to claim that a future state of existence brought about by constitutional reform will amount to a massive net loss. It is to issue a warning that there is no point in trying to evaluate such an envisaged state because it is not even remotely possible that a projection of intellectual constructs could ever be translated into an actual set of conditions. A negative defence like this depends essentially upon fear for its force of argument. It is precisely because the implications and ramifications of constitutional meddling cannot be foreseen that it is considered to be so dangerous to experiment in such an area of political life. Despite appearances to the contrary, constitutional reformers are accused in effect of engaging in a process of blind destruction in the faint hope that something constructive might be achieved at the end of the transformation. Reformist arguments in support of an alternative constitutional order are simply dismissed as a device to allay fears over the main strategy of dismantling the present constitution. To negative defenders of the constitution, the reformers are literally stupid, duplicitous and dangerous in recklessly and wantonly initiating a process that will be open-ended, irreversible and destructive. Constitutional reform on such a scale is never worth the risk – even if it can later be shown to have produced a satisfactory outcome. One successful precedent may be the last.

The prevailing predisposition of those who are drawn to such a negative defence is one in which premeditated change releases gravitational forces of degradation and dissolution. The mission, therefore, is one of a clarion call for caution in the face of beguiling promises of progress and modernisation. It is to look always one step beyond what are taken to be the myopic simplicities of the reformers' limited grasp of history. It is to issue reminders that political experimentations are not always as benign as they may appear and that they can be thoroughly malignant in effect. It is to characterise any serious attempt to transform the constitution as a dangerously misguided subversion of the constitutional order of society. The precipitous nature of such a prospectus is seen to warrant a proportional response like that given by John Major at a meeting of Conservative MPs on 2 December 1994. The prime minister accused Tony Blair and New Labour of 'teenage madness'. By endorsing such an 'extensive package of constitutional reform', it would spell the 'beginning of the end for Britain'. Major declared that 'you can't shake our constitution around as if it were a cocktail at an Islington dinner party'.[74]

A negative defence of the constitution, therefore, relies for its effect upon a pre-existing sense of constitutional holism in which any substantive reform threatens the organic indivisibility of the entire structure. The constitution is regarded as possessing an a *priori* systemic integrity which can only be sustained by a systematic adherence to that which is already present and functionally operational. All major alternatives pose immense risks because no assurance can ever be given that intended consequences will not be accompanied by unintended and even unimaginable consequences. The latter are necessarily assumed to be negative, undesirable and threatening. Action taken on the constitution is seen to be literally precipitous because it places the constitution on a precipice in which the security of constitutional certainty is outweighed by the constitutional uncertainty of the unknown and the unknowable. Even though the British constitution is in many respects indeterminate in nature, the proponents of negative defence turn this characteristic to their advantage by affirming the need to avoid compounding the constitution's familiar opaqueness with any attempt to inject into it an alien source of actual imprecision under the guise of theoretical imprecision. As a consequence, the negative defence is used to condemn the lack of constitutional restraint on the part of those committed to the inherently damaging objective of constitutional reform. Just as reform becomes a euphemism for destruction, so reformers are seen as Jacobins in Fabian clothing.

Conclusion

Constitutions are monuments to social conservatism and as such the means by which to defend them are almost invariably conservative in character. To Jonathan Clark, 'the point about constitutional forms is that they embody values'. As such, the 'love affair of the British with their national institutions is no limp romanticism but an appreciation of the way that institutions embody and perpetuate, as well as symbolise, a certain way of doing things.'[75] This is not to say that the maintenance of the British constitution can be equated with the interests and behaviour of the Conservative party or a Conservative government. As we shall see in the following chapter, many in the Labour party have been, and remain, sceptical of the benefits to be accrued from constitutional reform. They see every advantage in keeping the access points to government and the operation of political authority as they have been since the democratisation of the franchise. According to this view, the British constitution is there to facilitate political radicalism, not to provide a substitute for it.

It is the case that the defining principles behind a right-of-centre defence may not be the same as those prompting a left-of-centre defence of the constitution. The fomer is more likely to be drawn from a traditionalist scepticism of change and especially of change induced by rationalist schemes of political experimentation. By the same token, it is probable that the latter is derived from an impulse to further social and economic progress by using the state rather than by questioning it. It may well be that a left-of-centre defender of the constitution would find it difficult to embrace the sceptical disposition towards any general improvement in the condition of society with the same thoroughness as the traditional conservative. Nevertheless, on the basis of other political priorities, the absence of evidence relating to a constitutional breakdown, and the fundamental and overriding value attached to the democratic authority of the House of Commons, the net position of such a proponent would closely correspond to the pessimistic caution of those with a more traditionalist attachment to the constitution. Constitutional conservatism, therefore, is not exclusive to the customary parameters of political conservatism. As a consequence, the constitution has not had to depend upon Conservative governments for its continued viability. The attachment to its precepts, structures and modes of operation can be found across the political spectrum. As a result, the defensive positions described above have formed the foundation of a succession of unholy alliances in which party loyalty and strategy have regularly been superseded by a collective desire to prevent the constitution from becoming a contentious political issue.

The corollary of such a fluid and responsive political constitution has always been a supportive understanding of the 'rules of the game' which are needlessly jeopardised by any serious attempt to formalise them, let alone to devise a set of alternatives. To those with these instincts for constitutional conservatism, Michael Oakeshott's injunction that 'there is no such thing as an unqualified improvement'[76] is peculiarly appropriate. Any case for change in such an area always remains merely a *prima facie* case, constantly outweighed by the fear that the constitution could completely unravel through capricious intervention. If there is such a property as constitutional fundamentalism in the British system, then its central characteristic is one of mutability and pragmatism bounded by the collective self-restraint of the participants. To defend it is to support those changes to the constitution that can be construed as being incidental to the normal dynamics of political exchange and to reject those attempts to reduce the scope of such adaptive evolution through the direct and artificial reformulation of the constitutional structure. To support the British constitution is to accept the implication of its essential 'unwrittenness'. It is to champion digression and evasion even in the very act of its own defence for the British constitution equates constitutionality with derivative *ex post facto* change, thereby leaving premeditated intentional change as the illogical and illegitimate inversion of constitutional development. By the same token, an explicit analysis and detailed evaluation in support of the British constitution is almost a contradiction in terms because by employing a positivist approach it overlooks, and even risks dismissing, the main strengths and defining characteristics of such a constitution. To support the British constitution is to promote a particular way of looking at a constitution. In the same way that it requires intuitive means to render its idiosyncrasies intelligible, the constitution itself is seen as being only really defensible as an expression of collective intuition. Defending such an entity, therefore, does not just depend upon making a case for something which cannot easily be made explicit. It relies upon identifying, reaffirming and sustaining a set of attitudes capable of supporting such an intangible constitution on the basis both of trust in respect to those operating it and of faith in respect to its underlying existence as a coherent, effective and defensible constitution. Trust and faith of this order are possible with consensus but, as the 1990s have shown, it is more difficult to sustain an intuitive constitutional defence in a period when the constitution is continually the subject of close scrutiny and political dispute.

Notes

1   Peter Madgwick and Diana Woodhouse, *The Law and Politics of the Constitution* (Hemel Hempstead: Harvester Wheatsheaf, 1995), p. 340.
2   The Economist Election Briefing (London: *The Economist*, 1997), p. 9.
3   John Patten, 'Just Keep Rolling Along', *The Spectator*, 30 January 1993.
4   Philip Norton, 'In Defence of the Constitution: A Riposte to the Radicals' in Philip Norton (ed.), *New Directions in British Politics?: Essays on the Evolving Constitution* (Aldershot: Edward Elgar, 1991), p. 157.
5   *Ibid.*, p. 159. See also Philip Norton, 'The Changing Constitution – Part 2', *Contemporary Record*, vol. 3, no. 2 (November 1989), pp. 9–11; R. A. W. Rhodes, 'Now Nobody Understands the System: The Changing Face of Local Government' in Norton (ed.), *New Directions in British Politics*, pp. 83–112; R. A. W. Rhodes, *Understanding Governance: Policy Networks, Governance, Reflexivity and Accountability* (Buckingham: Open University Press, 1997).
6   John Redwood, 'The Crowning Glory', *The Guardian*, 26 June 1996.
7   Norton, 'In Defence of the Constitution', pp. 159–60.
8   Philip Norton, *The Constitution in Flux* (Oxford: Martin Robertson, 1982), p. 1.
9   Gillian Peele, 'Comparing Constitutions' in Gillian Peele and Dennis Kavanagh (eds), *Comparative Government and Politics: Essays in Honour of S. E. Finer* (London: Heinemann, 1984), p. 204.

10 Ferdinand Mount, 'The Recovery of the Constitution', transcript of the Second Sovereignty Lecture, 11 May 1992 (London: The Charter 88 Trust, 1992), p. 1.

11 Redwood, 'The Crowning Glory'.

12 Michael Foley, *The Silence of Constitutions: Gaps, 'Abeyances' and Political Temperament in the Maintenance of Government* (London: Routledge, 1989).

13 David Willetts, *Modern Conservatism* (London: Penguin, 1992), p. 153.

14 Robert Alexander, *The Voice of the People: A Constitution for Tomorrow* (London: Weidenfeld and Nicolson, 1997).

15 Lord McCluskey, 'An Enormous Power', *The Listener*, 4 December 1986.

16 Clive Ponting, *Secrecy in Britain* (Oxford: Basil Blackwell, 1990), p. 69.

17 Clive Ponting, *The Right To Know: The Inside Story of the Belgrano Affair* (London: Sphere, 1985), p. 57.

18 Rodney Austin, 'Freedom of Information: The Constitutional Impact' in Jeffrey Jowell and Dawn Oliver (eds), *The Changing Constitution*, 3rd edn (Oxford: Clarendon, 1994), p. 429.

19 Stephen Ward, 'Code of Openness Fails to Catch the Public Imagination', *The Independent*, 15 March 1995.

20 'Constitutional Clash', *The Times*, 3 February 1997.

21 Andrew Lansley and Richard Wilson, *Conservatives and the Constitution* (London: Conservative 2000 Foundation), p. 222.

22 *Ibid.*, p. 223.

23 *Ibid.*, p. 223.

24 Peter Hennessy, *Hidden Wiring: Unearthing the British Constitution* (London: Victor Gollanz, 1996), p. 205.

25 *Ibid.*

26 *Ibid.*, pp. 206–7.

27 David Cannadine (review of *Hidden Wiring* by Peter Hennessy) *The Independent*, 21 October 1995.

28 Walter Ellis review of *Hidden Wiring* by Peter Hennessy), *Sunday Times*, 22 October 1995.

29 Cannadine (review of *Hidden Wiring* by Peter Hennessy).

30 Ben Pimlott, letter to *The Guardian*, 5 December 1990.

31 *Ibid.*

32 K. D. Ewing and C. A. Gearty, *Freedom Under Thatcher* (Oxford: Clarendon, 1990), p. 268.

33 *Ibid.*, p. 275.

34 Conor Gearty, 'Wrongs of a Bill of Rights', *New Statesman and Society*, 20 July 1990.

35 *Ibid.*

36 Ewing and Gearty, *Freedom Under Thatcher*, p. 274.

37 Stephen Sedley, 'Charter 88: Wrongs and Rights' in Geoff Andrews (ed.), *Citizenship* (London: Lawrence and Wishart, 1991), p. 226.

38 *Ibid.*, p. 224.

39 *Ibid.*

40 *Ibid.*

41 *Ibid.*, pp. 224–5. See also Paul Hirst, *After Thatcher* (London: Collins, 1989), pp. 51–81.

42 Jonathan C. D. Clark, 'Back to Edwardian Values', *The Times*, 17 July 1996.
43 Jonathan C. D. Clark, 'No Need to Man the Barricades', *The Times*, 2 January 1992.
44 Norton, 'In Defence of the Constitution, p. 159–60. See also Philip Norton, 'The Glorious Revolution of 1688: Its Continuing Relevance', *Parliamentary Affairs*, vol. 42, no. 2 (April 1989), pp. 142–7.
45 Norton, 'In Defence of the Constitution, p. 167. See also Philip Norton, 'Should Britain Have a Written Constitution?', *Talking Politics*, vol. 1, no. 1 (1988), pp. 8–13.
46 Patten, 'Just Keep Rolling Along'.
47 Quoted in Philip Webster, 'Heath Heads Tory Revolt over Nolan', *Daily Telegraph*, 19 May 1995.
48 *Ibid.*
49 J. Enoch Powell, 'There's No Legislating for Honour' *The Times* 19 May 1995.
50 Willetts, *Modern Conservatism*, p. 155.
51 *Ibid.*, p. 151.
52 Max Beloff, 'Beware of Prattling Reformers', *The Independent*, 9 October 1991.
53 *Ibid.* See also Max Beloff, 'No Better Recipe for Conflict', *The Times*, 9 August 1997.
54 Charles Moore, 'The Muddled Voice of Moderation', *Daily Telegraph*, 18 March 1997.
55 *Ibid.*
56 Jonathan C. D. Clark, BBC Television, *The State of Democracy*, 4 July 1989.
57 *Ibid.*
58 Mattthew D'Ancona, 'Uprooting the Constitution', Sunday Telegraph, 6 January 1997.
59 Beloff, 'Beware of Prattling Reformers'
60 Alan Duncan, letter to *The Times*, 22 May 1995.
61 David Willetts, *Why Vote Conservative?* (London: Penguin, 1997), p. 64.
62 *Ibid.*, p. 65.
63 *Ibid.*
64 Beloff, 'Beware of Prattling Reformers'.
65 Patten, 'Just Keep Rolling Along'.
66 Beloff, 'Beware of Prattling Reformers'.
67 Quoted in Paul Anderson and Nyta Mann, *Safety First: The Making of New Labour* (London: Granta, 1997), p. 429.
68 Daniel Hannan, 'An Inglorious Revolution', *Daily Telegraph* 8 March 1997.
69 'Honeymoon Plans', *The Times*, 10 February 1997.
70 John Major, *Speech on the Constitution*, given to the Centre for Policy Studies, 26 June 1996.
71 Hannan, 'An Inglorious Revolution'.
72 Norton, *The Constitution in Flux*, p. 283.
73 Roger Scruton, *The Meaning of Conservatism* (London: Macmillan, 1980), p. 46.
74 Quoted in Philip Webster, 'Feuds Could Cost Us Power, says Major', *The Times*, 3 December 1994.
75 Jonathan C. D. Clark, 'Back to Edwardian Values, *The Times*, 17 July 1996.
76 Michael Oakeshott, *Rationalism in Politics and Other Essays* (London: Methuen, 1967), p. 171.

6

The 1997 general election and the dynamics of constitutional change

Up until recently, constitutional reform has been a minority issue of marginal political significance. It typified those noble causes which can command widespread assent but which remain lodged in the twilight of those important issues that never manage to make the transition to the status of urgent priority. Large-scale constitutional reform has been the subject of sober discussion for a generation but it has only become a sustained point of controversy and a compelling factor in the political and electoral calculations of the major parties since the mid-1990s. As Labour consolidated both its commitment to constitutional reform and its lead in the opinion polls, it offered the prospect of fundamental constitutional change being undertaken by a reform government. By the same token, conscious of the threat of imminent constitutional subversion, the sceptics and critics of reform deployed their arguments with a greater degree of urgency than before. Prior to the 1997 general election, the debate on the constitution was fully engaged. In fact, the issue of the constitution divided the two main parties more than any other and set in motion a process in which a Labour victory could legitimately be equated with a mandate for constitutional change. This period represented the culmination of the campaign of advocacy for the renovation of the British constitution. Given that the Labour party was always the one political organisation capable of actually securing change in the area and given that it had accepted constitutional reform as a central theme in its programme, the general election assumed a significance to the British constitution unparalleled by any development since World War II.

From the point of view of this study, the period prior to the 1997 general election and immediately following the landslide victory for Labour represents a pivotal time both for the development of constitutional politics in Britain and for the understanding of the methods, considerations and contingencies of constructing and securing an agenda of constitutional reform. Such a climactic period offers a series of analytical opportunities. It provides a basis on which to examine the relationship between different constitutional fuels and the composition of an actual reform roster. It permits an assessment to be made of the pressures supporting constitutional reform and the limits of its application when the potential for change is conditioned by political considerations. It affords the opportunity not only to assess the central characteristics of a constitutional debate conducted within a context of imminent change, but to gauge the effect of public opinion, party interests and government priorities upon different components of the reform agenda. The transition from the decline of the Conservative hegemony to the establishment of a Labour administration provides a litmus test of the actual potential for premeditated structural change within the British constitution. The onset of a reform government committed to constitutional change offers the prospect of insights into the depth of party and public commitment to such an issue; into the effect of the arguments and strategies in defence of the current constitutional arrangements; and into the limitations of the agenda as an organising theme for an administration committed to programmatic change.

The objective of this chapter is to use these opportunities of analysis to acquire an understanding of the distinguishing features and defining properties of what is an emergent form of politics centred upon the constitution. The evolving configuration of such a politics, together with its internal and external dynamics, and its rules of engagement, techniques of persuasion and factors of assessment become clearer in the period following the general election. But in order to grasp the nature of such a politics, it is necessary to review its immediate formative influences by examining the mobilisation of forces in the pre-election period and their deployment during the election itself.[1]

Constitutional reform and Labour suspicions

The issue of constitutional reform has in many respects been of secondary importance to the Labour party. As a mass organisation formed and developed outside Parliament upon democratic principles, the party has always regarded itself as sufficiently progressive in its own right to provide the state with a necessary injection of democratic values whenever a Labour government is installed in office. In this light, the solution to many problems pertaining to the British constitution has been the establishment of a Labour administration whose electoral authority places it in a position to mould the operational properties of government to its construction of the public interest. Constitutional values in such a context have been historically reducible to instrumental values in servicing the policy programme of an explicitly reformist party.

Labour's roots lay in socialism and especially in parliamentary socialism where, through electoral competition, the full panoply of state powers is made available to whichever party prevails. As a radical movement dedicated to transformative societal change, the Labour party has traditionally adhered to a particular conception of representation which has always carried with it implications for the British constitution. The socialist theory of representation is drawn from a vision of society that is polarised into two main classes. The antagonism between these classes defines the electoral battle but, whereas 'Tory democracy' is based upon the House of Commons representing local communities with individual parliamentarians being given specific mandates, the socialist theory of elections gives greater emphasis to the party as a collective force and to the parliamentarian as an agent of the party. Mandates are not local and individual in character but are based upon the party's collective ethos and programme for social reconstruction. The Labour MP is thus assumed to be the beneficiary of a party campaign based upon an ideologically rigorous conception of social forces, a mass-based organisation of support and a unified programme of policies providing a clear and decisive framework of electoral choice. The party outside Parliament, therefore, expects the party inside Parliament to reflect the policy decisions of the movement that generates, finances and mobilises the party's electoral campaigns. Samuel Beer describes the principle of such a conception of representation and the expectations that flow from it in the following terms:

> Socialist thought ... makes the party the main device by which voters take the initiative. According to this theory of democracy, voters organize or join a political party and by means of its conference agree on a program. Candidates elected on this program must stand by it. This is precisely how they fulfil their responsibility to the electorate. In short, if British democracy is 'government by the people,' then program-making by a party conference is a perfectly reasonable device for putting into effect this basic principle. The internal structure of the party depends upon the function that party is expected to perform in the system as a whole.[2]

The claims made on behalf both of Labour's intra-party democracy and its democratic expression of a wider public interest has led to perennial tensions between the extra-parliamentary party and the Parliamentary Labour Party (PLP). The former can claim to be the active and originating element in the formulation of the party programme and the sovereign entity from which the party draws its political and electoral resources. The latter can not only claim the right to interpret and apply the programme in the light of contemporary contingencies but can also assert a higher democratic status drawn from their electoral credentials as MPs. The friction between such claims can be especially severe during periods of Labour government when the PLP is divided between backbenchers and ministers, thereby compounding the contested categories of democratic priority and political legitimacy.

The effect of such traditional disjunctions and disputes has been to diminish the perceived value of any further checks and balances that might arise from constitutional reform. During the twentieth century, Labour governments have been of relatively short duration and for a party committed to a radical agenda of social and economic change, a further dimension of reform can seem to be an unnecessary encumbrance, especially when the consequences of such changes are likely to lead to an increase in the restraints upon governmental action. As a consequence, a powerful impulse in the Labour movement has been to regard constitutional reform as a distraction based upon a misconception. The notion that the constitution is basically neutral in operation is alleged to be as false as the assertion that liberal democracy is equally blind to the established structures of power, meaning and value in society. Labour is not simply another party in an all inclusive interplay of pluralist forces. Labour's historic *raison d'être* is to confront the inequities and injustices that characterise the infrastructure of a capitalist society. Given the pervasive influence of the predominant forces in such a society, the constitutional arrangements necessarily reflect the interests entrenched within the social order. Public discontent may appear to be accommodated through these arrangements but the institutional devices give only the impression of popular participation and political debate. In effect, they are designed merely to absorb and deflect pressures for radical change. Adherents to this view acknowledge the merits of enhancing the opportunities for the public to influence government policy by registering dissent and presenting alternatives. However, they are not prepared to purchase this increment in liberal democracy at the price of strengthening, or at least of not challenging, the already elaborate infrastructure of social, economic and political checks against any socialist government and its programme. According to this perspective, liberal democratic society is by definition strongly biased against a party with socialist origins, traditions and instincts. There are already sufficient checks in the system to resist, retard, deflect, delay and even reverse a socialist programme. The self-imposition of any additional constitutional checks, however well intentioned on civil libertarian grounds, would serve only to undermine Labour governments both now and in the future. For the Labour party to give emphasis to constitutional reform would amount not only to a waste of valuable political resources for an organisation dedicated to an altogether more extensive agenda of structural change, but to a form of graduated emasculation by making any future Labour administration even more vulnerable than before to the subversion of vested interests and minority obstruction. In essence, because the 'British left has sought to capture the state, not to reform it ... Labour has been at least as constitutionally conservative as its political opponents, and often more so.'[3]

Another reason why the subject of constitutional reform should be of only marginal significance to the Labour party is because of the negative experiences the issue has generated in the recent past. Apart from the political and ideological objections to such an issue, the party's previous associations with the theme of constitutional reform have been damaging not only to party unity but also to its reputation for organisational competence. In 1968, for example, the Wilson government introduced a measure to reform the House of Lords by phasing out the hereditary principle, ensuring a working majority for the government of the day and diminishing the chamber's powers of delay. The Parliament (No. 2) Bill passed the first and second reading stages but then became bogged down in protracted procedural disputes in the Committee of the Whole House where an 'unholy alliance' of left-wing Labour MPs and right-wing Conservative members frustrated the government. After 80 hours in Committee deliberating upon a few clauses, the coalition of those who felt the legislation went too far (e.g. Enoch Powell) and those who believed it did not go far enough (e.g. Michael Foot) finally succeeded in April 1969 in killing the bill. For a reform which had initially aroused little public controversy, the Wilson government had been humbled into submission by the Labour party's own lack of unity. The issue opened up serious fissures within the PLP and was instrumental in creating an impression of poetical ineptitude at which point '[a]gainst a background of visible prime ministerial weakness, the Government entered a phase of near-anarchy'.[4] Following such an experience, it would be nearly 30 years before another Labour prime minister would seriously reconsider reforming the upper chamber.

Another example of constitutional experimentation being directly associated with damage to both party and government is provided by the 1975 referendum on Britain's renegotiated terms of membership to the European Economic Community (EEC). The referendum was a classic case of constitutional innovation on pragmatic grounds. Ostensibly it was a device by which the Wilson government's revision of the terms could be finalised by investing it with a form of democratic legitimacy. In essence, it was a method of managing an issue which divided the Labour party to such an extent that it threatened to produce an internal schism. But the price of such remedial invention was high. The principle of collective cabinet responsibility had to be relaxed because cabinet ministers were so deeply split on the issue. This led to an intensification of the division with pro-Europeans like Roy Jenkins, Shirley Williams and George Thomson joining EEC supporters in other parties to campaign against the 'No' vote organisation that contained Tony Benn, Michael Foot, Peter Shore and Barbara Castle as well as many trade union leaders. The 'Britain in Europe' campaign prevailed in the vote, thereby in one sense vindicating both Wilson's policy package and the referendum strategy. Nonetheless, in another sense the departure from constitutional practice also served to demonstrate and even to institutionalise the depth of division within the governing party, and to reveal how an issue like Europe could cut across traditional party lines and undermine the party system's dynamics of political representation, programmatic choice and decisive government. The referendum was an 'intriguing constitutional device'[5] which provided an alternative expression and organisation of public opinion and which led commentators 'impressed by the spectacle of the Labour man, Roy Jenkins, the Conservative Heath, and the Liberal leader Thorpe participating in the same campaign on the same platform to urge the need for more coalition-minded or bipartisan politics in place of sterile conflict between time-worn and somewhat discredited parties'.[6]

Probably the most explicit case of linkage between constitutional innovation and Labour party discomfiture, and the one episode of constitutional reform which has done more than any other to generate caution within the party over this area of policy, remains that of devolution for Scotland and Wales in 1979. Responding to electoral pressure from the Scottish National Party (SNP) and Plaid Cymru in two of Labour's heartlands, the Callaghan government proposed a scheme of devolved government for Scotland and Wales which passed its second reading in December 1976 but which did not receive full parliamentary approval until July 1978. Just as the Kilbrandon Commission, set up in 1968 to study the constitutional feasibility of devolution, had failed to reach a consensus on the issue when it offered no fewer than four models of possible devolution, so the Labour government's legislation had failed to resolve a controversy which it had itself helped to fuel through its own impulse to move into the field of the United Kingdom's constitutional structure. The issue exerted so much strain upon party allegiances that it led to a host of cross-party alliances and to a high incidence of cross-party voting. The legislation was criticised for consuming excessive government time within the already restricted schedules of the House of Commons and for being so poorly drafted that it risked constitutional and administrative chaos were it to be implemented. Serious questions relating to the future role of the Secretaries of State for Scotland and Wales, and the constitutional implications of the relationship between the projected assemblies and Parliament at Westminster, were left largely unaddressed. The most serious constitutional problem of all was the 'West Lothian Question' which referred to the anomaly of English MPs being unable to vote in the House of Commons on those Scottish issues within the remit of a devolved government, even though Scottish MPs would retain the right to vote on English matters in the traditional way. More pertinent to Labour were the suggested solutions to the 'West Lothian' question – namely, a reduction in the number of Scottish MPs at Westminster, or a ban on Scottish members participating in decisions concerning English and Welsh affairs. But solutions on these lines would come at a very high political cost. question: 'The former would make it less likely that Labour would win a Commons majority, while the latter would tend to give Labour's opponents a majority on English and Welsh affairs even when the party had a Commons majority.'[7] For the party sponsoring the change, devolution was accused of generating more divisions than it promised to heal. It became clear that the referendums in Scotland and Wales, which the legislation had provided for, would be decisive in determining the viability of the devolution measures.[8]

The referendums were held on 1 March 1979 and prompted campaigns which revealed to the fullest extent the issue's capacity to disrupt and divide the Labour party. Nowhere was this more painfully evident than in Wales. The party was in a state of near civil war as those who were in favour of devolution on grounds of government loyalty, or political prudence, or nationalist fervour confronted the 'No' campaigners who were not only wary of the cultural and linguistic *imperium* among the pro-devolutionists but resistant to the projected effects that smaller units would have upon a socialist agenda. It would be difficult, for example, to envisage coherent forms of central planning within such a fractured state. Furthermore, a devolved government would be unable to confront international organisations, multinational corporations or central bureaucracies in the interests of Wales. To an opponent like Neil Kinnock, it was vital to preserve British solidarity, in order to protect working people in Wales and elsewhere:

> I believe that the emancipation of the class which I came to this House to represent, unapologetically, can best be achieved in a single nation and in a single economic unit, by which I mean a unit where we can have a brotherhood of all nations and have the combined strength of working class people throughout the whole of the United Kingdom brought to bear against any bully, any executive, any foreign power and bureaucratic arrangement, be it in Brussels or in Washington, and any would-be colonizer, either an industrial colonizer or a political colonizer.[9]

The pro-devolutionists claimed that Wales had already suffered from internal colonisation by the English and that it was time for the subject nations of the Celtic periphery to recover their cultural and political autonomy. The fervour with which nationalists defended the devolution proposal was equally matched by those who objected profoundly to having their Welshness disputed on the grounds of their opposition to devolution. To them, devolution was an arcane distraction from the serious social and economic issues of the late twentieth century and as such served only to defer the urgent action required to respond to them. Modern problems of alienation, frustration and opportunity were not simply a function of the distance between citizen and government, and, therefore, could not be resolved by direct and de-centralised democracy. Problems of this dimension required not only organisational power on the same scale but purposive remedial policy driven from a protective centre.

It was the intensity of those disputes over devolution within the Welsh Labour party which had forced the government to accept the principle of a referendum prior to the implementation of its devolution legislation. These same divisions led in turn to a decisive vote of no confidence in the Labour government's proposals when Labour strongholds like West Glamorgan and Gwent rejected the devolution measure by 81.3 per cent to 18.7 per cent and by 87.9 per cent to 12.1 per cent respectively. Both the Scottish and Welsh schemes for devolution were dismissed by their respective electorates. In Wales, there was an overall 4 to 1 majority against the measure and although devolution secured the support of 51.6 per cent of the voters in Scotland the level of acceptance came nowhere near the required 40 per cent threshold of the electorate. Devolution had been an expensive anti-climax for a Labour government which had taken over two years to finalise the legislation. It had generated confusion, fear and cynicism as opposing camps drew upon national distinctions and cultural prejudices in an attempt either to inspire or to scare voters into supporting their respective positions. The Labour government was seen to have mismanaged the issue by giving it a political prominence that was ultimately unwarranted and deeply damaging. The support for devolution in opinion polls dropped dramatically as the referendum campaigns progressed, leading to a point where in Scotland over 36 per cent of the electorate failed to vote. During the wider consideration of the devolution proposals, the economy had improved, especially in Scotland and, as a consequence, the nationalist threat to the Labour vote subsided. Nevertheless, even though Labour seemed to need devolution less at the time of the referendums than it had done prior to the campaigns, the party still suffered when its devolution measures were rejected by the very people whom they were designed to benefit. On the one hand, the devolution episode left a legacy of acrimony and betrayal by those most closely involved in the debate, while on the other it constituted a piece of tedious and distracting ephemera to the large majority of English MPs who were least involved in the issue. Just as devolution became discredited by failure, so the government that sponsored and underwrote the policy was seen to have become ingrown and out of touch. Even though the devolution debacle was not directly pertinent to the vote of confidence on 28 March 1979 which led to the collapse of the Callaghan government, it had become a constituent element of the *fin de siècle* atmosphere that afflicted what was to become the last Labour administration for 18 years. Devolution had been an attempt to devise a way of protecting the support for the Labour party in Scotland and Wales even at the risk of inducing a process that could have led to national separation. In the event, the experiment in the territorial reorganisation of British government was an irrelevance not just because Labour lost the 1979 general election but because, notwithstanding the absence of devolved government, Plaid Cymru lost half its seats and the SNP's parliamentary representation slumped by over three-quarters in the process.

The Labour party's lack of composure with constitutional change has not been confined to its experiences as a government struggling to prevail against a profusion of countervailing forces in the 1970s. In the early 1980s, reactive survival tactics in government had given way to proactive voluntarist reform of the party's own constitution. Once again, constitutional innovation precipitated serious problems, even for a party with a deep tradition of internal constitutionalism. The culmination of a drive by the party's left wing for radical changes in Labour's constitution came in 1981 when at a special conference it was agreed that the party leader would be selected by an electoral college and that all Labour MPs would have to submit themselves to a mandatory re-selection procedure within the lifetime of a single parliament. Although a third reform giving control of the party's manifesto to the National Executive Committee failed to win approval, the Wembley conference marked a victory for extra-parliamentary pressure within the party. The PLP and the Labour leadership were now required to be more responsive and accountable to the party's rank and file. But the convulsions occasioned by such an assault upon the party's machinery provoked such a depth of division that it immediately led to the Limehouse Declaration (January 1981) when the 'Gang of Three' (i.e. Roy Jenkins, Shirley Williams, William Rodgers) supported by nine other Labour MPs effectively launched the Social Democratic Party (SDP). Within a year, it was evident that the constitutional experiment in intra-party democracy had precipitated the most serious schism in the history of the Labour movement, with 26 MPs defecting to join the SDP. Worse was to follow. Labour's support fell from 46 per cent in January 1981 to a record low of 23.5 per cent by the end of the year. In September 1981 an electoral alliance was formed between the SDP and the Liberal party. Moreover, by March 1982, the Alliance had won three by-elections.[10] Prior to the 1983 general election, the Alliance threatened to become the main opposition party in British politics. Labour had to fight a rearguard action in the election simply to sustain its status as the primary source of an alternative government. In the event, it succeeded in prevailing over the SDP–Liberal coalition by 27.6 per cent of the popular vote to 25.4 per cent, but in the process it lost 60 seats mostly to the Conservatives and established such a low base of parliamentary representation (209) that it effectively discounted any serious prospect of a Labour government for the rest of the decade.[11]

The final reason for Labour's ambivalence towards constitutional reform has been the issue's close association with minority parties, marginal movements and lost causes. It is not merely that constitutional reform is seen as

unnecessary and divisive for a party requiring unity to achieve more explicitly substantive social and economic measures. It is widely regarded as both
a cause and an effect of party failure. In effect, the issue of constitutional
reform is seen as the loser's option – indeed very often the only available
option for a party with no hope of achieving the power to secure any programme of reform. For Labour to become embroiled in such an abstract, elusive and digressive theme is to risk its status as the cutting edge of social
transformation, and to identify the party with a form, a substance and a
style of politics which is largely at odds with the drives that animate its supporters and with the traditional precedents of winning elections.

The Labour party's origins lay in radical critique and social antagonism
and its identity has, until very recently, been defined by the use of the state
to confront vested economic and social interests with the objective of
achieving a more equitable and cohesive society. The ideological and ethical grandeur of such an agenda has historically regarded constitutional
reform as a largely irrelevant issue. As signifying the 'rules of the game', the
constitution affords not only a valuable legitimacy to any Labour government but permits such a government to amend constitutional arrangements
should the need arise. The constitution, therefore, provides a point of access
to government and with it the entry to parliamentary sovereignty that will
allow the rules to be changed in accordance with the political needs,
resources and prudence of the governing party. It is the prospect and even
imminence of such power in an established two-party system which fosters
a non-reform logic within the main reform party – i.e. when in power the
party has no need of constitutional reform; when out of power its whole
status as the 'government in waiting' is thrown into doubt by resorting to
such an issue. When the main opposition party in a predominantly two-
party system begins questioning the rules of the game, it denotes the existence of pressure upon its position as a viable alternative administration. In
effect, a commitment to constitutional reform can damage an opposition
party because it can be equated with a lack of self-belief in its ability to
replace a sitting government. In trying to optimise its political standing as
a main party, it risks taking on the appearance of a third party.

Constitutional reform therefore is commonly seen to be a defining characteristic of the kind of free-wheeling disaffection and licentious radicalism
of minority parties which have no serious prospect of ever forming an
administration, or sharing in governmental responsibilities. Much of the
raison d'être of third parties is provided by a sense of unwarranted exclusion
from the mainstream of British politics. They combine an evident minority
status with claims of representing a deeper or more historically rooted construction of the public interest. They infuse the standard interplay of established political forces with an ethical sub-text of representational injustice,
political unaccountability, and local, regional or national disfranchisement.

Free from the constraints of prospective governmental responsibility, a body like the Liberal party and its successor the Liberal Democrat party have had the freedom of action to pursue the flaws within the British constitution and to publicise the commensurate need to address them as problems requiring corrective action to preserve the democratic integrity of the system. It is its very distance from government which gives such an organisation its roving commission to engage in severe political and moral criticisms of both the constitution and its primary users. Guilt by association is extended to the Labour party as well as to the Conservative party because together they are seen as forming a duopoly of restrictive practices.

For 20 years, Labour party strategists have been conscious of the capacity of Liberal, Alliance and Liberal Democrat forces to prevent the election, or the re-election, of a left-of-centre government. They have had to acknowledge the responsiveness of the Liberal Democrats and other minor parties to grievances and issues that have not traditionally been high on Labour's agenda of priorities. They have had to recognise that an issue like constitutional reform arouses different forms of political interest and taps alternative sites of political support to that normally associated with Labour's conventional style of electoral campaigning. It is because of the clear resonance of such an issue in key areas that party managers have increasingly been prompted into giving serious consideration to forms of pre-emptive accommodation. Nevertheless, in undertaking such adjustments they have been confronted by a series of problems.

First, by endorsing parts or even all of the constitutional reform agenda, Labour runs the risk of looking unduly reactive for an allegedly innovative and autonomous party. It is seen to have come late and reluctantly to a set of issues which are popularly identified with other parties and with the Liberal Democrats in particular. Second, in adopting the terms of ethical engagement in the campaign to enhance the state of liberal democracy, the Labour party can appear to be acting disingenuously. When Liberal Democrats advocate electoral reform, for example, the moral force of their argument is supported by the party's evident status as a victim of the 'first-past-the-post' system. The palpable injustice of the latter helps to obscure the party's clear self-interest in seeking to change the system of representation. The Labour party on the other hand has not only been a prime beneficiary of the current system, but has traditionally shown very little interest in the merits of proportional representation (PR). Whenever Labour considers changing its position in an area like electoral reform, therefore, it can appear to be governed more by political advantage rather than by principles of justice and equity. While the Liberal Democrats can seem ostensibly objective and only subsequently self-regarding in their attachment to reform, the risk for Labour lies in the process of perception being reversed, stripping the party of any benefit of the doubt and leaving it in the position of defending itself against the charge of pursuing ideals for purely partisan motives.

Another problem for Labour in moving onto territory prepared by others is that it will almost invariably find itself occupying a central position between the Conservative minimalist view of constitutional reform and the maximalist stance of the Liberal Democrats. In such a context, the centre does not always represent the optimal location for attracting political support. On the contrary, where constitutional change is concerned it can be seen as a no-win position in which Labour's reformist credentials are depicted as cynical equivocation by the polarised flanks on either side. The effects of such a political and moral 'squeeze' were painfully evident in the 1992 general election when Labour's intermediate position on electoral reform looked like an improvised and ultimately ambiguous manoeuvre designed to attract support both from those Liberal Democrats well disposed towards Labour and from wavering Conservatives who were nevertheless nervous over the prospect of a divisive Labour government. Even though opinion research in 1991 had suggested that a Labour endorsement of PR might be worth between 2 and 4 percentage points of additional voter support, electoral reform remained a highly divisive issue within the party. A period of respite had been achieved after the 1987 general election through the formation of a party committee of inquiry under Professor Raymond Plant to examine options for introducing PR to the elections for the projected regional assemblies and the chamber designed to replace the House of Lords. But in 1990 the party conference insisted that the remit of the Plant inquiry be extended to consider the electoral arrangements of the House of Commons, and the issue began to acquire an unavoidable prominence. By 1991, '[e]lectoral reform, hitherto "undiscussable" in the Labour Party, was at last on the agenda'.[12] The party leader, Neil Kinnock, was privately sympathetic to PR but, because most of the shadow cabinet including the deputy leader were opposed to it, he followed a policy of judicious silence, referring only to the need for a full debate inside the party. As Labour moved cautiously in late 1991 and early 1992 towards forms of PR for the proposed Scottish assembly and the projected replacement of the House of Lords, the question of whether electoral reform could or should be excluded from the House of Commons in the light of such precedents became progressively more pressing. Labour's initial position of arguing that differing electoral systems suited different levels of government quickly proved to be intellectually untenable. The prime minister moved promptly to exploit the Labour party's disarray. John Major clearly established the Conservative position as early as October 1991 when in his speech to the party conference he ruled out any changes to the electoral system and, with it, any prospect of a post-election deal with the Liberal Democrats. The Labour position remained altogether more elusive and apparently less principled, intended as it was to maintain party unity while keeping the door open to the possibility of future co-operation with the Liberal Democrats.

During the campaign, the Labour leadership not only hinted at the introduction of PR for European elections but declared that the Plant committee could be enlarged to include representatives from the Liberal Democrat party. The 'wait-and-see' line from Labour in one sense appeared equivocal, especially after Neil Kinnock refused to divulge his personal position on PR in the *Granada 500* television programme three days prior to the election. In another sense, Labour's signals on PR to the Liberal Democrats could be viewed as a direct and even cynical attempt to form an implicit alliance by which to enhance its campaign to capture government power. Roy Hattersley recalls the problems incurred by the sudden emphasis upon constitutional reform:

> During the 1992 general election, Labour certainly wanted to poach Liberal votes. We wanted to poach Tory votes as well, but we were less successful in that endeavour. Unfortunately, we actually lost support by what appeared to be a sudden conversion to constitutional reform. The proposals set out during two press conferences (exactly a week before polling day) had been official party policy for years. But the unexpected enthusiasm with which the plans were advocated appeared to be the product of sudden panic.[13]

John Major integrated Labour's allusions to electoral reform into his overall strategy of defending the integrity of the United Kingdom and its constitution. Conservative party strategists portrayed Labour's positional flexibility as a sign of weakness: 'They look like losers,' commented a senior Tory.[14] Meanwhile, John Major made a virtue of his early stand against PR and reaffirmed his intransigence with increasing vigour towards the end of the campaign. He asserted that he would rather be hounded out of office than compromise his principles by conceding PR to the Liberal Democrats in order for the Conservatives to remain in power. 'I would rather quit politics,' he said, 'rather than accept a measure which would subvert the constitution.'[15] The Conservatives portrayed themselves as offering clarity, irrespective of conditions. Labour, on the other hand, was placed in a position of attempting to press its claims as a credible and trustworthy alternative government, while needing to adjust continually to changing scenarios of possible electoral outcomes in what was becoming a last-minute scramble for seats. The authors of the Nuffield College study of the 1992 general election concluded that the PR episode had been badly handled by the Labour leadership. '[I]f the party was going to raise electoral reform then it should have broached the subject much earlier in the parliament, perhaps in the policy review or in Mr Kinnock's 1991 conference speech, or most positively in the manifesto.'[16] Those participating in the election agreed. In the questionnaire conducted by the Nuffield survey, 'many Labour candidates were quick to condemn the proportional representation (PR) initiative in the last days of the campaign, on the grounds that it showed weakness, or distracted attention from the NHS or a counter-attack on tax, or simply because they opposed PR. Conservatives claimed that Labour betrayed its lack of confidence and was mistaken to introduce such an issue so late in the campaign.'[17]

Labour's preparation for the 1997 general election was heavily conditioned by the post-mortem of the 1992 general election. Although the late swing to the Conservatives was the result of a variety of factors, it occurred during, and was subsequently closely associated with, a period of the election campaign when the issue of constitutional reform achieved maximum exposure. The prospect of a hung parliament generated a ferment of constitutional speculation that was ostensibly related to PR but which indirectly embraced the entire agenda of constitutional change. In effect, the 1992 general election not only gave graphic expression to the opportunities and the costs of the constitutional issue, but underlined the requisite need on the part of all the main parties to take stock and to devise strategies by which to maximise the benefits and minimise the dangers of such an issue in preparation for the next election.

For the Conservatives, constitutional reform was perceived to be a negative asset. John Major used the authority of the premiership to its fullest extent to set the face of the Conservative party unequivocally against reform. Such a conspicuous defence of the status quo had four key merits. First, it provided a focus for party loyalty. 'The need to sustain the fragile unity of the party, following the fall-out from the Maastricht treaty and the UK's forced and unseemly withdrawal from the ERM, meant that much rhetoric had to be expended in defence of Britain's national and parliamentary sovereignty in order to maintain the government's narrow majority in the House of Commons.'[18] Second, it allowed the Conservatives to distract attention away from the large scale *de facto* changes already made to the constitution by successive Conservative administrations. Third, it allowed the party to unite behind a strong United Kingdom position, thereby affording common ground both to pro- and anti-Europeanists, while simultaneously concealing the depth of the party's division on the European integration issue. Fourth, it provided a definitive and coherent position from which to confront Labour. After 13 years in government, the defence of the British constitution was an issue which allowed the Conservatives to engage in a populist assault upon the promises of the opposition. Labour's constitutional proposals were described as an indiscriminate subversion of the entire fabric of both the British constitution and the United Kingdom. In like manner, reforms in such areas as devolution, regional government, PR and the House of Lords were used to characterise Labour's entire programme as indeterminate, unpredictable and even dangerous. The phrase 'defence of the constitution' carried with it the implicit suggestion of unseen and sinister forces at work within the constitutional order. This subversive imagery was simply extended across the board so that the constitution became the clinching exemplification of Labour and its reputedly hidden agenda for British society. The attribution of a reckless radicalism to Labour allowed the Conservatives to indulge in an uninhibited exercise of negative campaigning during the election. For example, Labour and the Liberal Democrats' devolution packages were claimed to risk the break-up of the United Kingdom just at a time when the combined weight of the Union's constituent nations was needed to help shape international decisions like the European Community agreement at Maastricht.[19] PR would also threaten the product of three hundred years of constitutional history by ensuring that the British government would be so weak that it could no longer be able to take strong decisions such as those which launched the Falklands expedition and Britain's participation in the Gulf War.[20] John Major accused Paddy Ashdown of 'flirting with the constitution'[21] by seeking to secure PR through a post-election deal with Labour that would distort the electoral verdict in favour of a contrived victory for the two defeated minority parties. He warned the voters in Bath: 'Beware Mr Ashdown. He is the doorkeeper to a Labour government. Don't look at the man; look through the door. The most famous door in the world is No. 10 Downing Street. Don't let Mr Ashdown open it for Mr Kinnock.'[22] A few days later, the insinuations became more defamatory with John Major observing that 'some sorts of PR would let in very tiny minorities with extremely unrepresentative views – the National Front, yes, the Communist party, yes – all alien to the way our constitution has run for over 200 years'.[23] The *coup de grâce* was left to Kenneth Baker:

> Proportional representation has helped the fascists to march again in Europe. It is a terrible warning to us about what could happen if we threw away our system of first past the post elections. That is what Mr Ashdown wants to do. It is what Mr Kinnock is prepared to do as the price of power. If PR turned out to have the same results in Britain, it would be a pact with the devil.[24]

In the event, the Conservatives won the election with a working majority, thereby precluding any prospect of party collaboration for constitutional gains. Notwithstanding the result, the Conservative campaign had highlighted the problems that may have ensued if a hung parliament had induced forms of negotiated co-operation between Labour and the Liberal Democrats.

The Liberal Democrats found that as the campaign progressed they were being pushed into a discreditable corner along with Labour by the Tories' dramatised rejection of any constitutional reform under any circumstances. This enforced proximity with Labour was no doubt more congenial to the

Liberal Democratic leadership than being placed adjacent to the Conservative government, but nevertheless a rapprochement with either of the other two main parties posed a danger to the electoral potential of such a third party. Even if the leadership were more closely aligned to Labour than to the Conservatives, it was known that a large proportion of the pool of soft Liberal Democratic support would be disaffected Conservative voters seeking an alternative means of political expression. A *Sunday Telegraph*/Gallup poll,[25] published only four days before polling day, showed that if minor parties were to hold the balance of power, 45 per cent of Liberal Democrat supporters favoured keeping the Tories in power compared to 41 per cent who preferred the Liberal Democrats' leverage being used in favour of the Labour option.

Mindful that the anti-Labour voters in their ranks would react strongly against the prospect of acting as a Trojan horse for the Labour party in a hung parliament, the Liberal Democrats tried to distance themselves from Labour by underlining the differences on economic policy between the two parties. However, this response only played into the Conservatives' hands because it gave credence to the notion that the Labour and Liberal Democrat parties were prepared to consider some form of co-operation for the sake of acquiring power even though they were fundamentally at odds over policy. The Liberal Democrats were seen to have run a successful campaign especially in respect to their proposal linking a penny increase in income tax to plans to improve the education system. Nevertheless, the party still had to confront the traditional 'wasted vote' argument. The difficulty in the 1992 election was that the most effective solution to such an argument merely created another problem. The prospect of Liberal Democrat votes being translated into an effective share of government generated misgivings that the Liberal Democrats were seeking to exploit what was a conspicuous minority position to revise the outcome of the election and to exploit the constitutional weakness of a hung parliament, in order to secure what would be irreversible changes to the constitution.

For Labour, the 1992 general election demonstrated the difficulty of controlling the issue of constitutional reform in an electoral setting. It showed that the tactical device of accumulating specific commitments to future reform on a particularistic basis could unravel under pressure without a strategic set of organising principles to provide a thematic structure of reform. In essence, the election revealed that constitutional reform was not a 'no-cost', or even a 'low-cost', policy, but an issue area that could backfire on the party in the intensity of electoral competition. It is true that the Labour party was placed in a difficult position because of the exact circumstances of the 1992 election. After a period of enforced modernisation from the centre, the party had succeeded in creating a more centrist image for itself in order to allay the fears it had generated over its radicalism in the early and mid-1980s. In 1992, Labour was finally in contention for a general election victory, but the trace elements of public distrust remained and therefore the opposition party received as much critical attention as the government throughout the period preceding and during the election. When Labour moved ahead of the Conservatives in three opinion polls ten days before the election, the emphasis of public assessment shifted away from the government's record and more towards the trustworthiness and competence of the Labour party. Even though the Conservatives were highly vulnerable on their record and especially so in the midst of a recession, they succeeded in making Labour the focus of critical attention.

After 13 years in opposition, the Labour party had to maximise its potential for acquiring power, but in doing so it laid itself open to assault for opportunism and deviousness. Labour may have led in the polls but such an advantage would probably diminish as polling day became imminent. Moreover, even if such a lead were to be maintained it was unlikely to produce a working majority. Labour strategists, therefore, were faced with a general need to allay fears over the prospect of a Labour government and a specific need to make preparations for the possibility of a hung parliament. The references to considering PR were intended to answer both these needs but, as described above, they were given an unfavourable interpretation in the hostile atmosphere of a general election. With the Conservative government fighting for its life and with its strategy of bringing Labour into disrepute over what the Conservatives were describing as Labour's surreptitious taxation policies, Labour's discrete and finely tuned positions on constitutional reform were simply bundled together as a politically motivated attack on parliamentary sovereignty and, thereby, on the British constitution as a whole. Labour quickly discovered that it was difficult to retain its various nuances on constitutional reform when confronted with the sweepingly visceral condemnation by a Conservative government that was intent upon making it a gut issue. The party also learnt that in this particular policy area the Liberal Democrats constituted a genuine third force which made strategic planning difficult. This was not only because Labour risked being stuck in the equivocal centre of an issue suffused with high principle, but because the Conservative government's opposition to reform was so implacable that it made Labour look as if it would take the reform initiative from the Liberal Democrats merely for the sake of achieving government – i.e. that Labour would agree to the paradox of new constitutional restraints upon power in order to acquire power. Finally, the election revealed how difficult it was for an opposition to use constitutional reform to challenge the conservatism of the constitution, especially when compounded by a Conservative government intent upon a policy of flamboyant resistance to reform. After a sustained period of one-party government, the main opposition party may feel the need for supplementary assistance in the form of constitutional change, or for some form of cross-party co-operation on the basis of such a change, but it is precisely because of the extended tenure of such a government that any transition to a new government must be seen as having been clearly, decisively and legitimately secured.

The 1997 general election and the constitutional agenda

The onset of a further five years of Conservative government made the issue of constitutional reform even more pertinent to political debate in Britain. But while the advocates of constitutional change had the advantage of a continuing fuel supply to maintain a public awareness of the constitution as an instrument of political dissent, they had the disadvantage of knowing that the only real chance of substantive reform lay with an alignment of the centre left which would be difficult to accomplish after the debacle over PR in the 1992 general election. While reformers and reformist organisations within the party – most notably Robin Cook, Jeff Rooker and the renovated Labour Campaign for Electoral Reform – sought to press the issue of PR, they were more than countered by those members, especially in the trade unions, who remained sceptical of such a radical departure from tradition. The conversion of the Labour party to constitutional change was still the optimum strategy for the reform lobby, but Labour remained cautious in spirit despite its public attachment to several non-PR items of the reform agenda. Party strategists were mindful of the effective irreversibility of previous commitments to constitutional change (e.g. devolution, bill of rights). They were also aware of their use as agents of party cohesion and as rallying points in opposition challenges to the government. Nevertheless, the party leadership also knew constitutional reform was a sensitive issue that was difficult to fine-tune in the public domain and especially during an election campaign when political motives and institutional consequences were particularly vulnerable to corrosively negative constructions by both Conservative and Liberal Democratic parties.

While the issue of the constitution had acquired an inertial force within the party, it had not reached the level of being a clearly marked priority. The Kinnock–Hattersley leadership of the party had always suffered from a collective ambiguity on the issue of the constitution. Roy Hattersley was uninhibited in his dismissal of constitutional reform as radical chic. Needing to maximise consensus within the party, Neil Kinnock was more elusive on the subject and preferred to reserve his position pending developments. Labour may have accumulated a number of commitments to constitutional change, but the view expressed by Perry Anderson reflected a widespread scepticism surrounding Labour's reticence over the constitution. Labour's acknowledgement of the need for constitutional reform did not in Anderson's view 'touch the two central arrangements at Westminster. The Labour

establishment continues to refuse any serious commitment to either electoral reform or a written constitution. It visibly still hopes to utilize the pre-
democratic structures of the British State, as Thatcher has done, for its own
ends.'[26] The constitutional reform lobby rightfully suspected the Labour
leadership of not being true believers. In 1990, Stuart Weir bitterly complained that Kinnock retained 'a narrow view of party advantage' in respect
to the issue of the constitution. At a time when 'Thatcher's ruthless
exploitation of the power of big government' was provoking a reappraisal of
the state of British democracy, the Labour party had placed itself at a disadvantage of its own making'. Weir continued:

> [T]he party has ... swallowed the nonsense about "strong government" and
> believes in it still even though Thatcher's governments since 1979 have vividly
> shown the damage that "strong government" can do to the social fabric and
> well-being of the nation. Right and left. Hattersley and Benn alike, Labour
> politicians remain loyal to an electoral and parliamentary system that renders
> them the weaker of the two main parties but at least gives them a near monop-
> oly of the opposition.[27]

Stuart Weir's analysis was accurate but his prescription of Labour attaching
itself fully to the theme of democratic revival was premature As Patrick Seyd
notes: 'During most of the late 1980s and the early 1990s, conventional
wisdom among the Labour leadership appeared to be that constitutional
reform was an issue of interest only to the "chattering classes" and therefore of little electoral significance.'[28] The leadership of John Smith (1992–94)
was more encouraging to the reform movement because he sustained a clear
engagement with the general issue. For example, he agreed to associate himself publicly with Charter 88 when in March 1993 he participated in the
first Charter 88 debate. In his speech to the reform group, the Labour leader
openly acknowledged that the constitution had become an issue requiring
urgent action: 'Our crumbling constitution can no longer be dismissed as a
side-show. It is at the heart of what is wrong with this country.'[29] He went
on to affirm the need for devolution, a freedom of information act, the revival
of local democracy and the incorporation into British law of the European
Convention on Human Rights. It was an address of 'such boldness and
explicit argument' that Andrew Marr believed it would be 'a hard speech to
walk away from, or forget'.[30] The occasion was in essence a recognition of
the part that Charter 88 and other reform groups had had in raising the
party's consciousness over the thematic and campaigning potential of institutional change. But notwithstanding such public professions of faith in the
need for constitutional reform, the precise nature and depth of the Labour
party's agenda remained unclear. The need for reform had been accepted in
principle, but it was difficult to ascertain whether the agenda had been
assimilated as a defining conviction and a strategic priority within the party.

The party had accumulated a set of diagnostic and prescriptive positions but there remained no controlling theme that integrated them together into a discernible programme, or geared them both into the party's traditional policy positions and into its contemporary social and economic plans. Their level of coherence, emphasis and urgency remained open to question up to and during the mid-term of the 1992–97 parliament.

In the hiatus following John Smith's death on 12 May 1994, the party was distracted first by a prolonged leadership election procedure and then by Tony Blair's campaign to change the party's own constitution. Labour was in effect affiliated to the theme of constitutional reform but detached from the task of establishing its exact objectives and of pursuing all the implications of such an extensive yet nominal programme for change. At the end of 1994, William Rees-Mogg balefully observed that under John Smith, the Labour party 'fell into the hands of lawyers ... [who] love proposals for constitutional reform'. He summed up Labour's subsequent predicament of no fewer than eleven items of reform in the following terms:

> So here are 11 areas of constitutional reform, each of which is open to endless debate, at a general election, in Parliament, in the courts. Some of the reforms would be popular, some not, but all will tend to distract attention from the Labour Party's other policies, which matter far more to the public. They could also give Labour a cranky image. There are ... 11 Pandora's boxes, each with its own booby-trap inside. Worst of all, these proposals would take almost all the time of the next parliament, if Labour were elected, in hair-splitting arguments which would delight the lawyers, bore the public, and split the party.[31]

These were not unreasonable conclusions. Labour was spread thin across a morass of agenda items without having really analysed their relationship to the party's long-term political objectives or their capacity to impact upon one another both in theory and in practice.

It was not until the issue of Clause Four had been resolved in April 1995 that Tony Blair was able to give his full attention to the strategic planning for the forthcoming general election and to the place of constitutional reform in the party's next challenge for government. It was clear to the new leader that the raft of constitutional proposals which he had inherited was not an unqualified benefit to the party. For example, such an agenda always carried the potential for opening up old divisions within the party over its historic mission and overall political rationale. It also had the capacity to absorb extensive political resources, to de-rail parliamentary schedules, to propagate immense problems over detail and to lead to severe difficulties over each proposal's relationship to the other elements of the agenda. Furthermore, as constitutional reforms would always be high-profile measures, the party leadership would invariably be charged either with incompetence for courting party disunity, or with authoritarian over-reaction in stifling open debate.

It was also evident that the Conservatives would seek to make their defence of the constitution a key election issue. John Major remained convinced that his dire warnings over constitutional dissolution and the impending break-up of the United Kingdom during the 1992 general election had been instrumental in producing a decisive late swing to the Tories. Even though no evidence exists to support such a claim, the prime minister was convinced of its effectiveness and was determined that the strategy should be redeployed next time around. A principled defence of the constitution would not only give the party a theme upon which to unify as conservatives set against reckless and irreversible changes, but would afford a means of nationalist solidarity to act as a counter-weight to the Tory split over Europe. It was also thought that the issue would allow the party to drive wedges both within the Labour party, and between Labour and the Liberal Democrats. As for the Conservatives, the party proceeded on the assumption that it had a natural advantage over constitutional affairs. 'These are great issues,' said the prime minister in a speech to party agents before the Conservative conference in 1995. 'But they are *our* issues. This is *our* ground.'[32] The self-belief in the party's natural proprietorship of constitutional management would, in John Major's view, allow the party to dictate the terms of the debate and to rally middle-class Tory waverers in the process. Labour's constitutional plans would be used not only to portray the party as unfit to govern but also to signify the continued existence of a deeply embedded and generic radicalism within its organisation. In this context, the constitution could and would be used by the Conservatives to open up the much sought after 'clear blue water' between the government and Blair's New Labour.

Tony Blair for his part was aware that while the issue of the constitution appeared to be running with Labour, it could quickly become a policy liability. Even though Labour had established a prodigious lead in the polls,[33] the party leadership and its strategists proceeded on the assumption that such an advantage was unsustainable and that, in the forthcoming general election, the Conservatives would again mobilise the 'Middle England' vote and close the gap. Blair felt he was placed in the invidious position of possessing a sufficient poll lead for his party to have the status of a government-in-waiting, while at the same time knowing that such a poll advantage was precarious and unreliable. He was also actively conscious that such a solid lead inverted the customary government–opposition relationship into a 'reverse incumbency' effect that would allow the Conservatives to attack Labour for its policies and past record and to keep the spotlight firmly on the question of Labour's trustworthiness and competence as a party of government.

Constitutional reform typified the kind of issue which the Conservatives would attempt to use in order to subvert Labour's claim to government. This is not to say that Labour was without some advantages over the Tories in this issue. For example, the Conservative government could be depicted as having been not only an inattentive trustee of the constitution, but an active agent in the corruption of the political system. The Conservatives were also vulnerable to the charge of double standards by standing on the principle of 'no change', while at the same time claiming credit for major constitutional changes during the period of Conservative government and defending future constitutional innovations as legitimate on the grounds that they would be conceived and implemented by the next Conservative government. At another level, conservative resistance to a specific scheme like devolution in Scotland was 'likely to seem atavistic and undemocratic'.[34] Bearing in mind the marginal Tory presence in Scotland, the act of 'pumping up English nationalism by warning of the break-up of the United Kingdom could look merely self-interested'.[35] Notwithstanding such weaknesses, the Labour party leadership had to proceed on the assumption that for constitutional issues to become electoral assets they had to be treated with caution. It was necessary to establish Labour's position as early and as clearly as possible on a number of key constitutional issues, but it was also politically prudent to defer decisions and to retain options in order to take account of shifting political conditions. Even more important for Labour's chances in the approaching election was the need for some kind of rapprochement with the party which more than any other had fostered an enduring intimacy with the whole theme of constitutional reform. The Liberal Democrats had publicly squeezed Labour on constitutional reform in 1992 and had again split the centre left in doing so. It now made sense for Labour not only to clarify the centre ground it shared with the Liberal Democrats on constitutional reform, but to use it to develop the main theme and to provide the guiding objective of a collaborative exercise between the two parties.

Although it was probable that Labour could win without Liberal Democrat support, it was equally the case that with minimal concessions the party could significantly enhance its chances of electoral penetration. Co-operation with Liberal Democrats on the sensitive issue of constitutional reform would act as a mutual defence alliance against Conservative attempts to divide and rule the centre left. Apart from protecting the coherence and integrity of Labour's own constitutional agenda from Liberal Democratic ambushes, a co-operative strategy would also protect the issue itself from becoming defined by the Liberal Democrats and, thereby, characterised by that party's often *avant garde* image. An 'understanding' between the parties would allow them to develop the theme of a popular movement not only against Tory government but against any repetition of what the Tories had inflicted upon the system of government. By breaking down the Liberal Democrats' position of 'equidistance' between the main parties, Labour would be afforded something of an amnesty from Liberal Democratic assaults while at the same time ensuring that the undoubted polemical and electoral skills of the Liberal Democrats would be targeted almost exclusively upon the Tories. Such visible evidence of a new politics of partnership would not be limited to the acquisition of governmental power. A convergence with the Liberal Democrats had the potential of helping Labour maintain power. By March 1996, Labour leaders were having to react to speculation over plans of a post-election coalition with the Liberal Democrats. On 17 March 1996, for example, the *Sunday Times* carried the following front page report: 'Tony Blair has signalled for the first time that he might support changes to Britain's electoral system ... Blair's move ... will fuel fears among Labour left-wingers that he intends to form a post-election coalition with the Lib Dems if he wins power. Although Labour leaders deny such plans, some senior figures are attracted by the idea of working closely with the Lib Dems. This could enable a Blair government to survive possible rebellions by left-wing MPs.'[36] An alternative construction of such a coalition could support the hypothesis of an alliance of the left giving security to a radical government to pursue egalitarian policies without continually having to appease the antagonisms of suburban floaters. Whatever the motives or projected scenarios, Labour strategists had shown clear signs of having been persuaded of the benefits of collaboration over a year prior to the general election .

For the Liberal Democrats, the general election promised to provide the optimal conditions for the party to consider a form of co-operation with Labour. It was likely, yet not certain, that Labour would win the election. The Liberal Democrats were poised to inflict maximum damage upon Conservative seats. Their tally of Tory scalps could prove decisive in a tight election. The Liberal Democrats' capacity to organise tactical voting in areas where Labour were the main challengers to the Tories would provide additional leverage. The Liberal Democrats' bargaining position may not have been strong, but in conditions that were expected to be volatile it was sufficient to be taken into account by Labour and, therefore, by the Liberal Democrats themselves. It was already safe to predict that the party would increase its number of seats by attacking the Conservatives rather than Labour. A Liberal Democrat candidate explained the logic in a party magazine: 'There are very few seats where we come a good second to Labour, suggesting that if we don't make significant gains this time, it is going to be an awful lot harder next time ... There appear to be very few seats that will easily fall our way by attacking Blair.'[37] By the same token, it was also safe to predict that the Liberal Democratic share of the vote would decline because of the resurgence of the Labour party as a centre-left organisation. In the circumstances, the opportunity to clarify, and therefore to maximise, the anti-Tory message combined with the chance of a share in government, prompted the Liberal Democrats to give serious consideration to the idea of a collaborative undertaking.

Constitutional reform would be the touchstone of Labour–Liberal Democratic co-operation. It was the primary reason for and the chief means of any form of convergence. But even though they had comparable agendas of reform, these in themselves were not enough to ensure the basis of joint enterprise. Incidental replication was not the same as mutual interest, let alone the existence of parallel commitment. To the Liberal Democrats, constitutional reform was a passion. It was integral to its entire identity as a party and reforming movement. It was not only 'the central plank of their programme ... it remain[ed] their unique selling point'.[38] The Liberal Democrats had extensive and detailed experience of the issues raised by constitutional reform and were watchful of other parties' interest in the theme even though they knew that for constitutional reform to become a reality it would always require the sponsorship of one of the main parties. The Liberal Democrats were also aware that the previous Lib–Lab pact (1977–79) had yielded nothing from the Callaghan government. They gleaned that the Labour party under Blair was as ambiguous as ever on constitutional reform. Policy legacies had been acknowledged, statements of interest had been registered and undertakings requiring serious consideration had been promised, but the Liberal Democrats were concerned over whether these amounted to an absolute commitment, or an exercise in 'bean counting' whereby individual constituencies of complaint had been accommodated by flamboyant yet spurious allusions to future action. It was evident that devolution for Scotland was an imperative item for Labour, but doubt remained over the relationship between the rest of the reform agenda and Labour's conception of its vital interests. Given the traditional support by 'old Labour' of the central state as an instrument of social change and given that the Labour party remained deeply split over the most important item of constitutional reform to the Liberal Democrats (i.e. PR), it was necessary for New Labour as the senior partner in any future collaboration to reveal itself publicly and emphatically on the issue of constitutional change.

It is unlikely that the Labour leadership was intent solely upon laying down markers for co-operation with the Liberal Democrats in the action undertaken during February 1996. Nonetheless, this was one of the consequences of Tony Blair's attempt to confront the issue of constitutional reform head on and to incorporate it explicitly into his vision of a new Britain. February 1996 marked the period when the Labour leadership embarked upon a strategy not just to quell doubts over the party's commitment to constitutional reform, but to elevate the issue into a defining theme and a prevailing priority of the new Labour party. Under the aegis of Blair's leadership, constitutional reform would no longer have the reputation of being a set of uncomfortable and ill-matched appendages to Labour party policy. The theme would now occupy centre stage as a collective conviction exemplifying the substance and methods of Blair's highly personalised conception of leadership. In his John Smith memorial lecture in February 1996, Blair took the opportunity to publicise his personal commitment to constitutional reform by recommitting his party to the restructuring of the House of Lords, the establishment of Welsh and Scottish assemblies, the passage of a freedom of information act, the revival of local government, the reform of the House of Commons, a referendum on the voting system and the incorporation of the European Convention on Human Rights into British law. Blair reiterated the reformist canon that Britain possessed 'the most centralised government of any large state in the western world'[39] and that decisional processes fundamentally affected both the substance of political decisions and their social and economic consequences. He used this arena to fuse together a critique of the constitution with the development of his personal vision of a 'stakeholding society'[40] which would enhance individual responsibility, social cohesion and political participation. In doing so, Blair may have risked irritating those on the left wing of his party by giving weight to their charges that he was intent not so much upon reforming socialism, as on replacing it with something more akin to the organicist illusions of one-nation Toryism. Blair attempted to confront this objection in an article that accompanied the lecture:

> Of course we have to change the Government if we want to turn the country around, but we also have to change the way things are run so that people exercise more power over those they elect and what is done in their name – not just a new set of politicians but a new politics ... Some people say that political reform only interests the chattering classes – it may an issue around the Hampstead dinner tables, but not something most people are interested in. That was not John Smith's view, nor is it mine. That attitude only benefits the Tories and the Establishment who run most things at the moment. They don't want the majority to think about these issues. But the fact is they matter to everyone because they are about power – who holds it, who uses it and how people can control it.[41]

Simply to compete for the temporary proprietorship of an unquestioned monolith of central power was to Blair no longer sufficient to achieve real change. By using constitutional reform not merely as a platform but as a litmus test of his leadership motif, Blair staked his reputation and prestige upon the cause of constitutional reform in a way that no previous Labour leader had done. Constitutional change could no longer be regarded as a peripheral anomaly or even as an aberrational necessity to Labour's rationale. The issue had now assumed a central location within the attributed seamlessness of Blair's seminal idea on society and the economy.

These signals of New Labour's thinking on the constitution were reaffirmed and fine-tuned in subsequent speeches and articles. The most authoritative compendium of the party's outlook at this time is provided by Peter Mandelson and Roger Liddle's *The Blair Revolution*. In it, they lay down the controlling beliefs and operational strategy of the leadership. They acknowledge that until recently Labour had distanced itself from the debate on the constitution, and those who remain opposed to constitutional change 'plead with Labour not to take any notice of theorists whose fancy schemes will first limit Labour's ability to win power on its own and then limit its ability to use that power, once obtained, to effect real change'.[42] Mandelson and Little recognise that although this is an understandable reaction, it is nevertheless a mistaken one. They issue the following injunction.

> This attitude is wrong. Tony Blair's ambitious project for national renewal cannot draw the line at Westminster and Whitehall. The case for constitutional change cannot stop with the internal machinery of the Labour Party: Labour politicians need to look at their ways of working in government. They must demonstrate convincingly that they recognise the public's deep-seated disillusionment with politics, and that it will be unacceptable for the same old show to go on with only different-coloured rosettes. As Blair himself put it, 'A government of national renewal requires a national renewal of government' ... The only way to make people understand the party's new seriousness about political reform is to state this quite openly and explain why it is integral to New Labour's governing approach.[43]

They go on to accept that one of the implications of such an ambitious programme of modernisation is the likelihood of some form of power-sharing. Given that New Labour is engaged in a long-term cultural crusade both to decrease polarisation and centralisation, and to increase trust and partnership within society as a whole, a Labour government would require at best two full terms of office and, therefore, the capacity to withstand short-term setbacks and long-term critical attrition. Radicalism requires security. 'For those ... stuck in the traditional confines of narrow party politics, this requires a lot of hard thought, inevitably including consideration of Labour's relations with the Liberal Democrats'[44]. Mandelson and Little give emphasis to the common ground between the parties and conclude that 'the overlap between the two parties has become obvious'[45] and as a consequence '[t]here is no barrier to co-operation in terms of principle or policy'.[46]

Labour's excursions into the field of constitutional reform set both the terms of public debate and the pattern of political engagement during the run-up to the general election. While the Conservatives remained hopeful that the constitutional issue would prove to be the holy grail of electoral redemption, they were continually placed in disarray by Labour's lack of indiscipline, by its graduated suggestiveness of reform and by the Conservatives' own divisions over the best way to counter the constitutional issue. By the time of Tony Blair's John Smith lecture, the prime minister had mobilised the entire cabinet to confront New Labour's constitutional agenda. The party chairman, Brian Mawhinney, led the charge by slamming into Blair's proposals and proclaiming them to be 'fashionable left wing prejudices in defiance of the wisdom of the ages'.[47] This negative response reflected Major's basic stonewall strategy, yet even the prime minister realised the constitutional stasis would not always be promising ground to defend. As *The Economist* remarked on 29 June 1996: '"It's the constitution stupid" does not seem much of a rallying call to voters.'[48] John Major wished to bring the public's attention to his government's own 'gentle and evolutionary'[49] innovations but knew that this could be misinterpreted as providing evidence of the need to make the constitution less responsive to government policy. He also wanted to flag the possibility of future Conservative movement on the constitution but again this ran the risk of compromising his attack on Labour and of diverting the focus of his position as supreme defender of the British constitution. The tensions generated by these separate impulses were exemplified in an interview for *The Independent* on 17 November 1995. During the course of the discussion, the prime minister simultaneously embraced all these positions. He gave notice of his intention to introduce a new package of constitutional reform for Scotland that would afford 'better access to government' and an improved responsiveness at Westminster to Scottish interests. He praised his government's achievements in 'incremental evolutionary reforms'. 'I would defy any dispassionate judge to go over any single parliament in recent years and find as many moves from previously fixed positions on constitutional issues.'[50] Finally, he reassessed his irreconcilable opposition to devolution and used it to characterise Labour's inexperience and irresponsibility in constitutional affairs. In his view, Labour's proposals would

> provide a platform for a separatist party to gain a majority in Scotland and claim a mandate for separation. Once that demon rears its head it is very difficult to deal with as we have seen in different parts of the world ... What I fear is happening ... is that the Labour party are offering a proposition for Scotland to keep the Scottish Nationalists at bay because it is in Labour's political interests to do so. And they have not considered the long term view of what opportunities that might give the separatist party to turn Scotland into a separate nation.[51]

Major's position threatened to become minimal, equivocal and negative at the same time. Such a posture allowed Blair to wrong-foot the prime minister in open confrontation. For example, during the winter of 1995–96, the prime minister attempted to establish his position as a moderate reformer with plans to readdress the territorial problem of British government through such measures as making ministers appear at meetings of the Scottish Grand Committee held north of the border. Such modest moves were sidelined by Tony Blair's John Smith lecture which poured an enriched mixture of constitutional reform ideas straight into the arena of public debate.

An even more pointed example of both John Major's discomfort and the political use of constitutional reform came on 26 June 1996 when the Conservative leader attempted to wrest the initiative on the issue with a carefully crafted defence of the British constitution. In a lecture to the Centre for Policy Studies, he sought to expose the problematic and dangerous nature of Labour's constitutional agenda. The ambiguities and disjunctions generated by reform in this area were alleged to be so technically and democratically insoluble that they merely served to reaffirm the interior authenticity of the current constitutional arrangements. According to the prime minister, Labour had set in motion 'the most thorough debate on the constitution for a generation'[52] and he 'intend[ed] to make sure that the issues at stake in the constitutional debate [were] properly understood'.[53]

> [I]t's too easy to take for granted the traditions and institutions that make us a nation. Our constitutional fabric has been woven over the centuries. It's the product of hundreds of years of knowledge, experience and history. It's been stable, but not static ... Out of this evolutionary change has grown one of the finest, strongest and most admired constitutions in the world. I'm all for practical change that would solve real problems or improve the way our constitution works. But pointless fiddling with our constitution wouldn't solve any problems. It would just create new ones. In the end, it would begin to unstitch our way of life. One group of politicians could unravel what generations of our predecessors have created.[54]

Ironically in a keynote address on the constitutional debate, John Major gave emphasis to the need to defend the constitution from debate by reaffirming the virtues of the political constitution, in which discussion was primarily directed to political divisions and choices, and only incidentally related to constitutional considerations.

> Vigorous politics offers the best safeguard of individual freedoms. And in Britain it is our Parliament ... that is, and should be, at the centre of that democratic, political process. That's why piecemeal reforms that threaten to erode the power and supremacy of Parliament are dangerous ... In our constitution, Parliament is supreme, because the people are supreme. Parliament is the process through which the representatives of the people control the Executive ... I know that some people argue that the freedom of the individual would be better protected if Britain had a written constitution or a new bill of rights, setting out a list of fundamental rights. I don't agree ... It's no exaggeration to say that we believe our individual freedom is absolute, unless restrained by law. It's a way of life. And we have no need for a bill of rights because we have freedom.[55]

But despite the best efforts of John Major to stamp his mark on the issue, it was to no avail for he was immediately upstaged by the Labour leadership's dramatic shift of position on devolution. The shadow Secretaries for the Scottish and Welsh Offices pledged that an incoming Labour government would not only publish White Papers on devolution but would hold referendums on them within a few weeks of an election victory. This bold stroke was an instant rebuttal to the Conservative strategy of trying to unpick Labour's devolution position by warnings of 'tartan taxes' and claims of democratic illegitimacy. Aware that the uncertainty over its devolution policy was threatening to damage its plans for building a reputation for trust, competence and openness, the leadership raised devolution to a top priority for a Labour government with an explicit commitment to move quickly on the issue. In order to prevent any further sniping from the Conservatives over the question of democratic consent to constitutional change, the leadership also reversed its earlier position on the needlessness of referendums. In Scotland, Labour's pledge to hold a referendum on the assembly proposal, together with an extra referendum question on its tax-raising powers, caused consternation within the Scottish Labour party. It had been understood that the general election result would act as a *de facto* referendum and that devolution would not be subjected to any possible delaying or wrecking mechanisms. This position was regarded as valid because of the extensive consultative work which had already been completed by the Scottish Constitutional Convention in its efforts to achieve a consensus position on devolution. Moreover, the referendum device evoked bitter memories of the 1979 devolution failure when the wrecking amendment of a 40 per cent threshold of the electorate's approval was seen to have denied an assembly for Scotland. Despite all these factors, and not least the objection that New Labour's London-based strategists had not even consulted the Scottish Labour party on the decision, the leadership was determined to close down Conservative arguments on the legitimacy of its reform position even if such a strategy risked generating internal party suspicions over the extent of the party's commitment to devolution. To the leadership, it was preferable to achieve constitutional reform by means as publicly uncontentious as possible, irrespective of the contention generated within the Scottish Labour party. This decisive action largely defused the issue and left John Major with little alternative than to rely upon purely negative techniques of campaigning in this issue area. His attempts to engage in reform or in defences of past constitutional novelties were as a consequence progressively abandoned in favour of a conservative appeal to constitutional continuity and a stance of projecting doomsday scenarios for Labour's constitutional agenda.

For New Labour, partial ambiguity may not have been an effective position in confronting the Conservatives but it was a vital ingredient in its relationship with the Liberal Democrats. To acquire anything approaching a working relationship with the Liberal Democrat party, it was necessary to reach an understanding on the one issue upon which all Liberal Democrats were united in their agreement as to its top priority and the one issue on which Labour was deeply divided. Even though the two parties shared a virtually identical reform agenda on the constitution, their differences over PR always threatened the possibilities of co-operation. Tony Blair's objections to PR were well known: 'Some feel strongly about the case for reform and point to the Tory governments elected on a minority of the vote and the fact that smaller parties get squeezed under the current system. I do not dismiss such arguments but I have never been persuaded that under proportional representation we can avoid a situation where small parties end up wielding disproportionate power.'[56] By March 1996, Blair was beginning to shift ground on the issue by signalling that for the first time he would seriously consider a limited reform of the electoral system. In July, Blair for the first time pledged to hold a referendum on electoral reform in the lifetime of Labour's first parliament.[57] At the same time, Paddy Ashdown mooted the idea of a ten-year partnership in government if Blair accepted the Liberal Democrats' *full* programme of constitutional reform. The political possibilities and mutual advantages of collaboration were given visible expression by the formation of an eight-member Joint Consultative Committee on Constitutional Reform (JCCR) co-chaired by Robin Cook and Robert Maclennan. The JCCR was a means by which the two parties could not only seriously examine the grounds for collaboration, but monitor and respond to the changing political emphases and nuances of the rapidly emerging politics of constitutional reform. The question of PR and prime ministerial authority was always going to be a sticking point because of Blair's ambivalence over the issue. The Liberal Democrats harboured a number of fears:

- that Labour would opt for a minimal Alternative Vote reform which the Liberal Democrats argued was not a genuine form of PR.
- that Blair would retreat from the referendum pledge, and with it from any electoral reform, if Labour secured a large majority in the election.
- that Blair would follow John Smith's precedent of proposing a referendum on PR with the intention of reducing the pressure within the party for electoral reform.
- that Blair would neither commit himself in favour of, nor campaign for, PR in a referendum, thereby denying the proposal the full backing of the government.
- that Labour would postpone electoral reform to a second or third term of office.

During late 1996 and early 1997, Paddy Ashdown pressed the Labour leader to make a personal commitment to PR and to give an undertaking that a Labour cabinet would campaign in favour of reform. The Liberal Democrats knew that as the election period approached their bargaining position would not be strong because the polls continued to point to a large Labour victory. It was difficult for Ashdown to make a referendum the price of co-operation with Labour when a hung parliament looked increasingly less likely. Nevertheless, expectations of constitutional reform had been raised by both parties and in the view of the Liberal Democrats. 'a failure by Mr Blair to move would jeopardise any agreement and seriously undermine efforts by both parties to convince the electorate that its constitutional programme is achievable'.[58] Some in the party believed that the referendum-based logic of Blair's constitutional programme would lead Labour's prime minister – however reluctantly – into both a referendum on PR and a supporting role in such a pivotal reform. Others were more suspicious and their doubts were fuelled by reports like that presented in *The Times* on 2 February 1997: 'Labour's election manifesto will give no commitment on the timing of a referendum. Nor would a Labour government's first Queen's Speech contain anything about PR ... Mr Blair's instinctive opposition to PR is hardening. He has indicated that he would campaign against it if a referendum were held and at a recent briefing meeting with Shadow Cabinet members, he argued firmly against changing the first-past-the-post system of electing MPs.'[59] An editorial leader depicted Labour's decision to 'retreat from a referendum [as] an overdue recognition not just of the weakness of the case for proportional representation, but also the unwieldy scale of Labour's constitutional reform package'.[60] But the original article also reported that Mr Blair was sensitive to the possible ramifications of the PR issue and was determined to avoid a repetition of events in 1992.[61]

The Liberal Democrats hoped either that their prospective contribution to the constitutional reform issue would be sufficiently appreciated by Labour, or else that their capacity to disrupt and even to de-rail Labour's crowded parliamentary schedule (e.g. the legislation to set up both devolved Scottish and Welsh assemblies and the referendum arrangements for their acceptance) would be regarded as a sufficient deterrent to prompt Blair into making concessions on the PR front. Negotiations between the two parties culminated in the report of the JCCR which was presented at a press conference on 7 March 1997 by Robin Cook and Robert Maclennan. Cook described the outcome as heralding 'an ambitious programme of reform which will be as important as any of the great reform parliaments of the last century'. He went on to say in reference to a Labour government that 'in the judgement of history it will be given a strategic importance as the government which gave Britain a modern constitution fit for the 21st century'.[62] The document amounted to a Liberal Democratic affirmation of the senior partner's agenda and priorities (i.e. (i) Scottish and Welsh devolution through referendums; (ii) the incorporation of the European Convention on Human Rights into British law; (iii) an elected authority and mayor for London; (iv) the abolition of the voting rights of hereditary peers; (v) a freedom of information act; (vi) the formation of an alternative scheme to Westminster's first-past-the-post system, together with a referendum to determine the public's preference over whether or not to shift to the new scheme of voting). More significantly, the potentially explosive issue of PR on which the entire constitutional reform agenda could well have foundered was resolved in time for the election.

In one respect, Ashdown had given way in that he was willing to approve the joint agreement even though there was no set timetable for the PR referendum measure to be achieved and no promise of prime ministerial or cabinet support for reform in a referendum campaign. Moreover, the agreement between the parties did not extend to laying down any set of priorities between the enumerated items on the joint agenda for reform. In another respect, the Liberal Democrats were encouraged by Labour's formal reiteration of PR for the Scottish and Welsh assemblies and by its acceptance in principle of PR for the European Parliament in 1999. But the major impulse to agreement on the Liberal Democratic side was a key concession by Labour – namely, an undertaking that a future referendum on the electoral system for the House of Commons would be structured as a choice between the current first-past-the-post system and a substantive PR scheme, and not a marginal reform like the Alternative Vote system. For this shift of position, *The Guardian* believed that the joint authors of the agreement warranted praise because it turned 'an otherwise largely managerial report into something of potentially epochal importance for the reform of corrupt British politics'.[63] To a close observer of the protracted and convoluted manoeuvres with the party over constitutional reform and one who had often despaired over the absence of a controlling scheme of convictions that would animate the issue and relieve it from its limited base, Labour's rapprochement with the Liberal Democrats was 'extraordinary ... by any historical standards'.[64] After 18 years, what a Labour government would mean 'suddenly leaped the chasm from speculation to imminent fact'.[65] Hugo Young was at last convinced that the major opposition party was serious over constitutional reform: 'The voice of Labour is no longer coloured by caution and compromise ... [H]ere for once, new government means the plausible chance of a new Britain. There is, after all, a Big Idea and this is it, beginning with the concordat that promotes it'.[66]

The Labour–Liberal Democrat agreement was important to both parties in their preparation for the 1997 general election. It provided tangible evidence of the feasibility of the 'new politics' which lay at the heart of Tony Blair's and Paddy Ashdown's strategy of electoral appeal. More importantly, the agreement afforded mutual security to the respective parties in an area which had the potential of becoming a source of instability and vulnerability. Given that Labour had shifted emphatically to the centre in most sectors of substantive policy and given that constitutional reform remained the one major area in which the two main parties could be clearly differentiated from one another, the leadership was intent upon avoiding a squeeze between the Conservatives and the Liberal Democrats over this issue. A confrontation with the Tories was unavoidable, but friction with the Liberal Democrats carried greater risks. They had the capacity to exploit electoral publicity to challenge the logical coherence of Labour's reform proposals, to question the party's depth of commitment to constitutional change, to query its presence in the centre ground of British politics, and to disrupt the delicate ganglia of internal balances and subtle amnesties that were so central to New Labour's drive for a unified front. The Labour leadership was determined to organise an electoral campaign that would maximise the level of integration within the party and minimise the risk of policy positions unravelling under public scrutiny. It had sought to be as explicit and as restrained as possible in as many areas as possible, including even that of taxation and public expenditure. Constitutional reform, however, was inherently more unpredictable as a policy area.

Although Labour had specified a set of reforms, party strategists were aware that the proposals generated a host of questions over timing, priorities, techniques, procedures, substance, implications and commitment. Labour's plans were not only unprecedented in scope for a major party, but were exceptionally open-ended in nature, being that they were designed to revise elements of a highly inter-connected set of institutional arrangements. To this extent, they were out of step with the foreclosed ethos of the rest of the manifesto. The leadership wished to take full advantage of the public disquiet over the machinery of government and of the radical frisson evoked by the theme of constitutional reform. But it was also concerned over the issue's potential to engender unforeseen and unpleasant developments that might damage the party's carefully restored reputation for political and organisational competence. Axiomatic condemnations of constitutional reform by the Conservative party might be countered on principles and abstract grounds. Such attacks would help to reduce internal party discord by demonstrating to the left wing that New Labour was still able to arouse fierce conservative antipathy. While the imagery of iconoclasm might be to Labour's advantage, it was when the dimension of constitutional reform shifted to the nuts and bolts of actual change that Labour would become more vulnerable. It was here that New Labour would be open to the type of technically sophisticated and searching criticism more likely to come from the Liberal Democrats – the one party with the longest and most extensive experience of constitutional reform and the one organisation whose relationship with Labour would arguably provide the litmus test of Tony Blair's seriousness of intent on constitutional change. The Liberal Democrats' traditional attachment to the issue of constitutional reform established the logic of a national alliance on this issue. Even though the Labour leadership may not have considered the active support of the Liberal Democrats to be crucial to its electoral strategy, the absence of active Liberal Democratic opposition to Labour's constitutional reform agenda was considered to be sufficiently important for Blair to change his position on PR and, as became evident after the election, to offer the Liberal Democrat leadership seats on the cabinet committee dealing with constitutional reform.

A number of factors contributed to the Labour–Liberal Democrat non-aggression pact over constitutional reform during the 1997 general election. Labour and the Liberal Democrats were conscious of maximising their respective positions in the light of the possibility of a hung parliament. Both parties were aware of the danger of dissipating the potential for anti-Tory voting by excessive public wrangling with one another over the one issue likely to divide them. An agreement on constitutional reform concentrated the attack upon the Conservative government and released the full potential of condemning the administration on the grounds of how it had mis-used and abused the constitution. The main opposition parties were also conscious of maximising their respective positions in preparation for the quite plausible electoral outcome of a hung parliament. Having abandoned their policy of 'equidistance' between the major parties, the Liberal Democrats possessed a clear preference for gravitating towards New Labour in any hung parliament. With Blair's public assurances on the Liberal Democrats' gut issue and his private promise of a Liberal Democratic role in a future Labour government, Paddy Ashdown was in a position to campaign almost exclusively against the Conservative government. Labour, on the other hand, was secure in the knowledge that its constitutional reform agenda would only receive serious criticism from one source and that in the event of a hung parliament, there would be no unseemly bargaining and eleventh-hour trials of strength between Blair and Ashdown to secure a Labour government. From a longer perspective, the Labour–Liberal Democrat agreement offered further advantages to the Labour leadership. For example, it opened up the possibility of an eventual centre-left realignment and with it a broader-based progressive party. This would not only allow constitutional reform to be secured but make any newly established checks and balances more legitimate and workable by being the evident outcome of a consensus between different parties, rather than simply a consequence of traditional party government. In the short-term immediacy of a general election, however, the Labour–Liberal Democrat agreement succeeded in providing Tony Blair with a single yet critical asset in the campaign. In combination with the work of the Scottish Constitutional Convention on devolution, it defused the issue of constitutional reform on the centre left and, in doing so, not only largely denuded it of a mobilising capacity but removed it from serious electoral contention.

Immediately prior to the election, it was widely believed that because the 'distance' between the Tories and the opposition parties [was] genuinely wide ... few subjects [were] likely to be more contested in the election campaign than that of constitutional reform'.[67] And yet in spite of the myriad references to the 'clear blue water' between the major parties on constitutional reform and the heightened expectations of partisan engagement over the issue, the subject of constitutional change was conspicuous by its virtual absence during the campaign. This is not to say that no discussion of constitutional issues occurred, but taking into account the scale and likelihood of New Labour's constitutional agenda, the level of debate was disproportionately low. A number of reasons can be advanced to explain such an apparent paradox. For example, the Labour–Liberal Democrat accord and the Scottish Constitutional Convention had both succeeded in establishing constitutional packages across party divisions prior to the general election. The Liberal Democrats in 1997 were also loath to highlight the injustices of the first-past-the-post system, or to give PR a central role in its campaign priorities, not just because of the party advantage to be accrued in a Labour victory, but because in this election the Liberal Democrats were poised to make large gains in seats with a reduced share of the popular vote. Another salient factor was the sleaze issue which highlighted the current defects of institutional self-regulation to such an extent that it was easily extrapolated to smear the political system as a whole and to generate increased levels of public cynicism over the conduct of politics. The case for constitutional reform having already been proven was also supported by the preponderance of public agreement with the need for items like a bill of rights, a freedom of information act and a written constitution. Notwithstanding the significance of these types of influence, the key factors behind the muted debate on the constitution in the general election lay with New Labour's own highly developed caution over the entire theme of constitutional change.

Even though Tony Blair had consistently made constitutional reform a defining element of New Labour's commitment to democratic renewal, party strategists remained wary of the issue and of its political dynamics. On the one hand, constitutional reform could be construed a positive theme allowing Labour to tap the popular, if largely unstructured, scepticism over the political system and to give a radical edge to Labour's otherwise inhibited policy platform. In this guise, the agenda of constitutional change not only gave New Labour a patina of conspicuous adventurism outside the parameters of Old Labour, but provided a highly recognisable point of reference for the party's claims to be at variance with the status quo. Given the high public approval ratings of individual items of constitutional reform, and the fact that the Conservatives had been in government for 18 years on the basis of successive minority votes and were seen to be clinging on to power to the very end, party managers might have concluded that Labour had the licence to engage in a free-wheeling campaign on constitutional reform that would demonstrate the party's responsiveness to popular anxieties and its commitment to modernise the substance of citizenship. It became clear that party strategists did not view constitutional reform in this light. Instead, they gravitated to another and altogether more sceptical perspective of the issue. In this light, constitutional reform was viewed as a nebulous and mainly non-transferable asset. It allowed the party to ride the surges of populist outrage over incidents of sleaze and governmental excess, and to share in the impulses of 'anti-politics' that accompanied public demands for new forms of government. But it was not regarded as an issue that would arouse solid and dependable support, or one that would translate public interest into electoral leverage. On the contrary, it was widely viewed either as an ephemeral distraction to more pivotal issues or as a substantive theme in its own right but one likely to unravel in unpredictable and counter-productive ways. According to these kinds of perspectives, constitutional reform could provide a frisson of subversive exhilaration within Labour's programme but one that always had to be kept within very tight bounds. Elements of constitutional reform might attract very high levels of public approval, but such popular endorsements would remain extremely soft in character and could not be relied upon to provide independent sources of electoral support when attention was drawn away from generalised principles of government to more specific and material policy options. In effect, constitutional reform featured a classic disjunction between high approval and low salience. Moreover, taking into account the way that constitutional reform was treated as a melange of single issues and the fact that single issues have a tendency to fade once an election campaign commences, it was safe to conclude that an appeal based heavily upon constitutional proposals would not be an effective electoral strategy.

To many in the Labour party, constitutional reform was an ostensibly attractive issue, but one that consisted of highly fissionable material. Reform in such an area was by definition constitutionally open-ended and, as such, it was imperative to enclose it politically – or at least to provide the appearance of its being ring-fenced for the purposes of internal party management and external party unity. Extensive efforts had been made since the previous general election to maximise agreement within the party over the issue. A network of accords and understandings had been constructed that would not only provide a pre-emptive clarity to cater for any contingent challenges to its coherence but ensure that Labour's policy positions in such a fissionable area were welded tight in armoured plated security. Labour strategists were well aware that its agenda of constitutional reform would not secure an election victory, but they were equally conscious of the way in which such a sensitive issue might lose an election if the party were to mishandle it. The party was publicly committed to reform. It had maximised the extent to which it was possible to defuse the issue within the party and between its other allies in this particular sector. It was confident that under the narcosis of a general election, with its attendant imperatives of party unity and campaigning discipline, it could manage the issue within the context of electoral confrontation. But it was this very element of regulated commitment and quiet control that provoked concern among constitutional reformers during the election period. They were anxious that the very caution of New Labour's risk-averse campaign might militate against the mobilisation of public opinion and imagination which they believed was necessary to establish a mandate for systemic change.

Constitutional reformers recognised that the Labour party never had been and never would be at one on the substance or priority of change in this area. They knew that Labour was sensitive over being encumbered with a radicalism that could not effectively be sold to the public in that it did not provide any substantive reason for floating voters to abandon the Conservative party. Moreover, it was an issue which could depress the party's appeal in the more traditional areas like health and education. Reformers could appreciate that while there might be 'clear blue water' between the two main parties on constitutional reform, Labour was concerned about becoming fully immersed in it, especially as John Major was intent upon focusing the Conservative campaign precisely on this area. Legitimate though these anxieties were, reform supporters believed that they should not prevail over the need actively to pursue the reform agenda. According to this perspective, it was important for Labour to live up to its reform commitments by vigorously and explicitly campaigning on the issue not just on ethical grounds of honouring its stated principles but on self-interested grounds of electoral advantage and political defence.

The asserted equation between constitutional reform and political prudence was examined in length by Anthony Barnett at the beginning of the campaign period. Although in his opinion, 'Labour want[ed] to fight the election on other issues,'[68] it was necessary for the party publicly to demonstrate its commitment to reform. The party strategists were so nervous over creating a backlash of swing voters returning to the Conservatives that they risked 'destroying the hope factor',[69] in order to eliminate the 'fear factor' of a Labour government. Barnett perceived that New Labour was locked into constitutional reform and that the only course of action was forward towards a positive campaign to mobilise the public's allegiance to what would be a new *de facto* constitutional settlement. Labour could not, and should not, drift while having such a pivotal cargo in its hold. To do so risked the vessel itself because it would leave it open to the destructive energies of Tory counter-claims that Labour did not mean what it said, or alternatively was convinced of the reform agenda but sought to conceal its radicalism. Either way, the chief casualty would be Labour's credentials of trust and even competence: 'It could prove a disaster if Labour were to "deny" that a bill of rights, a Scottish parliament, abolition of hereditary peers, a freedom of information act, a referendum on the voting system, together add up to significant change. They would look evasive if not lying, because they would be evasive and lying. A contemporary democratic agenda does mean a new settlement. Is this what Labour wants? Deny it, and they are caught. Accept it and they will have to explain themselves.'[70] Barnett concluded that the latter was the only viable option both politically as an electorally effective tactic and constitutionally as a means of acquiring a viable reconstruction of Britain's governing arrangements. Labour had accumulated an agenda of constitutional reform which demanded a commensurate commitment to principle. To give the appearance of being pusillanimous and vacillating while professing itself to be an engine of reform risked squandering the historical opportunity for material change provided by the 1997 general election:

> If the Tories hammer at the issue, Labour could break and run ... Labour needs to justify the reforms it wants and say how it will lead the country in a fast-changing world ... If Labour's constitutional reforms mean anything, they mean more and better democracy. It should not be afraid of saying so; it needs to give purpose to its method ... The process needs time and must place confidence in the people. If Labour is too afraid to say this then, indeed, it should never have embraced reform in the first place.[71]

Anthony Barnett's precepts may have been valid, but his prescriptions were more open to doubt. His analysis accurately reflected the disquiet of the constitutional reformers over the low profile given to the issue in the campaign. Nevertheless, the themes raised in such calls to action threw into high relief many of the deeply problematic complexities which affect an opposition party seeking to defeat a government by legitimating itself as an alternative government, at the very same time that it was attempting to de-legitimise part of the contemporary fabric of precisely that constitutional system which would facilitate a change of administration.

Five problems for Labour's constitutional challenge

Far from simply revealing how Labour had faltered in its campaign for constitutional reform, the 1997 general election in fact gave graphic illustration of both the intrinsic difficulties of confronting the issue of constitutional reform and the rapid emergence of a politics of the British constitution which would come to characterise and to condition the processes of constitutional change in the new Labour government. As the election progressed, the properties of these intrinsic difficulties and their role in the evolutionary dynamics of political engagement over the constitution became more explicit. They are considered below.

The party asymmetry problem

A central difficulty for an opposition centre-left force in confronting the constitution was that it was opposed by a conservative administration which could not only draw on its experience in government to challenge the feasibility of reform in such an area but integrate its defence into an overall conservative outlook upon any consciously designed and rationally informed change in society. This was why John Major thought that the constitutional reform proposals of New Labour and the Liberal Democrats would play into Tory hands. Richard Norton-Taylor and Laurence Neville were left in no doubt that the further the debate was developed, the more the Conservatives thought they could gain advantage from it: 'Major believes the constitutional agenda belongs to the Conservatives. That is not to say that the Conservatives have an agenda other than the maintenance of the status quo, but Major believes the issue can only benefit the Tories at the polls. He may be right ... A Conservative rallying call to defend all that made Britain great may become a powerful one if there is sufficient doubt in the minds of the voters.'[72] The customary practicality of the Conservative party could be claimed to be at one with the pragmatic and experiential nature of the British constitution. Even when the Conservatives were seen to be behaving in a doctrinaire manner, thereby prompting a more comprehensive critique both of the Conservative government and of the constitutional structure, the Tories were able to condemn any organised assault upon the constitution as ideological extremism. Constitutional change produced by Conservative governments could be and was defended on grounds of collateral damage in a political struggle and not as a premeditated attempt to revise constitutional arrangements. Constitutional alteration in such circumstances was incidental, instrumental and derivative.

With no real precedent or actual device for operationalising the constitution or constitutional tradition as a means of confronting the government *en masse*, an opposition party like Labour with its own heritage of radical intellectualism would always face difficulties in attempting to use the constitution as a form of political leverage. Such a strategy would run the risk of appearing to be either deluded in trying to create a material issue out of an avowedly ethereal entity, or else dangerous in rushing to subvert a constitution from the outside for political gain. In short, a greater correlation is often assumed to exist between the Conservative party and the defence of existing constitutional and institutional arrangements than that between the Labour party and the project of counter-evolutionary constitutional innovation. Thus, while the Conservatives had the advantage of government and the influence to define and rationalise the constitution, Labour had the uphill task not just of establishing the constitution as a political issue but of winning the argument in favour of change. To raise the theme of constitutional reform while in opposition, therefore, required the Labour party to confront the Conservative charges of technical *naïveté* and myopic dogmatism, and to challenge the general tradition of evolutionary change by cumulative government decisions.

Opposition parties may be part of the political environment within which an established administration operates but they are not integral to those governmental choices which shape a political constitution. They may condition or shape such choices, but in general opposition parties are 'outsiders' in the reactive and improvised dynamics of the British constitution. It is difficult enough for an opposition to challenge governments on or through the constitution but for a Labour opposition in particular, and especially one that has been in opposition for an extended period, the problems can be extensive. It is not simply the substance of change which is called into question, but the background, manner, motives and credentials of the reformers. The logic of such a constitution invokes a *Catch 22* conundrum upon those who would set out conspicuously to engage in a drive for reform. If Labour's constitutional critique were to be seen as a principled and genuine prescription for systemic change, then it could be challenged as being dangerously out of sync with the underlying dynamic of the British constitution. If on the other hand, Labour were to use the themes of constitutional reform as an instrument of party gain and party interest in the pursuit of power and a programme of policies, then such a strategy would needlessly lay the party open to Conservative accusations of political duplicity and wanton uncertainty. Such complaints would succeed only in jeopardising the party's prospects for office and, thereby, the rest of the party's objectives. Political resources would be wasted on both counts, leaving silence on the constitution as the only viable alternative.

While Conservative governments in the past have used this strategy to secure large-scale, if implicit, constitutional changes in the explicit pursuit of other objectives, New Labour would find it difficult to ignore the issue in 1997. Apart from the fact that the party had inherited and adopted a range of constitutional proposals which it could not easily relinquish, its association with constitutional reform invested the party's programme with a sense of radical purpose and political distinction. But in having adopted constitutional reform as a priority issue, New Labour was confronted with the asymmetry of the theme in political argument and electoral strategy – namely, the inherent problem of a left-of-centre opposition party seeking to arouse interest in the constitution as a reform issue being confronted by a right-of-centre governing party relying upon the traditional instinct of regarding the constitution not merely as a non-issue, but as a non-subject in terms of political engagement. Notwithstanding the evidence of systemic malfunction and public cynicism, both the responsibility for raising the constitution as political issue and the burden of proof required to substantiate the necessity of improvement continued to lay with the centre-left opposition. The latter may have possessed the initiative but, as the next two problems will demonstrate, the strategic and tactical advantages within a constitutional culture predisposed to a muddled and improvised continuity remain with that party which is not in the habit of asking searching questions about intuitions of governance.

The macro–micro problem

The macro–micro difficulty of constitutional reform is related to the party asymmetry problem but leads to a different dimension of constitutional politics. It pertains to the core question of what kind of constitution exists in Britain, which inevitably leads to the secondary question of how you reform it. The customary response to these questions is to treat the constitution as a generic summation of precedents, traditions, conventions and decisions that have a singular entity in name only. Its holistic nature is almost invariably seen to be a derivative of its multiple, pragmatic and particulate properties. Accordingly the weight of analysis and understanding is concentrated upon the plurality of discrete items of constitutional activity. Insofar as the constitution can be said to exist, therefore, it is taken to be an aggregate rather than a fixed essence of fundamental axioms.

This traditional evolutionary perspective incurs severe difficulties upon those who would seek to change it. In order to turn the constitution into a political issue, it is necessary to make, or to imply, a case for systemic criticism and therefore a sense of holistic character. Not to make such a case would not only reduce the gravity of the issue but make the alleged defects within the constitution partial in character and, therefore, amenable to the normal piecemeal remedies of the political constitution. As far as the reform agencies, and to a lesser extent the opposition parties, were concerned the bits of the constitution which were faulty were so numerous and so chronic in nature that the self-corrective mechanisms of the current system were no longer sufficient to restore public trust in the operation of the whole. The logic of such a critique and such a raft of reforms demanded some organising principles of change to make sense of, and to co-ordinate, the diversity of individual claims for change. Apart from the fact that no language or conceptual framework existed in the British political tradition to cater for a sweeping challenge to the idea and practice of the British constitution, the difficulties of providing a rationale of reform were exacerbated by the disciplines of a general election campaign.

Labour, as the key player in the constitutional reform agenda, was particularly susceptible to the problem of the shifting nature of the macro and micro dimensions within the constitutional issue. By giving political impetus to an array of reform proposals, Labour exposed itself to the complaint that it had no over-arching principles that would give definition and focus to the multiplicity of meddling interventions. Its plans for constitutional reform could then be presented as a mindless patchwork of *ad hoc* responses to a set of centre-left lobby interests. By condemning Labour for its lack of any design in its proliferation of reforms and for the absence of any sign of the organic nature of a functioning constitution, the macro dimension could be employed to challenge and to caricature the micro of the reform agenda. Even though Labour might claim that an emphasis on the micro was wholly legitimate within the parameters of the political constitution, there was a point at which the sheer volume of reform pledges would imply a need to explain their logic within a constitutional structure being indicted by the very pressures for systemic change. The problem for Labour was that the same argument could be applied in reverse – namely, that the micro dimension could be deployed by its opponents to confront any attempts by Labour to declare a macro rationale to constitutional reform. If Labour were to make a case for the coherence of their reforms from first principles, they would lay themselves open to charges of placing dogma over practicality, destruction over growth, and speculation over experience. New Labour would be parodied for its reckless inexperience and immaturity in not having due regard for the practicalities and complexities of governance. Labour and its reformist allies could then be declared naive and even unconstitutional for dismissing the significance of the tangible, the practical and the accommodating within the political and administrative realism required for a functioning constitutional system.

Both these countervailing strategies were used against Labour during the election campaign. Both were equally amenable to conservative opposition tactics. If Labour's macro position was unclear then it was elicited by implication either from de-constructing the meaning of phrases like 'democratic renewal' and 'constitutional modernisation', or from reconstructing old Labour's attachment to ideological nostrums. These real or imagined constructions could and were confronted by Tory antidotes of hard-headed empiricism for the 'real' business of government. By the same token, New Labour's fascination with constitutional change was attacked on high Tory grounds of failing to understand the meaning of a constitution or to appreciate the value of continuity and inter-relatedness in a governing structure. Labour was often stretched across these two dimensions of critique as the attacks oscillated between them. Conservative inconsistency over the usage of macro and micro defences was not an issue because they could both be individually justified on grounds of conservative principle and collectively defended on the basis of an indiscriminate assault to save the British constitution. Once again, party asymmetry was present in respect to the burden of proof in such an issue.

While both macro and micro techniques were employed in an effort to squeeze Labour into a 'no-win' position, it had become evident by the end of the campaign that the macro critique of the reform package had become the predominant pattern. In one way, it is always more likely for the micro-dimensional aspect of change to be more apparent than macro-dimensional principles that inform it. Any reform will inevitably have something of a patchwork quality to it because of the dynamics of political accommodation, the fragmented nature of the legislative process and the pragmatic character of the British constitution itself. Conservative opponents of constitutional reform, therefore, would always be in a position to summon up a macro critique by virtue of the very nature of the channels of political deliberation and engagement. But another factor was present in the ultimate preponderance of the macro defence. This is the difficulty of sustaining an attack upon reformers on purely micro-dimensional grounds in an electoral context. Professional politicians may be able to foresee a host of specific material problems and to predict a profusion of detailed complexities in the eventuality of a new government coming into office committed to constitutional change. Such projections can be used in an attempt to impugn the managerial and political competence of an alternative government. However, in the intensity of an election campaign the speculative and technical analysis of the minutiae of reform positions and consequences carries little purchase, especially when constitutional reforms are seen to be an ostensible good. The preferred choice, and arguably the only option, was for the Conservatives to concentrate in the end on the macro dimension in the form of an emotive appeal to save the United Kingdom from the disintegration that would ensue from a plethora of measures which were alleged to be myopic in conception and unpredictable in their collective effect.

The logical trap problem

Another difficulty that afflicted Labour during the general election, and which would become a feature of the constitutional debate during the Labour government, was the problem posed by the interior logic of the reform proposals. The British constitution, like all viable constitutions, is only sustainable by virtue of the conventions of usage which conceal its ambiguities, disjunctions and anomalies. The British constitution, more than most and arguably more than any other constitution, is dependent upon precisely these protective devices that maintain its inconsistencies and contradictions in abeyance. It is these devices which are threatened by reform. In raising the issue of large-scale constitutional change, it is impossible to avoid subjecting the constitution to close critical analysis which strips away much of the outer protective layers of the constitution's idiosyncrasies. The more reforms that are advocated and the greater the emphasis given to them, the more penetrating is the critique which justifies the assault. But in denuding the constitution of its reputation as a logical structure, it raises expectations – logical expectations – that if it requires such sweeping reform then by virtue of the very indictment presented against it any modifications to the constitution should conform to a consistent pattern drawn from fundamental organising principles. The problem with unpacking something which does not have an internal coherence is that it presents reformers with the challenge not just of providing an intellectually consistent substitute, but of squaring the proposals with the criteria and licence unleashed by the reformers' own catalyst of critical analysis.

Constitutional criticism has a multiplier effect in that partial complaint leads quickly to assertions of systemic disorder. By the same token, proposals for constitutional change have a similar multiplier effect in which new schemes of constitutional design stimulate the critical and comparative faculties to produce accelerated progressions of initial positions. Proposals in such a densely packed space as a constitution will always generate more questions than answers. Intellectual curiosity is engaged by the critical prelude to reform solutions and, as a consequence, the internal logic of the proposals, together with their relationship to one another, is traced through to their conclusions. Even though Labour sought to close down debate on its constitutional position within the party, it could not prevent the ramifying properties of the projected alterations to the constitution being examined by interested parties. To party strategists, there was a political and electoral logic to the exact shape and wording to New Labour's design for constitutional change. Such a logic might be able to confine constitutional speculation within demarcated limits during the general election, but such a constraint was always artificial and it did not, and could not, constrain the analytical drive to examine the premises and applications of the reform principles and plans. Party managers found that the external logic of Labour's disciplined restraint over constitutional reform could not be replicated at the intellectual and analytical levels. Proposals for constitutional change on such a scale generated their own dynamics. They prompted investigations into their interior logic not simply by detractors looking for negatives, but by friends, allies and neutrals who were intent upon throwing further light upon the nature and potential of the reforms.

Just as Labour found that it could not circumscribe the de-construction of its own proposals, it also discovered that in its stated endeavour to eradicate many of the British constitution's old anomalies it could not protect itself from the charge of attempting to inject a fresh dose of incoherence into the British system. The logic of a reform designed to provide an answer in one area, for example, could simply be extended to pose problems in others where the elicited principle of reform had not been consistently applied. A case in point was provided by the party's plans for devolution in Wales which were substantively different to its proposed devolution measures for

Scotland. Sound political and historical reasons could be advanced to justify the difference in treatment, yet the disparity in the juxtaposed reforms not only prompted demands for equal treatment for Wales but cast doubt on the logical coherence of the whole devolution package. A concerned editorial in *New Statesman and Society* summed up the problem:

> Labour's commitment to legislate for a tax-raising parliament for Scotland and an assembly for Wales in the first year of government threatens to bog down its legislative programme in interminable constitutional wrangling. We cannot assume that a considerable number of English Labour MPs will not balk at the privileged position being granted to Scotland, in particular. In the same manner, there are already those in Wales demanding parity between a Scottish parliament and a Welsh assembly. In this way, a constitutional innovation that may seem eminently justifiable in one part of the state soon tends to generalise itself on a 'sauce for the gander' basis. Labour's present proposals offer no rational limit to such extensions and they will provide scope for endless complications and further ammunition for the Tories.[73]

The very expectation of logical coherence, raised by the prospect of constitutional change through conscious design, leads to a profusion of questions when that expectation falls short, as it always will, of full realisation. Even a cursory examination of Labour's reform proposals raises a profusion of genuinely analytical inquiries over the ambiguity of the 'West Lothian' question; the lack of uniformity over Welsh and Scottish devolution; the puzzle over how a reformed House of Lords would reflect the share of votes in a preceding general election; the difficulty of reconciling a new second chamber with the constitutional pre-eminence of the House of Commons; the problematic status of a bill of rights in a system of parliamentary sovereignty; the inconsistency of PR provision in different elections within the British system; the lack of clarity over the status and criteria of exemptions in any freedom of information legislation; the prospect of regional governments with different powers and divergent forms of democratic legitimacy; the logical difficulties of employing referendums (e.g. Scottish and Welsh devolution) to provide mandates for pre-legislative proposals; the constitutional ramifications for the power and authority of Parliament of multiple referendums; and the constitutional uncertainty over the relationships between local and regional governments, between a London assembly with an elected mayor and Westminster, and most notably between Parliament and a Scottish parliament.

The unprecedented scale of the reform proposals in such a previously opaque area generated a host of controversies over the relationships between means and ends, between intentions and outcomes, and between premises and conclusions. The unavoidably experimental nature of constitutional reform helped to generate the logical themes that were applied to the prospectus for change. This is not to imply that there was only one form of logical analysis which was apposite to such a subject. Logical inquiry could be applied to pursuing chains of extrapolation, in order to identify the configuration of a future outcome, or to isolate an intrinsic flaw in the mechanics of a proposed arrangement. Logic could be applied to the techniques of reform, or to the integral properties of a reform, or to the projected outcomes of reform. The use of logical reasoning from conditional premises could lead just as easily to claims of an empirical grasp of a net effect, as to an admission of speculative vacuity. Such predictive reasoning could close subjects down or open them up. For example, as the general election approached, it became commonplace to read analyses of the PR controversy that possessed the interior design of a regression analysis. If PR were to be introduced for the Scottish and Welsh assemblies, then it would have to be conceded for the elections to the European Parliament. By the same token, 'if PR were demystified via Europe, how could this fail to have a bearing on the referendum for Westminster?'[74] The consequence would be a progressive abandonment of the first-past-the-post system through a cumulative process of inertial change. An initial reform would evoke a chain reaction of further reforms as the objections to, and constraints against, any additional innovation would diminish with each advance of PR into successive fields of electoral organisation. Logical analysis in this respect revealed a pattern of uniformity derived from a reform that was construed to be self-replicating in nature.

But the logical progression from the thin end to the thick end of a wedge could also at times lead to utter uncertainty: 'If Scotland stays in the United Kingdom, how can a Scottish parliament be reconciled with the Westminster Parliament, or with the position of Wales and the English regions? Should we change the British electoral system? If so, how? What sort of upper house would work best? These are all constitutional questions which Labour will be able to open, but not to close.'[75] Logical projections could expose and amplify inherent flaws in the reforms or in their relationships to one another, or in their connection with the totality of the British constitution. The case for the reform of the House of Lords, for example, may be well founded but any change will inevitably have implications for the rest of the system: 'If the new body is to become a vigorous chamber and a credible check on constitutional excesses, it will need to be largely elected. But reform of the Lords on these lines would also require reforms of the Commons. A new senate could hardly be given greater power to alter Bills than backbench MPs now enjoy.'[76] By the same token: 'How can the composition of a legislative chamber be decided without a clear notion of its proposed powers and functions? And how can this be known when the powers and scope of the House of Commons itself remain to be decided.'[77] Clearly, the usage, standards and motives of such logical inquiry were varied. Just as the rigour of the logic could be disputed, so the results of such analysis could be contested. But this is to miss the point. It was the belief in the necessary existence of an interior logic to such a set of challenges to the notional coherence of the British constitution that impelled a commensurate response to determine the nature of what would be in essence a different constitution. If the reforms were couched as irreversible, then the key to their properties lay in the ability to capture the future implications of constitutional change. The main problem with such analyses is that constitutions are not blueprints and constitutional revisions are even less so. They are invariably leaps into the dark, requiring improvisation and mid-course corrections. Any proposal for significant change will generate a multiplicity of precise questions and a dearth of exact answers and this is especially so in the highly inter-related context of constitutional change. Nevertheless, it is precisely this area which generates expectations of comprehensive coherence, mechanistic rigour and calculable precision, and with it a compulsive drive to subject all reform to logical inquiry. The professional politicians in New Labour knew that constitutional change would ramify into a profusion of logical extensions that would overload any instant rebuttal strategy. The optimum response was one of subduing controversy by not engaging in such speculation and keeping the party's focus fixed on the enumeration of self-contained items of constitutional reform and the deferment of difficult questions until such time that Labour was back in government and its priorities were clearer. The party was progressively encircled by commentators and analysts who had deduced that Labour had not only failed to answer serious questions over constitutional reform, but had not even posed them and, therefore, were oblivious to the dangers elicited from the logic of its project. Notwithstanding the pressure for disclosure and self-analysis, the critiques failed to engage. Labour withstood the assault and managed to square the circle of ring fencing that which had no outer limits of critical inquiry. But in achieving such integration, paradoxically, the party was assisted by another intrinsic problem in advocating constitutional reform in a general election.

The 'lilac' problem

Under Tony Blair's leadership, the Labour party had been repositioned at the centre of British politics. This positional strategy incommoded the Liberal Democrats in particular who increasingly found their identity as the centre party to be under threat. In some instances, New Labour had so crowded the middle ground that the Liberal Democrats had come to occupy the radical margin very often by default. In no issue area was this more evident than in constitutional reform where a clear three-way balance emerged with the Liberal Democrats on the left advocating comprehensive constitutional change, Labour pressing for selective reforms and the Conservative party resolutely denying the need for constitutional experimentation. Because this issue was generally recognised to be the one area that clearly differentiated the two main parties and the one policy sector which provided the basis of a *de facto* alliance between Labour and the Liberal Democrats, constitutional reform possessed a high visibility which generated several tactical advantages for Labour. At the same time, the very juxtaposition of *Liberal Democrats*, *Labour* and *Conservatives* in this area produced what will be referred as the *lilac* problem.

In order to capture the distribution of positions along the radical-conservative continuum, the parties' respective policy packages on the constitution are summarised in Table 6.1. While the Liberal Democrats' uninhibited approach to policy-making in the field had continued undiminished, and the Conservatives had maintained their clarity of opposition to constitutional change, New Labour had moved to a position that defined the centre. It was bold and cautious at the same time. It argued its case on the basis of a balance between reform and continuity. Its language was radical, yet its approach was eclectic and graduated in style. It offered leadership without anxiety or danger. It propounded the need to refute the negativism of the Conservatives but it drew back from the casual excesses of the Liberal Democrats' adventurism in constitutional reform. This central position afforded Labour a number of electoral benefits. For example, it made the party's position on constitutional reform appear moderate and responsible. By the same token, it made the issue of constitutional change itself seem mainstream. A major party which had no pedigree of constitutional challenge had now settled upon the need for structural change as a key component of its programme. New Labour had reinvented the party by conspicuously jettisoning much of its old radical baggage and scripting an appeal from market research and focus groups to create a centrist identity. It had amassed a large poll lead over the previous four and half years and was now poised to displace the Conservatives after 18 years. In the process, New Labour had come to define the centre ground and by 1997 its general appeal effectively transmuted the party's agenda on constitutional reform into a benign, middle-ground response to problems made starkly evident by the deficiencies of Conservative government. During the general election, Labour was able to use its newly acquired reputation for moderation to de-radicalise the issue of constitutional reform and to limit the extent to which the party's position could be unpacked and disaggregated by its adversaries. The anaesthetic properties of this position allowed Labour to maintain party unity in the drive to keep the focus upon the government's record and away from the party's own plans. In an issue which lent itself to extreme positions, Labour remained notably devoid of extremism.

Nevertheless, the benefits of such centralism came at a price. Despite its reputation for radicalism and its language of change and innovation, New

Table 6.1 *The three main parties' adopted positions on constitutional reform in the 1997 general election*

Liberal Democrat	Labour	Conservative
For a written constitution	Against a written constitution	Against a written constitution
For a bill of rights	Against a bill of rights	Against a bill of rights
For the incorporation of the European Convention on Human Rights into British law	For the incorporation of the European Convention on Human Rights into British law	Against the incorporation of the European Convention on Human Rights into British law
For a broad Freedom of Information Act	For a broad Freedom of Information Act	Against a Freedom of Information Act
For parliamentary reform including four year terms, reduced membership and enhanced executive scrutiny	For limited parliamentary reform (e.g. Prime Minister's Questions)	For limited reform but not to the composition or powers of Parliament
For the replacement of the House of Lords	For a phased reform of the House of Lords	Against reform of the House of Lords
For powerful devolved parliaments in Scotland and Wales	For devolution with tax powers in Scotland, but not in Wales and only after affirmative referendums	Against devolution
For elected assemblies in the regions and London	For elected assemblies in the regions and London but only after affirmative referendums	Against any additional tiers of government
For the enhancment of local government with tax-raising powers	For a general strengthening of local government	Against any change to the current system of local government
For electoral reform and especially PR for Westminster	For a PR-based reform to be presented in a referendum during the first Parliament	Against any PR-based reform to the electoral system

Source: The 1997 Liberal Democrat manifesto, the 1997 Labour Party manifesto and the 1997 Conservative Party manifesto.

Labour seemed to draw away from its own litmus test of modernisation through constitutional reform. Its balanced approach suggested equivocation between the polar opposites of the Conservative party and the Liberal Democrats. In fact, Labour's half way house made the other two parties appear comparable because of the uncompromising nature of their positions and the implication of a clear allegiance to principle. In an issue area suffused in principle, New Labour risked the appearance of lacking commitment through the variable nature of its reform proposals. The *lilac* problem exposed Labour to the criticism that constitutional reform by its very nature required the clear identification of first principles which could be applied consistently and coherently to produce a viable constitution, informed and structured according to a core of thematic axioms. It can be argued that constitutional reform has to be systematic in order to rank as a genuine reform of the constitution. In this light, 'softly-softly may catchee the election', but it would not secure a different constitution. Constitutional change required fundamental debate, in which the policies of the party most likely to win are subjected to exhaustive review and intensive deliberation. New Labour's *lilac* centrism may have been electorally more prudent than any clarion call to unbridled reform, but this posture only partly answered the criticism over a lack of debate because it presupposed that the issue of constitutional reform could never be lifted out of its quiescent state and made into a rallying call for popular support.

There was another and more substantive argument hiding underneath this assertion. Notwithstanding whether or not constitutional reform could produce electoral dividends, it was prudent for any prospective government committed to constitutional reform to conduct its election campaign in such a way that it could subsequently claim a mandate for change. This would give the momentum not merely for the passage of reform legislation, but for the process of assimilation and consolidation that would need to follow a restructuring of this magnitude. Critics and allies thought that Labour were in danger of succumbing to caution and forsaking the opportunity of creating a durable constituency of reform for its period in government. Even prior to the election, the Labour leadership was seen to be devaluing the mandate properties of the vote by its decision to press for separate referendums on Scottish and Welsh devolution. This amounted to a U-turn from its previous position which had construed a future general election victory as incorporating consent for devolution as part of the Labour manifesto. To Andrew Marr, New Labour's circumspection over the constitution would only be judicious in the short term. By failing to enthuse and agitate for constitutional change Labour endangered both the cause of constitutional change and the party's long-term self-interest:

> Mr Major is bellowing about the constitution in danger, in order to shore up his press support; Mr Blair is talking too quietly about reform for the same reason ... It follows that there could be nothing more damaging to Labour's relations with the press than the admission that Mr Blair is thinking of electoral reform. Why? Because that would threaten the Tory right's chances of taking power again in the early 2000s – and perhaps ever. For the rightist press, four years of Mr Blair might be tolerable; but a radical realignment of politics in favour of the centre-left certainly would not be ... As an unabashed

enthusiast for political reform, I am worried that the combination of flag-waving hyperbole from Mr Major – however silly – and nervous throat-clearing from the other side – however sensible – may fatally damage the cause ... The Opposition has learnt quite a lot from [the prime minister] in the past few years. Perhaps ... they need to learn one lesson more: you cannot crusade in a whisper.[78]

The *lilac* disposition of New Labour's proposals may have defused the issue inside the party but it was also a major influence in damping down the constitutional debate in the country as a whole. It is true that the prospect of constitutional change was given a high news value in the coverage of the election (see Table 6.2). Nevertheless the theme was mainly restricted to the sub-field of devolution and the Scottish dimension in particular, with the 'implications for England receiv[ing] little attention'.[79] In general, the issue of constitutional reform only 'intruded intermittently in the campaign'.[80] This was reflected both in the content and in the style of Labour's strategy. Tony Blair had assumed the role of the party's chief spokesperson and negotiator in the field of constitutional reform, and yet as Peter Riddell noted, the party leader 'did not make one major speech, or hold any national press conference, on constitutional reform during the election. His advisers believe[d] that English voters [were] not very interested in these issues.'[81] Andrew Puddephatt of Charter 88 could not conceal his disappointment over the conduct of the election: 'Many people assumed that the general election would focus on "democracy". The joint talks between the Liberal Democrats and Labour on democratic reform seemed to indicate a new seriousness of intent ... Instead we heard the sound of silence'.[82]

New Labour was seen to be safe and, as such, its muted endorsement of constitutional change was viewed in the same vein. But to both the Conservatives and the Liberal Democrats, constitutional change was inherently unsafe. To the former, it was positively dangerous. To the latter, constitutional reform had to be radical or else it was nothing. To the reformers, the 1997 general election amounted to the best chance for serious reform in over half a century, but for such an opportunity to be grasped, it was necessary for the public to be mobilised and energised in support of change. According to this perspective, New Labour needed to be in the vanguard of the challenge to the British constitution. It was necessary for the party to create the momentum for the agenda to be carried through in government. Given the regularly recorded majorities for constitutional reform recorded in opinion polls, such a role might be construed as sound electoral politics. Labour strategists, however, could point out that strong opinion poll support for items of constitutional change would not necessarily translate into party support in the general election. This was confirmed in polls conducted during the election period. In an *Independent on Sunday*/MORI poll, for example, respondents were asked to state the issues which they thought would

Table 6.2 *Relative prominence of issues in news coverage (1997 General Election)*

	BBC	ITV	C4	R4	All 1997
Europe	1	1	1	1	1
Constitution	2	3	2	3	2
Sleaze	3	2	5=	2	3
Education	4	4	3	5	4
Taxation	6	5	10	4	5
NHS	7	9	5=	6	6
Pensions	5	6	9	7	7
The economy	8	13	7	9=	8=
Employment	13=	10	4	9=	8=
Law and order	9	8	8	8	10
Northern Ireland	12	7	11	14	11
Public expenditure	13=	12	6	13	12

Source: Butler and Kavanagh, *The British General Election 1997* (Houndmills: Macmillan, 1997), p. 140.

be very important to them in helping to decide which party to vote for. (See Table 6.3.) Constitutional reform in the shape of devolution came 'right at the bottom of the first 15 issues that [would] affect the outcome of the election',[83] with only 10 per cent of respondents describing the issue as being very important in determining electoral choice. Among women, the over 55s and those questioned in the DE social class, the figure drops to between 6 and 7 per cent. Even animal welfare received a higher estimate of voting decisiveness with a 12 per cent response overall, which incorporated a level of 14 per cent among women, thus making the issue twice as pivotal to that of constitutional reform. This being so, it could be claimed by party managers that the policy of subdued advocacy was appropriate in the conditions and that any attempt to inject fervour into the issue during a general election would be counter-productive. Nevertheless, such effective self-effacement came at a price. New Labour's *lilac*-hued support of constitutional reform may have appeared suitably anodyne in the harsh monochrome of a debate dominated by Conservative and Liberal Democratic principles, but by risking little in the election, the party risked gaining little in government, thereby relinquishing unrepeatable opportunities for securing irreversible changes to the constitution.

Table 6.3 *The decisiveness of individual issues in electoral choice (1997 General Election)*

Which of these issues do you think will be very important to you in helping to decide which party to vote for?

%	All	Men	Women	18–24	25–34	35–54	55+	AB	C1	C2	DE
1 Health care	70	62	76	51	73	75	69	70	70	73	66
2 Education	62	57	66	58	71	71	48	67	64	61	56
3 Law & order	50	50	50	42	50	52	50	49	51	58	43
4 Unemployment	45	45	46	56	52	49	34	42	45	50	45
5 Pensions	42	39	44	21	28	41	58	40	41	41	44
6 Taxation	35	36	34	39	45	37	24	41	39	36	25
7 Economy	32	36	28	21	42	37	25	47	39	28	18
8 Housing	28	26	30	32	33	30	21	21	28	31	29
9 Europe	24	28	20	23	24	25	24	36	29	23	12
10 Environment	24	23	25	28	29	24	19	35	24	21	17
11 Transport	21	23	20	27	24	18	21	24	25	22	15
12 Animal welfare	12	9	14	9	13	12	12	8	11	13	14
13 Northern Ireland	11	13	10	15	10	13	9	14	11	11	9
14 Trade unions	10	12	7	12	10	10	8	11	11	10	7
15 Devolution	10	13	7	10	13	12	6	11	14	9	6

Source: The *Independent on Sunday*/MORI poll published in the *Independent on Sunday*, 6 April 1997. MORI interviewed 1069 individuals between 2 April 1997 and 3 April 1997.

The 'political constitution' question

The final problem with which the Labour leadership had to contend was the challenge of managing a party close to victory after a prolonged period in the wilderness, while at the same time making the issue of change in the constitutional arrangements of governmental power a defining theme of the party's appeal. Labour was being asked to jettison its traditional ambivalence over the constitution at precisely the time when it was poised to become the chief beneficiary of the unreconstructed political constitutionalism of the British system. Notwithstanding the claim that New Labour's position on constitutional reform may have been a key component of its enhanced electoral appeal, many sectors of the party retained a traditionalist attachment to the clarity afforded by the political constitution in the acquisition of power by an opposition party. This jaundiced view of constitutional reform as an alien distraction from the party's push for office reached the highest echelons of the organisation. It was well known that most of the senior figures in the shadow cabinet were less than enthusiastic on the subject. Matthew d'Ancona's observations typified the nature of what had become a public secret. 'John Prescott's instinctive position on proportional representation was summed up by an uncharacteristically lucid remark to one campaigner for constitutional change: "I'm not in f——ing favour of f——ing PR for anything *[sic]*. Like many of his Old Labour comrades, he has always been suspicious that proposals for electoral reform are a bourgeois ploy to realign his party with the Liberal Democrats and to weaken what little remains of its socialism.'[84] But as Andrew Rawnsley graphically points out, such scepticism was not confined to Old Labour: 'Some of [Blair's] ... closest aides do not and never did give much of a toss for constitutional reform. If I had a pound for every time I have heard it dismissed as an anal obsession of *Guardian* and *Observer* readers, I would be writing this column from my 50-room mansion.'[85] Reports of this kind were only to be expected in a system that assigns such a pivotal significance to a single, simple and decisive electoral exercise. According to the precepts of Britain's political constitution, a transition of power produces in effect a *de facto* revision of the British constitution in the extent to which a new government is empowered to provide political solutions to problems that had only been accessible prior to the election through constitutional contention. A new administration can by its very existence in office diminish and even eliminate many of the political pressures supporting constitutional reform. For example, given Labour's strong presence in the regions, a Labour victory in a general election would probably have the immediate effect of reducing the demand for regional devolution generated by the perceived Southern bias of Tory governments over the previous 18 years. In the words of Martin Wainwright, Labour's strengths in the North and the Midlands would be a 'useful card in avoiding any substantial devolution of real power ... [T]he presence of a prime minister in County Durham and his deputy in Hull would probably mean more to many Joe Punters than the right to vote for a regional assemblyman/woman at Darlington.'[86]

In this respect, the advocacy of constitutional reform by an opposition party can be seen as a reflection of its own political weakness. By the same token, the solution to such weakness in the form of an interchange of power very often serves to highlight the weakness of the constitutional reform position through its dependency upon opposition forces which only have the capacity to make constitutional changes once they are no longer in opposition. This dynamic typifies the paradoxical nature of the constitutional reform issue in such a political constitution. The more dependent the constitutional reform issue is upon the sponsorship of an alternative government, the more it is placed in jeopardy when the latter acquires government status. The nearer an opposition force like New Labour is to power and the greater the likelihood of a working majority, then the less need there is for constitutional reform to be retained as a high priority. The less decisive the win, the greater the difficulty of securing constitutional reform through parliament. The more decisive the win, the larger the opportunity for the governing party to secure more of its social and economic agenda and, therefore, the less incentive to jeopardise such an opportunity with the disruption of constitutional reform. The greater the achievement in social and economic policy, the more plausible the traditional claims of constitutional neutrality and responsiveness, and the more implausible the professed need for fundamental change.

The paradoxical character of the constitutional reform issue in the constitutional framework of the British system can have the effect of undermining the logic of the arguments made in support of constitutional change. For example, by highlighting the way that Conservative governments had misused or abused governmental power in order to advance the cause of constitutional reform, it tends to link such pathologies to a particular government. When constitutional deficiencies are juxtaposed in this way with party government – and it is difficult to prevent such an association being made in the British system – then they can be resolved logically by the establishment of a Labour government. Because constitutional problems are necessarily implicated in inter-party dialogue and strategy, it is difficult for constitutional problems to transcend this dimension and to be treated as wholly structural or procedural issues. The reductionist properties of political constitutionalism have the effect of giving constitutional critique a party-based dimension, leading ineluctably to the prospect of a Labour win being seen as a solution in its own right. Just as Labour's lead in the polls prior to the election could in part be attributed to the popularisation and severity of the analysis of governmental power, so Labour's victory could effectively demolish such anxieties to the extent of making constitutional reform even less likely than before. In this way, constitutional reform could be seen as an ancillary device for an opposition party, only to become a piece of superfluous exotica once that party had acquired the prize of governmental responsibility and, with it, the prerogative of redefining the public interest.

Conclusion

Sufficient ambiguity existed over Labour's position in relation to these problems for John Major to make the issue of the constitution his key campaigning theme. In a concerted attempt to use Labour's reform proposals to typify the opposition's *naïveté* in every dimension of governance, Major deployed the political influence of the premiership to focus public attention upon the alleged anomalies and contradictions of Labour's claim to power. The prime minister took personal responsibility for closing the gap between what he took to be the dangerous nature of the opposition's plans and the somnolent atmosphere surrounding the issue in the election. He sought to extract the benefits that should accrue to a government facing an opposition that had opened itself up to the multifaceted jeopardy of constitutional reform. Major believed that this was his issue and that a populist intervention by the prime minister acting as a crisis-manager would turn the tide towards the Conservatives in the same way as he believed his eleventh-hour appeals to the integrity of the United Kingdom had secured a late swing in 1992. Major planned a repetition in 1997 by carefully nurturing the issue during the election in preparation for a full-scale assault during the final week of the campaign. He drew upon the dangers, the needlessness, the incoherence and the cost of Labour's project. The prime minister alternated between macro and micro critiques; he attacked the logic of the intended arrangements together with their short- and long-term consequences; he questioned the motives behind Labour's plans and the legitimacy of its alliance with the Liberal Democrats; and he sought to fuel suspicion over the existence of a hidden agenda. The prime minister was central to the Conservative strategy of building up a sense of fear over the prospect of a Labour government. It was a plan that relied upon fusing three fears into an amalgam of anxiety. 'This week we have seen that Britain faces three great threats: the [trade] union threat, the federalist threat and today the separatist threat. Labour will be soft on all three funded by the unions ... Labour would destroy British prosperity, risk dividing Britain and put us on a escalator to a federal Europe.'[87] Labour was accused of courting all three of these vices but the central and defining threat remained that of constitutional change: 'We have to raise this issue, it's one issue that rises above the normal run of politics ... There's a great battle being fought at the moment ... a battle about the nature of the United Kingdom itself.'[88] Labour was indicted not merely for supporting constitutional reform but more significantly for openly thinking about the British constitution, for encouraging public speculation and debate over its properties and for failing to comprehend the possible ramifications of such constitutional self-examination. Major warned the country that 'Labour would throw a bone to the yapping dogs of Welsh and Scottish separatism in the vain hope they might then follow Labour. They would gerrymander Britain and play party politics with our nation for pure political advantage. A thousand days of Labour government could ditch a thousand years of British history. It's a poor bargain. Better to keep the history and ditch Labour.'[89] By the final week of the campaign, the tone had become even more strident and alarmist.

> The message I would give you, to the British nation, we have 72 hours to save the union, 72 hours to make sure that the nature of our government is not changed irrevocably for the worse, with power draining away from Westminster. There are 72 hours in which to save the Union, 72 hours to make sure that the system of Government that has prevailed in this country for a very long time is protected and enshrined, and ... not broken up and divided in one direction towards the EU and the other to a devolved Parliament across the United Kingdom.[90]

The prime minister could not have been more emphatic in staking his public prestige and professional reputation upon a direct appeal to the electorate's conservative and nationalist instincts to protect the British constitution by defeating New Labour. To question part of the constitution was to question all of it which was in its turn the equivalent of subverting it and throwing the United Kingdom into turmoil.

And yet in spite of John Major's best efforts to galvanise the electorate in defence of the constitution, the public was not sufficiently roused to allow any doubts over Labour's constitutional agenda to distract attention from the government's overall record as the primary consideration in the choice between parties. The Conservatives hammered away at the issue in an attempt to dramatise the residual radicalism of New Labour, to intimidate the floating voters over Labour's 'hidden agenda' and to generate splits between the opposition parties and especially within the Labour party itself. But just as party ranks held firm under the onslaught, so the issue of constitutional reform remained largely dormant in the electorate at large. Labour may have feared that the issue could have become its Achilles' heel, but the 69 per cent of the electorate who voted against the Conservative party had either dismissed it as a pivotal issue, or had over the prolonged pre-election period already assimilated constitutional reform as the necessary concomitant of a change in government. Whatever the exact salience of the theme in the minds of the voters, two aspects of the issue were very clear. First, Labour had won an emphatic victory in the 1997 general election and had done so with an explicit manifesto commitment to extensive constitutional reform. Second, the decisiveness of the win was not matched by the clarity of what it signified in the area of constitutional reform. The election had not resolved any of the questions, arguments or problems surrounding the issue. It had merely established the configuration of the issues and had reaffirmed that the politics of constitutional change were complex and contingent upon a set of highly fluid and reactive conditions. The problem, over constitutional reform which had confronted Labour in opposition and during the campaign were not settled by the election victory. They were simply transposed to a new context where their dynamics continued to structure the processes of change and to draw out the full implications of the politics of constitutional reform.

Notes

1 I am indebted to a number of individuals who agreed to provide background information, on a non-attributable basis, relating to campaign strategy and electoral calculation.

2 Samuel Beer, *Modern British Politics: A Study of Parties and Pressure Groups* (London: Faber, 1965), p. 90. See also Anthony Wright, 'British Socialists and the British Constitution', *Parliamentary Affairs*, vol. 43, no. 3 (July 1990), pp. 322–40.

3 Vernon Bogdanor, 'Labour and the Constitution, Part I: The Record', in Brian Brivati and Tim Bale (eds), *New Labour in Power: Precedents and Prospects* (London: Routledge, 1997), p. 112.

4 Ben Pimlott, *Harold Wilson* (London: Harper Collins, 1992), p. 533.

5 Kenneth O. Morgan, *The People's Peace: British History 1945–1989* (Oxford: Oxford University Press, 1990), p. 366.

6 *Ibid.*, p. 366.

7 Paul Anderson and Nyta Mann, *Safety First: The Making of New Labour* (London: Granta, 1997), p. 278.

8 For an excellent commentary on the political and constitutional problems posed by devolution, see Vernon Bogdanor, 'The English Constitution and Devolution' in Vernon Bogdanor (ed.), *Politics and the British Constitution* (Aldershot: Dartmouth, 1996), pp. 183–94 and Vernon Bogdanor, 'Devolution: The Constitutional Problems' in Bogdanor (ed.), *Politics and the British Constitution*, pp. 195–212.

9 Quoted in Robert Harris, *The Making of Neil Kinnock* (London: Faber and Faber, 1984), p. 100.

10 They were Croydon North West (22 October 1981), Crosby (26 November 1981) and Glasgow Hillhead (23 March 1982).

11 See Ivor Crewe and Anthony King, *The Birth, Life and Death of the Social Democratic Party* (Oxford: Oxford University Press, 1995).

12 David Butler and Dennis Kavanagh, *The British General Election of 1992*

(Houndmills: Macmillan, 1992), p. 52.

13 Roy Hattersley, 'Love Affairs of State', *The Guardian*, 10 January 1997.

14 Quoted in Michael Jones and Andrew Grice, 'Britain Set for Hung Parliament with Labour the Largest Party', *Sunday Times*, 5 April 1992.

15 Quoted in Jones and Grice, 'Britain Set for Hung Parliament', *Sunday Times*, 5 April 1992.

16 Butler and Kavanagh, *The British General Election 1992*, p. 253.

17 *Ibid.*, pp. 252–3.

18 Trevor Smith 'Citizenship, Community and Constitutionalism', *Parliamentary Affairs*, vol. 49, no. 2 (April 1996), p. 269.

19 See Toby Helm, 'Don't Forget the Strengths of the Union, says Major', *Sunday Telegraph*, 23 February 1992.

20 See Robin Oakley, 'Major Gambles with Attack on Hung Parliament', *Daily Telegraph*, 7 April 1992.

21 Quoted in Oakley, 'Major Gambles', *Daily Telegraph*, 7 April 1992.

22 Quoted in George Jones, 'Major Warns of Liberal Democrat Trojan Horse', *Daily Telegraph*, 2 April 1992.

23 Quoted in Michael Jones and Andrew Grice, 'Britain Set for Hung Parliament', *Sunday Times*, 5 April 1992.

24 Quoted in George Jones, 'Baker Raises Fear of "Pact with Devil"', *Daily Telegraph* 7 April 1992.

25 *Sunday Telegraph*, 5 April 1992.

26 Perry Anderson, *English Questions* (London: Verso, 1992), p. 348.

27 Stuart Weir, 'Labour Puts Democracy in the Back Seat', *Sunday Times*, 9 September 1990.

28 Patrick Seyd, 'Tony Blair and New Labour', in Anthony King, David Denver, Iain McLean, Pippa Norris, Philip Norton, David Sanders and Patrick Seyd, *New Labour Triumphs: Britain at the Polls* (Chatham: Chatham House, 1988), p. 64.

29 Charter 88, *News Briefing*.

30 Andrew Marr, 'Mr Smith Shows the Zeal of the Nearly Converted', *The Independent*, 2 March 1993.

31 William Rees-Mogg, 'Too Many Promises', *The Times*, 22 December 1994.

32 Quoted in Anthony Barnett, 'Changing the Rules', *New Statesman and Society*, 16 February 1996.

33 Labour had an average lead of 17.42 points over the Conservatives during the 1994–95 period. See the aggregate of ICM polls in Martin Linton (ed.), *The Election: A Voters' Guide* (London: Fourth Estate, 1997), pp. 56–8.

34 'Constitutional politics', *The Economist*, 29 June 1996, p. 20.

35 *Ibid.*

36 Andrew Grice, 'Blair Shifts Ground on Voting Reform'.

37 Quoted in Andrew Marr, 'Changing the Chemistry of Politics', *The Independent*, 2 April 1996.

38 Trevor Smith, 'Post-modern Politics and the Case for Constitutional Renewal', *Political Quarterly*, vol. 65, no. 2 (April–June 1994), p. 134.

39 Tony Blair, 'John Smith Memorial Lecture' in Tony Blair, *New Statesman Special Selection from New Britain: My Vision of a Young Country* (London: Fourth Estate, 1996), p. 78.

40   *Ibid.*, pp. 82, 86.
41   Tony Blair, 'Power to the People Must Be Our Aim', *The Independent*, 7 February 1996.
42   Peter Mandelson and Roger Liddle, *The Blair Revolution: Can New Labour Deliver?* (London: Faber, 1996), p. 191.
43   Mandelson and Liddle, *The Blair Revolution*, p. 191, 192.
44   *Ibid.*, p. 206.
45   *Ibid.*
46   *Ibid.*, p. 207.
47   Quoted in Barnett, 'Changing the Rules'.
48   'The Tug for the Flag', *The Economist*, 29 June 1996.
49   Quoted in 'Major Plans Wide-ranging Reforms for Scotland', *The Independent*, 17 November 1995.
50   Quoted in 'John Major: Watch Me, Then Judge Me', *The Independent*, 17 November 1995.
51   Quoted in *ibid.*
52   John Major, *Speech on the Constitution*, given to the Centre for Policy Studies, 26 June 1996.
53   *Ibid.*
54   *Ibid.*
55   *Ibid.*
56   Quoted in Robert Shrimsley, 'Blair Shifts His Stance on Electoral Reforms', *Daily Telegraph*, 18 March 1996.
57   See Tony Blair's interview with *New Statesman and Society*, 5 July 1996.
58   Patrick Wintour, 'Labour Set for Historic Poll Deal', *The Observer*, 5 January 1997.
59   Jill Sherman, 'Blair Pulls Back from Voting Reforms', *The Times*, 10 February 1997.
60   'Honeymoon Democrats', *The Times*, 10 February 1997.
61   Sherman, 'Blair Pulls Back'.
62   Quoted in Ewan MacAskill, 'Ashdown Rules Out Labour Merger', *The Guardian*, 6 March 1997.
63   'Two Parties Are Better Than One', *The Guardian*, 6 March 1997.
64   Hugo Young, 'At Last – A Big Idea for a New Britain', *The Guardian*, 6 March 1997.
65   *Ibid.*
66   *Ibid.*
67   *The Economist Election Briefing* (London: *The Economist*, 1997), p. 9.
68   Anthony Barnett, 'Blair's Fear of the Fear Factor', *The Independent*, 20 February 1997.
69   *Ibid.*
70   *Ibid.*
71   *Ibid.*
72   Linton, *The Election*, p. 62.
73   'Unfinished Business', *New Statesman and Society*, 6 February 1996.
74   Hugo Young, 'Voting Revolution Labour Can't Control', *The Guardian*, 10 June 1997.

75 William Rees-Mogg, 'Labour is Going to Sea in a Sieve', *The Times*, 10 March 1997.

76 'Dangers of Lords Reform', *Financial Times*, 14 January 1998.

77 Max Beloff, 'No Better Recipe for Conflict', *The Times*, 9 August 1997.

78 Andrew Marr, 'The Voices That May Dash All Hopes of Reform', *The Independent*, 19 February 1997.

79 David Butler and Dennis Kavanagh, *The British General Election of 1997* (Houndmills: Macmillan, 1997), p. 140.

80 *Ibid.*, p. 109. In the indexes to Butler and Kavanagh, *The British General Election 1997* and King *et al.*, *New Labour Triumphs*, page references to the subject of the constitution amount to eight and two respectively – i.e. ten references out of a combined total of 603 pages in the two works which equates to 1.67 per cent of the base.

81 Peter Riddell, 'Our Ostrich MPs and the Constitution', *The Times*, 7 July 1997.

82 Andrew Puddephatt, 'Instead We Heard the Sound of Silence', *Citizens*, no. 19 (May 1997).

83 Stephen Fay, 'More Women, Honesty and a New Set of Faces, Please', *Independent on Sunday*, 6 April 1997.

84 Matthew D'Ancona, 'There's More to PR Than Public Relations', *Sunday Telegraph*, 27 July 1997.

85 Andrew Rawnsley, 'The Great Democrat Must Keep His PR pledge', *The Observer* 13 July 1997.

86 Linton, *The Election*, p. 68.

87 Quoted in Rachel Sylvester and Joy Copley, 'Major Stakes Victory on the Future of the Union', *Daily Telegraph*, 23 April 1997.

88 Quoted in *ibid.*

89 Quoted in Anthony Bevins, 'Major Launches Crusade to Save Constitution', *The Independent*, 15 February 1997.

90 Quoted in Philip Webster, Jane Landale and Arthur Leatley, '72 Hours Left to Save UK, says Major', *The Independent*, 29 April 1997.

The politics of the British constitution

Labour's carefully laid contingency plans for a hung parliament were rendered null and void by the landslide victory on 1 May 1997. An incoming Labour administration would not be afflicted by the constitutional uncertainty of a dependence upon a third party. Instead, the sheer scale of New Labour's parliamentary pre-eminence ensured that any constitutional ambiguity would be of its own making in the form of the party's manifesto commitments to comprehensive constitutional change. Even though the theme of constitutional reform had not been given emphasis during the election campaign, the victory was widely interpreted as an affirmation of the need for, and support of, the modernisation of the British way of government. Given that the issue of constitutional change represented the area in which the Conservative and Labour parties were most clearly differentiated from each other and given the decisive nature of the Conservative defeat, there was a strong *prima facie* case for implying a logical connection between the Conservative government's rejection of constitutional change and its fall from power. By the same token, Labour's attachment to constitutional reform prior to the election at least suggested the existence of a mandate to proceed with its reform agenda following the election triumph.

To the supporters of constitutional reform, New Labour's win represented a breakthrough for the campaign to revise the British constitution. The party was seen to be not only politically committed to reform, but morally obligated to pursue the agenda because of the specific promises made to engage in constitutional renovation and because of the backing given to the party by the reform lobby. Reformers could point to the continuation of high levels of public support for constitutional change even though the issue had been largely eclipsed by other themes in the election. For example, a MORI poll published by *The Economist* two days after the election demonstrated that the preponderance of support for constitutional reform over opposition to constitutional change had remained intact (see Table 7.1). Supporters of reform felt able to declare in the aftermath of the election victory that 'the

Table 7.1 *'What people really want': The Economist/MORI poll*

Constitutional changes % favouring	Strongly support	Tend to support	Neither	Tend to oppose	Strongly oppose
Creating a Scottish parliament	13	32	22	15	10
Removing voting-rights of hereditary peers	21	26	22	12	8
Holding referendum on voting system	18	32	18	18	6
Locally elected mayors	29	44	14	7	1
Removing constitutional powers of monarchy	8	11	14	22	40
Bill of rights	28	42	12	9	2
Proportional representation	27	38	11	11	6
Freedom of information act	35	42	7	7	3

Source: The Economist, 3 May 1997. MORI interviewed a sample of 962 adults aged 18+ in 171 constituencies between April 25 and April 28 1997.

constitution will dominate the first half of the Blair Government as it has no Parliament since the Asquith era. This is exhilarating to those who believe the updating of British democracy is sorely overdue'.[1] Yet there were no guarantees that this would occur. Electoral mandates are highly contestable concepts and it is governments which reserve the right to make and to use such constructions according to their own priorities, needs and judgements. Reformers could attempt to establish the issue as the collective embodiment of electoral achievement and to define it as a necessary *raison d'être* of the new Labour government. But such efforts were heavily conditioned by the knowledge that they were not only exercises in *ex post facto* rationalisation but devices to insinuate a clear policy imperative from a diffuse process of general legitimation. Despite the content of the Labour manifesto and the language of Labour's electoral commitments, the British constitution remained intact. The general election had transferred the power of the state to the Labour cabinet and, with it, the prerogative rights to determine what policies were now in the public interest and whether previous obligations were provisional, conditional or optional.

It was conceivable that constitutional reform would have been marginalised in the euphoria of an historic Labour victory. It was known that a majority of senior cabinet ministers was on record as having grave reservations over many aspects of the issue. Nevertheless, the new prime minister had publicly associated himself with constitutional reform and had explicitly linked it to his overall theme of the transformation of British society. The litmus test of the new government's allegiance to the issue would be the Queen's Speech laying out the government's programme for the first session of the new parliament. This would mark out the new government's point of embarkation and define its programmatic themes and priorities. In what was Labour's first Queen's Speech for a generation, constitutional reform was clearly established as a major subject of legislation. The government declared that devolution for Scotland and Wales would be its chief priority during the first session. Moreover, the size of the Labour majority allowed the government to opt for the grand strategy of pressing ahead with all the necessary stages of the devolutionary process – including the referendums – in as small a time frame as possible. In addition to devolution, the government proposed the incorporation of the European Convention of Human Rights into British law and the establishment of a directly elected strategic authority and mayor for London. Collectively, these measures on the constitution represented the most radical element of New Labour's programme for the first session. Given that the new government was conspicuously cautious in the major areas of social, economic and industrial policy, radicalism in the field of constitutional change was particularly significant. The prime minister himself explicitly reaffirmed the claim to a linkage between the source of the new government's authority and its programme of constitutional reform: 'Our mandate is clear: to modernise what is outdated and to make fair what is unjust, and to do both by the best means available'.[2] *The Observer* reflected the atmosphere of anticipation that was prompted by the government's stated intention to move the focus of the political agenda to structural change in the political system.

> Last week saw the biggest programme of constitutional modernisation Britain has witnessed since the First World War. The State is to be recast, together with an entrenchment of fundamental liberties that seemed inconceivable seven or eight years ago. Tony Blair's economic and social programme may be more minimalist and conservative, but his political reforming efforts are genuinely ambitious. History is in the making ... The challenge is to prepare for politics after the Great Reform Parliament.[3]

And yet, in spite of the excitement aroused by the government's commitment to concerted change, doubts remained over the scale and depth of New Labour's attachment to diminishing the prize of governmental power that it had so recently acquired. A number of previously stated commitments were left out of the first wave of legislation set for the opening 18-month session of parliament. Instead of a freedom of information act, there would only be a government white paper. The reform of the House of Lords was reserved for another session. The government was silent over the introduction of proportional representation (PR) for the 1999 European elections and announced no provisions to honour its pledge to set up a commission of inquiry into the possible means of introducing PR, or to hold a referendum on a change to the traditional electoral system. It is true that the new administration was able to offer plausible reasons for these anxieties. Freedom of information legislation was said to be complex and far-reaching and, as a result, would require extensive consultation within Whitehall and the public sector in general. The absence of the bill to remove the voting rights of hereditary peers in the House of Lords was rationalised by ministers as an incentive to the Lords not to obstruct Labour's programme during the first session. It could also be claimed that the government already had a full schedule of constitutional reform and that to include more items in the initial stage of a parliament would only create serious political and timetabling problems that might jeopardise the passage and consolidation of the primary reform measures in the field of the constitution. Furthermore, it had to be borne in mind that Labour had not been expecting a landslide majority and, therefore, had not planned for a fuller constitutional agenda that such a majority may have warranted. As a final defence, the government was in a position to assert that its reform package was a first step in what would be a continuing process of constitutional modernisation. In effect, the implication was that because constitutional reform was necessarily systemic in nature, any starting point was a tacit acceptance of the full journey. Some reforms would have to wait until later sessions but, because Labour had already introduced a series of constitutional measures, this was sufficient in the government's view to affirm good faith and the presence of a general across-the-board flotation of a comprehensive constitutional agenda to be pursued over a sustained period.

In the early weeks of the new government, the leadership took further actions to enhance its reputation for constitutional change. For example, the government proposed a series of changes to the legislative process that were intended not only to make more efficient use of Parliament's time and energy but to raise the level of legislative scrutiny and critical review. For example, it was proposed that some bills would be published in draft form to allow for easier amendments during the pre-legislative consultation process and that there should be a 'roll-over' of unfinished bills into succeeding sessions of Parliament. The government also tried to demonstrate its innovative capacity by the decisions to transfer the control of interest rates to the Bank of England and to nominate Paddy Ashdown and other leading Liberal Democrats to become members of the cabinet committee considering constitutional reform. Furthermore, following a brief period of pressure from some elements of the media, the government ended the hiatus over the arrangements for the 1999 European elections by announcing that they would after all be conducted through a system of PR. This was one of the issues which *The Guardian* had earlier described as being 'ominous by their absence' – i.e. 'questions where delay is either not an option or where it is a guarantee of further problems'.[4]

But notwithstanding the radicalism of the original agenda for constitutional reform in the Queen's Speech, the urgency with which measures like devolution for Scotland and Wales were being put through Parliament, the provision of supplementary constitutional measures and the intimations of more reform to come in future sessions of Parliament, the misgivings over the full extent of Labour's reform programme quickly began to show signs of turning into scepticism. According to John Lloyd, a close observer of the evolution of the constitutional issue within the Labour party, concern over the momentum of reform had become widespread after only ten weeks of the new government. He refers to the 'post-modernisers' in the Labour party who accept only part of the modernisers' ethos of the need for 'more transparent and rational systems of parliamentary, electoral and representative procedures'. 'Post-modernisers' may accept the political value and rhetorical force of constitutional reform, but wish to exclude change in such controversial and expansive areas as the monarchy, the electoral system for Westminster and the principle of parliamentary supremacy. By late July 1997, it was evident to Lloyd that the 'post-modernisers' were making their presence felt in the priorities of the new government:

> In this relatively plastic period the alarmed conviction is growing in the minds of the constitutional modernisers that their colleagues are working quietly to put barriers and flashing red lights across many of the highways leading to radical reform. Change, they believe, will soon be limited to areas where an irrevocable commitment has been made – as Scots devolution [sic] – or where the change can be represented as both modernising and popular – as the ending of the right of hereditary peers to vote on legislation.[5]

The Observer was even more critical. Within two months of its acclamation of the new government's historic role in the modernisation of the British constitution, the paper had become suspicious of New Labour's attachment to the cause. The indictment was extensive:

> If anything is New Labour's Big Idea, it is democratic renewal ... But the Big Idea is becoming shrouded in big delay and big uncertainty. Reform of the House of Lords has been shelved until at least the second session. So has a Freedom of Information Bill; last week, even the more modest White Paper was put back, with dark muttering about 'senior civil servants' being 'strongly opposed' and a government spokesman saying that Ministers needed more 'experience of government' before they introduced it. Stories of Cabinet moves by an 'English lobby' to water down the Scottish devolution White Paper are rife. Similar conflict is reported over the proposed incorporation of the European Convention on Human Rights. Proportional representation for the European elections – a key test of Labour's pluralistic impulses – is also in the balance. The cap-

ping regime has been retained for local councils, making a mockery of local democracy. And the commission on PR for Westminster, agreed with the Liberal Democrats before the election, has yet to be appointed ... [T]he drift is unsettling. All of the reforms were in Labour's manifesto. Most had been discussed ad nauseam while Labour was in Opposition and required little more than the deployment of legal draftsmen ... As for parliamentary time, a government with a majority of 179 has little excuse for inactivity.[6]

Speculation over the reasons for such incipient disillusionment tended to revolve around individual personalities, contemporary events and immediate political forces. Nevertheless, the underlying problems for the incoming Labour government in this field were more fundamental in character. They were not only comparable to, but derived from the same difficulties that the party had confronted in opposition while developing an agenda of constitutional reform. In effect, New Labour's experience in government demonstrated the prevailing continuity of the problems attached to the issue of change in this area of political activity. But such problems signified something even more fundamental in the nature of the issue area. The reappearance of these difficulties indicated the presence, and clarified the identity, of what was a rapidly developing framework of constitutional politics in the United Kingdom.

The picture to emerge during this formative period of a self-professed reform administration was that of a government with a programme for graduated constitutional change co-existing first with a well-organised public campaign for constitutional transformation, and second with a countervailing force of articulate scepticism and traditionalist reaction. It was during the first six months of the Labour government when the post-election licence and momentum for innovation was at its greatest, and where the expectations and fears of radical change were at their highest, that the terms of engagement in the struggle over constitutional change were established. It was in this key period that a new matrix of conditions was formed that would set the parameters of constitutional change not merely for Labour's first parliament, or for its first term of office, or even for the entirety of its term of office, but for the foreseeable future of British politics. It was not that the incoming Labour government represented some point of culmination in the long campaign to modernise the British constitution. It was that the new government provided the catalyst that enabled the interior properties and functional characteristics of the constitutional issue to be both fully revealed and at the same time decisively realised. Whatever had been implicit in the issue was now there to be observed and assessed. Its usages and dynamics, its ways and means, its strategies and conventions, and its effects upon the nature of political contention had become more evident than ever before.

This new matrix of constitutional politics fused together a number of elements which had existed prior to the Blair administration but which had not been fully engaged with one another until the onset of a government committed to the reform of the constitution. The first ingredient was the supply of constitutional fuels which had generated a growing consciousness of the need for constitutional change during the years of Conservative hegemony. Constitutional critique had become a highly effective device of political dissent and opposition. So much so that during the Thatcher period, it carried the risk of being typecast as a uniquely anti-Thatcher strategy that would fade as her premiership declined and the strident use of her executive authority diminished into the more emollient exterior features of the Major administration. But contrary to many expectations, the potential energy of the separate fuels continued to increase in volume especially in the period following the 1992 general election when the Conservatives appeared to have become a permanent fixture in government. The issues which fuelled constitutional speculation gathered momentum and became an established stimulus to an alternative prospectus for the structure and operation of government. Because such a prospectus became closely linked to the programme of New Labour, it could be conjectured that an election victory for Labour would in some way undermine, or even eliminate, the need for a new constitutional settlement. Because a landslide win for Labour could be construed as a *de facto* resettlement, then it might be thought that the very existence of a Labour government would drastically reduce the energy potential of the constitutional fuels. In the light of previous experience and under other circumstances, this most probably would have been the case. But by 1997, the fuels had been primed far too long and the core temperatures were too high to be extinguished even by a new government geared openly to a radical reconstruction of the constitution.

It is true that there were variations in core temperatures as different fuels had distinctive profiles of ignition and controversy (see chapter 3). But it is equally true that the characteristics of each fuel remained in place in spite of the change of government. A Labour government may initially have reduced the intensity of the pressure for constitutional reform – not least by deferring to the need for change in a number of areas – but even a new reformist administration in its honeymoon period could not eliminate any of the ten fuels. Some fuels (*e.g. electoral inequity, centralisation, external imposition, transcendent innovation, traditional anomalies*) remained wholly intact. Other fuels were less thematic and more incident driven and, therefore, their effect would as usual be dependent upon future instances of *governmental excess, governmental misuse, systemic dysfunction, personal misconduct and secrecy.* The heightened sensitivity towards all such constitutional issues ensured that they would remain salient triggers to political dispute. Whether it is through the collective memory of past disputes, the assimilation of constitutional precepts, or the establishment of a political language of constitutional argument, the effect of these fuels over the recent past has been to invest contemporary politics with a continuous current of constitutional evaluation. It quickly became evident that the maintenance of constitutional critique and the pressure for constitutional reform would not be dependent upon the Labour government. During its period of opposition, an entire hinterland of interest groups, political activists, social commentators, radical lawyers, committed journalists and other constitutional partisans developed their arguments, organisation and political penetration to an extent sufficient to maintain the issue of constitutional change, irrespective of government opposition and even government sponsorship.

Whenever the Labour government is perceived to reduce its commitment to constitutional change, or to weaken its resolve in pursuing individual items of reform, the slack is now sure to be taken up by the various elements of what has become a very sophisticated, attentive, suspicious, articulate and durable lobby for constitutional reform. When the government announced in the Queen's Speech that it would be presenting only a White Paper on freedom of information in the first session rather than a bill, those elements of the media that had been most closely involved in the movement for constitutional reform gave notice that they were not prepared to give the Blair administration the benefit of the doubt. Even though the government had only been in office for a matter of days and had already flagged its intention to introduce a series of substantive measures, the reform lobby immediately focused upon what it regarded as a suspicious omission. It was pointed out that while in opposition Blair himself had repeatedly endorsed the principle of freedom of information. In a keynote speech on constitutional reform on 7 February 1996, Blair had alluded to the central significance to the freedom of information: 'The first right of a citizen in any mature democracy should be the right of a freedom of information. It is time to sweep away the cobwebs of secrecy which hang over far too much government activity ... If trust in the people means anything then there can be no argument against a Freedom of Information Act which will give people rights of public information.'[7] But even in the afterglow of a dramatic election victory, the supporters of reform were not prepared to be lulled into hopeful patience by general promises or by expectations of trust. On 8 May 1997, *The Independent* splashed the banner headline 'Blair stalls on open government.'[8] Others quickly followed. *New Statesman*, for example, gave more space to what was missing in the Queen's Speech than to what it contained. Under the injunction 'Take the lid off, Tony', it raised the question of good faith. 'Coupled with the emergent centralising, disciplinarian tendencies of the government ... there is now a whisper that perhaps Blair doesn't mean what he says about modern, open, decentralised government.'[9] Richard Norton-Taylor in *The Guardian* was more direct:

The Labour front bench delighted in what Scott uncovered about the tatty, dishonest, amoral, workings of the Conservative government ... Will the new government still warm to Scott, a supporter of an FoI Act, when he attacks 'the secrecy with which the Government chooses to surround its inner workings, with light cast only by designer leaks and investigative journalists?' ... The Government yesterday argued that it would be better to start from scratch. It will be ironic indeed if the FoI Bill which finally emerges amounts to little more than putting in statutory form the Conservatives' code of practice on open government, with its many exemptions, which has been in place since 1994. We shall be waiting.[10]

For sympathisers of reform, it was clear that, notwithstanding the change of administration, critical vigilance would remain a key component of the campaign for constitutional modernisation. This point was eloquently expressed in the Joseph Rowntree Reform Trust's review of the first six months of the Blair government. The opening period had been promising but there could be no room for complacency. '[I]f anything, its flying start increases the pressure on reformers to keep the new government on its toes. The reform movement cannot relax. Turning reformist thinking into action therefore remains a priority for the coming period and this means maintaining the momentum ... [P]olitics is too important to be left to politicians'.[11] In his book *This Time*, Anthony Barnett also reflects on the need to maximise the potential of New Labour's mandate before the intoxication of government or the absorbent properties of constitutional tradition begin to conceal the identity of 'the core issue ... [of] democracy versus the old regime'.[12] The danger as he sees it lies with those who are so impatient to engage in new social and economic measures that they 'disregard the need for constitutional measures, which they feel force them to look backward at the clinging tentacles of ancient institutions. They see the past as a distraction. "Let us use the trusty sword of the absolute sovereignty of Parliament to cut our way into the future", they shout, not realising that its blade faces the wrong way.'[13] Partial reform is no substitute for a new democratic settlement. In fact, the need for such a settlement, and the pressure to achieve it, have a higher priority than they had before. As Barnett notes, the 'need for a written constitution is more important now that Britain has a government that is altering the unwritten one so radically'.[14]

The effects of other constitutional fuels well primed and sustained in operation, even with a change of government, were given graphic illustration by the Labour government's decision to exempt Formula One motor-racing from what was in every other respect a general ban on tobacco advertising. The prime minister had made the decision on the exemption following a meeting on October 16 1997 with Formual Ones's chief promoter Bernie Eccleston. The subsequent release of information that Mr Eccleston had made a personal donation of £1 million to the Labour party prior to the election, and had made reference to the prospect of a further donation following the election, exposed both the Labour government and the Labour leadership to allegations of a conflict of interest and of personal misconduct. In this incident, the new government had its first experience of how constitutional fuels that had been developed as critical devices against the previous Tory regime, could be applied with equal vigour to a Labour administration. It was not merely that such fuels were theoretically reversible in their application. It was that they became so with such rapidity after such an extensive period when the opposition parties had successfully associated sleaze with the pathology of a Conservative government in decline. *Governmental misuse* and *personal misconduct* had become so intrinsically identified with the era of Conservative government that it was difficult to conceive of such charges being used as constitutional fuels against any other government. And yet, having been instrumental in creating the groundswell of suspicion over the economic motives and ethical standards of Conservative politicians, the Labour government found that the criteria of standards once so effectively employed against the Conservatives could be used against itself.

Bearing in mind the strong element of moral revival in the development of New Labour, it may have been supposed that an incoming Labour government would be most resistant to the constitutional fuels of *governmental misuse* and *personal misconduct*. But the success that New Labour had achieved with the politicisation of morality during John Major's second administration, proved to be two-edged as the Labour government was accused of trading influence for cash. In Tony Blair's most uncomfortable session of prime minister's questions in the House of Commons since taking office, the independent MP Martin Bell, who owed his very presence in the chamber to the campaign against Tory sleaze, asked the prime minister: 'Have we slain one dragon only to have another take its place with a red rose in its mouth?'[15] The U-turn on Formula One was damaging to the government not just because of how it could be portrayed but because of the way it had been revealed:

> New Labour ... was presented to the electorate as the party of openness, honesty and transparency, confronting a Conservative Government whose sleaziness had made it incapable of inspiring people ... Its promise was to squeeze sleaze out of public life; it recognised a lack of trust in politicians and promised to rebuild it ... Now it has been shown to be evasive on facts, grudgingly conceding information only under pressure and threatening towards those who pressed it for an honest account. This was the kind of reaction we had come to expect from the Tories.[16]

Such an issue tapped so easily and so immediately into the channels of conditioned reflexes which had been developed prior to 1 May 1997 that Blair found it difficult to reverse the tide of suspicion. *The Times* soberly declared that Tony Blair had not learnt from the mistakes of the Major administration: 'In order to avoid being accused of succumbing to undue influence, the Prime Minister should have taken the greatest pains to consult, explain and open up decision-making. Instead, we have seen shiftiness and cover-up. For many supporters of Mr Blair, this week will mark the beginning of disillusionment.'[17] *The Guardian* was even more jaundiced: '[A] Labour government stands accused of running a cash-for-policy operation tailored to the needs of few corporate big boys with large wallets. When such role reversals are possible, we are living in strange times ... If this had happened in the last days of Major era we know what we would have called it: sleaze.'[18] Ultimately, the prime minister felt compelled to appear in a televised interview in order to explain himself and to apologise for the handling of the issue.[19] He took the opportunity to promote the idea that the Committee on Public Standards in Public Life should investigate the issue of party funding in general. In this respect, the Labour government was no different to the Conservative government in that it had been driven by the public reaction to individual events to make decisions that would be likely to have significant long-term constitutional implications. No sooner had the Formula One affair subsided than the government was confronted by further allegations of sleaze including the revelation of the Paymaster General's interest in a £12.75 million offshore trust fund (30 November 1997); the arrest of the Labour MP for Glasgow Govan, Mohammed Sawar, for electoral fraud (16 December 1997); and the publicity surrounding the break-up of the Foreign Secretary's marriage, culminating in the charge (27 January 1998) that Robin Cook had dismissed the civil servant who acted as his appointments secretary at the Foreign Office in order to give his mistress, Gaynor Regan, the position. In July 1998, the Labour government was confronted with accusations that lobbyists, who had previously been aides to Tony Blair, Gordon Brown and Peter Mandelson, had used their insider knowledge of the administration to provide their clients with confidential government information, access to ministers and advisers, and assistance in securing places on government task forces engaged in formulating policy. These types of allegation, in the conjunction with those already under ivestigation (e.g. the activities of Labour MPs Donald Dixon (Jarrow), Tommy Graham (Renfrew West) and Irene Adams (Paisley North) in the circumstances leading to the suicide on 28 July 1997 of Gordon McMaster, the Labour MP for Paisley South; and the suspension from the party of nine Glasgow councillors at the centre of a scandal involving the misuse of public funds) dramatically confirmed the continuity of the *governmental misuse* and *personal misconduct* fuels. In May 1998, it became evident that the fuel of *secrecy* had also retained its force. Foreign Office officials and ministers were accused of complicity in conspiring to break a United Nations arms embargo on Sierra

Leone by granting an export licence to Sandline International that allowed the company to supply weapons to the British-backed forces of President Kabbah. Officials and ministers were accused of a 'cover up' that involved misleading the House of Commons and witholding information to a parliamentary select committee. The claims of official concealment set in motion a long investigation into a question that had become very familiar over the final years of the Conservative period of office – namely, 'who knew what and when?'

What holds true for constitutional fuels also holds true for the content of constitutional discourse in this matrix of prospective, incipient and actual change. The arguments for and against constitutional reform had been thoroughly rehearsed prior to the establishment of a Labour government. The arguments in favour of reform may not always have been made or received with the full conviction that they would ever be used to substantiate actual change. Nevertheless, the various propositions supporting measures to protect, or to restore, or to modernise the constitution had been repeatedly deployed throughout the 1990s and had, as a consequence, acclimatised the public to the currency of constitutional critique and corrective reform. By the same token, the arguments against change may initially have been perfunctory in style, depending more upon the force of constitutional inertia than on the actual merits of the claims refuting the need for change. Nevertheless, as the case for constitutional reform became more forceful and persistent, the case against it became more urgent, leading to a commensurate drive to make arguments more sensitively attuned to the level of threat and to recognise the reasons for the increase in constitutional anxiety. By the time that Labour had achieved office, the respective positions and supportive arguments on constitutional reform had been thoroughly assimilated in the lexicon of contemporary British politics. The different rationales for change and the variants of positive, concessionary and negative defence were now firmly established as the dominant medium of political exchange and evaluation in the issue area. To this extent, the election made no difference, other than the fact that the political balance of the arguments had been reversed with the demise of the Conservative government. The substance of the respective arguments, however, remained intact and have continued to inform and structure debate on the subject.

Another element in the matrix of constitutional politics is provided by the operational and managerial problems which confronted the Labour party in opposition (see pp. 226–44) and which have continued to condition its reponses to the constitutional issue in government. The Labour administration remains subject to the 'macro-micro' problem in its efforts to promote its constitutional agenda. It is regularly criticised for its piecemeal approach to constitutional change and for presenting measures 'as if they had no connection to each other'.[20] By the same token, the government has had to guard itself from appearing to be driven either by dogma or by mantra. Whether the complaints pertain to 'democratisation', 'modernisation' or 'renewal', the Labour administration has had to tread a careful line between possessing organising principles of reform and recognising the need for pragmatism, responsiveness and even improvisation. In spite of Labour's accession to power, the problem of party asymmetry also continues to be a factor. The political initiative may have shifted to a reforming centre-left government, but the level of public tolerance for sustained constitutional innovation and experimentation remains untested. Given the traditions of continuity and incrementalism in the British constitution, the burden of proof continues to lie with the party of change even in the aftermath of an emphatic election victory. It is true that in the honeymoon period of the incoming Labour government, many of the arguments over constitutional reform appeared to have been won by the sheer scale of the victory. However, such a mandate would always be provisional in nature and contested in time. The Labour leadership was always aware that after a period of reform activity, the political advantage would be reserved to favour the scepticism of conservative philosophy. While Labour would endeavour to guard against any resumption of a perceived affinity between constitutionalism and the conservative ethic, it would be a continual challenge to maintain constitutional change as a party asset. After having raised the stakes of constitutional reform and profited from the credit of long-awaited changes to the constitution, a reforming government like that of New Labour would inevitably be held culpable for the political disruption and unfulfilled expectations that are integral to any substantive reconstruction of a constitution. Once Labour had crossed the line from opposition dissent and reformist abstraction to the sponsorship of material change through the agency of governing power, it acquired a blanket accountability. Every palpable consequence that could be attributed to constitutional reform, directly or indirectly, by accident or design, would henceforth be regarded as the exclusive responsibility of the Labour government. Such a generalised process of attribution will always permit conservative scepticism to leach back into favour under the guise of a need for a more conservative management of the constitution to secure a resumption of equilibrium.

An administration engaged in constitutional reform will never be far away from the effects of the 'logical trap' problem. If the critical analysis and logical projection of New Labour's policy positions were rife during its period of opposition, then they have become doubly intense when those proposals are part of an active government agenda. Their imminence concentrates the mind and turns constitutional analysis from idle speculation into a rigorous examination of the relationships between intentions and outcomes, between premises and conclusions, and between techniques and objectives. The disjunctions and anomalies that may have been inherent in an opposition's roster of reform proposals have not only been made explicit in government, but have been exacerbated by the government's need to attend to some reforms before others. Political priorities, parliamentary schedules, or logistical imperatives, however, do not always correspond with constitutional logic. It might be claimed, for example, that the government was disorganised and disingenuous in proposing the abolition of the heredity peer's voting rights in the House of Lords without first deciding upon the future rationale of a reformed second chamber and, in particular, its legislative relationship with a House of Commons whose own basis of representation was under review. It could also be argued, that from the point of view of the overall integrity of the programme to restructure the British constitution, a freedom of information act or a bill of rights should have had a higher priority than devolution for Scotland or Wales.

Logical anomalies have not been restricted to the selection of priorities. The issue of devolution, for example, raised the logical conundrum of a pre-legislative referendum, where the Scottish and Welsh electorates were consulted on the principle of devolution but not on the final parliamentary product of de-centralised government. In what was presented as a participatory exercise in constitutional change, the voters were in essence being asked to 'asked to sign a constitutional ... blank cheque and then to rely on the Government to fill in the details later'.[21] In effect, the referendums on devolution served to underline not only the non-binding character of such devices upon the central government, but also the lack of consultative leverage on the substance of legislation. Far from authorising devolution, the referendums merely triggered parliamentary action on the provisional and conditional delegation of authority from the centre on a basis that was non-negotiable in Scotland and Wales. The White Paper on devolution even reaffirmed that because the British constitution is a subject reserved to the United Kingdom parliament, the issue of national independence for Scotland or Wales would always be determined in Westminster.

Another synthesis of opposites was discernible in the coalitions between the Labour party and the SNP in the referendum on Scottish devolution, and between Labour and Plaid Cymru in the Welsh campaign. In both cross-party exercises, the Labour teams promoted the theme that devolution was the best way to protect the integrity of the United Kingdom. For example, in his final appeal to Welsh voters, the prime minister underlined the link between devolution and unionism: 'No-one could believe I would do anything to weaken the United Kingdom ... Devolution is the exact opposite of separatism.'[22] At the same time, their nationalist partners in Scotland and Wales openly campaigned for devolution as the first stage towards independence. The net effect was a logically confounding result in which the 'Yes' vote could be construed as an approval of two diametrically opposed outcomes. Confusion was to be further compounded by the European sub-text to any process of devolution in which greater independence from London on the part of Scotland and Wales would immediately be compromised by the direct application of European Union directives in a host of key policy areas. A further inconsistency was also evident in the different provisions for devolution in Scotland and Wales despite the fact that the measures were prompted by the need to give recognition to the national dimension in each area. Direct reference to nationality in the composite entity of the United Kingdom usually carries with it an implication of equity and comparability, but in the case of Wales there was a clear disparity in the level of devolution on offer. Sound political and historical reasons may have existed to account for the separate treatment but in the context of the objective of constitutional de-centralisation, the presence of two models raised difficult questions over the organising rationale of a process that was designed ultimately to be extended to the English regions. The government has sought to turn inequity in this field into the virtue of variety: 'Reforms must be right for their time and place. Reflecting the wishes of this kingdom will inevitably lead to different solutions in different parts of our country ... [T]he pace of change will be determined by local conditions.'[23] Notwithstanding the procedural consistency of democratic consent in this area, the effect of such licensed diversity will be to generate, under the rubric of constitutional reform, a host of constitutional inconsistencies between different parts in the United Kingdom.

It should also be pointed out that these inconsistencies are not limited simply to change. Devolved governments will carry the risk of replicating elements of the Westminster/Whitehall structure which, when given new expression in a scheme motivated by national and political renewal, will throw traditional arrangements into critical relief. On occasions, the process may well throw up exaggerated replicas where elements of one constitutional reform generate outcomes which are diametrically opposed to another. For example, in March 1998 it was disclosed that within the legislation relating to Welsh devolution was a provision extending the Official Secrets Act to members of the proposed new Welsh Assembly. Because members would have access to government documents, they would technically be crown servants and therefore were to be placed under the same secrecy rules as government ministers, civil servants, police officers and members of the armed services. This would be the 'first time Britain's powerful secrets laws have been imposed on elected representatives'[24]and as a result it could be claimed that Clause 79 of the bill would not only effectively curtail the Assembly membership's freedom of expression, but extend the remit of closed government at precisely the time when the government was publicly committed to securing passage of freedom of information legislation as part of its constitutional reform programme.

The logical examination and extrapolation of governmental promises, proposals and positions, together with analyses of issue inter-relationships and assessments of possible scenarios, have come to occupy a central role in the consideration of all aspects of constitutional reform. The Labour government has continually had to contend with projections of current and past positions into future conditions of either a determinate or indeterminate nature. But the calculation of cause and effect in the area has not been the exclusive preserve of the opposition parties. The government itself has to look to the political ramifications of constitutional change, in order to protect its interests and options. This has been especially important in respect to the *lilac* problem. Labour's-centre ground position on constitutional reform has continued from opposition into government. It is true that the Conservatives have softened their outright opposition to constitutional change and in some instances have accommodated the need for some reform.[25] For example, the party has had to concede that the devolution referendums have made the Scottish and Welsh assemblies an irreversible feature of Britain's governing arrangements. Conservatives quickly declared that they would engage in the electoral campaign for seats in the new assemblies. Given the provision of a PR component in the assembly structures, Conservatives were likely to benefit from another constitutional reform which they had steadfastly opposed in government. The need to engage with conviction in the constitutional experiment of devolution prompted some Scottish Conservatives to reconsider their attachment to the party in England and its historic opposition to devolution. But despite these instances of assimilation, the Conservative party general has remained highly sceptical of the programme of constitutional modernisation and, accordingly, reserves the right to use the theme against the government for political advantage. The Conservative strategy is one of graduated response in which the party will participate in new constitutional forms and moderate its original objections, while disclaiming any responsibility for the consequences of such reforms and positioning itself to take advantage of any political disarray or public fatigue engendered by them.

The Liberal Democrats, on the other hand, have witnessed a series of assaults upon the central state by a government which shares many if not most of its agenda items on constitutional reform. The party has achieved a role in a government with the establishment of a Lib–Lab cabinet committee on constitutional change. The large increase in the contingent of Liberal Democrat MPs, many of whom owed their seats to Labour supporters voting tactically to maximise the anti-Tory swing, has enhanced its position in Westminster and persuaded many in the Labour party that a convergence between the two parties is not only possible, but necessary for Labour to establish a progressive alliance that would marginalise the Tories on a long-term basis. In many respects, constitutional reform is the handmaiden of such a prospective alliance. Apart from the joint experiences of the two parties in such contexts as the Scottish Constitutional Convention and the 'Yes' vote campaigns in Scotland and Wales, it could be foreseen that both parties would have to work together within a coalition in Edinburgh, in order to provide a stable and coherent majority in a PR-based Scottish assembly. But in other respects, constitutional reform threw the differences between the parties into high relief. This was particularly so in the tectonic manoeuvrings over the issue of PR for Westminster – an issue widely regarded as potentially 'the most fundamental change in Britain's constitution'.[26] What was the gut issue for the third party was also the most sensitive for Labour as it would seriously affect its future capacity to form a government on its own. The Liberal Democrats had a straight preference for the most proportional system to be endorsed and actively supported by the prime minister in the promised referendum on electoral change. The Labour leadership was proportionately more cautious in seeking to retain Liberal Democratic good will, whilst wavering between no change, minimal change and moderate change.

As the political stakes were so high on such an issue, the consideration given to PR was pervaded by calculations of party advantage and by projections of political cycles. For the Liberal Democratic leadership, it was worthwhile to suppress its opposition role in the hope of working towards a joint agreement on PR that would irredeemably strengthen the Liberal Democrats' leverage on future governments. Paddy Ashdown's hopes for a centre-left coalition, however, generated anxieties in his party over its future identity. Critics believed that he was being either patronised or consumed by Labour – i.e. that the Liberal Democrats were being kept quiet by tokens of high office and false promises, or were simply being taken over in an asset-stripping exercise. These tensions were palpable in the Liberal Democrats' post-election party conference when sceptics and dissidents asked the same questions over New Labour's intentions that anxious Labour party members were to ask in their own party conference two weeks later. What concerned both parties was the extent to which Blair was engaged in a project to achieve a partnership in a genuinely pluralistic multi-party style of politics, or in the creation of a hegemonic party that would outmanoeuvre and absorb the Liberal Democrats for Labour's own long-term security – even at the expense of creating splits in Labour, the Liberal Democrat and even the Conservative parties. In his leader's speech to the 1997 party conference, Ashdown warned the Liberal Democrats that the position of working with the prime minister to 'change the culture of British politics' would not always be easy: 'No doubt we shall not always agree with every detail of the Government's proposals on constitutional reform and no doubt, not everything we do agree to will match every dotted "i" and crossed "t" of every Liberal Democrat policy. And that may mean compromises. And I will find that as tough as any of you'.[27] The disclosure was greeted in total silence by an audience which was unaccustomed to compromising constitutional reform and its own identity with the requirement of acquiring a stake in government.

At the time of writing (October 1998), the strongest likelihood is that a referendum on a presented PR option will not be held until 2000 and that, even if a 'yes' vote were secured, the arrangements for a new system would not be in place until after the next general election. Given the delays involved in appointing a commission to formulate a choice of a 'broadly proportional' voting system and the high probability that the selected PR option would not be the Liberal Democrats' preferred choice, it is likely that Lib–Lab co-operation at the cabinet committee level would decline following such an outcome, thereby leaving the Liberal Democrats to resume their position on the radical wing of the constitutional debate. While a marginal reform of the electoral system might 'suddenly look overwhelmingly attractive' to Labour as the 'best way of overcoming the threat of "third term blues"'[28], it is equally probable that the Liberal Democrats would come increasingly to recognise that the window of opportunity for constitutional reform would be closing and that it would be necessary to resume a more distant posture to what would be seen as a government with a decreasing interest in the reform of governing structures. Whatever reforms are achieved in the area of the constitution and whatever changes are made to the dynamics of party competition, one aspect will almost certainly remain constant – namely, the continuation of the *lilac* factor during the course of the Labour government and the persistence of a constitutional agenda which Liberal Democrats will always regard as peculiarly their own.

Finally, the 'political constitution' problem will remain a conditioning agent in the matrix of constitutional politics. Any government, even one committed to reform, will find that the opportunity, time frame and appetite for disruptive change will be limited not only to cycles of innovation and consolidation but by the irresistible displacement of old agendas with new events and the need to respond to them. For a new government coming into office after a protracted period in opposition during which it developed a roster of radical proposals, the transition would be bound to incorporate a change of perspective from opposition licence to governmental responsibility – from the self-interest of complaint and condemnation to the self-interest of caution and security. Even the incoming administration of New Labour, supported by a landslide majority of seats and with an identity centred upon a change in the culture of British politics, knew that the momentum for constitutional change would be limited by time, tolerance and resources. Constitutional reform may have been an effective rallying device in the mobilisation of opposition forces, but there were numerous realists in the party who still adhered to the authoritarian traditions of the political constitution and who were loth to risk the standing of the new government in unnecessarily lavish adventures of constitutional reconstruction.

Prior to the election, there had been many agnostics on constitutional reform in the shadow cabinet. Following the election, it was to be expected that senior ministers would become distracted by their new departmental responsibilities, that they would come to appreciate the limits of parliamentary time and political resources, and that they would realise the need to make priorities and to front-load what were considered to be the important proposals at the expense of the more dispensable measures. These transitions duly occurred. During the first few months of the Labour government, there was a growing realisation within the party and the administration that constitutional reform was neither cost-free nor neutral in terms of governmental management. Running a government was now seen to be a rocky road. Account had to be taken of a profusion of changing external conditions in a highly volatile environment. The unexpected death of Diana, Princess of Wales, for example, threatened completely to de-rail both the debate and the referendum campaign over Scottish devolution, as normal political conduct was formally suspended for period of national mourning immediately prior to the vote. Account also had to be taken of the political impact of constitutional reform measures upon New Labour. A case in point was provided in the aftermath of the referendum on Welsh devolution when the government's plans only survived by a margin of 50.3 per cent to 49.7 per cent. Because the 'Yes' campaign had been sponsored by the government as a *de facto* vote of confidence in the Blair administration, a rejection of its proposals would have severely undermined the political authority of both the new government and the prime minister. As a consequence of the outcome of the Welsh referendum, plans for English regional devolution were shelved by ministers who 'feared the prospect of a series of divisive and time-consuming referendums disrupting the legislative programme'.[29] In effect, the government had to abandon an item of constitutional reform which it had accepted in opposition. Having achieved governmental status, New Labour could not countenance the risk of a political defeat in the pursuit of the reform – even though such a defeat would only have occurred in the 'free vote' circumstances of a referendum. *The Guardian* may have complained that the decision demonstrated the need for 'Labour ... to have its feet held to the fire',[30] but New Labour in office, like any other government, had interests of its own that superseded policy pledges like those to constitutional reform. Such political caution was reinforced by the signs that the decisive referendum vote in favour of Scottish devolution (74.3 per cent to 25 per cent) had led not to the anticipated flattening out of SNP attachment, but to an increase in public support of both the party and its programme of national independence. Contrary to expectations, the SNP had by June 1998 risen to become the most popular party in Scotland, thereby posing a direct threat to Labour's power base not just in Scotland but in Westminster as well.

In spite of the government's sustained commitment to constitutional reform, therefore, it became evident that New Labour's graduation to government would temper its drive for constitutional change. The issue had continued to create tensions beneath the surface and had demonstrated that the old impulses of the political constitution could not be discounted. The sceptical view of constitutional reform from within the government saw it as a high-profile issue where the risks outweighed any of the benefits. Change in such a sensitive area would always be regarded as endangering the unity of the party by prompting close ties with the Liberal Democrats. The issue of constitutional reform threatened to make government even more difficult than it already was by unnecessarily encumbering its operational discretion and policy choices with disabling handicaps and obligations of its own making. Given the traditional doctrine of the British constitution – i.e. that a Labour victory would effectively have resolved many of the issues previously supporting the case for constitutional reform – then the government might well see itself as justified in marginalising its prior commitments as part of an ineluctable process of maturation from opposition to government. Far from eliminating these ancient drives, constitutional reform amounted to a litmus test of their continued existence.

The tension between Labour's declared objective of constitutional modernisation and its acquisition of governmental authority was typified by the imbroglio over a freedom of information act. Even though freedom of information had been promoted by the Labour leadership in opposition as an indispensable component of constitutional modernisation, 'implying it would be a top priority',[31] and even though parts of the media had been 'told that a Freedom of Information Bill would be included in Labour's first-year programme',[32] the item was conspicuously absent from the government's plans for the first session of Parliament. Reasons for the omission ranged from reports that ministers required more time to arrive at a set of satisfactory draft proposals to the difficulties of controlling the costs of information provision; from the problems of administration and appeals procedures to the effects of Freedom of Information upon decision-making, collective responsibility and civil service impartiality; and from difficulties over defining exemptions and protecting commercial and governmental confidentiality to the pressures of parliamentary time and the constraints of government priorities. Many of these reasons were widely considered to be merely pretexts for a new government's rite of passage into secrecy as a necessary instrument in the management of the state. That a Labour government would risk public opprobrium for deleting what would have been a low-cost item of constitutional reform and one to which the party and the leadership had repeatedly committed itself in opposition was seen as a measure of New

Labour's graduation into the authoritarian mores of government. Amid reports that civil servants and senior ministers were arguing for delays of three to four years before the need to honour the manifesto pledge, proponents of Freedom of Information were claiming that the time being requested to finalise the legislation was unnecessary. They pointed out that the legislation was already available, the groundwork had already been completed, the issues had been extensively examined in the debates on Mark Fisher's private member's bill on open government in 1993, the large Labour majority would facilitate prompt legislative action and that delay in such circumstances would inflict long-term damage to the cause. In the words of Maurice Frankel, the director of the Campaign for the Freedom of Information, 'the longer they wait, the more diluted it could well become'.[33] Richard Norton-Taylor was less restrained in his depiction of the dynamic: '[T]he longer the wait, the more ministers will be attracted to secrecy. Secrecy is an addictive drug. It is the opium of the people in the dark. The more they get used to it the more they crave it. It protects them from criticism'.[34] The struggle within the government over this issue prompted one insider to ruminate on the dynamics of reform.

> So why the delay? Ministers claim their self-imposed timetable was too ambitious, and they have not been able to devote enough time to scrutinising the draft prepared by officials. Why, then, did Labour commit itself to the legislation? Perhaps because that's the fated role of opposition politics. Oppositions hope to increase their own power by making governments more accountable – and believe that such accountability will embarrass the ruling party and contribute to its downfall ... Installed in power, it seems that the government may have discovered other more important priorities, though time will tell.[35]

Six months on from the initial disappointment of the Queen's Speech, campaigners for a freedom of information had not been assuaged by the government's assurances of future action. By the end of November 1997, Anthony Barnett had become convinced that Labour, in wanting 'to rule from above' and to be 'even more royal than the Queen', was going slow on the freedom of information. 'Ministers are making all too obvious attempts to retain the old British royalist regime of secrecy and prerogative power that it inherited ... [I]nstead of launching a public campaign for this popular measure, the decisive arguments are taking place behind closed doors and apparently about how to limit it.'[36] That a Freedom of information measure would eventually emerge from the Whitehall machine as a piece of priority legislation was not in doubt and indeed a freedom of information White Paper was duly launched on 11 December 1997. In the event, even though it would 'not please advocates of open government in every respect', the proposal was 'much bolder than expected, and bolder than it had to be merely to meet the promise contained in Labour's election manifesto'.[37] Nevertheless, the suspicions over the delays and evasions were not dispelled. By October 1998, FOI appeared again to be in retreat with legislation deferred, exemptions extended and with responsibility for the Bill transferred to the Home Office – i.e. the department most resistant to the measure.

This matrix of constitutional fuels, political argument and operational dynamics will continue to shape the political forces surrounding the British constitution and with it the future development of the constitution itself. The various balances between the component factors will vary over time depending upon a range of political, institutional and legal conditions but the basic constituents of the matrix will remain in evidence and provide the framework within which the constitution will increasingly become an established medium of political dispute and a central object of competing claims of legitimacy. This is not to say that the matrix will remain static and unresponsive to changing political circumstances. On the contrary, the conflation of forces within it will ensure that, although the constitution will become a more determinable entity in terms of formal principles, documented powers and declared rights, it will also become more open-ended than ever before, not just because it is being propelled along several major new fronts, but because it generates new forms of friction and conflict as it proceeds. Constitutionalism does not replace politics and, as such, it is not possible to make predictions concerning future decisions over the constitution. Nonetheless, it is possible to examine the implications already observable in the matrix and to formulate a number of propositions that seem very likely to be central to the development of the politics that now surrounds the constitution. What follows, therefore, is not a set of projections concerning the future course of substantive constitutional change. It is an exercise in drawing upon the insights gained into the political dynamics of the constitutional issue, in order to elicit something of the nature of that politics beyond the immediacy of the current reform agenda. The logic of the properties and forces present in the matrix prompt the following four propositions that are presented in the spirit of the entire enterprise of this study – namely, to grasp the nature and ramifications of a style of politics which in Britain is unfamiliar, unorthodox, unrecognised and as yet unassimilated.

Proposition 1:

The progression of constitutional reform will inevitably reach a point of disjunction with the passage of the political cycle.

Just as the products of constitutional reform materialise in new institutions and legal forms, so the probability is that the political resources of the sponsoring government will be in a state of decline. Most public policies have a considerable time lag between inception and application, but in the case of constitutional reform the 'lead time' is considerable. The sheer complexity of the enabling legislation, combined with the need to take into account the political, administrative and legal ramifications of such systemic interventions, as well as the requirement in some instances for pre-legislative referendums, mean that constitutional change is necessarily slow to come on stream. Given the irreversible character of reform in this area, the unpredictability of the final outcome, and the level of political risk to a sponsoring government's reputation for competence, constitutional reform measures will be treated with such great caution as to allow the maximum period of time for problems to be identified and addressed. In this case, because the very identity of New Labour had been closely associated with the theme of constitutional change and because the Labour government had secured a decisive parliamentary majority following the 1997 general election, constitutional measures would not only be integral to the government's agenda but conspicuously prominent as a set of Labour priorities. As a consequence, constitutional reform has been attainable at the price of clear and indisputable accountability. The emphasis upon caution in constitutional change is, therefore, a function both of the intricate nature of legislation in this area and of the need for governments to minimise the political costs of such excursions into uncharted waters.

This is not to say that all forms of constitutional reform are necessarily the same in respect to their initial complexity. Some items of innovation are clearly amenable to technically elegant solutions (e.g. a change in the electoral system, or a revision in the voting rights of hereditary peers). Other reforms involve prolific preparatory exercises in planning and designing a set of comprehensive changes to the nature and allocation of powers, structures, procedures and functions. Reforms such as devolution and the incorporation of European Convention on Human Rights into British law each involve very careful analyses of the projected problems with the intention of securing a successful transition from one intricate state of existence to another. But notwithstanding the variation in front-loading, whether it be in terms of parliamentary timetables, political priorities, administrative logistics or legislative complexity, what remains the defining characteristic of legislation in the field of constitutional revision is the extent to which it is open-ended, evolutionary and non-predictive in character. However finite the original investment may seem, there is always a high preponderance of back-loading over front-loading in constitutional reform. There is no such thing as a simple corrective device or self-contained adjustment in such a multifaceted and inter-connected context.

Governments may be able to precipitate change, and in some cases to influence the pace of change, but to control the precise substance of change is beyond them. The short-term calculations for and against different forms of PR, for example, will largely preclude consideration of either the long-term implications of such a reform, or the lateral consequences of PR in ostensibly unrelated areas of political activity. On other occasions, the negative disposition against a particular aspect of the constitution may outweigh consideration of the constructive alternatives and their wider repercussions. The anomalies of the House of Lords, for example, can generate strong public support for reform but little consensus upon what changes are required and little understanding of the knock-on effects of a reformed second chamber upon the interior balances of the constitution. The need to give adequate reflection to such negative-driven and apparently simplistic reform again demands political time and space. Where incrementalism is possible, then it is prudent for governments to take it. A case in point is provided by the incorporation of the European Convention on Human Rights into British law. The arrangement might have fuelled the logic of creating a rights-based culture by allowing the courts to resolve any conflict between parliamentary legislation and the provisions of the convention explicitly and conclusively in favour of the latter. To grant the courts the power to strike down an Act of Parliament would not only raise the possibility of creating tension between the judicial and legislative functions of the respective institutions, but challenge the axiomatic principle of parliamentary sovereignty upon which the rationale of the British constitution rests. Under the Labour government's proposals, it was envisaged that the courts would be able to declare a law to be incompatible with the convention. It was assumed that this would provide the necessary stimulus for the government to revise the offending legislation. By adopting such a device, the government intended to provide a gradual transition to a system more sensitive to individual rights, but in a way that would not disturb the anchorage of parliamentary sovereignty. As the White Paper made clear: 'A finding by the European Court of Human Rights of a violation of a Convention right does not have the effect of automatically changing United Kingdom law and practice: that is a matter for the United Kingdom Government and Parliament.'[38] The Human Rights Bill offered the prospect of a possible progression to a full bill of rights with entrenched liberties, protected by courts empowered to invalidate government actions. By the same token, the incorporation of the convention would provide the opportunity for the government first to reduce the pressure for more radical reform, second to achieve a measure of change without raising fundamental questions over the royal prerogative or parliamentary sovereignty, and third to allow time for the cultural assimilation of the convention's principles while monitoring the ramifications of such a shift from the common law tradition.

The net effect of all these factors in the consideration and provision of constitutional reform is that notwithstanding the political priority given to revising the constitutional arrangements, the intentional and unintentional delays in achieving change will mean that the rate of constitutional reform will accelerate at a time when the government's political standing is likely to falter. Proceeding on the basis that governments tend to run into difficulties by the mid-term of a parliament, then in the case of the Labour government its mid-term blues in the late 1990s to 2000 period will coincide with the first effects of those constitutional reforms that were secured in the afterglow of its electoral triumph in 1997 (e.g. the establishment of a Scottish parliament and Welsh assembly, the presence of the European Convention on Human Rights in British law, the provision of PR in the elections to the European Parliament, the Scottish parliament and the Welsh assembly, the transfer of monetary policy to the Bank of England). If it is assumed that the Labour government is re-elected for a second term of office, it is likely that a similar effect will be repeated not simply as a result of a second tranche of reforms working through the system, but because after such a prolonged period of government (i.e. six to eight years) the fuller effects of the initial reforms will be in evidence. The cultural change heralded by the government as the *raison d'être* of the reforming initiative will be seeping through the system for good or ill, and the sense of irreversibility in such a velvet revolution will be intense. The correlation of declining public approval and constitutional change may be purely circumstantial and have no substantive relationship to one another. However, this seems unlikely in the circumstances, especially when constitutional change is the flagship of New Labour and when the reform agenda has been so closely identified with the programme and purpose of the Blair government. The political dynamics of these circumstances suggest the existence of another proposition.

Proposition 2 :

Just as the sponsoring government will claim credit for securing constitutional reforms, so it will be seen as directly culpable for all the consequences of such experimentation.

The onset of cumulative constitutional change will not only coincide with downturns in the government's popularity, it will in all probability act as a material influence upon the dynamics of public fatigue. The problem for the Labour government in this respect is fivefold. First, the constitutional reforms of the Blair government will always be seen as Labour's babies. Notwithstanding the true diversity of their origins, the reforms will be inextricably identified with the Labour government and this association will increase in depth over time. In contrast to almost any other area of public policy, the Blair's reforms to the constitution do not build upon any pre-existing infrastructure of governmental action, experience or organisation. In the heavy continuity of the British constitution, such changes represent a profound and deliberate discontinuity in the evolution of the political system. They were conceived and designed by a government which, while facing some political pressures for constitutional change, will nevertheless increasingly come to be seen as having engaged in voluntarist action to pursue its own agenda.

Second, the presumption of Labour's autonomy will intensify as the aggregate effects of multiple reforms become evident. The onrush of change will inevitably lead to an accumulation of retrospective references for explanation and blame leading back to the attributed point of inception. Constitutional reform will generate a profusion of political phenomena, each one of which can be justifiably assigned a Labour patent. Time will deepen and sharpen accountability as congenitally open-ended flagship reforms will allow a case to be made for every discernible consequence to be reduced to a consciously intended outcome from a consciously intended process. Third, the only alternative to such a blanket attribution of deliberate culpability will be the arguably more damaging blanket attribution of unintentional accountability, where the government is accused of negligence in not foreseeing the full ramifications of its own reforms. Even at the initial stage of the government's campaign for constitutional reform, anxieties were being expressed over the concealed implications of Labour's choices in the field. In making 'referendums the normal recourse for major constitutional change', for example, the Labour government was warned that it 'may not realise quite what forces it is unleashing'.[39] Legislation to integrate the European Convention on Human Rights into British law was another case where the government was regularly accused of myopia. *The Times*, for example, speculated on the extent to which 'this Bill could shift the balance between Parliament and the courts, irreversibly and in ways that may not be evident for some years'.[40] This type of observation, made at the outset of the Blair government, will grow in volume as the implications of constitutional reform assume a greater material presence. Given Labour's historic vulnerability on the issue of governmental competence, it is more likely that the government's opponents will seek to exploit the vagaries of constitutional reform outcomes with a generic criticism of Labour's capacity for effective government.

Fourth, because constitutional reform was originally promoted as an instrument of national renewal and economic growth, any faltering in the national economy or in the regional economies will be linked directly to the experiment in constitutional innovation. Having talked up the conjunction between renovated government and the development of the economy, and having given constitutional reform such a high profile in Labour's programme, the government will find it difficult to off-load responsibility to structural considerations out of its control. Having itself set the criteria for constitutional culpability, it will be difficult for the government either to disprove any linkage between constitutional reform and economic reversals, or to improve the state of the association to a now more sceptical public. It is likely that future economic crises will be the occasion when the government is attacked either for offering a false prospectus on the nexus between political reform and economic performance, or for being distracted from the management of the economy by constitutional changes that would at such times and in such a context be seen as increasingly superfluous.

Fifth, even though the declared objective of many of the constitutional reforms may have been to enhance democratic citizenship and participation by allowing decision-making to be devolved to communities, or by strengthening the legal safeguards of individual liberties, or by removing electoral and institutional anomalies, the fact remains that in politics those on the losing side of a dispute will look for outlets of disappointment and blame – even if they are reformed structures of constitutional government. The greater the impact of such reforms, the more counter-factuals will flow from those claiming that changes made in the name of the people had frustrated measures that would otherwise have been secured and would have served the public interest.

As a consequence both of these dynamics and those referred to in proposition 1, a government that sponsors constitutional change can expect to suffer a backlash because of it – whether it is warranted or not. If constitutional reform is back-loaded, so are its the political costs. It is almost certain that in the mid-to late term of the Blair government, constitutional fatigue will become evident. With the likelihood of diminished public approval, fewer political resources and a declining interest in constitutional reform both inside and outside Westminster, the leadership will be aware of the need to protect the political interests and governing credentials of the administration from the massive fall-out of accountability over the constitution, while at the same time seeking to reaffirm the principle of a long-term commitment to the remainder of the constitutional agenda. The chief problem with such an assurance is that if such items were capable of postponement during the honeymoon, then they are even more likely to be deferred when the government is suffering from the squeeze of middle age – between the demands of noisy young reforms and the timeless obligations to the venerable issues of social and economic policy.

Proposition 3:

Constitutional innovation may initially consist of discrete legislative measures but reform is a continuous process with no finite boundaries.

After many years of gestation, the transition from a policy idea to legislative enactment may seem like the culmination of a campaign for reform but it is in reality only the beginning of a continuing progression of appeals and

counter-claims, refinements and extensions, as well as elucidation and evaluation. It may be the case that the Labour party's attachment to the reform
agenda owes less to the impulse for a revised constitutional settlement and
more to the idea of constitutional reform being a device by which to close
down disruptive constitutional questions and promptly remove their digressive properties from the political stage. It may also be the case that the 'Blair
government's instincts seem to be gradualist and piecemeal, reforming the
existing unitary state rather than creating a new constitution'.[41] And yet,
despite the reservations and limited horizons of its chief patron, reform legislation on such a scale in such a complex context as constitutional law is
never the end of the journey, so much as the point of embarkation. Constitutional measures may be sold as decisive responses to a variety of constitutional fuels, but they lead instead to a proliferation of self-replicating
agendas, as politics increasingly assumes the character of legal disputation.
Enabling legislation will be de-constructed for implied meanings, inherent
powers and concealed limitations. Any declaration of rights will become the
source of extensive case law and political analysis in which integral concepts, ethical priorities and legal criteria are openly contested. The impact
of constitutional reform will invariably create a profusion of debates over
the injustice or otherwise of inclusions, exclusions, contingencies and
exemptions. The very act of altering the constitution, for example, will not
only throw into high relief the residual problems left conspicuously
untouched by reform, but create an expectation that such problems should
be addressed with an urgency that had previously been absent. Constitutional change will spawn demands for further changes in order to eliminate
new inequities, to address new forms of discrimination, and to remove new
anomalies. Constitutional reform will also generate demarcation disputes
between different public authorities and political institutions. It will lead to
inquiries into the empirical and normative aspects of the inter-relationships
between the different constituent elements of a redistributed system of
power. Even the reforms themselves will produce clashes between their separate objectives, methods and priorities.

Constitutional change, therefore, will not only raise a host of critical questions over the perceived state of the constitution's balances, but stimulate a
series of corrective solutions to restore, improve or refashion such equilib-
ria. Constitutional differentials between, for example, Parliament and the
courts over the interpretation of the European Convention on Human
Rights, or between Westminster and Edinburgh over the meaning and
mechanics of devolution, will become the subject of intense political and
legal analysis. But constitutional disputes will not just be limited to these
types of tectonic plate questions. They will apply downwards in scale by progression to address issues like the need for uniform standards and equitable
treatment. For example, when Lord Nolan retired from the Committee on

Standards in Public Life in November 1997, he advocated that the Committee should inquire into the ethical implications of the new institutions to be created by constitutional reform (e.g. the Scottish parliament, the Welsh assembly, the new London authority and the reformed House of Lords).[42] In similiar vein, Andrew Adonis has argued that once proportional representation has been established at the level of the Scottish parliament and Welsh assembly, the same electoral system should be extended to local councils as a matter of logical and political consistency. It would not only help to displace entrenched Labour majorities but would help to prevent the occurrence of a possibly de-stabilising imbalance between local authorities and the new national assemblies.[43]

When all this potential for domestic constitutional controversy is combined with the unremitting consequences of European integration, then the result will be an exponential growth in the understanding of the constitution as a perpetual political issue. And as the Conservative party becomes more adept both at turning constitutional fuels to its own purposes and at exploiting the burgeoning opportunities of constitutional reform for party advantage, the circle of constitutional politics will be closed. As a consequence, a culture of constitutional consciousness will be fixed in the British system. This may not quite be the culture originally envisaged by New Labour, but it will represent a cultural shift in British politics where the emphasis lies increasingly upon a fusion of law and politics, in which the constitution becomes an endlessly interpretable construct in the service of political dispute. That the constitution is in permanent turmoil will become a thoroughly mundane fact of political life.

The political constitution, 'whose operation depends upon the strength of political factors'[44] will increasingly be interwoven with constitutional politics, in which the changing structure and dynamics of the constitution will act as a separate and originating source of political claims and strategies. This is not to say that the constitution will achieve an overriding position in the conduct of British politics. In many respects, 'British voters are unlikely to find their passions being roused by constitutional questions'.[45] By the same token, constitutional changes are 'unlikely to act as a focus for the immediate electoral battles ahead'.[46] But this is to equate politics with electoral politics. The prominence afforded to the issue of the constitution, especially in a reforming period, will have numerous ramifications which will impinge upon the normal political conduct. As a conditioning agent and as a factor of political calculation, the constitution will progressively be released from its traditionally derivative identity and become more of an independent and generative agency of sustainable conflict. Observers may criticise New Labour's reform activities as 'missing ... any semblance of a comprehensive constitutional settlement',[47] but in a system of constitutional politics such finality is a chimera in a necessarily open-ended and contingent context, in which constitutional arguments increasingly become both the medium of political exchange and the currency of positional advantage. In the same way that constitutional reform cannot be dismissed as being simply analogous to a breakdown in the political stability and fixed categories of the two-party system,[48] so the consequences of constitutional reform cannot be reduced to the premeditated projections of a ruling party. Even for a sponsoring government with a 179-seat majority, constitutional reform brings uncertainty in its wake and, with it, a new politics that cannot simply be regarded as an extension of those political forces that initially gave rise to constitutional change.

Proposition 4:

The incidence of constitutional reform will set in motion an increasing disparity between the traditional precepts and habits of parliamentary sovereignty and the rationale of a constitutional sovereignty implicit in the claims and contexts of successive changes to the constitutional arrangements.

The instinctive consensus which used to surround the British constitution has been progressively eroded to the point where large scale reforms are widely seen as being both necessary and realisable. Selective reforms provide correctives to a set of separate deficiencies. But no matter how many changes are made or how substantial they might be, they will neither amount to a new constitution coherently organised around clear and consistent principles of structure and operation, nor embody a constitutional settlement capable of generating and sustaining a social consensus upon the means of governance. Instead, the proliferation of changes will lead to a hybrid constitutional culture in which the claims of modernisation and democratisation made on behalf of the reforms will co-exist with the more familiar anchorages of the traditional British constitution. Even in the midst of one of the most intensive and productive periods of reform in British constitutional history, it is clear that the conventions of political conduct and public appraisal show few signs of adapting towards a more rigorous regime of constitutional constraint.

The logic of the reforms may be directed towards a more de-centralised, open and democratically sensitive government, together with a more rights-based and activist conception of citizenship. Nevertheless, the Blair administration, even when it has been instrumental in securing constitutional reform, has simultaneously raised concern not merely over the level of retained central control, but over the top-down methods employed to introduce constitutional change designed to limit the discretion of central government. Whether it is the usage of *pre*-legislative referendums, the dependence uopn non-statutory executive 'concordats' to resolve anomolies arising from constitutional reform, the retention of rate-capping powers, the continued dependence of Scottish and Welsh devolved government upon Treasury block grants, the maintenance of the executive's unhindered appointment process to bodies like the Monetary Policy Committee of the Bank of England, the reserved discretion of Parliament in correcting legislation found to be in contravention of the European Convention on Human Rights, or the resistance to granting any independent revenue-raising powers to the Welsh assembly or to the projected London authority, the Labour government has not, in its rush for constitutional reforms, demonstrated a dedication to a systematic reform of the constitution. Its constitutional changes have been selective and arguably even eclectic in nature. Furthermore, its priorities in the reform agenda have often been driven by party interests.

In what has been an optimal period of constitutional reform, when a new government has been actively pursuing its manifesto pledges of reform, it has been noteworthy that no political resources have been expended on presenting any kind of challenge to the ultimate authority of parliamentary sovereignty. It may well be the case that the Blair administration has had 'nothing to gain from the change[s] in terms of narrow self-interest'.[49] It may equally be true that the government has underestimated or miscalculated the radical repercussions of its reform achievements, and that as a result is drifting into constitutional disarray unaware of the logical and political implications of its adjustments. What it cannot be accused of, however, is negligence over protecting the core axiom of parliamentary sovereignty from the viral influences of constitutional reform. On the contrary, the Labour government has been careful to preserve the final authority of Parliament in its devolution proposals, and its plans to entrench the European Convention on Human Rights into British law; it has deferred plans for a bill of rights; it has ignored calls for a written constitution and for the executive's usage of crown prerogative to be curtailed; and it has shown consummate caution over any changes either to the electoral system or to the role of the second chamber that might threaten the security of old stable party majorities in the House of Commons and, thereby, the provision of strong central government.

Anxieties over the level of constitutional reform have been matched by the lasting effects of the methods used to achieve them. Given New Labour's large majority of seats in the House of Commons and the organisational discipline engendered by the leadership in support of its political projects, many constitutional reforms have been given a greater ease of passage than could ever have been predicted prior to the election. This has led to complaints that New Labour is pursuing a new type of constitutionalism through the very techniques of the old discredited constitutionalism it is professing to replace. Reforms are claimed to have been driven through the House of

Commons using the attributed authority of an electoral mandate, the discipline of the Parliamentary Labour Party and the organisational deficiencies of a depleted and demoralised Conservative party. The implicit irony was captured by the Director of Charter 88, Andrew Pudephatt, in his denunciation of the Labour government's decision in June 1997 to use the guillotine procedure to limit debate on the Referendums (Scotland and Wales) Bill.

> The Labour party argues that this has happened often in the past ... But it was not right then, and it is not right now. Constitutional reform is an important issue ... We are pleased that change is on the political agenda. But we certainly do not want things handed down to us. We want to see the arguments for change made in public. We want to see consultation, open discussion and a willingness to answer opponents of reform. Changes to our governing arrangements can't simply be announced by those who govern. If they are, there will be no understanding of what the reforms have to offer us, and no appreciation of the progress that has been made ... All these changes are promised by Labour. But how they come about is as important as what they guarantee.[50]

Intimations of a repetition of the Thatcher paradox (i.e. the stated need to enhance central control in order to increase individual freedom) are unmistakable and have been accompanied by assertions that Parliament is being marginalised, that the cabinet is in decline and the centralisation of policy and political strategy under Tony Blair represents the antithesis of countervailing powers and government limitation.[51] Even New Labour's usage of the referendum for constitutional change has come under attack. Notwithstanding the elements of popular participation and direct choice provided by the device, referendums are claimed to enhance democratic centralism at the expense of the institutional arrangements of deliberation and consent. They are also said to reduce complex issues to simple questions and to compound them with the government's political standing, producing in effect a series of constrained and structured choices.

The stated rationale of the constitutional reform agenda centres upon the idea that government would become more plural in character, sharing powers between different levels and assigning responsibilities to more localised, specialised and democratised centres of decision-making. But the practice does not bear out the theory. The behaviour of the Labour government reveals the difficulties of replacing one constitutional culture with another. Old habits die hard. Habits of thought die harder. Habits of constitutional thought possess an even greater resistance. Apart from the questions over whether constitutional change through massive parliamentary dominance provides an appropriate basis for a new constitution, or whether a series of discrete measures can collectively bring a new constitution into existence, it is the continuing presence of those traditions associated with the principles of the political constitution which pose the most severe limitations upon the development of a separate constitutional dimension in British politics. Bearing in mind the substance of propositions 2 and 3, it will become increasingly likely that the constitutional reforms set in motion by New Labour will not only ramify in effect but will be closely associated with the party of their inception. As the open-ended and even capricious consequences of constitutional reform become increasingly evident with the onset of jurisdictional disputes, contested powers, judicial interventions, legal arguments, and political campaigns for constitutional clarification or amendment, the probability arises that such chronic uncertainty, protracted conflict resolution and confused accountability will lead to a backlash against the demands of constitutional modernisation. At present, elements of two differing conceptions of constitutionalism are discernible within the same system. On the one hand is that constitutionalism which gives critical emphasis to the negative properties and anomalies of the traditional constitution and which underlines the concomitant need to replace them with a system of governance more sensitive to individual rights, enhanced democratic representation and structural self-constraint. On the other hand is the pragmatic, improvised and openly evolutionary character of the political constitution which is grounded both in the adaptability of traditional institutions and processes to democratic forces, and in the common law theme of power constrained by social convention and collective self-discipline. The latter can accommodate some of the formal, positive and mechanistic elements of the former, but there is a limit to the assimilative properties of even the political constitution.

At present when constitutional change carries with it the excitement of promises and prospective solutions, the tension between the two constitutionalisms is largely concealed. But to a growing extent, the change incurred by constitutional reform will begin to multiply and then to confound and, ultimately, to challenge the traditions of the political constitution. Reforms, which at the time of passage may have seemed to be, not least to their New Labour sponsors, the culmination of a process, will increasingly be seen as merely the beginning of a chain reaction of developments that will require formidable levels of adjustment. The proliferation and fissile character of constitutional reform will in all likelihood lead to a measure of public fatigue with the demands of such fundamental change. In a political culture accustomed to the political reductionism of the traditional British constitution and to the adaptive immediacy of institutional forms and policy outcomes, it will increasingly become a strain to accommodate the complexity and elongated time frames of a more substantive constitution. Instead of the customary flexibility of the political constitution which can essentially be characterised as an agreed medium of political exchange, the effect of constitutional reform will be to introduce elements of an altogether more rigorous constitutionalism with an authority and identity distinct from the more derivative properties of the old constitution. This enriched type of constitutionalism is not merely less responsive to the pressures and outcomes of electoral democracy, it is in a variety of ways actively resistant to the clarifying and decisive simplicities of manifestos, mandates and party governments co-opting the powers of the state. While measures like devolution for Scotland and Wales and adoption of the European Convention on Human Rights cannot be equated with federalism and a bill of rights, there is sufficient scope for the erosion of those axioms connected to parliamentary sovereignty to generate a sense of disjunction between the old and the new – the simple and the complex. For example, while central government may attempt to off-load responsibility for a range of public services, especially in Scotland and Wales, it is far from clear whether public habits of attributing ultimate and often blanket culpability to central government will become calibrated in line with the decision-making authority of newly de-centralised structures – i.e. 'whether actual voters are willing to accept that all power does not stem from London'.[52] Likewise, the possible problems arising from the restriction of the central government's discretion through the effects of the European Convention on Human Rights or freedom of information legislation may well be viewed not as a necessary feature of an enhanced constitutionalism of shared powers and reciprocal checks but as a testament to the government's own incompetence for introducing such self-imposed frustrations in the first place.

The backlash against what is deemed to be a class of constitutional change out of character with previous British norms is likely to assume a number of forms. One type of backlash would be based on a reaction against any adverse political consequences of reform and against any other perceived disadvantage that might be attributed to the effects of reform. A second variant would place the emphasis of objection upon the consumption of political resources and public time in continual constitutional disputes over the textual analysis of fundamental statutes and the interpretation of their original intent and meaning. A third type of backlash would centre upon what has allegedly been lost by the exaggerated interest in constitutional reform as a social and political panacea. It is very probable that the Conservative party, for example, will exploit the opportunities afforded by the new constitutional structures to reinstate itself as a serious force in British politics. It may even surpass New Labour in its efforts to modernise itself and it is certain that it will seek to turn the constitutional reforms that it had originally opposed to its own advantage (e.g. holding a primary election to select the party's candidate for London mayor; extending devolution to an English parliament). At the same time, the party will maintain its traditional allegiance to a pre-European Union and pre-New Labour state of mind. In doing so, it will foster a nationalist nostalgia for the British constitution (circa 1950) in embodying the nation's identity. The

Conservatives will run with both the hare and the hounds by fully engaging in the reformed arrangements,[53] while at the same time offering a sceptical outlook upon the enterprise, using the reforms themselves to attribute any negative aspects to the incompetence of their political opponents, and positioning themselves to take full advantage of any public intolerance with constitutional innovation and any movement to equate its antidote with a return to the ancient clarity of a singular and incontestable sovereignty.

While the Conservative backlash will be shaped by notions of constitutional and national restoration, the reaction on the left is likely to be defined by an increasing conviction that constitutional politics represent a permanent and compelling digression to urgent social and economic issues. Notwithstanding the claims made on behalf of constitutional reform for enhanced democracy and governmental responsiveness, the fear on the left is that British politics will become disengaged from serious national questions by what is seen as a neo-liberal obsession with market forces and a related preoccupation with procedural methodology at the expense of substantive policy objectives. The exasperation with the allegedly limited visions of constitutional reform is epitomised by Peter Wilby's reactions to Vernon Bogdanor's carefully researched treatise on the subject. According to Wilby, the trouble with constitutional reformers is that they are invariably 'political nerds', who overlook the fact that 'genuinely popular feeling is increasingly channelled into single issue, direct action campaigns'. In spite of their good intentions, constitutional reformers 'fail to connect with anything that the rest of us find important: the power of Rupert Murdoch to dominate our media, the power of the big City investors to enforce the poverty line wages; the power of motorists to change the world's weather ... Perhaps this explains why politicians make constitutional reform sound so complex: it puts off the evil day when they have to do anything useful.'[54] The backlash on the left will be prompted by a growing belief in the missed opportunities stemming from the surreptitious veto of alternative agendas by what will be seen to be a myopic concern for the instrumental marginalia of politics. The programme of constitutional reform will accordingly be interpreted in such quarters not merely as an abandonment of social democracy but as a *de facto* regression to nineteenth-century liberal values and priorities, creating a deepening disjunction between a progressively ingrown, and arguably irrelevant, constitutionalism and the challenges of global issues, regional integration and construction of new autonomies within and across societies.[55]

Given the nature of these reservations and the political potential they offer for the critique of constitutional reform, the chances are high that the relative weighting given to the various constitutional fuels will alter over time, and that an eleventh fuel to the constitutional debate will become apparent – namely, the constitutional fuel of constitutional fatigue. Such a

fuel will be prompted by the irritations, resentments and frustrations ensuing from the afterburn of multiple reforms which have yet to be consolidated, let alone absorbed. A negative fuel like this will help to create a
counter-weight to the claims of past reforms and to the dynamics impelling
an ongoing succession of further reforms designed to refine and to extend
the process of change. The reaction may be expressed in terms of a need for
retrenchment, or a desire to escape from the enclosed horizons of legal and
institutional dispute, or simply a bridling against the paradox of a loss of
political autonomy in the cause of securing reforms purportedly designed to
achieve a greater measure of constitutional autonomy. Irrespective of how
the reaction is presented, the net effect will be the same. It will lead to the
creation of a flourishing duality of constitutional cultures.

Notwithstanding the criticism of constitutional renovation and the objections lodged against its ramifications, the current process of establishing an
explicitly constitutional dimension will not be reversed or abandoned. Too
many interests and commitments are already engaged in the project of
assigning to the constitution a separate identity and authority to that of the
government. While some may see this development as a way of insulating
British liberties from the reach of the European Union, most view the European dimension as being instrumental in conditioning the British system to
a greater emphasis upon rights, citizenship and shared powers.[56] The
dynamics set in motion by the European Union and the European Convention on Human Rights, and by Britain's own constitutional innovations will
maintain and extend this dimension of the British constitution. At the same
time, the customs and impulses associated with the political constitution
will continue to make their presence felt in what will be in effect an increasingly distinct set of attachments and attitudes. Far from fading away, these
traditions and norms will continue to act as a set of first principles whose
axiomatic properties will remain at variance with the guiding themes of the
other constitutional culture. The political constitution will remain a source
of political authority and a focus of concerted action. It will continue to offer
the prospect of clear majoritarian solutions, decisive collective action and
periodic antidotes to the legal fastidiousness associated with the culture of
the constitutional dimension. Despite their differences, these two cultures
will co-exist with one another. They may possess different premises and
divergent operational principles. They may appeal to different values, or to
different combinations of values, at different times. On some occasions, for
example, there will be populist surges against the constitutional dimension
and its accoutrements of intermediary filters and aggregate appeals. At the
other times such populist fervour will be directed against effective government action and in favour of restraint to give protection to minority rights
or to prevent any erosion of traditional conventions of political conduct.
Despite these differences, the two cultures will collectively constitute a gen-

uine duality, in which their separate characteristics and attributes will effectively run in parallel to one another in a mutually complementary arrangement that draws upon different currents of constitutional support. The exact relationship between the two components will remain forever imprecise. There will be no final constitutional settlement because there are no final solutions to such a duality. But a workable and even flourishing constitution does not require even the pretence of comprehensive answers.

Now and in the foreseeable future the politics of the British constitution will not simply be confined to the contested outcomes and projections of constitutional change. It will extend to the ongoing tension between these two constitutional cultures and their respective claims to the proprietorship of the constitution. In the final analysis, political arguments over the British constitution will be governed by the even deeper question of whether the constitutional arrangements in Britain can any longer support a singular frame of reference. This raises the issue of whether the holistic precepts of constitutionalism will ultimately have to give way to an irreducible duality of constitutions, whose interactions and points of equilibrium provide the only accessible means of acquiring the only available condition of constitutionalism in contemporary British circumstances.

Notes

1   Simon Jenkins, 'A Constitutional Adventure', *The Times*, 3 May 1997.
2   Quoted in Philip Webster, 'Blair Pledges Shake-up of the Welfare State', *The Times*, 15 May 1997.
3   'Parliament of the Great Reform', *The Observer*, 18 May 1997.
4   'First Steps on a Long Track', *The Guardian*, 15 May 1997.
5   John Lloyd, 'Labour Needs a Genius of the Constitution', *The Times*, 20 July 1997.
6   'Labour's Big Idea Shrouded in Delay', *The Observer*, 13 July 1997.
7   Tony Blair, 'John Smith Memorial Lecture' in Tony Blair, *New Statesman Special Selection from New Britain: My Vision of a Young Country* (London: Fourth Estate, 1996), pp. 82–3.
8   *The Independent*, 8 May 1997.
9   'Take the Lid Off, Tony', *New Statesman*, 16 May 1997.
10 Richard Norton-Taylor, 'Watch Out: Secrecy's About (Again), *The Guardian*, 9 May 1997.
11 *Trusting in Change*, 2nd edn (York: The Joseph Rowntree Reform Trust, 1998), p. 27.
12 Anthony Barnett, *This Time: Our Constitutional Revolution* (London: Vintage, 1997), p. 319.
13 *Ibid.*, p. 155.
14 *Ibid.*, p. 6.

15 Quoted in George Jones, 'Turmoil for Blair over Sports Cash', *Daily Telegraph*, 13 November 1997.

16 John Lloyd, 'Has Labour Sold Its Soul for a Bernie?', *The Times*, 14 November 1997.

17 'Disillusion Day', *The Times*, 14 November 1997.

18 'Labour's First Whiff of Sleaze', *The Guardian*, 10 November 1997.

19 BBC 1, *On The Record*, broadcast on 19 November, 1997.

20 Peter Riddell, 'Our Ostrich MPs and the Constitution', *The Times*, 7 July 1997.

21 Robert Hodge, 'You are Being Asked to Follow like Sheep and Replicate the Scotland Vote', *Daily Post*, 18 September 1997.

22 Tony Blair, 'No-one Could Believe I Would Do Anything to Weaken the United Kingdom', *Daily Post*, 18 September 1997.

23 Donald Dewar, 'Dewar on Devolution', *The Economist*, 4 October 1997.

24 Valerie Elliot, 'Welsh Assembly Members to Face Secrets Gag', *The Times*, 6 March 1998. For more on the anomolies created by the altered institutional and operational relationships between Westminster, Whitehall and the new assemblies see Barry K. Winetrobe, 'Government of Wales Bill. Operational Aspects of the National Assembly', Research Paper No. 97/132 (London: House of Commons Library, 1997).

25 Under William Hague's leadership, the Conservative party has even attempted to outflank New Labour's commitment to reform. On rare occasions, this takes the form of a direct challenge to the Labour government's credentials on constitutional change (e.g. Hague's proposal of an all-elected House of Lords). The more customary challenge has been that of using internal changes to the Conservative party's structure, in order to demonstrate a greater commitment to organisational democracy (e.g. the Conservatives' adoption of new rules on leadership selection which will be determined by the party membership on the basis of one-member-one-vote ballot, in contrast to the Labour's tripartite system of trade unions, constituency parties and MPs and MEPs; the establishment of membership referendums on key policy positions; and the provision of a Conservative primary election for the selection of the party's candidate for the post of London mayor).

26 'Last Gasp for First Past the Post', *The Economist*, 31 May 1997.

27 Quoted in Anthony Bevins, 'Ashdown Stands Up for the New Politics', *The Independent*, 25 September 1997.

28 Anthony Howard, 'In the Long Run We Are All Radical', *The Times*, 2 September 1997.

28 Andrew Price, 'Devolution Plans Put on Hold', *The Times*, 22 September 1997.

30 'An Alliance for Change', *The Guardian*, 22 September 1997.

31 Norton-Taylor, 'Watch Out'.

32 Anthony Bevins, 'Blair Stalls on Open Government', *The Independent*, 8 May 1997.

33 Quoted in Anthony Bevins, 'Blair Stalls on Open Government'.

34 Norton-Taylor, 'Watch Out'.

35 Derek Draper, *Blair's 100 Days* (London: Faber, 1997), pp. 168–9.

36 Anthony Barnett, 'New Labour. New Queen. Same Old Secrecy', *The Observer*, 23 November 1997.

37 'Pandora's Box', *The Economist*, 13 December 1997.
38 *Rights Brought Home: The Human Rights Bill*, Cm 3782 (London: Stationery Office, 1997), p. 5.
39 'Vote, Vote, Vote for More Democracy', *The Observer*, 15 May 1997.
40 'The Bill for Rights,' *The Times*, 25 October 1997.
41 Peter Riddell, *Parliament Under Pressure* (London: Victor Gollanz, 1998), p. 131.
42 See Peter Riddell, 'How Nolan's Successor Can Keep Up the Good work', *The Times*, 6 November 1997.
43 Andrew Adonis, *Voting in Proportion: Electoral Reform for Scotland's Councils* (Edinburgh: Scottish Councli Foundation, 1998).
44 Vernon Bogdanor, 'The Political Constitution' in Vernon Bogdanor (ed.), *Politics and the British Constitution* (Aldershot: Dartmouth, 1996), p. 19.
45 David Sanders, 'The New Electoral Battleground' in Anthony King (ed.), *New Labour Triumphs: Britain at the Polls* (Chatham, N.J.: Chatham House, 1998), p. 241.
46 *Ibid.*
47 Anthony King, 'Changing Britain's Guard', *The World in 1998* (London: *The Economist*, 1997), p. 26.
48 Bogdanor, 'The Political Constitution' in Bogdanor, *Politics and the British Constitution*, pp. 3–20.
49 Donald Dewar, quoted in John Kampfner and Robert Wright, 'No Parish Council', *Financial Times*, 25 July 1997.
50 Andrew Pudephatt, 'Memo to Blair: You're Treading Dangerously', *The Guardian*, 5 June 1997.
51 For example, see Riddell, *Parliament Under Pressure*; John Redwood, 'Labour is Killing Off Our Parliament', *Daily Telegraph*, 12 September 1997.
52 Peter Riddell, BBC Radio 4, *Analysis*, 15 January 1998.
53 With the intellectual emancipation of the Conservative party's political decline in 1997, there has arisen a more uninhibited conservative consideration to the libertarian and Thatcherite possibilities of constitutional reform in providing a permanent restriction on the power of the state. The Centre for Policy Studies, for example, called in February 1998 for 'total devolution – with Westminster reduced to a federal parliament responsible for foreign policy and defence' (*The Guardian*, 18 February 1998). See also Bill Emmott and David Manasian, 'Rights for the Right', *Prospect*, March 1997, pp. 26–30.
54 Peter Wilby, 'Two Forbidden Words' review of *Power and the People: A Guide to Constitutional Reform* by Vernon Bogdanor, *Independent on Sunday*, 10 August 1997
55 For an examination of the extension of constitutional reform to Europe as a whole, see Frank Vibert, *Europe: A Constitution for the New Millenium* (Aldershot: Dartmouth, 1997).
56 See John Pinder, 'European Citizenship: A Project in Need of Completion' in Colin Crouch and David Marquand (eds), *Reinventing Collective Action: From the Global to the Local* (Oxford: Blackwell, 1995), pp. 112–22.

Index